FREEDOM IN EXILE
The Autobiography of the Dalai Lama

Contents

Maps

(Maps drawn by Hanni Bailey)

Foreword

Dalai Lama means different things to different people. To some it means that I am a living Buddha, the earthly manifestation of Avalokiteshvara, Bodhisattva of Compassion. To others it means that I am a 'god-king'. During the late 1950's it meant that I was a Vice-President of the Standing Committee of the National People's Congress of the People's Republic of China. Then when I escaped into exile, I was called a counter-revolutionary and a parasite. But none of these are my ideas. To me 'Dalai Lama' is a title that signifies the office I hold. I myself am just a human being, and incidentally a Tibetan, who chooses to be a Buddhist monk.

It is as a simple monk that I offer this story of my life, though it is by no means a book about Buddhism. I have two main reasons for doing so. Firstly, an increasing number of people have shown an interest in learning something about the Dalai Lama. Secondly, there are a number of historical events about which I wish to set the record straight.

Because of constraints on my time, I have decided to tell my story directly in English. It has not been easy, for my ability to express myself in this language is limited. Furthermore, I am aware that some of the subtler implications of what I say may not be precisely what I intended. But the same would be true in a translation from Tibetan. I should also add that I have at my disposal only limited resources for research and my memory is as fallible as anyone else's. That said, I wish to offer my thanks to the concerned officers of the Tibetan Government in Exile and to Mr Alexander Norman for their assistance in these areas.

Nine years have passed since first publication of my autobiography. It is thus almost half a century since Tibet was invaded and I have lived well over half my life as a refugee.

To coincide with the release of *Kundun*, the film based on my life story, my publishers requested that I add a new chapter to this book. In doing so I have taken the opportunity to record the events of the past ten years which seem relevant.

Dharamsala
10 March 1998

Holder of the White Lotus

O

I FLED TIBET on 31 March 1959. Since then I have lived in exile in India. During the period 1949–50, the People's Republic of China sent an army to invade my country. For almost a decade I remained as political as well as spiritual leader of my people and tried to re-establish peaceful relations between our two nations. But the task proved impossible. I came to the unhappy conclusion that I could serve my people better from outside.

When I look back to the time when Tibet was still a free country, I realise that those were the best years of my life. Today I am definitely happy, but inevitably the existence I now lead is very different from the one I was brought up to. And although there is clearly no use indulging in feelings of nostalgia, still I cannot help feeling sad whenever I think of the past. It reminds me of the terrible suffering of my people. The old Tibet was not perfect. Yet at the same time, it is true to say that our way of life was something quite remarkable. Certainly there was much that was worth preserving that is now lost for ever.

I have said that the words Dalai Lama mean different things to different people, that for me they refer only to the office I hold. Actually, *Dalai* is a Mongolian word meaning 'ocean' and *Lama* is a Tibetan term corresponding to the Indian word *guru*, which denotes a teacher. Together, the words *Dalai* and *Lama* are sometimes loosely translated as 'Ocean of Wisdom'. But this is due to a misunderstanding I feel. Originally, *Dalai* was a partial translation of Sonam Gyatso, the Third Dalai Lama's name: *Gyatso* means ocean in Tibetan. A further, unfortunate misunderstanding is due to the Chinese rendering of the word *lama* as *huo-fou*, which has the connotation of a 'living Buddha'. This is wrong. Tibetan Buddhism recognises no such thing. It only accepts that certain beings, of whom the Dalai Lama is one, can choose the manner of their rebirth. Such people are called *tulkus* (incarnations).

Of course, whilst I lived in Tibet, being Dalai Lama meant a great deal. It meant that I lived a life far removed from the toil and discomfort of the vast majority of my people. Everywhere I went, I was accompanied by a retinue of servants. I was surrounded by government ministers and advisors clad in sumptuous silk robes, men drawn from the most exalted and aristocratic families in the land. My daily companions were brilliant scholars and highly realised religious adepts. And every time I left the Potala, the magnificent, 1,000-chambered winter palace of the Dalai Lamas, I was escorted by a procession of hundreds of people.

At the head of the column came a *Ngagpa*, a man carrying a symbolic 'wheel of life'. He was followed by a party of *tatara*, horsemen dressed in colourful, traditional costumes and carrying flags. Behind them were porters carrying my songbirds in cages and my personal belongings all wrapped up in yellow silk. Next came a section of monks from Namgyal, the Dalai Lama's own monastery. Each carried a banner decorated with sacred texts. Behind them followed musicians mounted on horseback. Then followed two groups of monk officials, first a subordinate section who acted as bearers, then monks of the *Tsedrung* order who were members of the Government. Behind these came a posse of horses from the Dalai Lama's own stables, all nicely turned out, caparisoned and led by their grooms.

There followed another troop of horses which carried the seals of state. I myself came next, carried in a yellow palanquin, which was pulled by twenty men, all officers in the army and dressed in green cloaks with red hats. Unlike the most senior officials, who wore their hair up, these had a single, long pigtail running down their backs. The palanquin itself, which was yellow in colour (to denote monasticism), was supported by a further eight men wearing long coats of yellow silk. Alongside it rode the four members of the *Kashag*, the Dalai Lama's inner Cabinet, attended by the

Kusun Depon, head of the Dalai Lama's bodyguard, and the *Makchi*, Commander-in-Chief of Tibet's tiny army. Both of these marched carrying their swords sternly at the salute. They wore a uniform comprised of blue trousers and yellow tunic covered with gold braid. On their heads they wore a tasselled topi. Surrounding this, the main party, there was an escort of *sing gha*, the monastic police. These terrifying-looking men were all at least six feet tall and wore heavy padding, which lent them an even more impressive appearance. In their hands they carried long whips, which they did not hesitate to use.

Behind my palanquin came my two Tutors, Senior and Junior (the former being the Regent of Tibet before I attained my majority). Then came my parents and other members of my family. They were followed by a large party of lay officials, both nobles and commoners, marshalled according to rank.

Invariably almost the entire population of Lhasa, the capital, came to try to catch a glimpse of me whenever I went out. There was an awed silence and often there were tears as people lowered their heads or prostrated themselves on the ground when I passed.

It was a life very different from the one I had known as a small boy. I was born on 6 July 1935 and named Lhamo Thondup. This means, literally, 'Wish-Fulfilling Goddess'. Tibetan names of people, places and things are often picturesque in translation. For example, Tsangpo, the name of one of Tibet's most important rivers – and source of India's mighty Brahmaputra – means 'The Purifier'. The name of our village was Taktser: Roaring Tiger. It was a small and poor settlement which stood on a hill overlooking a broad valley. Its pastures had not been settled or farmed for long, only grazed by nomads. The reason for this was the unpredictability of the weather in that area. During my early childhood, my family was one of twenty or so making a precarious living from the land there.

Taktser is situated in far north-eastern Tibet, in the province of Amdo. Geographically, Tibet can be divided into four principal areas. To the north-west lies the Changtang, an area of frozen desert which runs east–west for over eight hundred miles. It is almost

A M D O

L.Kokonor

Siling
•Kumbum
Taktser

Golmud

Tashikiel

Machu

Drichu (Yangtse)

C H I N A

M T S

E   T

Zachu (Mekong)

RETING GOMPA

Chamdo
•10 640 FT

Karze

K H A M

Dhar-tsedo

SERA
GANDEN
Lhasa
Tsethang
L.Yamdrok

L.Lhamoi
Lhatso

Lhuntse Dzong

AN

Bomdila
Tezpur

I N D I A

ESCAPE ROUTE
FROM TIBET

Kyichu
Lhasa
12 090 FT

Tsethang •

Lhuntse Dzong
Mang
-mang   Jhora

Tapo Pass

Bomdila

Tezpur

devoid of vegetation and only a few hardy nomads live amidst its desolation. To the south of the Changtang lie the provinces of U and Tsang. This area is bordered to the south and south-west by the mighty Himalayas. To the east of U-Tsang lies the province of Kham, which is the most fertile and hence most populous region in the country. To the north of Kham is situated Amdo. On the eastern borders of both Kham and Amdo lies Tibet's national boundary with China. At the time of my birth, a Muslim warlord, Ma Bufeng, had recently succeeded in establishing in Amdo a regional government loyal to the Chinese Republic.

My parents were small farmers: not peasants exactly, for they were not tied to any master; but they were by no means nobility. They leased a small amount of land and worked it themselves. The main crops in Tibet are barley and buckwheat and my parents grew both of these, together with potatoes. But quite often their year's work went to ruin due to heavy hailstorms or to drought. They also kept a number of animals, which were a more reliable source of produce. I remember that we had five or six *dzomos* (a cross between a yak and a cow) for milking and a number of footloose chickens for laying. There was a mixed flock of perhaps eighty sheep and goats, and my father nearly always had one or two or even three horses, of which he was very fond. Finally, my family kept a couple of yaks.

The yak is one of Nature's gifts to mankind. It can survive at any altitude above 10,000 feet, so it is ideally suited to Tibet. Below that they tend to die. Both as a beast of burden and as a source of milk (in the case of the female, which is called a *dri*), and meat, the yak is truly a staple of high-altitude farming. The barley which my parents grew is another Tibetan staple. When roasted and ground down into a fine flour, it becomes *tsampa*. There is rarely a meal served in Tibet which does not include *tsampa* and, even in exile, I continue to have it every day. It is not eaten as flour, of course. You must first combine it with liquid, usually tea, but milk (which I prefer) or yoghurt or even *chang* (Tibetan beer) will do. Then, working it with your fingers around your bowl, you roll it into small balls. Otherwise it can be used as a base for porridge. To a Tibetan, it is very tasty though, in my experience, few foreigners like it. The Chinese in particular do not care for it at all.

Most of what my parents grew on the farm was used solely to feed us. But my father would occasionally trade grain or a few sheep either with passing nomads or down at Siling, the nearest town and capital of Amdo, which lay three hours away by horse. Currency was not much in use in these far-flung rural areas and most trade was conducted by barter. Thus my father would exchange the season's surplus for tea, sugar, cotton cloth, a few ornaments perhaps, and maybe some iron utensils. Occasionally he would come back with a new horse, which delighted him. He had a very good feel for them and had quite a reputation locally as a healer of horses.

The house I was born in was typical of our area of Tibet. It was built of stone and mud with a flat roof along three sides of a square. Its only unusual feature was the guttering, which was made from branches of juniper wood, gouged out to make a channel for rain water. Directly in front of it, between the two 'arms' or wings, there was a small yard in the middle of which was a tall flagpole. From this hung a banner, secured top and bottom, on which were written innumerable prayers.

The animals were kept behind the house. Inside were six rooms: a kitchen, where we spent most of our time when indoors; a prayer-room with a small altar, where we would all gather to make offerings at the beginning of the day; my parents' room; a spare room for any guests we might have; a storeroom for our provisions; and finally a byre for the cattle. There was no bedroom for us children. As a baby, I slept with my mother; then, later, in the kitchen, by the stove. For furniture, we had no chairs or beds as such, but there were raised areas for sleeping in both my parents' room and the spare room. There were also a number of cupboards made of gaily painted wood. The floors were likewise wooden and neatly laid with planks.

My father was a man of medium height with a very quick temper. I remember pulling at his moustache once and being hit hard for my trouble. Yet he was a kind man too and he never bore grudges. An interesting story was told about him at the time of my birth. He had been ill for a number of weeks and was confined to his bed. No one knew what was wrong with him and people started to fear for his life. But on the day I was born, he suddenly began to recover, for no obvious reason. It cannot have been excitement at becoming a father since my mother had already given birth to eight children, although only four had survived. (Of necessity, farming families like ours believed in large families and my mother bore sixteen children in all, of whom seven lived.) At the time of writing, Lobsang Samten, my immediate elder brother, and Tsering Dolma, my eldest sister, are no longer living, but my two other older brothers, my younger sister and my younger brother are still alive and well.

My mother was undoubtedly one of the kindest people I have ever known. She was truly wonderful and was loved, I am quite certain, by all who knew her. She was very compassionate. Once, I remember being told, there was a terrible famine in nearby China. As a result, many poor Chinese people were driven over the border in search of food. One day, a couple appeared at our door, carrying in their arms a dead child. They begged my mother for food, which she readily gave them. Then she pointed at their child and asked whether they wanted help to bury it. When they had caught her meaning, they shook their heads and made clear that they intended to eat it. My mother was horrified and at once invited them in and emptied the entire contents of the larder before regretfully sending them on their way. Even if it meant giving away the family's own food so that we ourselves went hungry, she never let any beggars go empty-handed.

Tsering Dolma, the eldest child, was eighteen years older than me. At the time of my birth she helped my mother run the house and acted as my midwife. When she delivered me, she noticed that one of my eyes was not properly open. Without hesitating, she put her thumb on the reluctant lid and forced it wide – fortunately without ill effect. Tsering Dolma was also responsible for giving me my first meal, which, by tradition, was a liquid made from the bark of a particular bush that grew locally. This was believed to ensure a healthy child. It certainly worked in my case. In later years, my sister told me that I was a very dirty baby. No sooner had she taken me in her arms than I made a mess!

I did not have much to do with any of my three elder brothers. Thupten Jigme Norbu, the eldest, had already been recognised as the reincarnation of a high lama, Taktser Rinpoché (Rinpoché is the title given to spiritual masters and means, literally, 'Precious One'), and was installed at Kumbum, a famous monastery several hours away by horse. My next brother, Gyalo Thondup, was eight years older than me and by the time I was born he was away at school in a neighbouring village. Only my immediate elder brother, Lobsang Samten, remained behind. He was three years older than me. But then he too was sent to Kumbum to be a monk, so I hardly knew him at home.

Of course, no one had any idea that I might be anything other than an ordinary baby. It was almost unthinkable that more than one *tulku* could be born into the same family and certainly my parents had no idea that I would be proclaimed Dalai Lama. My father's recovery from illness was auspicious, but it was not taken to be of great significance. I myself likewise had no particular intimation of what lay ahead. My earliest memories are very ordinary. Some people put great emphasis on a person's first recollections, but I do not. Amongst mine I remember, for example, observing a group of children fighting and running to join in with the weaker side. I also remember the first time I saw a camel. These are quite common in parts of Mongolia and occasionally they were brought over the border. It looked huge and majestic and very frightening. I also recall discovering one day that I had worms – a common affliction in the East.

One thing that I remember enjoying particularly as a very young boy was going into the hen coop to collect the eggs with my mother and then staying behind. I liked to sit in the hens' nest and make clucking noises. Another favourite occupation of mine as an infant was to pack things in a bag as if I was about to go on a long journey. 'I'm going to Lhasa, I'm going to Lhasa,' I would say. This, coupled with my insistence that I be allowed always to sit at the head of the table, was later said to be an indication that I must have known that I was destined for greater things. I also had a number of dreams as a small child that were open to a similar interpretation, but I cannot say categorically that I knew of my future all along. Later on, my mother told me several stories which could be taken as signs of high birth. For example, I never allowed anyone but her to handle my bowl. Nor did I ever show fear of strangers.

Before going on to tell about my discovery as Dalai Lama, I must first say something about Buddhism and its history in Tibet. The founder of Buddhism was an historical figure, Siddhartha, who came to be recognised as the Buddha Shakyamuni. He was born more than 2,500 years ago. His teachings, now known as the *Dharma*, or Buddhism, were introduced to Tibet during the fourth century AD. They took several centuries to supplant the native Bon religion and become fully established, but eventually the country was so thoroughly converted that Buddhist principles governed all society, at every level. And whilst Tibetans are by nature quite aggressive people and quite warlike, their increasing interest in religious practice was a major factor in bringing about the country's isolation. Before then, Tibet possessed a vast empire, which dominated Central Asia with territories covering large parts of northern India, Nepal and Bhutan in the south. It also included much Chinese territory. In 763 AD, Tibetan forces actually captured the Chinese capital, where they extracted promises of tribute and other concessions. However, as Tibetans' enthusiasm for Buddhism increased, Tibet's relations with her neighbours became of a spiritual rather than a political nature. This was especially true of China, where a 'priest–patron' relationship developed. The Manchu Emperors, who were Buddhists, referred to the Dalai Lama as 'King of Expounding Buddhism'.

The fundamental precept of Buddhism is Interdependence or the Law of Cause and Effect. This simply states that everything which an individual being experiences is derived through action from motivation. Motivation is thus the root of both action and experience. From this understanding are derived the Buddhist theories of consciousness and rebirth.

The first holds that, because cause gives rise to effect which in turn becomes the cause of further effect, consciousness must be continual. It flows on and on, gathering experiences and impressions from one moment to the next. At the point of physical death, it follows that a being's consciousness contains an imprint of all these past experiences and impressions, and the actions which preceded them. This is known as *karma*, which means 'action'. It is thus consciousness, with its attendant *karma*, which then becomes 'reborn' in a new body – animal, human or divine.

So, to give a simple example, a person who has spent his or her life mistreating animals could quite easily be reborn in the next life as a dog belonging to someone who is unkind to animals. Similarly, meritorious conduct in this life will assist in a favourable rebirth in the next.

Buddhists further believe that because the basic nature of consciousness is neutral, it is possible to escape from the unending cycle of birth, suffering, death and rebirth that life inevitably entails, but only when all negative *karma* has been eliminated along with all worldly attachments. When this point is reached, the consciousness in question is believed to attain first liberation and then ultimately Buddhahood. However, according to Buddhism in the Tibetan tradition, a being that achieves Buddhahood, although freed from *Samsara*, the 'wheel of suffering', as the phenomenon of existence is known, will continue to return to work for the benefit of all other sentient beings until such time as each one is similarly liberated.

Now in my own case, I am held to be the reincarnation of each of the previous thirteen Dalai Lamas of Tibet (the first having been born in 1351 AD), who are in turn considered to be manifestations of Avalokiteshvara, or Chenrezig, Bodhisattva of Compassion, holder of the White Lotus. Thus I am believed also to be a manifestation of Chenrezig, in fact the seventy-fourth in a lineage that can be traced back to a Brahmin boy who lived in the time of Buddha Shakyamuni. I am often asked whether I truly believe this. The answer is not simple to give. But as a fifty-six year old, when I consider my experiences during this present life, and given my Buddhist beliefs, I have no difficulty accepting that I am spiritually connected both to the thirteen previous Dalai Lamas, to Chenrezig and to the Buddha himself.

When I was not quite three years old, a search party that had been sent out by the Government to find the new incarnation of the Dalai Lama arrived at Kumbum monastery. It had been led there by a number of signs. One of these concerned the embalmed body of my predecessor, Thupten Gyatso, the Thirteenth Dalai Lama, who had died aged fifty-seven in 1933. During its period of sitting in state, the head was discovered to have turned from facing south to north-east. Shortly after that the Regent, himself a senior lama, had a vision. Looking into the waters of the sacred lake, Lhamoi Lhatso, in southern Tibet, he clearly saw the Tibetan letters *Ah*, *Ka* and *Ma* float into view. These were followed by the image of a three-storeyed monastery with a turquoise and gold roof and a path running from it to a hill. Finally, he saw a small house with strangely shaped guttering. He was sure that the letter *Ah* referred to Amdo, the north-eastern province, so it was there that the search party was sent.

By the time they reached Kumbum, the members of the search party felt that they were on the right track. It seemed likely that if the letter *Ah* referred to Amdo, then *Ka* must indicate the monastery at Kumbum – which was indeed three-storeyed and turquoise-roofed. They now only needed to locate a hill and a house with peculiar guttering. So they began to search the neighbouring villages. When they saw the gnarled branches of juniper wood on the roof of my parents' house, they were certain that the new Dalai Lama would not be far away. Nevertheless, rather than reveal the purpose of their visit, the group asked only to stay the night. The leader of the party, Kewtsang Rinpoché, then pretended to be a servant and spent much of the evening observing and playing with the youngest child in the house.

The child recognised him and called out 'Sera lama, Sera lama'. Sera was Kewtsang Rinpoché's monastery. Next day they left – only to return a few days later as a formal deputation. This time they brought with them a number of things that had belonged to my predecessor, together with several similar items that did not. In every case, the infant correctly identified those belonging to the Thirteenth Dalai Lama saying, 'It's mine. It's mine.' This more or less convinced the search party that they had found the new incarnation. However, there was another candidate to be seen before a final decision could be reached. But it was not long before the boy from Taktser was acknowledged to be the new Dalai Lama. I was that child.

Needless to say, I do not remember very much of these events. I was too small. My only real recollection is of a man with piercing eyes. These turned out to belong to a man named Kenrap Tenzin, who became my Master of the Robes and later taught me to write.

As soon as the search party had concluded that the child from Taktser was the true incarnation of the Dalai Lama, word was sent back to Lhasa informing the Regent. It would be several months before official confirmation was received. Until then, I was to remain at home. In the meantime, Ma Bufeng, the local Governor, began to make trouble. But eventually I was taken by my parents to Kumbum monastery, where I was installed in a ceremony that took place at dawn. I remember this fact particularly as I was surprised to be woken and dressed before the sun had risen. I also remember being seated on a throne.

There now began a somewhat unhappy period of my life. My parents did not stay long and soon I was alone amongst these new and unfamiliar surroundings. It is very hard for a small child to be separated from its parents. However, there were two consolations to life at the monastery. First, my immediate elder brother Lobsang Samten was already there. Despite being only three years older than me, he took good care of me and we soon became firm friends. The second consolation was the fact that his teacher was a very kind old monk, who often held me inside his gown. On one occasion I recall that he gave me a peach. Yet for the most part I was quite unhappy. I did not understand what it meant to be Dalai Lama. As far as I knew, I was just one small boy among many. It was not unusual for children to enter the monastery at a very young age and I was treated just the same as all the others. A more painful memory is of one of my uncles, who was a monk at Kumbum. One evening, whilst he sat reading his prayers, I upset his book of scripture. As they still are today, this book was loose-leafed and the pages went everywhere. My father's brother picked me up and slapped me hard. He was extremely angry and I was terrified. For literally years afterwards I was haunted by his very dark, pock-marked face and fierce moustache. Thereafter, whenever I caught sight of him, I became very frightened.

When it became clear that I would eventually be reunited with my parents and that together we would journey to Lhasa, I began to look to the future with more enthusiasm. As any child would be, I was thrilled at the prospect of travel. This did not come about for some eighteen months, however, because Ma Bufeng refused to let me be taken to Lhasa without payment of a large ransom. And having received it, he demanded more, although he did not get it. It was thus not until the summer of 1939 that I left for the capital.

When eventually the great day dawned, a week after my fourth birthday, I remember a tremendous feeling of optimism. The party was large. Not only did it consist of my parents and my brother Lobsang Samten, but the members of the search party and a number of pilgrims came too. There were also several government officials in attendance, together with a great number of muleteers and scouts. These men spent their lives working the caravan routes of Tibet and were indispensable to any long journey. They knew exactly where to cross each river and how much time it took to climb the mountain passes.

After a few days' travel, we left the area administered by Ma Bufeng and the Tibetan Government formally announced its acceptance of my candidature. We now entered some of the most remote and beautiful countryside in the world: gargantuan mountains flanking immense flat plains which we struggled over like insects. Occasionally, we came upon the icy rush of meltwater streams that we splashed noisily across. And every few days we would come to a tiny settlement huddled amongst a blaze of green pasture, or clinging as if by its fingers to a hillside. Sometimes we could see in the far distance a monastery perched impossibly on top of a cliff. But mostly, it was just arid, empty space with only savage dust-laden winds and angry hailstorms as reminders of Nature's living forces.

The journey to Lhasa took three months. I remember very little detail apart from a great sense of wonder at everything I saw: the vast herds of *drong* (wild yaks) ranging across the plains, the smaller groups of *kyang* (wild asses) and occasionally a shimmer of *gowa* and *nawa*, small deer which were so light and fast they might have been ghosts. I also loved the huge flocks of hooting geese we saw from time to time.

For most of the journey I travelled with Lobsang Samten in a sort of palanquin called a *dreljam* carried by a pair of mules. We spent a great deal of time squabbling and arguing, as small children do, and often came to blows. This put our conveyance in danger of overbalancing. At that point the driver would stop the animals and summon my mother. When she looked inside, she always found the same thing: Lobsang Samten in tears and me sitting there with a look of triumph on my face. For despite his greater age, I was the more forthright. Although we were really best friends, we were incapable of behaving well together. One or other of us would make a remark which led to an argument and finally to blows and tears – but the tears were always his and not mine. Lobsang Samten was so good-natured that he could not bring himself to use his superior strength against me.

At last, our party began to draw near to Lhasa. It was by now autumn. When we were within a few days' journey, a group of senior government officials came out to meet us and escorted our party on to the Doeguthang plain, two miles outside the gates of the capital. There, a huge tented encampment had been erected. In the centre was a blue and white structure called the *Macha*

Chenmo, the 'great Peacock'. It looked enormous to my eyes and enclosed an intricately carved wooden throne, which was only ever brought out for the purpose of welcoming the infant Dalai Lama back home.

The ceremony that followed, which conferred on me spiritual leadership of my people, lasted one whole day. But my memory of it is vague. I remember only a great sense of homecoming and endless crowds of people: I had never thought there could be so many. By all accounts, I behaved myself well for a four year old, even to one or two extremely senior monks who came to judge for themselves whether I really was the reincarnation of the Thirteenth Dalai Lama. Then, at the end of it all, I was taken off with Lobsang Samten to the Norbulingka (meaning Jewel Park) which lay just to the west of Lhasa itself.

Normally, it was used only as the summer palace of the Dalai Lama. But the Regent had decided to wait until the end of the following year before formally enthroning me at the Potala palace, the seat of the Tibetan Government. In the meantime, there was no need for me to live there. This turned out to be a generous move as the Norbulingka was much the more pleasant of the two places. It was surrounded by gardens and consisted of several smallish buildings which were light and airy inside. By contrast the Potala, which I could see towering magnificently above the city in the distance, was dark, cold and gloomy inside.

I thus enjoyed a whole year free from any responsibility, happily playing with my brother and seeing my parents quite regularly. It was the last temporal liberty I was ever to know.

CHAPTER TWO

The Lion Throne

○

I REMEMBER very little of that first winter. But one thing has stuck firmly in my mind. At the end of the last month of the year, it was traditional for the monks of Namgyal monastery to perform *cham*, a ritual dance which symbolised driving out the negative forces of the past year. However, because I had not yet been formally enthroned, the Government felt it would be inappropriate for me to go to the Potala to see it. Lobsang Samten, on the other hand, was taken by my mother. I was exceedingly envious of him. When he came back late that evening, he teased me with very full descriptions of the leapings and swoopings of extravagantly costumed dancers.

Throughout the following year, that is 1940, I remained at the Norbulingka. I saw a good deal of my parents during the spring and summer months. When I was proclaimed Dalai Lama, they automatically acquired the status of the highest nobility and with it considerable property. They also had the use of a house in the palace grounds during that period each year. Almost every day, I used to steal over, with an attendant, to spend time with them. This was not really allowed, but the Regent, who was responsible for me, chose to ignore these excursions. I particularly enjoyed going over at mealtimes. This was because, as a young boy destined to be a monk, certain foods such as eggs and pork were forbidden to me, so it was only at my parents' house that I ever had the chance to taste them. Once, I remember being caught in the act of eating eggs by the *Gyop Kenpo*, one of my senior officials. He was very shocked, and so was I. 'Go away,' I shouted at the top of my voice!

On another occasion, I remember sitting next to my father and watching him like a little dog as he ate some pork crackling, hoping that he would give me some – which he did. It was delicious. So, altogether, my first year in Lhasa was a very happy time. I was still not yet a monk and my education lay before me. Lobsang Samten, for his part, enjoyed a year off from the schooling he had begun at Kumbum.

During the winter of 1940, I was taken to the Potala, where I was officially installed as spiritual leader of Tibet. I do not recall anything particular about the ceremony this entailed, save that it was the first time I sat on the Lion Throne, a vast, jewel-encrusted and beautifully carved wooden structure that stood in the *Si shi phuntsog* (Hall of All Good Deeds of the Spiritual and Temporal World), the principal stateroom in the east wing of the Potala.

Soon after, I was taken to the Jokhang temple, in the middle of the city, where I was inducted as a novice monk. This involved a ceremony known as *taphue*, meaning 'cutting of the hair'. From now on, I was to be shaven-headed and attired in maroon monk's robes. Again, I do not remember much about the ceremony itself except that at one point, on seeing the flamboyant costumes of some ritual dancers, I completely forgot myself and blurted out excitedly to Lobsang Samten, 'Look over there!'

My locks were symbolically shorn by Reting Rinpoché, the Regent, who, in addition to his position as head of state until I reached my majority, was also appointed as my Senior Tutor. At first I was cautious in my attitude to him, but I came to like him very much. His most striking feature, I remember, was a continually blocked nose. As a person, he was quite imaginative, with a very relaxed mental disposition, a man who took things easily. He loved picnics and horses, as a result of which he became good friends with my father. Sadly though, during his years as Regent, he had become something of a controversial figure and the Government itself was by now quite corrupt. For example, the practice of buying and selling high positions was commonplace.

At the time of my induction, there were rumours that Reting Rinpoché was not fit to perform the hair-cutting ceremony. It was suggested that he had broken his vows of celibacy and was therefore no longer a monk. There was also open criticism of the way he had punished an official who had spoken against him in the National Assembly. Nevertheless, in accordance with ancient custom, I forfeited my name Lhamo Thondup and assumed his, Jamphel Yeshe, along with several others, so that my full name now became Jamphel Ngawang Lobsang Yeshe Tenzin Gyatso.

In addition to Reting Rinpoché as Senior Tutor, I was appointed a Junior Tutor, Tathag Rinpoché, who was an especially spiritual man and very warm and kind. After our lessons together, he would often indulge in casual talks and jokes which I greatly appreciated. Finally, during my early years, Kewtsang Rinpoché, leader of the search party, was given unofficial responsibility as a third tutor. He stood in for the others whenever either of them was away.

I was particularly fond of Kewtsang Rinpoché. Like myself, he was from Amdo. He was so kind that I could never take him seriously. During our lessons, instead of reciting what I was supposed to, I used to hang round his neck and say, 'You recite!' Later, he warned Trijang Rinpoché, who became my Junior Tutor when I was around nineteen years old, that he should take care not to smile or I would be certain to take advantage of him.

These arrangements did not last long, however, for soon after I began my novitiate, Reting Rinpoché gave up the Regency, mainly on account of his unpopularity. Despite my being only six years old, I was asked who I thought should replace him. I nominated Tathag Rinpoché. He then became my Senior Tutor and was replaced as Junior Tutor by Ling Rinpoché.

While Tathag Rinpoché was a very gentle man, Ling Rinpoché was very reserved and stern, and to begin with I was really scared of him. I became afraid even at the sight of his servant and quickly learned to recognise the sound of his footsteps – at which my heart missed a beat. But in the end I became friendly towards him and we developed a very good relationship. He became my closest confidante right up until his death in 1983.

As well as my tutors, three men were appointed to be my personal attendants, all of them monks. They were the *Chöpon*

Khenpo, Master of the Ritual, the *Sölpon Khenpo*, Master of the Kitchen and the *Simpon Khenpo*, Master of the Robes. This last was Kenrap Tenzin, the member of the search party whose piercing eyes had made such an impression on me.

When I was very young, I developed a close attachment to the Master of the Kitchen. So strong was it that he had to be in my sight at all times, even if it was only the bottom of his robe visible through a doorway or under the curtains which served as doors inside Tibetan houses. Luckily, he tolerated my behaviour. He was a very kind and simple man, and almost completely bald. He was not a very good storyteller, nor an enthusiastic playmate, but this did not matter one bit.

I have often wondered since about our relationship. I see it now as being like the bond between a kitten or some small animal and the person who feeds it. I sometimes think that the act of bringing food is one of the basic roots of all relationships.

Immediately after my induction as a novice monk, I began to receive my primary education. This consisted solely of learning to read. Lobsang Samten and I were both taught together. I remember our schoolrooms (one at the Potala and one at the Norbulingka) very well. On opposite walls hung two whips, a yellow silk one and a leather one. The former, we were told, was reserved for the Dalai Lama and the latter was for the Dalai Lama's brother. These instruments of torture terrified us both. It took only a glance from our teacher at one or other of these whips to make me shiver with fear. Happily, the yellow one was never used, although the leather one came off the wall once or twice. Poor Lobsang Samten! Unluckily for him, he was not such a good student as I was. But then again, I have a suspicion that his beatings might have followed the old Tibetan proverb: 'Hit the goat to scare the sheep.' He was made to suffer on my behalf.

Although neither Lobsang Samten nor I were allowed to have friends of our own age, we were never short of company. Both at the Norbulingka and the Potala were an ample staff of sweepers, or room attendants (you could not call them footmen). Mostly they were middle-aged men of little or no education, some of whom had come to the job after serving in the army. Their duty was to keep the rooms tidy and to see to it that the floors were polished. This last I was very particular about as I enjoyed skating on them. When Lobsang Samten was eventually taken away because the two of us behaved so badly together, these men were my only companions. But what companions they were! Despite their age, they played like children.

I was about eight when Lobsang Samten was sent to study at a private school. Naturally, this saddened me for he was my sole contact with my family. Now I only saw him during his school holidays at the time of the full moon. When he left after each visit, I remember standing at the window watching, my heart full of sorrow, as he disappeared into the distance.

Apart from these monthly reunions, I had only the occasional visits of my mother to look forward to. When she came, she was usually accompanied by my elder sister, Tsering Dolma. I particularly enjoyed these visits as they would invariably bring presents of food. My mother was a wonderful cook and was well known for her excellent bakery and pastry.

When I reached my early teens, my mother would also bring with her Tenzin Choegyal, my youngest brother. He is twelve years my junior and if there was ever a more unruly child than myself, then it was he. One of his favourite games was to take ponies on to the roof of our parents' house. I also well remember one occasion when, as a small boy, he sidled up to me to say that Mother had recently ordered pork from the slaughterman. This was forbidden for, whilst it was acceptable to buy meat, it was not acceptable to order it since that might lead to an animal being killed specially to fulfil your requirement.

Tibetans have a rather curious attitude towards eating non-vegetarian food. Buddhism does not necessarily prohibit the eating of meat, but it does say that animals should not be killed for food. In Tibetan society it was permissible to eat meat – indeed it was essential as, apart from *tsampa*, there was often not much else – but not to be involved in butchery in any way. This was left to others. Some of it was undertaken by Muslims, of whom there was a thriving community, with its own mosque, settled in Lhasa. Throughout Tibet, there must have been several thousand Muslims. About half came originally from Kashmir, the remainder from China.

On one occasion, when my mother did bring me a present of some meat (sausages filled with rice and mince – a Taktser speciality), I remember eating it all at once, because I knew that if I told any of my sweepers about it I would have to share it with them. The next day, I was extremely ill. Following this incident, the Master of the Kitchen almost lost his job. Tathag Rinpoché thought he must have been at fault, so I was compelled to admit the truth of the matter. It was a good lesson.

Although it is very beautiful, the Potala was not a nice place to live. It was built on a rocky outcrop known as the 'Red Hill', on the site of a smaller building, at the end of the time of the Great Fifth Dalai Lama, who ruled during the seventeenth century by the Christian calendar. When he died in 1682, it was still far from completion so Desi Sangye Gyatso, his faithful Prime Minister, concealed the fact of his death for fifteen years until it was finished, saying only that His Holiness had embarked on a long retreat.

The Potala itself was not just a palace. It contained within its walls not only government offices and numerous storerooms, but also Namgyal (which means 'The Victorious') monastery with its 175 monks and many chapels, and a school for young monks destined to become *Tsedrung* officials.

As a child, I was given the Great Fifth's own bedroom on the seventh (top) storey. It was pitifully cold and ill-lit and I doubt whether it can have been touched since his time. Everything in it was ancient and decrepit, and behind the drapes that hung across each of the four walls lay deposits of centuries-old dust. At one end of the room stood an altar. On it were set small butter lamps (bowls of rancid *dri* butter into which a wick was set and lighted) and little dishes of food and water placed in offering to the Buddhas. Every day these would be plundered by mice. I became very fond of these little creatures. They were very beautiful and showed no fear as they helped themselves to their daily rations. At night, as I lay in bed, I would hear these companions of mine running to and fro. Sometimes they came over to my bed. This was the only substantial piece of furniture in my room, other than the altar, and consisted of a large wooden box filled with cushions and surrounded by long, red curtains. The mice would clamber over these too, their urine dripping down as I snuggled under my blankets below.

My daily routine was much the same at both the Potala and the Norbulingka, although at the latter the timings were brought forward an hour because of the longer days during summer. But this was no hardship. I have never enjoyed getting up after sunrise. Once I remember oversleeping and waking up to find Lobsang Samten already outside, playing. I was furious.

At the Potala, I used to get up at around six o'clock in the morning. After dressing, I undertook a short period of prayer and meditation, which lasted about an hour. Then, just after seven, my breakfast was brought in. This invariably consisted of tea and *tsampa*, with honey or caramel. I then had my first period of study with Kenrap Tenzin. After I had learned to read and until I reached the age of thirteen, this was always penmanship. There are two principal written scripts for the Tibetan language, *Uchen* and *U-me*. One is for manuscripts and the other for official documents and personal communications. It was only necessary for me to know how to write *U-me*, but as I learned quite quickly I taught myself *Uchen* as well.

I can't help laughing when I think back on these early morning lessons. For whilst I sat under the attentive eye of my Master of the Robes, I could hear my Master of the Ritual next door chanting his prayers. The 'schoolroom' was actually just a veranda, with rows of potted plants, situated adjacent to my bedroom. It was often quite cold there, but it was light and offered good opportunities to study the *dungkar*, small, black birds with a vivid red beak that used to build their nests high up in the Potala. Meanwhile, the Master of the Ritual sat in my bedroom. Unfortunately, he had a habit of falling asleep whilst reciting these morning prayers.

When this happened, his voice trailed off rather like a gramophone player running down when the electricity has failed as his chanting turned to a mumble and finally stopped. Then there would be a pause until he woke up, whereupon he would start up again. Only then he would get into a muddle as he wouldn't know where he had left off, so quite often he repeated himself several times over. It was very comical. But there was a good side to this. When eventually I came to learn these prayers myself, I already knew them by heart.

After penmanship came memorisation. This simply consisted of learning a Buddhist text for recital later on in the day. I found this very boring as I learned fast. I should say, though, that I often forgot just as quickly.

At ten o'clock came a respite from the morning's lessons when there was a meeting for members of the Government, which I had to attend even at a very young age. From the beginning, I was groomed for the day when, in addition to my position as spiritual leader of Tibet, I would assume temporal leadership as well. At the Potala, the assembly hall where this took place was next door to my room: the officials came up from the government offices which were on the second and third floors of the building. The meetings themselves were quite formal occasions – during which people's duties for the day were read out to them – and, of course, protocol regarding myself was strictly observed. My Lord Chamberlain, the *Donyer Chenmo*, would come to my room and lead me to the hall where I was greeted first by the Regent and then the four members of the *Kashag*, each according to rank.

After the morning meeting with the Government, I returned to my rooms for further instruction. I was now joined by my Junior Tutor, to whom I recited the passage I had learned during the period of memorisation that morning. He then read out to me the text for the next day, explaining it to me in detail as he went along. This session lasted until around noon. At this point, a bell was rung (as it was every hour – except once when the ringer forgot, so he rang it thirteen times at one o'clock!). Also at noon, a conch was blown. Then followed the most important part of the young Dalai Lama's day: play.

I was very fortunate in that I had quite a good collection of toys. When I was very young, there was an official at Dromo, a village on the border with India, who used to send up imported toys to me, along with boxes of apples when they were available. Also, I used to be given gifts by the various foreign officials who came to Lhasa. One of my favourites was a Meccano set given to me by the head of the British Trade Mission, which had an office in the capital. As I grew older, I acquired several more sets of Meccano until by the time I was about fifteen I had them all, ranging from the easiest to the most difficult.

When I was seven years old, a deputation of two American officials came to Lhasa. They brought with them, in addition to a letter from President Roosevelt, a pair of beautiful singing birds and a magnificent gold watch. These were both welcome presents. I was not so impressed with the gifts brought to me by visiting Chinese officials, however. Bolts of silk were of no interest to a small boy.

Another favourite toy was a clockwork train set. I also had a very good set of lead soldiers, which, when I was older, I learned to melt down and recast as monks. In their original form, I enjoyed using them in wargames. I used to spend ages setting them out. Then, when battle was commenced, it took only minutes to devastate the beautiful formations that I had arranged them in. The same went for another game which involved making tiny models of tanks and aeroplanes from *tsampa* dough, or *pa*, as it is properly known.

First of all, I would hold a competition amongst my grown-up friends to see who could produce the best models. Each person was given an equal amount of dough and allowed, say, half an hour to build an army. I then judged the results. There was no danger of losing this stage of the game as I am quite dextrous. Often I would disqualify the others for making such bad models. I would then sell some of my models to my opponents for twice as much dough as it took to make them. In this way I contrived to end up with much the strongest forces and at the same time I was able to derive satisfaction from bartering. Then we joined battle. Up until now, I had had everything my own way, so this was when I generally lost. For my sweepers never gave quarter in any sort of competition. I often tried to use my position as Dalai Lama to my advantage, but it was no use. I played very forcefully. Quite often I lost my temper and used my fists, but they still did not give in. Sometimes they even made me cry.

Another favourite pursuit of mine was military drill, which I learned from Norbu Thondup, my favourite sweeper and one of those who had been in the army. I was always so full of energy as a boy that I enjoyed anything that involved physical activity. I loved one particular jumping game – which was officially banned – which involved running as fast as you could up a board set at an angle of about 45° and leaping off at the top. However, my tendency to aggression did once almost get me into serious trouble. I had found an old, ivory-topped swagger-stick amongst my predecessor's belongings. This I took for my own. One day, I was swinging it violently around my head when it slipped from my hand and went spinning hard into Lobsang Samten's face. He dropped to the floor with a crash. For a second, I was convinced that I had killed him. After a few stunned moments, he stood up, in floods of tears and with blood pouring from a terrible deep gash on his right eyebrow. This subsequently became infected and took a very long time to heal. Poor Lobsang Samten ended up with a prominent mark that scarred him for the rest of his life.

Shortly after one o'clock came a light lunch. Now it so happened that, because of the Potala's position, sunlight flooded the room at midday when my morning's studies ended. But by two o'clock it had begun to fade and the room fell back into shadow. I hated this moment: as the room sank back into shade, a shadow fell across my heart. My afternoon studies began soon after lunch. The first hour and a half consisted of a period of general education with my Junior Tutor. It was all he could do to hold my attention. I was a very reluctant pupil and disliked all subjects equally.

The curriculum that I studied was the same as that for all monks pursuing a doctorate in Buddhist studies. It was very unbalanced and in many ways totally inappropriate for the leader of a country during the late twentieth century. Altogether, my curriculum embraced five major and five minor subjects, the former being: logic; Tibetan art and culture; Sanskrit; medicine; and Buddhist philosophy. This last is the most important (and most difficult) and is subdivided into a further five categories: *Prajnaparamita*, the perfection of wisdom; *Madhyamika*, the philosophy of the Middle Way; *Vinaya*, the canon of monastic discipline; *Abidharma*, metaphysics; and *Pramana*, logic and epistemology.

The five minor subjects are poetry; music and drama; astrology; metre and phrasing; and synonyms. Actually, the doctorate itself is awarded on the basis only of Buddhist philosophy, logic and dialectics. For this reason, it was not until the mid-1970s that I studied Sanskrit grammar; and certain subjects, such as medicine, I have never studied other than in an informal way.

Fundamental to the Tibetan system of monastic education is dialectics, or the art of debating. Two disputants take turns in asking questions, which they pose to the accompaniment of stylised gestures. As the question is put, the interrogator brings his right hand up over his head and slaps it down on to his extended left hand and stamps his left foot on the ground. He then slides his right hand away from the left, close to the head of his opponent. The person who is being asked questions remains passive and concentrates on trying not only to answer, but also to turn the tables on his opponent, who is all the time pacing around him. Wit is an important part of these debates and high merit is earned by turning your opponent's postulates to your own humorous advantage. This makes dialectics a popular form of entertainment even amongst uneducated Tibetans who, though they might not follow the intellectual acrobatics involved, can still appreciate the fun and the spectacle. In the old days, it was not unusual to see nomads and other country people from far outside Lhasa spend part of their day watching learned debates in the courtyard of a monastery.

A monk's ability at this unique form of disputation is the criterion by which his intellectual achievements are judged. For this reason, as Dalai Lama, I had to have not only a good grounding in Buddhist philosophy and logic but also proficiency at debating. I therefore began to study subjects in earnest when I was ten years old and at twelve I was appointed two *tsenshap*, experts who coached me in the art of dialectics.

After the first of the afternoon periods of study, my tutor spent the next hour explaining how to debate the topic of the day. Then at four, tea was served. If there is anyone who drinks more tea than the British, it is the Tibetans. According to one Chinese statistic I came across recently, Tibet imported ten million tons of tea annually from China before the invasion. This cannot possibly be true as it implies that every Tibetan drank almost two tons per year. The figure was obviously invented to try to prove Tibet's economic dependence on China, but it does give an indication of our fondness for tea.

Having said that, I do not entirely share my countrymen's liking for it. In Tibetan society, tea is traditionally drunk salted and with *dri* butter in place of milk. This makes a very good and nourishing drink providing it is carefully prepared, but the taste depends very much on the quality of the butter. The Potala kitchens were regularly supplied with fresh, creamy butter and the brew they produced was excellent. But that was the only time I ever really enjoyed Tibetan tea. Today I generally drink it English style, in the mornings and evenings. During the afternoons, I drink plain hot water, a habit I picked up in China during the 1950s. Though this might sound insipid, it is in fact extremely healthy. Hot water is considered to be the first remedy in the Tibetan medical system.

After tea, the two *tsenshap* monks arrived and I spent the next hour and a bit debating abstract questions like, for example, what is the nature of Mind? At last the day's tribulations would come to an end at approximately half-past five. I cannot give accurate times as Tibetans do not have the same high regard for clocks as do some people and things tended to start and finish when convenient. Hurry was always avoided.

As soon as my tutor had gone, I would rush out on to the roof, if I was at the Potala, with my telescope. It held a magnificent view over Lhasa from the Chakpori Medical School nearby to the Holy City, that part of the capital which lay round the Jokhang temple, in the distance. However, I was much more interested in the village of Shöl, which lay far below at the foot of the Red Hill. For it was here that the state prison stood and this was the time when the prisoners were allowed to walk in the compound. I considered them to be my friends and kept a close eye on their movements. They knew this and whenever they caught sight of me threw themselves down in prostration. I recognised them all and always knew when someone was released or there was a new arrival. I also used to check the piles of firewood and fodder that lay in the courtyard.

After this inspection, there was time for more play inside – for example, drawing – before my evening meal, which was brought to me soon after seven. This consisted of tea (inevitably), broth, sometimes with a little meat, and yoghurt or *sho*, together with a generous supply of different varieties of bread baked by my mother and sent up to me fresh every week. My favourite was that made in the Amdo style – small round loaves with a hard crust and light and fluffy inside.

Quite often I managed to eat this meal with one or more of my sweepers. They were voracious eaters, all of them. Their bowls were big enough to hold a whole kettle's worth of tea. Other times, I ate with some monks from Namgyal monastery. Generally, however, I shared my meals with just my three monk attendants and sometimes the *Chikyab Kenpo*, my Chief of Staff. In the absence of the latter, they were always boisterous occasions, and very happy too. I especially remember evening meals in winter when we sat by the fire eating our hot broth by the light of flickering butter lamps and listening to the moan of a snow-laden wind outside.

After eating I would go down the seven flights of stairs into the courtyard, where I was supposed to recite scripture and pray as I walked. But when I was young and still carefree, I hardly ever did so. Instead, I would spend the time either thinking up stories or anticipating the ones that would be told to me before going to bed. Very often, these were of a supernatural nature, so it would be a very scared Dalai Lama who crept into his dark, vermin-infested bedroom at nine o'clock. One of the most frightening tales concerned giant owls which were supposed to snatch small boys after dark. This was based on an ancient fresco in the Jokhang temple. It made me very particular about being inside by nightfall.

My life both at the Potala and the Norbulingka was very routine. It only varied at the time of important festivals or when I undertook a retreat. During the latter, I was accompanied by one of my Tutors, though sometimes both, or other senior lamas from Namgyal monastery. Usually, I did one each year, during winter. Generally, they lasted three weeks, during which I had only one short lesson and was not allowed to play outside, just long periods of prayer and meditation conducted under supervision. As a child, I did not always enjoy this. I spent a lot of the time looking out of one or other of my bedroom windows. The one to the north faced Sera monastery, with mountains in the background. The one to the south faced into the great hall where the morning meetings with the Government were held.

This hall was hung with a collection of priceless, old *thangkas*, embroidered silk hangings depicting the life of Milarepa, one of Tibet's best-loved spiritual masters. I often used to gaze at these beautiful pictures. I wonder what happened to them.

The evenings during my retreats were even worse than the days, as it was at this time that young boys of my own age would drive their cows back home to the village of Shöl at the base of the Potala. I well remember sitting quietly saying *mantras* during the stillness of the fading light and hearing their songs as they returned from the pastures nearby. On a few occasions, I wished that I could change place with them. But gradually I came to appreciate the value of making retreats. Today I dearly wish I had more time for them.

Basically , I got on well with all of my tutors as I was quick to learn. I have quite a good mind, as I discovered with some satisfaction when I was put with some of Tibet's 'super scholars'. But mostly I just worked hard enough to keep out of trouble.

However, there came a time when my tutors became worried about my rate of progress. So Kenrap Tenzin organised a mock exam in which I was to compete with Norbu Thondup, my favourite sweeper. Unknown to me, Kenrap Tenzin had briefed him fully beforehand, with the result that I lost the contest. I was devastated, especially as my humiliation was public.

The trick succeeded and for a time I worked very hard out of sheer anger. But in the end my good intentions wore off and I slipped back into my old ways. It was not until I was given my majority that I realised how important my education was and thereafter began to take a proper interest in my studies. Today I regret my early idleness and always study for at least four hours a day. One thing that I think might have made a difference to my early schooling is some real competition. Because I had no class-mates, I never had anyone to measure myself against.

When I was about nine years old, I discovered amongst my predecessor's belongings two old, hand-cranked movie projectors and several rolls of film. At first, nobody could be found who knew how to operate them. Eventually, an old Chinese monk, who as a boy had been presented by his parents to the Thirteenth Dalai Lama when he visited China in 1908 and who now lived permanently at the Norbulingka, was discovered to be a good technician. He was a very kind man and very sincere, with a strict devotion to his religious calling, although, like many Chinese, he had a very bad temper.

One of the films was a newsreel of King George v's coronation, which impressed me very much with its rows and rows of splendidly uniformed soldiers from all over the world. Another contained intriguing trick photography which showed female dancers being somehow hatched out of eggs. But most interesting of all was a documentary about gold mining. From it, I learned what a dangerous occupation mining is, and under what difficult conditions miners work. Later, whenever I heard about the exploitation of the working class (which I often did during the years to come), I thought of this film.

Unfortunately, the old Chinese monk, with whom I had quickly become very good friends, died not very long after this important discovery. Luckily, I had by this time worked out how to use the projectors for myself, and in so doing gained my first experience of electricity and the workings of dynamos. This turned out to be very useful when I received a gift, apparently from the British Royal Family, of a modern electrical projector with its own generator. It was delivered via the British Trade Mission, and Reginald Fox, the assistant Trade Commissioner, came to show me how to use it.

Because of its altitude, many diseases common to other parts of the world are unknown in Tibet. However, there was one which was an ever-present danger: smallpox. When I was about ten years old, I was appointed a new, rather plump, doctor who, using imported medicine, vaccinated me against the disease. This was a very painful experience which, in addition to leaving me with four prominent scars on my arm, caused considerable pain and brought on a fever which lasted for about two weeks. I remember complaining a great deal about 'that fat doctor'.

My other personal physician at the time was nicknamed Doctor Lenin on account of his goatee beard. He was a small man with a huge appetite and an excellent sense of humour. I particularly valued him for his skill at storytelling. Both of these men were trained according to the traditional Tibetan system of medicine, about which I shall speak more in a later chapter.

Also when I was ten, the world war which had been raging for the past five years ended. I knew very little about it save that when it was over my Government sent a mission bearing gifts and a message of congratulations to the British Government in India. The officials were received by Lord Wavell, the Viceroy. The following year, a delegation was again sent to India to represent Tibet at a conference on Asian Relations.

Shortly afterwards, during the early spring of 1947, a very sad incident occurred which epitomises the way in which the selfish pursuit of personal interest amongst those in high office can have repercussions affecting the fate of a country.

One day, whilst I was watching a debate, I heard the sounds of shots being fired. The noise came from the north, in the direction of Sera monastery. I rushed outside, full of excitement at the prospect of doing some real work with my telescope. Yet, at the same time I was also very troubled as I realised that gunfire also meant killing. It turned out that Reting Rinpoché, who had announced his political retirement six years previously, had decided to claim the Regency back. He was supported in this by certain monks and lay officials who organised a plot against Tathag Rinpoché. This resulted in Reting Rinpoché's arrest and the death of a considerable number of his followers.

Reting Rinpoché was subsequently brought to the Potala, where he made a request that he be allowed to see me. Unfortunately, this was refused on my behalf and he died in prison not long afterwards. Naturally, as a minor, I had very little opportunity to become involved in judicial matters, but looking back, I sometimes wonder whether in this case I might not have been able to do something. Had I intervened in some way, it is possible that the destruction of Reting monastery, one of the oldest and most beautiful in Tibet, might have been prevented. All in all the whole affair was very silly. Yet, despite his mistakes, I still retain a deep personal respect for Reting Rinpoché as my first tutor and *guru*. After his death, his names were dropped from mine – until I restored them many years later on the instructions of the oracle.

Not long after these unhappy events, I went with Tathag Rinpoché to Drepung and Sera monasteries (which lie respectively about five miles west and three and a half miles north of Lhasa). Drepung was at that time the largest monastery in the world, with over seven thousand monks. Sera was not much smaller, with five thousand. This visit marked my public debut as a dialectician. I was to debate with the abbots of each of Drepung's three colleges and of Sera's two colleges. Because of the recent disturbances, extra security precautions were taken, which made me feel uncomfortable. In addition, I was very nervous to be going to these great seats of learning for the first time during this lifetime. Yet somehow, they were both very familiar to me and I became convinced of some connection from my previous lives. The debates, which were conducted before audiences of hundreds of monks, went off well enough, despite my nervousness.

Also, at around this time, I received from Tathag Rinpoché the special teaching of the Fifth Dalai Lama, which is considered to be particular to the Dalai Lama himself. It was received by the Great Fifth (as he is still known to all Tibetans) in a vision. In the following weeks, I had a number of unusual experiences, particularly in the form of dreams which, although they did not seem significant then, I now see as being very important.

One of the compensations of living in the Potala was that it contained numerous storerooms. These were far more interesting to a small boy than those rooms which contained silver or gold or priceless religious artefacts; more interesting even than the vast, jewel-encrusted tombs of each of my predecessors down in the vaults. I much preferred the armoury with its collection of old swords, flintlock guns and suits of armour. But even this was as nothing compared with the unimaginable treasures in the rooms containing some of my predecessor's belongings. Amongst these I found an old air rifle, complete with targets and ammunition, and the telescope, to which I have already referred, not to mention piles of illustrated books in English about the First World War. These fascinated me and provided the blueprints for the model ships, tanks and aeroplanes that I made. When I was older, I had parts of them translated into Tibetan.

I also found two pairs of European shoes. Even though my feet were far too small, I took them to wear, stuffing bits of cloth into the toes so that they fitted more or less. I was thrilled at the sound they made with their heavy, steel-capped heels.

One of the things I most enjoyed as a child was to take objects apart and then try to reassemble them. I became quite good at it. However, in the beginning, I was not always successful in my efforts. One of the items that I came across amongst my predecessor's belongings was an old musical box that had been given to him by the Tsar of Russia, with whom he had been on friendly terms. It was not working, so I decided to try to mend it. I found that the mainspring was overwound and jammed. As I poked at it with my screwdriver, the mechanism suddenly freed itself and unwound uncontrollably, flinging out all the thin shards of metal that made the music. I shall never forget the demonic symphony of noise as the bits went flying round the room. As I think back on this incident, I realise that I was lucky not to lose an eye. My face was right up close as I fiddled with the mechanism. I might have been mistaken in later life for Moshe Dayan!

I was very grateful to Thupten Gyatso, the Thirteenth Dalai Lama, for having been given so many wonderful gifts. Many of the sweepers at the Potala had served him during his lifetime, and from them I came to know something about his life. I learned that not only was he a highly accomplished spiritual master, but also a very able and far-sighted secular leader. I also came to know that he had twice been forced into exile by foreign invaders – first by the British, who sent in an army under the command of Colonel Younghusband in 1903, and secondly by the Manchus in 1910. In the first case, the British withdrew of their own accord, but in the second, the Manchu army was forcibly ejected during the winter of 1911–12.

My predecessor also took a great interest in modern technology. Amongst the things he imported to Tibet were an electrical generating plant, a mint for producing both coins and Tibet's first paper currency, and three cars. These were the sensation of Tibet. At the time, there was almost no wheeled transport in the country. Even horse-drawn wagons were virtually unknown. Of course they were known about, but the unyielding nature of the Tibetan land mass meant that pack animals were the only practical form of conveyance.

Thupten Gyatso was also visionary in other ways. After his second period of exile, he arranged for four young Tibetans to be sent to Britain for education. The experiment was successful, the boys did well – and were even received by the Royal Family, but sadly there was no follow-up. Had the practice of sending children abroad for education been implemented on a regular basis, as he intended, I am quite certain that Tibet's situation today would be very different. The Thirteenth Dalai Lama's reform of the army, which he recognised to be a vital deterrent, was likewise successful but unsustained after his death.

Another plan of his was to strengthen the Lhasa Government's authority in Kham. He realised that due to its distance from Lhasa, Kham in particular had been neglected by the central administration. He therefore proposed that the sons of local chieftains be brought to Lhasa for education and then sent back with government posts. He also wanted to encourage local recruitment for the army. But unfortunately, due to inertia, neither scheme materialised.

The Thirteenth Dalai Lama's political insight was also extraordinary. In his last written testament he warned that, unless there were radical changes,

> 'It may happen that here in Tibet, religion and government will be attacked both from without and within. Unless we guard our own country, it will now happen that the Dalai and Panchen Lamas, the Father and the Son, and all the revered holders of the Faith, will disappear and become nameless. Monks and their monasteries will be destroyed. The rule of law will be weakened. The lands and property of government officials will be seized. They themselves will be forced to serve their enemies or wander the country like beggars. All beings will be sunk in great hardship and overwhelming fear; the days and nights will drag on slowly in suffering.'

The Panchen Lamas referred to in the text represent, after the Dalai Lamas, the highest spiritual authority in Tibetan Buddhism. By tradition, their seat is Tashilhunpo monastery in Shigatse, the second largest city in Tibet.

Personally, the Thirteenth Dalai Lama was a very simple man. He did away with many old customs. For example, it used to be the case that whenever the Dalai Lama left his chambers, any servant who happened to be in the vicinity would immediately leave. He said that this procedure gave unnecessary trouble to people and made him reluctant to appear. So he abolished the rule.

As a child, I heard a number of stories about my predecessor that illustrate how down-to-earth he was. One of them, told to me by a very old man whose son was a monk at Namgyal monastery, concerned a time when a new building was being put up in the grounds of the Norbulingka. As usual, many members of the public came to lay a stone in the foundations to mark their respect and well-wishing. One day a nomad from faraway (the father of the person who told me this story) came to make a contribution. He had with him a very cantankerous mule, which, as soon as he turned his back to make the offering, sped off in search of freedom. Luckily, someone was walking in the opposite direction. The nomad called out to this person, asking him to grab the wandering mule. This the stranger did and brought it over. The nomad was at first delighted and then amazed, for his rescuer turned out to be none other than the Dalai Lama himself.

But the Thirteenth Dalai Lama was also very strict. He forbade the smoking of tobacco both at the Potala and in the grounds of the Norbulingka. However, there was one occasion when he was out walking and came to a place where some stonemasons were working. They did not see him and were talking amongst themselves. One of them complained loudly about the tobacco prohibition, saying that it was very good when a person is tired and hungry. He was going to chew some anyway. The Dalai Lama, on hearing this, turned away and left without making his presence known.

This does not mean that he was always lenient. If I have anything critical to say about him, it is that I feel he may have been a bit too autocratic. He was extremely severe with his high officials and came down heavily on them for the slightest mistake. He confined his generosity to simple people.

Thupten Gyatso's greatest achievements in the spiritual field concerned his dedication to raising the standard of scholarship in the monasteries (of which there were over six thousand in all Tibet). In doing so, he gave precedence to the most able monks, even if they were junior. Also, he personally ordained many thousands of novices. Right up until the 1970s, most of the senior monks had received their ordinations as *bikshus* from him.

Up until my early twenties, when I began to remain there permanently, I moved each year to the Norbulingka during early spring, returning to the Potala around six months later with the onset of winter. The day that I quit my gloomy room in the Potala was undoubtedly one of my favourite during the whole year. It began with a ceremony that lasted for two hours (which seemed like an eternity to me). Then came the great procession, which I did not much care for. I would rather have walked and enjoyed the countryside, whose fresh outpourings of natural beauty were just beginning to show themselves in delicate shoots of green.

The diversions at the Norbulingka were endless. It consisted of a beautiful park surrounded by a high wall. Within this there were a number of buildings which were lived in by the members of staff. There was also an inner wall, known as the Yellow Wall, beyond which no one but the Dalai Lama, his immediate household and certain monks were allowed. On the other side of it lay several more buildings, including the Dalai Lama's private residence which was surrounded by a well-kept garden.

I happily whiled away hours in the park walking through the beautiful gardens and watching some of the many animals and birds that lived there. Amongst these were, at one time or another, a herd of tame musk deer; at least six *dogkhyi*, enormous Tibetan mastiffs which acted as guard dogs; a Pekinese sent from Kumbum; a few mountain goats; a monkey; a handful of camels brought from Mongolia; two leopards and a very old and rather sad tiger (these last in pens, of course); several parrots; half-a-dozen peacocks; some cranes; a pair of golden geese; and about thirty, very unhappy Canada geese whose wings had been clipped so that they could not fly: I felt very sorry for them.

One of the parrots was very friendly with Kenrap Tenzin, my Master of the Robes. He used to feed it nuts. As it nibbled from his fingers, he used to stroke its head, at which the bird appeared to enter a state of ecstasy. I very much wanted this kind of friendliness and several times tried to get a similar response, but to no avail. So I took a stick to punish it. Of course, thereafter it fled at the sight of me. This was a very good lesson in how to make friends: not by force but by compassion.

Ling Rinpoché had a similarly good relationship with the monkey. It was friendly only with him. He used to feed it from his pocket, so that whenever the monkey saw him coming, it would scamper over and start delving amongst the folds of his robes.

I had slightly better luck in making friends with the fish which lived in a large, well-stocked lake. I used to stand at the edge and call them. If they responded, I rewarded them with small pieces of bread and pa. However, they had a tendency to disobedience and sometimes would ignore me. If this happened, I got very angry and, rather than throw them food, I would open up with an artillery barrage of rocks and stones. But when they did come over, I was very careful to see to it that the small ones got their fair share. If necessary, I would use a stick to prod the larger ones out of the way.

Once whilst I was playing at the edge of this lake, I caught sight of a lump of wood floating near the edge. I started to try to sink it with my fish-prodding stick. The next thing I knew, I was lying on the grass seeing stars. I had fallen in and started to drown. Luckily, one of my sweepers, an ex-soldier from far western Tibet, had been keeping an eye on me and came to the rescue.

Another attraction of the Norbulingka was its proximity to a tributary of the Kyichu river, which lay a few minutes' walk beyond the outer wall. As a small boy I used to go out incognito quite often, accompanied by an attendant, and walk to the water's edge. At first, this practice was ignored, but eventually Tathag Rinpoché put a stop to it. Unfortunately, protocol regarding the Dalai Lama was very strict. I was compelled to remain hidden away like an owl. In fact, the conservatism of Tibetan society at that time was such that it was considered improper for senior government ministers even to be seen looking down on to the street.

At the Norbulingka as at the Potala, I spent a great deal of time with the sweepers. Even at a very young age, I had a dislike of protocol and formality and much preferred the company of servants to that of, say, members of the Government. I particularly enjoyed being with my parents' servants, with whom I spent a lot of time whenever I went over to my family's house. Most of them came from Amdo and I liked very much to hear stories about my own village and others nearby.

I also enjoyed their company when we went and raided my parents' food stores. They were also glad of mine on these occasions, for obvious reasons: it was an exercise in mutual benefit. The best time for these forays was in late autumn when there would always be fresh supplies of delicious dried meat, which we dipped in chilli sauce. I liked this so much that, on one occasion, I ate far too much and soon afterwards I was violently sick. As I bent over, retching in agony, Kenrap Tenzin caught sight of me and gave some words of encouragement, something like, 'That's it. Get it all up. It's good for you.' I felt very foolish and did not thank him for his attention.

Although I was Dalai Lama, my parents' servants treated me just as they would any other small boy, as in fact did everyone except on formal occasions. I received no special treatment and no one was afraid to speak their mind to me. Accordingly, I learned at an early age that life was not always easy for my people. My sweepers likewise told me freely about themselves and the injustices they suffered at the hands of officials and high lamas. They also kept me in touch with all the gossip of the day. This often took the form of songs and ballads which people sang as they worked. So, although my childhood was quite lonely at times, and although at the age of about twelve Tathag Rinpoché forbade me from going any more to my parents' house, my early life was not in the least like Prince Siddhartha's or that of Pu Yi, the last Emperor of China. Besides, as I grew up I came into contact with a number of interesting people.

There were about ten Europeans living in Lhasa throughout my childhood. I did not see much of them and it was not until Lobsang Samten brought Heinrich Harrer to me that I had the chance to get to know an *inji*, as Westerners are known in Tibetan.

Amongst those settled in the capital when I was growing up were Sir Basil Gould, head of the British Trade Mission, and his successor, Hugh Richardson, who has since written some books about Tibet and with whom I have had several useful discussions since coming into exile. And, in addition to Reginald Fox, there was also a British medical officer, whose name I cannot recall. However, I shall never forget one occasion when this man was summoned to the Norbulingka to treat one of the peacocks which had a cyst under its eye. I watched him very carefully and listened in amazement as he spoke to it in reassuring tones using both Lhasa dialect and honorific Tibetan (which are virtually two distinct languages). It struck me as something very extraordinary when this strange man addressed the bird as 'Honourable peacock'!

Heinrich Harrer turned out to be a delightful person with blond hair such as I had never seen before. I nicknamed him *Gopse*, meaning 'yellow head'. As an Austrian, he had been interned during the Second World War, a prisoner of the British in India. But somehow he had managed to escape with a fellow prisoner named Peter Aufschnaiter. Together they had made their way to Lhasa. This was a great achievement, as Tibet was officially out of bounds to all foreigners, except the few who had special dispensation. It took them about five years living as nomads before they finally reached the capital. When they arrived, people were so impressed by their bravery and persistence that the Government permitted them to stay. Naturally, I was one of the first to hear of their arrival and I became quite curious to see what they were like, especially Harrer, as he quickly developed a reputation as an interesting and sociable person.

He spoke excellent colloquial Tibetan and had a wonderful sense of humour, although he was also full of respect and courtesy. As I began to get to know him better, he dropped the formality and became very forthright, except when my officials were present. I greatly valued this quality. We first met in 1948, I think, and for the next year and a half before he left Tibet I saw him regularly, usually once a week. From him I was able to learn something about the outside world and especially about Europe and the recent war. He also helped me with my English, which I had recently begun to study with one of my officials. I already knew the alphabet, which I had had translated into Tibetan phonetics, and was eager to learn more. Harrer assisted me in a number of practical ways as well.

For example, he helped me with the generator that was presented to me along with the electrical projector. It had turned out to be very old and sick. I have often wondered whether the British officials did not keep the generator intended for my use and pass on their own old one to me!

Another great enthusiasm of mine at this time was for the three cars that the Thirteenth Dalai Lama had imported into Tibet. Although there were no proper roads, he had used them occasionally for transport in and around Lhasa up until the time of his death. Thereafter they were not used and fell into disrepair. They now stood in a building at the Norbulingka. One of them was an American Dodge; the two others were both Baby Austins. All were of late 1920s' vintage. There was also a Willys jeep, which was acquired by the Tibetan Trade Mission that travelled to America in 1948, but which was rarely used.

As with the movie projectors, it took some time before I could trace anyone who knew anything about cars. But I was determined that they should be put back into service. Eventually a driver, Tashi Tsering, was found, another man with a very short temper, who came originally from Kalimpong, just south of the border with India. Between us we worked on the cars and finally, by plundering one of the Austins for parts, we got the other one going. Both the Dodge and the jeep were in better condition and they ran after only minor tinkering.

Of course, once we had the cars working, I was not allowed to go anywhere near them. But this became too much for me and one day, when I knew that my driver was away, I decided to take one of them out for a drive. Both the Dodge and the jeep required keys to start and these were in the possession of my driver.

However, the Baby Austin had magneto ignition and could be started by turning a crank handle.

Very gingerly, I reversed it out of its shed and proceeded to take a turn around the garden. Unfortunately, the Norbulingka park is full of trees and it was not very long before I collided with one of them. To my horror I saw that the glass of one of the headlamps was smashed. Unless I could repair it before the following day, my joyride would be discovered by my driver and I would be in trouble.

I managed to get the car back without further damage and at once began trying to repair the broken glass. To my further dismay I found that it was not ordinary glass, but tinted. So although I managed to find a piece that I was able to fashion well enough to fit, I was then faced with the problem of getting it to match the original. This I eventually succeeded in doing by smearing it with sugar syrup. In the end I was well pleased with my handiwork. But even so, I felt extremely guilty when I next saw my driver. I felt sure that he must know, or at least that he would find out, what had happened. But he never said a word. I shall never forget Tashi Tsering. He is still alive and now living in India, and although I rarely see him, I continue to regard him as a good friend.

The Tibetan calendar is rather complicated. It is based on a lunar month. Also, rather than centuries of hundreds of years, we follow a sixty-year cycle, each one of which is assigned to one of the five elements, whose order is earth, air, fire, water and iron; and one of twelve animals: the mouse, the ox, the tiger, the hare, the dragon, the serpent, the horse, the sheep, the monkey, the bird, the dog and the pig, again in order. Each of the elements comes twice, first in its male and then in its female aspect. They thus end with the tenth year. Then the first element is joined to the eleventh and twelfth animals, the second to the thirteenth and fourteenth animals, and so on. So for example, according to the Tibetan calendar, the year 2,000 AD will be the Iron Dragon year.

Throughout the centuries preceding Tibet's invasion by China, the seasons were marked by numerous festival days. Generally these had a religious significance, but they were celebrated by monks and laymen alike. For the latter, the time was passed in eating, drinking, singing, dancing and playing games, combined intermittently with prayer.

One of the most important of these events was the New Year celebration, or *Losar*, which comes in either February or March of the Western calendar. For me its particular significance was my annual, public meeting with Nechung, the state oracle. I shall discuss this in a later chapter, but essentially this gave me and the Government the opportunity to consult, via a medium, or *kuten*, with Dorje Drakden, the protector divinity of Tibet, about the coming year.

There was one festival that I had very mixed feelings about. This was *Monlam*, the Great Prayer Festival, which followed directly after *Losar* – the reason being that as Dalai Lama, I had, even at a very young age, to participate in its most important ceremony. The other bad thing about *Monlam* was the fact that I invariably had to endure a severe bout of flu, just as I do today whenever I go to Bodh Gaya in India, due to the dust. This was because I took up residence in rooms at the Jokhang temple, which were even more derelict than my room at the Potala.

The ceremony, or *puja*, that I feared so much took place in the afternoon, at the end of the first of two weeks devoted to *Monlam*. It followed a long discourse on the life of the Buddha Shakyamuni given by the Regent. The *puja* itself lasted for over four hours, after which I had to recite from memory a long and difficult passage of scripture. I was so nervous that I took in not a word of what came before. My Senior Tutor, the Regent, my Junior Tutor and the Masters of the Ritual, Robes and Kitchen were all equally anxious. Their main worry was that because I sat high up on a throne throughout the ceremony, no one could easily prompt me if I got stuck.

But remembering my lines was only half the problem. Because the proceedings went on for so long, I had an additional dread: I feared that my bladder might not hold out. In the end everything went well, even the first time when I was so young. But I remember being apoplectic with fear. It dulled my senses to the point where I no longer noticed what was going on around me. I ceased to be aware even of the pigeons which flew around the inside of the building, stealing from the offering plates. I only noticed them again when I was halfway through my oration.

When it was over I was ecstatically happy. Not only was the whole dreadful business over for another twelve months, but there now followed one of the best moments in the Dalai Lama's year. After the ceremony I was allowed outside to walk round the streets so that I could see the *thorma*, the huge, gaily coloured butter sculptures traditionally offered to the Buddhas on this day. There were also puppet shows and music played by military bands and an atmosphere of tremendous happiness amongst the people.

The Jokhang temple is the holiest shrine in all Tibet. It was built during the reign of King Songtsen Gampo in the seventh century AD to house a statue brought by one of his wives, Bhrikuti Devi, daughter of the Nepalese King Anshuriaruam. (Songtsen Gampo had four other wives, three of them Tibetan and one Chinese, Princess Wengchen Kongjo, daughter of the second Emperor of the Tang dynasty.) Over the centuries the temple was expanded and embellished considerably. One outstanding feature of the Jokhang is the stone monument which still stands at its entrance bearing witness to the historical power of Tibet. Its inscription, engraved in both Tibetan and Chinese, records the perpetual treaty concluded by Tibet and China in AD 821–2:

> 'The Great King of Tibet, the Miraculous Divine Lord, and the Great King of China, the Chinese Ruler Hwang-ti, being in the relationship of nephew and uncle, have conferred together for the alliance of their kingdoms. They have made and ratified a great agreement. Gods and men all know it and bear witness so that it may never be changed; and an account of the agreement has been engraved on this stone pillar to inform future ages and generations.

'The Miraculous Divine Lord Trisong Dretsen and the Chinese King Wen Wu Hsiao-te Hwang-ti, nephew and uncle, seeking in their far-reaching wisdom to prevent all causes of harm to the welfare of their countries now or in the future, have extended their benevolence impartially over all. With the single desire of acting for the peace and benefit of all their subjects they have agreed on the high purpose of ensuring lasting good; and they have made this great treaty in order to fulfil their decision to restore the former ancient friendship and mutual regard and the old relationship of friendly neighbourliness.

'Tibet and China shall abide by the frontiers of which they are now in occupation. All to the east is the country of Great China; and all to the west is, without question, the country of Great Tibet. Henceforth on neither side shall there be waging of war nor seizing of territory. If any person incurs suspicion he shall be arrested; his business shall be inquired into and he shall be escorted back.

'Now that the two kingdoms have been allied by this great treaty it is necessary that messengers should once again be sent by the old route to maintain communications and carry the exchange of friendly messages regarding the harmonious relations between the nephew and uncle. According to the old custom, horses shall be changed at the foot of the Chiang Chun pass, the frontier between Tibet and China. At the Suiyung barrier the Chinese shall meet Tibetan envoys and provide them with all facilities from there onwards. At Ch'ing-shui the Tibetans shall meet Chinese envoys and provide all facilities. On both sides they shall be treated with customary honour and respect in conformity with the friendly relations between nephew and uncle.

'Between the two countries no smoke nor dust shall be seen. There shall be no sudden alarms and the very word 'enemy' shall not be spoken. Even the frontier guards shall have no anxiety nor fear and shall enjoy land and bed at their ease. All shall live in peace and share the blessing of happiness for ten thousand years. The fame of this shall extend to all places reached by the sun and the moon.

'This solemn agreement has established a great epoch when Tibetans shall be happy in the land of Tibet, and Chinese in the land of China. So that it may never be changed, the Three Precious Jewels of Religion, the Assembly of Saints, the Sun and Moon, Planets and Stars have been invoked as witnesses. An oath has been taken with solemn words and with the sacrifice of animals; and the agreement has been ratified.

'If the parties do not act in accordance with this agreement or if they violate it, which ever it be, Tibet or China, nothing that the other party may do by way of retaliation shall be considered a breach of the treaty on their part.

'The Kings and Ministers of Tibet and China have taken the prescribed oath to this effect and the agreement has been written in detail. The two Kings have affixed their seals. The Ministers specially empowered to execute the agreement have inscribed their signatures and copies have been deposited in the royal records of each party.'

My room in the Jokhang was on the second storey, that is to say on the flat roof of the temple. From here, I was able to look down not only into the main part of the building itself but also into the market-place below. The window looking south gave me a view of the principal chamber, in which I could see monks chanting throughout the day. These monks were always very well behaved and diligent in their offices.

The view from the east window was very different, however. This one enabled me to look down into a courtyard where novice monks, like myself, gathered. I used to watch amazed as they played truant and sometimes even fought each other. When I was very young, I used to creep downstairs so that I could get a better view of them. I couldn't believe what I saw and heard. For a start, they did not chant their prayers as they were supposed to. They sang them – at least if they bothered to open their mouths at all. Quite a lot of them never seemed to do so and instead spent their whole time playing. Every so often a scuffle would break out. Then they would take out their wooden bowls and crack each other over the head. This scene provoked a curious reaction in me. On the one hand, I told myself that these monks were extremely stupid. On the other, I could not help envying them. They seemed not to have a care in the world. But when their fights became violent, I grew frightened and went away.

To the west, I could see out on to the market-place. This was easily my favourite view, but I had to spy out rather than look directly in case anyone saw me. If they did, everyone would come running over to prostrate themselves. I could only peer through the curtains, feeling like a criminal. I remember that the first or second time I stayed at the Jokhang, aged seven or eight, I disgraced myself rather badly. The sight of all those people down there was too much for me. I boldly poked my head through the curtain. But, as if this were not bad enough, I remember blowing bubbles of spit which fell on several people's heads as they threw themselves down to the ground far below! Afterwards, I am glad to say that the young Dalai Lama learned some self-discipline.

I loved peeping down on to the market stalls and remember once seeing a small wooden model of a gun. I sent someone to go out and buy it for me. I paid for it out of some of the offering money put out by pilgrims, which occasionally I used to help myself to, for I was not officially allowed to handle money. In fact, even to this day, I do not have direct dealings with it. All my income and expenditure is handled by my Private Office.

One of the other joys of staying at the Jokhang was the chance to make new friends amongst the sweepers there. As usual, all my spare time was spent in their company and I think that they were as sorry when I left as I was. However, I remember one year when the people with whom I had made such firm friends during the previous festival turned out not to be there any longer. I wondered why, as I was very much looking forward to seeing them all again. I demanded to know what had happened from the single one that remained. He told me that the other ten had all been sacked for theft. After I had gone last time, they let themselves into my apartment by climbing down through the ceiling skylight and made off with various items – gold butter lamps and the like. So much for the company I kept!

The last day of the *Monlam* festival was given over to outdoor activities. Firstly, a large statue of Maitreya, the Buddha to come, would lead a procession round the perimeter of the old city. This route was known as the *Lingkhor*. I have heard that it no longer exists thanks to Chinese development of the capital, but the *Barkhor*, or inner perimeter which runs around the immediate outside of the Jokhang, does still stand. In former times, devout pilgrims would prostrate themselves bodily along the entire length of the *Lingkhor* as a devotional duty.

Soon after the statue had completed its circuit, there would be a general commotion as people turned their attention to sporting activities. These were great fun and involved both horse races and running races for members of the public. The former were rather unusual in that the animals were riderless. They were released beyond Drepung monastery and guided towards the centre of Lhasa by their grooms and spectators. Just before the horses arrived, the would-be athletes competing in the running race would also set off over a shorter distance, also towards the city centre. This tended to result in enjoyable confusion as both arrived simultaneously. However, one year there was an unfortunate incident when some of the human competitors grabbed hold of the tails of passing horses and took a tow. Immediately after the races were over, the Lord Chamberlain accused those whom he thought were involved. Most of them were members of my household. I was very sorry when I heard they were likely to be punished. In the end, I was able, for once, to intervene on their behalf.

Certain aspects of the *Monlam* festival affected the entire population of Lhasa intimately. For, in accordance with ancient tradition, the civil administration of the city was given up to the abbot of Drepung monastery. He then appointed, from amongst his monks, a staff and policemen to maintain law and order. This was imposed strictly and any misdemeanours were punished with quite heavy fines. One of the things that was always insisted upon by the abbot was cleanliness. As a result, this was the time of year when every building was freshly whitewashed and the streets thoroughly cleaned.

One thing about the New Year that was important to me as a child was the tradition of baking *khabse* or *Losar* cookies. Every year, at the time of the festivities, my Master of the Kitchen would make batches of delicious pastry, fashioned into extravagant shapes and deep fried. One year, I decided to try my hand at some baking myself. Everything went well and I was quite impressed by my handiwork, so I told the Master of the Kitchen that I would come back to do some more next day.

This I did, but unfortunately the oil that was put out for my use on the second occasion was fresh and had not been properly boiled. As a result, when I dropped my mix into the pan, it erupted like a volcano. My right arm was covered in boiling oil, which caused immediate blistering. My chief memory of the event, however, is of one of the cooks, an elderly man who took a lot of snuff and was not easily excited, running over with something that looked like whipped cream which he started to apply to my arm. Normally he was a very jovial person, but on this occasion he was extremely flustered. I remember thinking how comical he looked with grains of snuff and bits of snot coming out of his nose, and a very serious expression on his heavily pock-marked face.

Of all the festivals, the one that I most enjoyed was the week-long opera festival, which began on the first day of the seventh month each year. This involved performances by various troupes of dancers, singers and actors from all over Tibet. They gave their performances on a paved area situated on the far side of, but adjacent to, the Yellow Wall. I myself watched the proceedings from a makeshift enclosure erected on the top of one of the buildings that abutted the wall on the inside. Amongst the other spectators were all the members of Government, and their wives – who used the occasion as an excuse to compete with one another in terms of jewellery and dress. However, this rivalry was not confined to the ladies. For this was also the favourite time of the sweepers at the Norbulingka. In the days preceding the festivities, they spent much time and energy borrowing and hiring clothes and ornaments, preferably coral, in which to parade. Their moment came when they carried forward vessels containing the flowers that were to be judged in a horticultural competition which was held during the festival.

I will never forget one of my sweepers, who always appeared wearing a special hat, of which he was immensely proud. It had a long, red silk tassel that he arranged artfully round his neck and over his shoulder.

Members of the public also came to watch the theatricals, although they did not have special seating arrangements unlike the government officials and aristocracy. As well as coming to see the performances, they came to marvel at the high officials in their ceremonial finery. They also used to take the opportunity to circumambulate, prayer-wheel in hand, the perimeter of the Yellow Wall. (A prayer-wheel consists of a cylinder, containing prayers, which is rotated whilst a person recites *mantras*.)

Many people other than Lhasans came too: tall, swashbuckling Khampas from the east, their long hair extravagantly braided with red tassels; Nepalese and Sikkimese traders from the south; and, of course, the small, gaunt figures of the nomad farmers. People dedicated themselves to having fun – something that Tibetans are naturally good at. We are for the most part quite simple people, who like nothing better than a good show and a good party. Even a few members of the monastic community joined in, though illegally and therefore in disguise.

It was such a happy time! People sat and talked during the performances, so familiar were they with the songs and dances that they knew every incident by heart. Almost everyone brought a picnic and tea and *chang* and they would come and go as they pleased. Young women suckled babies at their breasts. Children ran to and fro – shrieking and laughing – stopping only for seconds to stare wide-eyed as a new performer, clad in wild and colourful costume, made his entrance. At this too, the expressions of the old men who sat alone and stony-faced would brighten and for a

moment the old women would cease their chatter. Then everything would carry on as before. And all the while, the sun bore
steadily down through thin, exhilarating mountain air.

The only time you could be sure of everyone's complete attention was when satires were performed. Then the actors appeared
dressed as monks and nuns, high officials and even the state oracles
to lampoon public figures.

Other important festivals during the year included the festival
of *Mahakala* held on the eighth day of the third month. This was
when summer officially began and on that day all members of the
Government changed into summer dress. This was also the day
when I shifted from the Potala to the Norbulingka. On the
fifteenth day of the fifth month was *Zamling Chisang*, Universal
Prayer Day, which marked the beginning of a week-long holiday
period when most of the population of Lhasa who were not either
monks, nuns or members of the Government decamped in tents
to the plains outside Lhasa for a series of picnics and other social
amusements. Actually, I am fairly certain that some people who
were not supposed to attend this did so, but in disguise. Then on
the twenty-fifth day of the tenth month, which marked the death
of Tsonkapa, the great reformer of Buddhism in Tibet and founder
of the *Gelugpa* tradition, there was a special festival. It involved
torchlight processions and the lighting of innumerable butter
lamps throughout the land. This event also marked the day when
winter formally began, officials changed into winter dress and I
moved reluctantly back to the Potala. I longed to be old enough
to follow the example of my predecessor who, having participated
in this procession, used to return to the Norbulingka, which he
much preferred.

There were also a number of purely secular events held at
different times during the year, for example the horse fair, which
was held during the first month. There was likewise a particular
time of year, autumn, when nomads brought yaks to be sold to
the slaughtermen. This was a very sad time for me. I could not
bear to think of all those poor creatures going to their deaths. If
ever I saw animals being taken behind the Norbulingka on their

way to market, I always tried to buy them by sending someone out to act on my behalf. That way I was able to save their lives. Over the years I should imagine I must have rescued at least ten thousand animals, and probably many more. When I consider this, I realise that this extremely naughty child did do some good after all.

CHAPTER THREE

Invasion: The Storm Breaks

○

ON THE DAY before the opera festival of summer 1950, I was just coming out of the bathroom at the Norbulingka when I felt the earth beneath my feet begin to move. It was late evening and I had been chatting to one of my attendants whilst I washed before going to bed. The facilities were then situated in a small outbuilding a few yards from my quarters so I was outside when this happened. At first, I thought we must have had another earthquake as Tibet is quite prone to seismological activity. Sure enough, when I went back inside, I noticed that several pictures hanging on the wall were out of alignment. Just then, there was a terrific crash in the distance. I rushed back outside, followed by several sweepers. As we looked up into the sky, there was another crash and another. It was like an artillery barrage – which is what we assumed to be the cause of both the tremors and the noise: a test of some sort being carried out by the Tibetan army. In all, there were thirty to forty explosions.

Next day we learned that, far from being a military test, it was indeed some sort of natural phenomenon. Some people even reported seeing a strange red glow in the skies in the direction from which the noise came. It gradually emerged that people had experienced it throughout the length and breadth of Tibet: certainly in Chamdo, nearly 400 hundred miles to the east, and in Sakya, 300 miles away to the south-west. I have even heard that it was observed in Calcutta. As the scale of this strange event began to sink in, people naturally began to say that this was more than a simple earthquake: it was an omen.

Now from very early on, I have always had a great interest in science. So naturally, I wanted to find a scientific basis for this extraordinary event. When I saw Heinrich Harrer a few days later, I asked him what he thought was the explanation, not only for the earth tremors, but more importantly for the strange celestial phenomena. He told me he was certain that the two were related. It must be a cracking of the earth's crust caused by the upward movement of whole mountains.

To me, this sounded plausible, but unlikely. Why would a cracking of the earth's crust manifest itself as a glow in the night sky accompanied by thunderclaps and, furthermore, how could it be that it was witnessed over such immense distances? I did not think that Harrer's theories told the whole story. Even to this day I do not. Perhaps there is a scientific explanation, but my own feeling is that what happened is presently beyond science, something truly mysterious. In this case, I find it much easier to accept that what I witnessed was metaphysical. At any rate, warning from on high or mere rumblings from below, the situation in Tibet deteriorated rapidly thereafter.

As I have said, this event occurred just before the opera festival. Two days later, the omen, if that is what it was, began to fulfil itself. Towards evening, during one of the performances, I caught sight of a messenger running in my direction. On reaching my enclosure, he was immediately shown in to Tathag Rinpoché, the Regent, who occupied the other half. I realised at once that something was wrong. Under normal circumstances government matters would have had to wait until the following week. Naturally, I was almost beside myself with curiosity. What could this mean? Something dreadful must have happened. Yet being still so young and having no political power, I would have to wait until Tathag Rinpoché saw fit to tell me what was going on. However, I had already discovered that it was possible, by standing on a chest, to peep through a window set high up in the wall separating his room from mine. As the messenger went in, I hoisted myself up, and, holding my breath, began to spy on the Regent. I could see his face quite clearly as he read the letter. It became very grave. After a few minutes, he went out and I heard him give orders for the *Kashag* to be summoned.

I discovered in due course that the Regent's letter was in fact a telegram from the Governor of Kham, based in Chamdo, reporting a raid on a Tibetan post by Chinese soldiers, causing the death of the responsible officer. This was grave news indeed. Already the previous autumn there had been cross-border incursions by Chinese Communists, who stated their intention of liberating Tibet from the hands of imperialist aggressors – whatever that might mean. This was despite the fact that all Chinese officials living in Lhasa had been expelled in 1949.

It now looked as if the Chinese were making good their threat. If that were so, I was well aware that Tibet was in grave danger for our army mustered no more than 8,500 officers and men. It would be no match for the recently victorious People's Liberation Army (PLA).

I remember little else of that year's opera festival, save for the desolation I felt in my heart. Not even the magical dances performed to the slow beat of drums could hold my attention, the players in their elaborate costumes (some dressed to look like skeletons, representing Death) solemnly and rhythmically following an ancient choreography.

Two months later, in October, our worst fears were fulfilled. News reached Lhasa that an army of 80,000 soldiers of the PLA had crossed the Drichu river east of Chamdo. Reports on Chinese Radio announced that, on the anniversary of the Communists coming to power in China, the 'peaceful liberation' of Tibet had begun.

So the axe had fallen. And soon, Lhasa must fall. We could not possibly resist such an onslaught. In addition to its shortage of manpower, the Tibetan army suffered from having few modern weapons and almost no training. Throughout the Regency, it had been neglected. For Tibetans, despite their history, basically love peace and to be in the army was considered the lowest form of life: soldiers were held to be like butchers. And although some extra regiments were hurriedly sent from elsewhere in Tibet, and a new one was raised, the quality of troops sent to face the Chinese was not high.

It is useless to speculate on the possible result had things been otherwise. It is necessary only to say that the Chinese lost large numbers of men in their conquest of Tibet: in some areas, they did meet with fierce resistance and, in addition to direct casualties of war, they suffered greatly from difficulties of supply on the one hand and the harsh climate on the other. Many died from starvation; others must certainly have succumbed to altitude sickness, which has always plagued, and sometimes actually killed, foreigners in Tibet. But as to the fighting, no matter how large or how well prepared the Tibetan army had been, in the end its efforts would have been futile. For even then, the Chinese population was more than a hundred times larger than ours.

This threat to the freedom of Tibet did not go unnoticed in the world. The Indian Government, supported by the British Government, protested to the People's Republic of China and stated that the invasion was not in the interests of peace. On 7 November 1950, the *Kashag* and the Government appealed to the United Nations Organisation to intercede on our behalf. But sadly, Tibet, following her policy of peaceful isolation, had never sought to become a member and nothing came of this – nor from two further telegrams sent before the year was out.

As winter drew on and the news got worse, there began to be talk of giving the Dalai Lama his majority. People started to advocate my being given full temporal power – two years early. My sweepers reported to me that posters had been put up around Lhasa vilifying the Government and calling for my immediate enthronement, and there were songs to the same effect.

There were two schools of thought: one consisted of people who looked to me for leadership in this crisis; the other, of people who felt that I was still too young for such responsibility. I agreed with the latter group, but, unfortunately, I was not consulted. Instead, the Government decided that the matter should be put to the oracle. It was a very tense occasion, at the end of which the *kuten*, tottering under the weight of his huge, ceremonial head-dress, came over to where I sat and laid a *kata*, a white silk offering scarf, on my lap with the words '*Thu-la bap*', 'His time has come.'

Dorje Drakden had spoken. Tathag Rinpoché at once prepared to retire as Regent, though he was to remain as my Senior Tutor. It remained only for the state astrologers to select the day for my enthronement. They chose 17 November 1950 as the most auspicious date before the end of the year. I was rather saddened by these developments. A month ago I had been a carefree young man eagerly looking forward to the annual opera festival. Now I was faced with the immediate prospect of leading my country as it prepared for war. But in retrospect, I realise that I should not have been surprised. For several years now, the oracle had shown undisguised contempt for the Government whilst treating me with great politeness.

At the beginning of November, about a fortnight before the day of my investiture, my eldest brother arrived in Lhasa. I hardly knew him. As Taktser Rinpoché, he was by now abbot of Kumbum monastery where I had spent those first lonely eighteen months after my discovery. As soon as I set eyes on him, I knew that he had suffered greatly. He was in a terrible state, extremely tense and anxious. He stammered as he told me his story. Because Amdo, the province where we were both born, and in which Kumbum is situated, lies so close to China, it had quickly fallen under control of the Communists. Straight away, he had been put under duress. Restrictions were put on the activities of the monks and he himself was kept virtual prisoner in his monastery. At the same time, the Chinese endeavoured to indoctrinate him in the new Communist way of thinking and to try to subvert him. They had a plan whereby they would set him free to go to Lhasa if he would undertake to persuade me to accept Chinese rule. If I resisted, he was to kill me. They would then reward him.

That was a strange proposal. First of all, the idea of killing any living creature is anathema to Buddhists. So the suggestion that he might actually assassinate the Dalai Lama for personal gain showed how little understanding the Chinese had of the Tibetan character.

After a year during which my brother saw his community turned upside down by the Chinese, he gradually came to the conclusion that he must escape to Lhasa to warn me and the Government of what lay in store for Tibet if the Chinese conquered us. The only way he could do this was by pretending to go along with them. So finally he agreed to do their bidding.

I gasped as he told me this. Up until now, I had almost no knowledge of the Chinese. And of Communists I was almost entirely ignorant, although I was aware that they had been causing terrible hardship for the people of Mongolia. Aside from that, I knew only what I had gleaned from the pages of the odd copy of *Life* magazine that came into my hands. But my brother now made it clear that they were not only non-religious but were actually opposed to the practice of religion. I became very scared as Taktser Rinpoché told me that he was convinced that the only hope for us was to secure foreign support and to resist the Chinese by force of arms.

The Buddha forbade killing, but he indicated that under certain circumstances it could be justified. And to my brother's mind, the present circumstances justified it. He would therefore renounce his monastic vows, disrobe and go abroad as an emissary for Tibet. He would try to make contact with the Americans. It was certain, he felt, that they would support the idea of a free Tibet.

I was shocked to hear this, but before I could protest he urged me to leave Lhasa. Although a number of other people had said the same thing, not many held this view. But my brother begged me to take his advice, no matter what the majority might say. The danger was great, he said, and I must on no account fall into Chinese hands.

After our meeting, my brother had discussions with various members of the Government before leaving the capital. I saw him once or twice more, but could do nothing to persuade him to change his mind. His terrible experiences over the past year had convinced him that there was no other way. I did not brood on the matter, however, as I had preoccupations of my own. My enthronement ceremony was only a few days away.

To mark the occasion, I decided to grant a general amnesty. On the day of my accession, all prisoners were to be set free. This meant that the prison at Shöl would now be empty. I was pleased to have this opportunity, although there were times that I regretted it. I no longer had the pleasure of our tenuous friendship. When I trained my telescope on the compound, it was empty save for a few dogs scavenging for scraps. It was as if something was missing from my life.

On the morning of the 17th, I rose an hour or two earlier than usual, whilst it was still dark. As I dressed, my Master of the Robes handed me a piece of green cloth to tie round my waist. This was on the instructions of the astrologers, who deemed green to be an auspicious colour. I decided against breakfast as I knew that the ceremony would be a long one and I did not want to be distracted by any calls of nature. However, the astrologers had also stipulated that I must eat an apple before the proceedings began. I had difficulty forcing it down, I remember. That done, I went to the chapel where the enthronement was to take place at dawn.

It was to be a splendid occasion with the entire Government present, along with the various foreign officials resident in Lhasa all attired in their most formal and colourful regalia. Unfortunately, it was very dark so I was unable to see much detail. During the ceremony, I was handed the Golden Wheel symbolising my assumption of temporal power. However, there is not much more that I remember – save an insistent and growing need to relieve my bladder. I blamed the astrologers. Their idea of giving me an apple to eat was clearly at the root of the problem. I had never had much faith in them and this reinforced my bad opinion.

I have always felt that since the most important days of a person's life, those of their birth and death, cannot be set in consultation with astrologers, it is not worth bothering with any of the others. However, that is only my personal opinion. It does not mean that I think that the practice of astrology by Tibetans should be discontinued. It is very important from the point of view of our culture.

Anyway, my situation on this occasion went from bad to worse. I ended up by passing a message down to the Lord Chamberlain begging him to speed things up. But our ceremonies are long and complicated and I began to fear it would never end.

When eventually the proceedings drew to a close, I found myself undisputed leader of six million people facing the threat of a full-scale war. And I was still only fifteen years old. It was an impossible situation to be in, but I saw it as my duty to avoid this disaster if at all possible. My first task was to appoint two new Prime Ministers.

The reason for having to appoint two was that in our system of government, every post from Prime Minister down was duplicated, each being filled by both a layman and a monk. This derived from the time of the Great Fifth Dalai Lama, who was the first to assume temporal power in addition to his position as spiritual head of state. Unfortunately, although the arrangement had worked well enough in the past, it was hopelessly inadequate for the twentieth century. Besides, after almost twenty years of Regency, the Government had become quite corrupt, as I have already said.

Needless to say, few reforms were ever introduced. Not even the Dalai Lama could do this, for whatever he suggested had first to be referred to the Prime Ministers, then to the *Kashag*, then to each subordinate member of the Executive and finally to the National Assembly. If anyone objected to his proposals, it was extremely difficult for the matter to go any further.

The same happened when reforms were proposed by the National Assembly, except in reverse. In the event that a piece of legislation was finally presented to the Dalai Lama, he might then wish to make amendments, in which case these were written on to strips of parchment and stuck on to the original document, which was then sent back down the line for approval. But what made it even more difficult to instigate reforms was the religious community's fear of foreign influence, which they were convinced would damage Buddhism in Tibet.

I chose a man called Lobsang Tashi as the monk Prime Minister and an experienced lay administrator, Lukhangwa, as his opposite number.

That done, I decided in consultation with them and the *Kashag* to send delegations abroad to America, Great Britain and Nepal in the hope of persuading these countries to intervene on our behalf. Another was to go to China in the hope of negotiating a withdrawal. These missions left towards the end of the year. Shortly afterwards, with the Chinese consolidating their forces in the east, we decided that I should move to southern Tibet with the most senior members of Government. That way, if the situation deteriorated, I could easily seek exile across the border with India. Meanwhile, Lobsang Tashi and Lukhangwa were to remain in Lhasa in an acting capacity: I would take the seals of state with me.

Refuge in the South

o

THERE WAS much to organise and it was several weeks before we left. Moreover, all preparations had to be made secretly. My Prime Ministers feared that if word leaked out that the Dalai Lama was preparing to leave, there would be widespread panic. However, I am sure that many people must have realised what was happening as several large baggage trains were sent on ahead – some of which, unknown even to me, carried fifty or sixty strong-boxes of treasure, mostly gold biscuits and bars of silver from the vaults at the Potala. This was the idea of Kenrap Tenzin, my former Master of the Robes who had recently been promoted to *Chikyab Kenpo*. I was furious when I found out. Not that I minded about the treasure, but my youthful pride was wounded. I felt that by not telling me, Kenrap Tenzin was still treating me as a child.

I awaited the day of departure with a mixture of anxiety and anticipation. On the one hand, I was very unhappy at the prospect of abandoning my people. I felt a heavy responsibility towards them. On the other hand, I eagerly looked forward to travelling. To add to the excitement, the Lord Chamberlain decided that I should disguise myself and dress in layman's clothes. He was worried that people might actually try to prevent me from leaving when they found out what was happening. So he advised me to remain incognito. This delighted me. Not only would I now be able to see something of my country, but I would be able to do so as an ordinary observer, not as Dalai Lama.

We left Lhasa at dead of night. It was cold but very light, I remember. The stars in Tibet shine with a brightness I have not seen anywhere else in the world. It was also very still and my heart missed a beat every time one of the ponies stumbled as we made our way stealthily from the courtyard at the foot of the Potala, past the Norbulingka and Drepung monastery. Yet I was not really afraid.

Our final destination was Dromo (pronounced Tromo), which lay 200 miles away, just inside the border with Sikkim. The journey would take at least ten days, barring mishap. It was not long, however, before we ran into trouble. A few days after leaving Lhasa, we arrived at a remote village called Jang, where the monks of Ganden, Drepung and Sera were gathered for their winter debating camp. They realised as soon as they saw the size of our column that this was no ordinary move. Altogether we numbered at least two hundred people – of whom fifty were high officials – and a similar number of pack animals, and the monks guessed that I must be somewhere there.

Luckily, I was right at the front and my disguise proved effective. No one stopped me. But as I rode past, I could see that the monks were in a highly emotional state. Many had tears in their eyes. A few moments later, they stopped Ling Rinpoché who followed me. I glanced round and realised they were begging him to turn back with me. It was an extremely tense moment. Feelings were running high. The monks had such faith in me as their Precious Protector that they could not bear the thought of my leaving them. Ling Rinpoché explained that I did not intend to be away for long, and reluctantly the monks agreed to let us continue. Then, throwing themselves down on the track, they pleaded that I should return as soon as possible.

After this unfortunate incident we had no further trouble and I was able to make the most of the situation by going on ahead, still in disguise, and using every occasion I could to stop and talk with people. I realised that I now had a valuable opportunity to find out what life was really like for my fellow countrymen and women and managed to have a number of conversations during which I kept my identity secret. From these, I learned something about the petty injustices of life suffered by my people and resolved as soon as I could to set about making changes to help them.

*

We reached Gyantse (Tibet's fourth largest city) after almost a week of travel. Here it was impossible to maintain secrecy and hundreds turned out to greet me. A posse of shabby but enthusiastic Indian cavalry, which provided the escort for the Indian Trade Mission, also presented arms. But there was no time for formalities and we hurried on, arriving at Dromo in January 1951 after a journey of almost a fortnight.

We were all exhausted. But personally I felt a tremendous sense of excitement. The place itself was nothing special, consisting in fact of several villages quite close together, but its landscape was spectacular. It lay just at the point where the Amo-chu valley divides into two, at around 9,000 feet above sea level.

A river ran along the bottom of the valley, close enough to the village that its roar could be heard day and night. Not far from the water, the hills rose steeply. At some places, the river was bordered by vertical cliffs soaring straight up into the crystal blue sky. And in the near distance stood the mighty peaks which give Tibet both majesty and menace. Here and there were clumps of pine and thickets of rhododendron, peppering acres of green pasture. The climate, as I was to discover, was rather damp. Because it is situated so close to the Indian plains, Dromo is subject to monsoon rains. But even then the sun shines frequently, shouldering its way through massive cloud banks and washing the valleys in a sparkling, mystic light. I longed to explore the area and climb some of the more accessible mountains when they were carpeted with wild spring flowers, but for the time being there were several more months of winter.

On arrival in Dromo, I stayed first at the house of a local official – the one who had sent me toys and apples – before moving to Dungkhar, a small monastery situated on a hill with a view of the entire Dromo valley. It was not long before we were settled in and I was back into my usual routine of prayers, meditation, retreats and study. But although I could have wished for a bit more free time and although I missed some of my usual diversions in Lhasa, I felt that something within me had changed. This was perhaps in response to the sense of freedom I caught from being able to do away with much of the rigid protocol and formality that was so much a part of my life in Lhasa. And whilst I missed the company of my friends the sweepers, the void was filled by the extra responsibility I felt. One thing that the journey down had convinced me of was the need to study hard and learn as much as I could. I owed it to the faith of my people to be the best person I could be.

One significant event that took place soon after reaching Dromo was the arrival of a Sri Lankan monk, who had with him an important relic which I received at a very moving ceremony.

With Lukhangwa and Lobsang Tashi left behind in Lhasa, my main advisors were the *Kashag*, the Lord Chamberlain, Ling Rinpoché (now my Senior Tutor) and Trijang Rinpoché, the senior *tsenshap* who had recently been appointed my Junior Tutor. My eldest brother, Taktser Rinpoché, was also there. He had arrived a few weeks previously on his way to India.

Our first piece of bad news was that only one of the delegations sent abroad before I left Lhasa had reached its final destination: the one to China. Each of the others had been turned away. This was devastating. Tibet had always maintained the friendliest relations with Nepal and India. After all, they are our closest neighbours. As for Britain, thanks to Colonel Younghusband's expedition, there had been a British Trade Mission in Tibet for almost half a century. Even with Indian independence in 1947, the Mission at first continued to be run by the same Englishman, Hugh Richardson. So it was almost impossible to believe that the British Government was now agreeing that China had some claim to authority over Tibet. They seemed to have forgotten that in the past, for example when Younghusband concluded his treaty with the Tibetan Government, they had found it necessary to deal with Tibet as a fully sovereign state. Nor was this their position in 1914, when they convened a conference (the Simla Convention) to which Tibet and China were both invited independently. Besides, the English and Tibetan peoples had always had good relations. My countrymen and women found them to have a sense of decency, justice and humour which they respected very much.

As for America, in 1948 Washington had welcomed our trade delegation, which even had a meeting with the Vice-President. So they too had obviously changed their minds. I remember feeling great sorrow when I realised what this really meant: Tibet must expect to face the entire might of Communist China alone.

The next development, after the return of all but the one delegation within only a few weeks, was the arrival of a long report from Ngabo Ngawang Jigme, Governor of Chamdo. Most of the Chamdo region was by now in Chinese hands and the report had been taken to Lhasa by one of the area's leading merchants. He saw it safely into the hands of Lobsang Tashi and Lukhangwa, who in turn sent it on to me. It set out in painful and gloomy detail the nature of the Chinese threat and made clear that, unless some sort of settlement could be reached, troops of the PLA would soon march on Lhasa. There would inevitably be great loss of life if this happened and I wanted, at all cost, to avoid this.

Ngabo suggested that we had no alternative but to negotiate. If it was agreeable to the Tibetan Government, and if we would send some assistants, he proposed to go in person to try to open a dialogue with the Chinese in Peking. I contacted Lobsang Tashi and Lukhangwa in Lhasa to find out their opinion. They replied that they felt such negotiations should take place in Lhasa, but since the situation was desperate, they would have to agree to Peking as the venue.

Because he had shown no hesitation in offering himself for the task, I concluded that Ngabo, whom I knew to be a very decisive administrator, should go to the Chinese capital. Accordingly, I sent two officials from Dromo and two from Lhasa to accompany him. I hoped that he could make it clear to the Chinese leadership that Tibet did not require 'liberation', just continued peaceful relations with our great neighbour.

Meanwhile, spring came, and with it the outpourings of Nature. The hills were soon splashed with wild flowers; the grass took on an altogether new and richer shade of green; and the air became scented with fresh and surprising smells – of jasmine, honeysuckle and lavender. From my rooms in the monastery, I could look down towards the river where farmers came to graze their sheep, yaks and *dzomos*. And I could watch, enviously, the groups of picnickers that came almost daily to build a little fire and cook down by the water's edge. I was so enchanted with all that I saw that I felt brave enough to ask Ling Rinpoché for some time off. He must have felt the same way as, to my surprise, he granted me a holiday. I could not remember being happier as I spent several days roaming around the area. On one of my excursions I visited a Bon monastery. My only sadness was that I knew that troubled times lay ahead. It could not be long now before we heard from Ngabo in Peking. I half expected bad news, but nothing could have prepared me for the shock when it came.

At the monastery I had an old Bush radio receiver which ran off a six-volt battery. Every evening, I would listen to the Tibetan language broadcasts of Radio Peking. Sometimes I did so with one or other official, but often I listened alone. The majority of the broadcasts were taken up with propaganda about the 'Glorious Motherland', but I must say that I was very impressed with much of what I heard. There was constant talk of industrial progress and of the equality of all China's citizens. This seemed like the perfect combination of material and spiritual progress. However, one evening, as I sat alone, there was a very different sort of programme. A harsh, crackling voice announced that a Seventeen-Point 'Agreement' for the Peaceful Liberation of Tibet had that day been signed by representatives of the Government of the People's Republic of China and what they called the 'Local Government' of Tibet.

I could not believe my ears. I wanted to rush out and call everybody in, but I sat transfixed. The speaker described how 'over the last hundred years or more' aggressive imperialist forces had penetrated into Tibet and 'carried out all kinds of deceptions and provocations'. It added that 'under such conditions, the Tibetan nationality and people were plunged into the depths of enslavement and suffering'. I felt physically ill as I listened to this unbelievable mixture of lies and fanciful clichés.

But there was worse to come. Clause One of the 'Agreement' stated that 'The Tibetan people shall unite and drive out imperialist aggressive forces from Tibet. The Tibetan people shall return to the big family of the Motherland – the People's Republic of China.' What could it mean? The last foreign army to have been stationed on Tibetan soil was the Manchu army in 1912. As far as I was aware (and now know), there was no more than a handful of Europeans in Tibet at that time. And the idea of Tibet 'returning to the Motherland' was shameless invention. Tibet had never been part of China. In fact, as I have mentioned already, Tibet has ancient claims to large parts of China. On top of which, our respective peoples are ethnically and racially distinct. We do not speak the same language, nor is our script anything like the Chinese script. As the International Commission of Jurists stated subsequently in their report:

'Tibet's position on the expulsion of the Chinese in 1912 can fairly be described as one of de facto independence . . . it is therefore submitted that the events of 1911–12 mark the re-emergence of Tibet as a fully sovereign state, independent in fact and in law of Chinese control.'

What was most alarming, however, was that Ngabo had not been empowered to sign anything on my behalf, only to negotiate. I had kept the seals of state with me at Dromo to ensure that he could not. So he must have been coerced. But it was several more months before I heard the whole story. In the meantime, all we had to go on was the radio broadcast (repeated several times), together with a number of self-congratulatory sermons about the joys of Communism, the glory of Chairman Mao, the wonders of the People's Republic of China and all the good things that the Tibetan people could look forward to now that our destinies were united. It was quite silly.

The details of the Seventeen-Point 'Agreement' were chilling all the same. Clause Two announced that the 'Local Government' of Tibet would 'actively assist the People's Liberation Army to enter Tibet and consolidate the national defence'. This meant, so far as I could judge, that our forces were expected to surrender at once. Clause Eight continued the theme by saying that the Tibetan army was to be absorbed into the Chinese army – as if such a thing were possible. Then in Clause Fourteen we learned that, from now on, Tibet was to be deprived of all authority over the conduct of her external affairs. Interspersed with these more telling clauses were others assuring Tibet of religious freedom and protecting my position and the present political system. But for all these platitudes one thing was clear: from now on, the Land of Snows answered to the People's Republic of China.

As the unhappy reality of our position began to sink in, several people, notably Taktser Rinpoché in a long letter from Calcutta, urged me to leave for India at once. They argued that the only hope for Tibet lay in finding allies to help us fight the Chinese. When I reminded them that our missions to India, Nepal, Great Britain and the United States had already been turned back, they countered that once these countries realised the gravity of the situation, they would be sure to offer their support. They pointed out that the United States was implacably opposed to Communist expansionism and was already fighting a war in Korea for that very reason. I could see the logic of their arguments, but somehow felt the fact that America was already engaged in fighting on one front lessened the likelihood of her wanting to open up a second.

A few days later, a long telegram arrived from the delegation in Peking. It did not say very much beyond repeating what we had already heard on the radio. Obviously Ngabo was being prevented from telling the truth. Recently, some members of the delegation have related in their memoirs the full story of how they were forced to sign the 'Agreement' under duress and use counterfeit seals of the Tibetan state. But from Ngabo's telegram I could only guess at what had happened. However, he did say that the new Governor-General of Tibet, General Chiang Chin-wu, was en route to Dromo via India. We should expect him shortly.

There was nothing to do but wait. In the meantime, I received the abbots of the three great university monasteries, Ganden, Drepung and Sera, who had recently arrived. Having been told about the Seventeen-Point 'Agreement', they urged me to return to Lhasa as soon as possible. The Tibetan people were most anxious that I should return, they said. They were supported in this by both Lukhangwa and Lobsang Tashi, who had sent messages with them.

A few days later, I heard once more from Taktser Rinpoché, who had apparently succeeded in making contact with the American Consulate in Calcutta and been granted permission to visit the United States. Again he urged me to come to India, saying that the Americans were very anxious to make contact with Tibet. He suggested that if I were to go into exile, some arrangement for assistance could be negotiated between our two Governments. My brother concluded his letter by saying that it was imperative that I should arrive in India as soon as possible, adding that the Chinese delegation was already in Calcutta, en route to Dromo. The implication here was that if I did not make a move immediately, it would be too late.

At about this time, I also received a letter in similar vein from Heinrich Harrer, who had left Lhasa just before me and was now in Kalimpong. He firmly stated his view that I should seek exile in India – and was supported in this by a few of my officials. However, Ling Rinpoché was equally adamant that I should not.

So now I was faced with a dilemma. If my brother's letter was anything to go by, it seemed that there might, after all, be some hope of winning foreign support. But what would this mean for my people? Should I really leave before even meeting with the Chinese? And if I did, would our new-found allies see us through thick and thin? As I pondered these thoughts, I continuously came up against two particular considerations. Firstly, it was obvious to me that the most likely result of a pact with America or anyone else was war. And war meant bloodshed. Secondly, I reasoned that although America was a very powerful country, it was thousands of miles away. China, on the other hand, was our neighbour and, whilst materially less powerful than the United States, easily had numerical superiority. It might therefore take many years to resolve the dispute by armed struggle.

Furthermore, America was a democracy and I could not believe that her people would put up with unlimited casualties. It was easy to imagine a time when we Tibetans would be on our own once more. The result would then be the same, China would have her way and, in the interim, there would have been the loss of countless lives, Tibetan, Chinese and American, all to no purpose whatever. I therefore concluded that the best course of action was to stay put and await the arrival of the Chinese General. He must be human after all.

On 16 July 1951, the Chinese delegation duly reached Dromo. A messenger came running to the monastery to announce its imminent arrival. At this news, I felt both great excitement and great apprehension. What would they look like, these people? I was half convinced that they would all have horns on their heads. I went out on to the balcony and looked out eagerly down the valley towards the town, scanning the buildings with my telescope. It was a fine day, I remember, although it was the middle of the rainy season and water vapour rose in swirls from the ground as it warmed under the summer sun. Suddenly I spied movement. A group of my officials was heading in the direction of the monastery. With them, I could make out three men in drab grey suits. They looked very insignificant next to the Tibetans, who wore the traditional red and gold silk robes of high office.

Our meeting together was coldly civil. General Chiang Chin-wu began by asking me whether I had heard of the Seventeen-Point 'Agreement'. With the greatest reserve, I replied that I had. He then handed over a copy of it, together with two other documents. As he did so, I noticed that he was wearing a gold Rolex watch. Of these two supplementary documents, one dealt with the Tibetan army. The other explained what would happen if I elected to go into exile. It suggested that I would quickly realise that the Chinese had come in genuine friendship. I would then certainly want to return to my country. That being so, I would be welcomed back with open arms. Therefore, there was no point in leaving.

Next, General Chiang asked me when I intended to return to Lhasa. 'Soon,' I replied, not very helpfully, and continued to act as aloof as possible. It was obvious by his question that he wanted to travel back to Lhasa with me so that we could enter the city together, symbolically. In the end, my officials managed to avoid this and he set off a day or two after me.

My first impression, then, was rather as I had suspected. Regardless of all the suspicion and anxiety I felt beforehand, during our meeting it became clear that this man, although supposedly my enemy, was in fact just another human being, an ordinary person like myself. This realisation had a lasting impact on me. It was another important lesson.

Having now met General Chiang, I was a bit happier about the prospect of returning to Lhasa. Preparations were put in hand for my return, along with all of my officials, and we set off towards the end of the month. This time, no attempt was made at secrecy and I travelled in much more elaborate style than on the way down. At practically every major village en route, I stopped to give audiences and short teachings to the local population. This afforded me the chance personally to tell people about what was happening in Tibet, how we had been invaded by a foreign army but how the Chinese were proclaiming friendship. At the same time, I gave a short discourse on a religious text which I generally selected for its relevance to whatever else I had to say. I continue to use this formula right up to the present day. I find it a good way of showing that religion has a lot to tell us, no matter what situation we find ourselves in. However, I am better at it now than I was then. In those days I lacked confidence, although it improved every time I spoke in public. Also, I found, as every teacher does, that there is nothing like teaching to help one learn.

I was glad that there was so much to do on this journey. Otherwise I might have had time to feel sad. All of my family were abroad, except my father, who had died when I was twelve, and Lobsang Samten, who accompanied me now, and my only travelling companion outside the household was Tathag Rinpoché. He had come to visit me at Dromo to pass on certain important teachings and was now on his way back to his own monastery, which lay just outside Lhasa. He had aged considerably since I had last seen him during the previous winter, and now looked all of his seventy odd years. I was very happy to be in his company once more as not only was he an extremely kind man, but he was also a highly accomplished spiritual master. He was undoubtedly my most important *guru*. He initiated me into a great number of lineages and secret teachings, which had in turn been handed on to him by the most brilliant teachers of his day.

From Dromo we proceeded slowly to Gyantse, where the Indian cavalry turned out as before to present arms. But instead of hurrying through, I was able to remain for a few days. Then we set out for Samding monastery, home of Dorje Phagmo, one of the most important Bodhisattvas. It was also one of the most beautiful monasteries in all Tibet. The countryside on the way there was spectacular: cobalt blue lakes fringed with strips of lush green pasture on which thousands of sheep grazed. The views were more wonderful than anything I had ever seen, thanks to the crisp, clear summer light. Occasionally I caught sight of herds of deer and gazelle, which were in those days common throughout Tibet. I loved to see them stand nervously watching us approach, then spring away on their long sinuous legs.

For once I enjoyed being on horseback, though normally I am rather afraid of horses. I don't know why this should be as I can deal with almost any other creature, save caterpillars. I can pick up spiders and scorpions without hesitation, and I do not mind snakes very much, but I am not fond of horses and caterpillars leave me cold. Nevertheless, on this occasion, I thoroughly enjoyed riding across the open plains and was continually urging my mount on. It was actually a mule, called Grey Wheels, which had once belonged to Reting Rinpoché. It had excellent speed and stamina and I became quite good friends with it. The head groom did not approve of my choice, however. He considered it to be too small and undignified for the Dalai Lama to ride.

Samding monastery lay not far from the small town of Nangartse, which in turn is situated close to Yamdrok Lake, one of the most glorious stretches of water I have ever seen. Because there is no constant flow of water into and out of it, Yamdrok has a miraculous turquoise colour which quite startles the senses. Sadly, I heard recently that the Chinese are planning to drain its water for a hydro-electric project, though what the long-term effect of this might be I hardly dare think.

In those days, Samding was a thriving community. Interestingly, the head of its monastery was by tradition a woman. This is not so surprising as it may sound as in Tibet there was no special discrimination against women. For example, there was an important female spiritual teacher at a hermitage located close to Lhasa, who, during my childhood, was famous throughout Tibet. And although she was not a *tulku*, she is still revered to this day. There were also quite a lot of nunneries, but this was the only monastery to be headed by a nun.

What is perhaps curious is that Dorje Phagmo is named after Vajravarahi, a female deity known as the Adamantine Sow. Legend has it that Vajravarahi's manifestation had the body of a woman and the face of a pig. A story is told of how in the eighteenth century, when some Mongolian raiders came to Nangartse, their chief sent word demanding that the abbess come before him. He received a courteously negative reply. This angered him and he set off at once for the monastery. With his warriors, he forced his way inside and found the congregation hall full of monks; on the throne, at their head, was a big, wild pig.

At the time of my visit, the head of Samding monastery was a young girl of about my own age. When I arrived, she came to pay her respects to me. I remember her as a very shy, young girl with long plaits in her hair. Subsequently she escaped to India, but then, for reasons unclear to me, she returned to Lhasa, where for many years she was exploited by our new masters. Tragically, the monastery and all its subsidiary buildings were destroyed like thousands of others since the late 1950s, and its ancient tradition has vanished.

I remained for two or three days at Samding before setting out on the final leg of the journey to Lhasa. Before returning to the Norbulingka, I accompanied Tathag Rinpoché to his monastery, which lay a few hours outside the city gates. Very kindly, he vacated his rooms for me and moved out on to the grassy area behind the main building where debates were usually held. We met formally a number of times over the next few days. When we parted, I was quite sorry to be leaving him. I felt the deepest appreciation and respect for him. It saddened me very much that his reputation had been rather spoiled during his period of office as Regent. Even now I wonder whether it would not have been better if he had remained a lama and not been involved with politics. After all, he had no knowledge of government and no experience of administration. It was unreasonable to have expected him to do well at something for which he had received no training whatever. But that was Tibet. Because he was so well respected for his spiritual learning, it seemed only natural that he should be appointed to the second highest office in the land.

This was the last time that I saw Tathag Rinpoché alive. At our final meeting, he asked me not to feel bad about the prohibitions he had forced on me as a child. I felt very moved that such an old and venerable teacher should want to say this to me. Of course I understood.

I arrived back in Lhasa in the middle of August, after a nine-month absence. There was a big reception in my honour. It looked as if the entire population had turned out to see me and demonstrate its happiness at my return. I was deeply moved and, at the same time, extremely glad to be home. Only I knew full well that there had been many changes since the previous winter, that nothing was quite the same. It seemed that my people had similar feelings as, although they were full of joy, there was a note of hysteria in their enthusiasm. In the time that I had been away, reports had begun to reach the capital telling of atrocities against Tibetans in Amdo and Kham. Naturally, people were very much afraid of the future, though I knew that some felt that everything would be all right now that I was home.

On a personal level, I discovered to my great sadness that my favourite sweeper, Norbu Thondup, had died earlier in the year – the one who had been by far my most enthusiastic playmate. Throughout my childhood, this man had been a devoted friend and a constant source of fun. When I was small, he frightened me by pulling hideous faces; when I grew older, he joined me in my roughest games. We often came to blows during my mock battles and I remember being quite vicious towards him at times, even to the point of drawing blood with the swords of my lead soldiers when he caught me up in his arms during our playful skirmishes. But he always gave as good as he got and never for a moment lost his great sense of humour. Now, of course, there was nothing I could do for him, although I was able to be of some service to his children, a son and a daughter. As a Buddhist, I knew that there was not much use in grieving. Yet at the same time I realised that in a way Norbu Thondup's death symbolised the end of my childhood. There could be no going back. In a few days' time, I was due to meet the Chinese delegation again. I must do for my people whatever I could, no matter how little, ever mindful that the peaceful pursuit of religion is one of the most important things in life. And I was still just sixteen years old.

I received General Chiang Chin-wu at the headquarters of my bodyguard, in accordance with tradition. This put him in a ferocious temper and he demanded to know why I was meeting him here and not in a more informal place. He was not a foreigner, he insisted, and did not wish to be treated as one. The fact that he could not speak Tibetan was apparently lost on him. At first I was taken aback at the sight of his bulging eyes and vermilion cheeks as he spluttered and stammered, banging the table with his fist. I subsequently discovered that the General was frequently given to outbursts of temper like this. Meanwhile, I reminded myself that he was probably a good person underneath – which, in fact, he turned out to be, and quite straightforward too.

As for his expressions of anger, I soon discovered these outbursts to be quite usual amongst the Chinese. I think it is because of this that they are treated so reverentially by some people, particularly by Europeans and Americans who tend to control their emotions more thoroughly. Fortunately, my religious training helped me to keep a perspective on his behaviour: I could see that in some ways it is quite good to express anger like this. Although not always appropriate, it is usually better than pretending to be gentle and hiding resentment.

To begin with I did not have to deal with Chiang on a very frequent basis. I met with him perhaps once a month during the first year or two of the Chinese occupation. It was Lukhangwa, and Lobsang Tashi and the members of the *Kashag* who saw him most and they quickly learned to dislike his behaviour. They told me that he was arrogant, high-handed and without any sympathy for our different approach to life. Whenever we did meet, I saw for myself how he and his countrymen offended Tibetans at every turn.

I now see the first five or six weeks after my return to Lhasa from Dromo as a honeymoon period. It ended abruptly on 26 October 1951, when 3,000 troops of the Chinese 18th Route Army entered Lhasa. These were men who belonged to the division that had overcome our forces in Chamdo the previous year. With them came Generals Tan Kuan-sen and Chiang Kuo-ha, who, when they came for an audience, were accompanied by a Tibetan in national costume and fur hat. As they entered the room, this man made three formal prostrations. I thought this rather strange as he was evidently a member of the Chinese delegation. It turned out that he was the interpreter, and a loyal supporter of the Communists. When I later asked why he was not wearing the same Mao suits as his companions, he replied good-naturedly that I must not make the mistake of thinking that the Revolution was a revolution in dress; it was a revolution of ideas.

Also at around this time, my brother Gyalo Thondup arrived back in Lhasa. He did not stay long, but whilst in the city he met with the Chinese leadership several times. He then announced his intention to travel south, where my family had an estate given to them by the Government at the time of my enthronement. This visit to oversee the property was only a ruse, however, and I learned soon afterwards that he had slipped over the border into Assam, then known as NEFA, the North-Eastern Frontier Area. He intended to do what he could in the way of organising foreign support, but had not told me of his plans because he feared, on account of my age, that I might let his secret out in an unguarded moment.

Within a short time, a further large detachment of the PLA reached Lhasa. I well remember their arrival. Because of the altitude, sound carries over great distances in Tibet and, as a result, I heard the slow, insistent thud of martial drums in my room at the Potala long before I saw any soldiers. I rushed out on to the roof with my telescope, where I watched them approach in a long, snaking column enveloped in clouds of dust. When they reached the city walls, there was a flourish of red banners and posters depicting Chairman Mao and his deputy, Chu Te. Then came a fanfare of trumpets and tubas. It was all most impressive. So were the troops, who looked positively demonic.

Later, after I had got over a feeling of great uneasiness at the sight of all their red flags (this is, after all, Nature's colour for danger), I noticed that the soldiers were actually in a very poor state: their uniforms were ragged and they all looked under-nourished. It was this, together with the grime on their faces from the eternal dust of the Tibetan plains, that gave them their frightening appearance.

Throughout the winter of 1951–2, I continued with my studies much as usual, though more diligently. It was during this period that I began *Lam Rim* meditations. These relate to a text which expounds a stage-by-stage path to enlightenment through mental training. Since around the age of eight, I had begun, in tandem with my monastic education, to receive Tantric teachings such as these. In addition to scriptures, they consisted of secret, oral transmissions handed down by initiates. As the months went by, I began to notice some progress in myself as I laid down the foundations of my own, very slight, spiritual development.

Whilst making my annual retreat, at this time, I heard that Tathag Rinpoché had passed away. I very much wanted to attend his cremation, but could not, so I offered special prayers for him.

My other preoccupation that winter was to do all I could to encourage my Prime Ministers and *Kashag*. I reminded them of the Buddhist doctrine of Impermanence and pointed out that the present situation could not last for ever, even if it did last for our lifetimes. But privately, I followed events with increasing anxiety. The only happy occasion to look forward to was a visit by the Panchen Lama, who was due to reach Lhasa shortly.

Meanwhile, following the arrival of the last consignment of 20,000 troops, a serious food shortage was developing. The population of Lhasa had almost doubled in a matter of weeks, and it could not be long before our meagre resources gave out. At first the Chinese kept more or less to the provisions of the Seventeen-Point 'Agreement' which stated that the PLA should 'be fair in all buying and selling and shall not arbitrarily take a needle or thread from the people'. They paid for the grain the Government gave them and reimbursed the owners of houses that were requisitioned to quarter their officers.

However, this system of remuneration soon broke down. Money ceased to change hands and the Chinese began to demand food and lodging as of right. Very quickly, a crisis developed. Inflation took off. This was something that had never been experienced before and my people did not understand how the price of grain could double overnight. They were outraged and their previously passive hatred of the invaders turned abruptly to active derision. In the traditional way to drive out evil, they began to clap and spit whenever they saw groups of Chinese soldiers. Children began to throw rocks and stones, and even monks would wind the loose folds of their gowns into a bunch and use it for whipping any soldiers that came near.

At the same time, scurrilous songs were sung about General Chiang Chin-wu that made fun of his gold watch. And when it was discovered that many of his officers wore costly fur linings under their outwardly similar uniforms, Tibetans' contempt knew no bounds. This infuriated the Chinese, mostly I suspect because although they knew they were being laughed at, they could not understand what was being said. This hurt their pride. It was tantamount to losing face, the worst thing that can happen to a Chinese. The eventual result was an extremely amusing incident with General Chiang. One day he came to see me and demanded that I issue a proclamation banning any criticism of the Chinese, whether in songs or on posters, since these were 'reactionary' activities.

However, despite new laws prohibiting opposition to China, notices began to appear in the streets denouncing the presence of the Chinese. A popular resistance movement was formed. Finally, a six-point memorandum was drawn up and sent directly to General Chiang listing the people's grievances and demanding the removal of the garrison. This infuriated him. He suggested that the document was the work of 'imperialists' and accused the two Prime Ministers of leading a conspiracy. Tension mounted. Thinking that they could bypass Lobsang Tashi and Lukhangwa, the Chinese began to approach me directly. At first I refused to receive them without the two men being present. But when on one occasion Lobsang Tashi said something that particularly inflamed him, Chiang actually moved as if to strike my Prime Minister. Without thinking, I ran between the two men, yelling at them to stop at once. I was terrified. I had never seen adults behave like that. Thereafter, I consented to see the two factions separately.

The situation between the Chinese leaders and my two Prime Ministers continued to deteriorate as more and more officials and bureaucrats began to arrive from China. These men, far from allowing the Tibetan Government to look after its own affairs, as was stipulated in the Seventeen-Point 'Agreement', interfered incessantly. General Chiang called endless series of meetings between them and the *Kashag*, mainly with a view to discussing the permanent accommodation of these officials, his soldiers and their many thousand camels and other pack animals. Lobsang Tashi and Lukhangwa found it impossible to make him understand that not only were these demands unreasonable, but they were also not feasible.

When the General asked for a second disbursement of 2,000 tons of barley, they had to explain to him that no such quantity of food existed. Already the Tibetan population of the city lived in fear of scarcity and what little grain remained in the government warehouses could only feed the army for another two months at most. They told him that there could be no possible reason for wanting to maintain such large forces in Lhasa. If their purpose was to defend the nation, they should be sent to the borders. Only the officials need remain in the capital, with perhaps a regiment or so for an escort. The General took this quietly and answered politely, so they told me, but he did nothing.

After their suggestion that these troops be sent elsewhere, the two Prime Ministers became increasingly unpopular with General Chiang. To begin with he reserved his anger for Lobsang Tashi, the elder of the two, who knew some Chinese. This irritated the General and he was quick to accuse the monk of every imaginable crime, whilst simultaneously praising Lukhangwa, whom he saw as a potential ally.

It turned out, however, Lukhangwa was the man with the greater depth of character, despite his youth, and he never once tried to hide his true feelings from the General. Even on a personal level, he displayed the utmost contempt for the man. On one occasion, I remember being told, Chiang asked him casually how much tea he drank. 'It depends on the quality of the tea,' Lukhangwa replied. I laughed when I heard this, but realised that the situation between the two men must be very bad.

The climax of the drama occurred only a short while later when Chiang convened a meeting with the two Prime Ministers, the *Kashag* and all of his own officials. When it began, he announced that they were gathered to discuss the absorption of the Tibetan army into the PLA. This was too much for Lukhangwa. He said straight away that the idea was unacceptable. No matter that it was one of the provisions of the Seventeen-Point 'Agreement'. Its terms had already been broken so many times by the Chinese that it was a meaningless document. It was unthinkable, he said, that the Tibetan army would switch allegiance to the PLA.

Chiang listened quietly. 'In that case,' he said, 'we shall begin by doing nothing more than replacing the Tibetan flag with the Chinese flag.' 'It will only be pulled down and burned if you do,' replied Lukhangwa. 'And that will be embarrassing for you.' He went on to say that it was absurd for the Chinese, who had violated the integrity of Tibet, to expect to have friendly relations with Tibetans. 'You have already cracked a man's skull,' he said, 'and that crack has not yet healed. It is too soon to expect him to be your friend.' At this Chiang stormed out of the meeting. There would be another in three days' time.

Naturally I was not present at any of these conferences, but I was kept fully informed of everything that took place. It began to look as if I would be more directly involved very soon if the situation did not improve.

The meeting was convened three days later as planned. This time another general, Fan Ming, presided. He began by saying that he was sure that Lukhangwa wished to make an apology for what he had said last time. Lukhangwa corrected him at once. He had no intention of apologising. He stood by all that he had said, adding that he considered it his absolute duty to keep the Chinese fully informed of the Tibetan point of view. People were very disturbed at the presence of so many Chinese soldiers. Further-more, they were concerned that Chamdo had not been returned to the administration of the central Government and there were no signs that the PLA elsewhere in Tibet was about to return to China. As far as the proposals concerning the Tibetan army were concerned, there would certainly be trouble if they were accepted.

Fan Ming was outraged. He accused Lukhangwa of being in league with foreign imperialists and said that he would demand that the Dalai Lama have him removed from office. Lukhangwa replied that if the Dalai Lama requested it of him, he would gladly give up not only his office, but also his life. With that, the meeting ended in confusion.

Soon afterwards, I received a written report from the Chinese stating that it was clear that Lukhangwa was an imperialist reac-tionary who did not want to improve relations between China and Tibet and asking that he be removed from office. I also received a verbal suggestion from the *Kashag* saying that it would probably be for the best if I asked both Prime Ministers to resign. This saddened me greatly. They had both shown such loyalty and conviction, such honesty and sincerity, such love for the people they served.

When they came to see me to offer their resignations a day or so later, they had tears in their eyes. There were tears in mine too. But I realised that if I did not accept the situation, their lives would be in danger. So, with a heavy heart, I accepted their resignations, conscious only of my concern, if possible, to improve relations with the Chinese, with whom I must now deal directly. For the first time, I understood the true meaning of the word 'bully'.

It was about this time that the Panchen Lama reached Lhasa. Unfortunately for him, he had been raised under the eye of the Chinese and was only now on his way to Tashilhunpo monastery to take up his rightful position there. When he arrived, from Amdo Province, he did so with yet another large detachment of Chinese troops (his 'bodyguard'), along with his family and tutors.

Shortly after his arrival I received the young Panchen Lama at an official meeting followed by a private lunch at the Potala. I remember that he had with him a very pushy Chinese security officer, who tried to barge in on us when we were alone together. My own (ceremonial) bodyguards moved at once to stop this man, with the result that I almost had an ugly incident on my hands: the man was armed.

In the end, I did manage to have some time alone with the Panchen Lama and my impression was of a very honest and faithful young man. Being three years younger than me, and not yet in a position of authority, he retained an air of innocence and struck me as a very happy and pleasant person. I felt quite close to him. It was just as well that neither of us knew what a tragic life he would lead.

Not long after the Panchen Lama's visit, I was invited back to Tathag monastery, where I consecrated, very elaborately and thoroughly, in a ceremony lasting fifteen hours, the *stupa* (memorial) dedicated to my *guru*. I felt quite sad as I prostrated full length in front of it. Afterwards, I went on an excursion into the mountains and surrounding area, relieved to be free from the pressures of our unhappy situation. One interesting aspect of this visit was being shown a piece of Tathag Rinpoché's skull that had survived the flames of his cremation. On it could clearly be seen an imprint of the Tibetan character that corresponded to his protector divinity. Actually, this mysterious phenomenon is quite common amongst high lamas. The bones melt in such a way as to reveal characters, or sometimes images. In other cases, such as that of my predecessor, those imprints can actually be observed on the body itself.

After the forced resignations of Lukhangwa and Lobsang Tashi in early spring, 1952, there followed a period of uneasy truce with the Chinese authorities. I used this as an opportunity to establish the Reform Committee that I had had in mind since the journey to Dromo more than a year before. One of my main ambitions was to establish an independent judiciary.

As I have mentioned in the case of Reting Rinpoché, I was impotent as a minor to help people when they fell foul of the Government, though I should often have liked to. For example, I remember with sadness the case of a man who worked in the administration, discovered to have been hoarding gold-dust which was intended for use in making *thangkas*. I watched him through my telescope having his hands bound and then being set on a mule facing backwards and banished from the city. This was the traditional punishment for such crimes.

Sometimes I feel that I could have intervened more often. There was another similar incident that I witnessed at the Potala. From very early on I had identified several places where it was possible, by peeping through windows or skylights, to observe what was going on in rooms that I would not otherwise have seen inside. On one occasion, I saw by this means a hearing of the Regent's Secretariat which had met to consider the grievance of a certain tenant against his landlord. I clearly remember how miserable this poor man looked. He was quite elderly, short and bent, with grey hair and a thin moustache. Unluckily for him, his master's family was friendly with the Regent's (at the time still Reting Rinpoché) and his case was dismissed. My heart went out to him, but there was nothing I could do. So now, as I heard of similar cases of injustice, I became ever more convinced of the need for judicial reform.

I also wanted to do something about education. At the time, there was still no system of universal education. There were only a few schools in Lhasa and a tiny handful in rural areas, but for the most part the monasteries were the only centres of learning, and the education they provided was open only to the monastic community. Accordingly, I instructed the *Kashag* to put forward proposals for the development of a good educational programme.

Another area which I felt was in urgent need of reform was communications. In those days, there was not a single road in all Tibet and almost the only wheeled vehicles were the Thirteenth Dalai Lama's three cars. It was easy to see that many people would benefit enormously from a system of roads and transportation. But, like education, this was a long-term consideration and I realised that it would be many years before there could be progress here.

However, there were things that could be done which would bring immediate positive results. One was the abolition of inheritable debt. This, I had gathered both from my sweepers and from my talks en route to Dromo, was the the scourge of the peasant and rural community in Tibet. It meant that debt owing to a landlord by his tenants, perhaps acquired as a result of successive bad harvests, could be transferred from one generation to the next. As a result, many families were not able to make a decent living for themselves, let alone hope one day to be free. Almost as pernicious was the system whereby small landowners could borrow from the Government in times of need. Here too the debt was inheritable. So I decided firstly to abolish the principle of hereditary debt and secondly to write off all government loans that could not be repaid.

Knowing that these reforms might not be very popular with the nobility and people with vested interests, I persuaded the Lord Chamberlain to issue these decrees publicly, not in the usual way by putting up posters in public places. Instead, I had them distributed on paper that was printed on wooden blocks similar to those used for printing scripture. That way, there was a better chance the information would be widely disseminated. Anyone who might otherwise have tried to interfere would with any luck not have their suspicions raised until it was too late.

The terms of the Seventeen-Point 'Agreement' made it clear that 'the Local Government of Tibet shall carry out reforms of its own accord' and that these would not be subject to 'compulsion on the part of the authorities [i.e. the Chinese]'. However, although these early attempts at land reform brought immediate benefit to many thousands of my people, it soon became clear that our liberators had an altogether different approach to the organisation of agriculture. Already, collectivisation had begun in Amdo. Eventually, it was introduced throughout Tibet and was directly responsible for widespread famine and the deaths of hundreds of thousands of Tibetans from starvation. And although the authorities relented following the Cultural Revolution, the effects of collectivised farming are felt to this day. Many visitors to Tibet have commented on how small and underdeveloped the people in rural areas look, due to malnutrition. But all this lay in the future. In the meantime, I urged the Government to do all it could to rout out old and unproductive practices. I was determined to do all I could to propel Tibet into the twentieth century.

During the summer of 1953, so far as I can remember, I received the *Kalachakra* initiation from Ling Rinpoché. This is one of the most important initiations in the Tantric tradition, with special significance for world peace. And, unlike other Tantric rites, it is given before large public audiences. It is also very elaborate and takes a week to ten days to prepare, as well as three days actually to perform. One of its features is the construction, using individual grains of coloured sand, of a large *mandala*, a representation in two dimensions of a three-dimensional symbol. The first time I ever saw one of these *mandalas*, I almost lost my balance from just looking at it, so extraordinarily beautiful did it appear.

The initiation itself followed a month-long retreat. I recall it as a very moving experience that affected both Ling Rinpoché and myself. I felt extremely privileged to be participating in a tradition performed over countless generations by successions of highly realised spiritual masters. Whilst chanting the last verse of the dedication prayer, I was so moved that I choked with emotion, a fact that subsequently I came to regard as having been auspicious, though I thought nothing of it at the time. I now see it as being premonitory of my being able to give many more *Kalachakra* initiations than any of my predecessors, and in all parts of the world. This, despite my being by no means the most qualified to do so.

The following year, during *Monlam*, I received full ordination as a Buddhist *bikshu* in front of the statue of Chenrezig in the Jokhang temple. Again this was a very moving occasion, with Ling Rinpoché officiating. Then, that summer, at the request of a group of lay women, I performed the *Kalachakra* initiation ceremony for the first time during this lifetime.

I was very glad of this period of fragile rapprochement with the Chinese authorities. I used it to concentrate on my religious duties and began to give regular teachings, to both small and large groups. As a result, I began to build up a personal relationship with my people. And although at first I was somewhat anxious to be addressing public audiences, my self-confidence rapidly increased. I was aware, however, that outside Lhasa the Chinese were making life very hard for my people. At the same time, I could see for myself why my two Prime Ministers had been so scornful of the Chinese. For example, whenever General Chiang Chin-wu came to see me, he posted bodyguards outside the room – even though he must have known that sanctity of life is one of the cardinal rules of Buddhism.

Still, I took note of the Buddha's teaching that in one sense a supposed enemy is more valuable than a friend, for an enemy teaches you things, such as forbearance, that a friend generally does not. To this I added my firm belief that no matter how bad things become, they will eventually get better. In the end, the innate desire of all people for truth, justice and human understanding must triumph over ignorance and despair. So if the Chinese oppressed us, it could only strengthen us.

CHAPTER FIVE

In Communist China

○

ABOUT A YEAR after the departure from office of Lobsang Tashi and Lukhangwa, the Chinese suggested that the Government send some officials to China, to see for themselves how marvellous life was in the Glorious Motherland. A party was duly assembled and taken on a tour of the People's Republic. When they came back after many months, they submitted a report which was full of praise and admiration and lies. I realised at once that this document had been written under supervision, as by now I was used to the fact that it was often impossible to speak the truth in front of our new masters. I too had had to learn a similar form of communication: how to put on false appearances when dealing with the Chinese under difficult circumstances.

Not long after, in early 1954, I myself was invited to go to China. This seemed like an excellent idea. Not only would it enable me to meet with Chairman Mao in person, but also it would give me the opportunity to see something of the outside world. But few other Tibetans were happy with the idea. They were afraid that I might be kept in Peking and not allowed to return – some even felt that my life could be in danger and many did their best to dissuade me from going. I had no fear for myself, however, and I made up my mind to go no matter what anyone told me. Had I not been so decisive, I doubt whether the proposal would have come to anything.

In the end I set out, together with a retinue which included my family, my two tutors, my two *tsenshap* (a new one having been appointed after Trijang Rinpoché became Junior Tutor), the *Kashag* and a great many other officials. In all we numbered about five hundred. When we departed one morning during high summer, a formal farewell was held on the bank of the Kyichu river, with musical bands and a parade of officials. Tens of thousands of people attended, many carrying religious banners and burning incense to wish me a safe journey and a happy return.

In those days, there was still no bridge over the Kyichu and we crossed in animal-skin coracles, to the accompaniment of chanting by Namgyal monks positioned on the other side. As I climbed aboard my own special vessel, which consisted of two of these coracles strapped together, and turned to wave goodbye to my people, I could see that they were in a highly emotional state. Many were crying and it looked as if some were on the point of throwing themselves into the water, convinced that they were seeing me for the last time. I myself felt a mixture of sadness and excitement, just as I had on leaving for Dromo four years previously. It was heartbreaking to see my people so distraught. At the same time, the prospect of the adventure that lay ahead was very thrilling to a young man of nineteen.

The distance from Lhasa to Peking is approaching two thousand miles. In 1954, there were still no roads connecting the two countries, although the Chinese had begun work on one called the Qinghai highway, using Tibetan forced labour. The first part was complete, which enabled me to travel a short way in the Thirteenth Dalai Lama's Dodge car. It too had been transported across the river.

My first stop was at Ganden monastery, about thirty-five miles from Lhasa, where I took the opportunity to remain for a few days. This was another moving experience for me. Ganden is the third of Tibet's great university monasteries. When I left to continue my journey to China, I noticed something very strange. A statue of one of the protector divinities of Tibet, which is represented as having a buffalo's head, had clearly moved. When I had first seen it, it was looking down with a rather subdued look on its face. Now, it was facing East, with a very ferocious expression. (Similarly, I heard that at the time of my escape into exile, the walls of one chapel at Ganden ran with blood.)

I resumed my journey by car. But it was not long before I had to exchange this stately form of transport for a mule: the road had been washed away as soon as we reached the Kongpo region, and many bridges were down. The going quickly became very dangerous. There was constant flooding from mountain streams carrying melted snow and there were frequent landslides. Rocks and boulders often came thundering down amongst us. Being late summer, there was some heavy rainfall and there were long stretches when the mud came halfway to a person's knees. I felt very sorry for the older people, who sometimes struggled to keep up.

Altogether conditions were very bad. Our Tibetan guides tried very hard to persuade the Chinese who escorted us to alter course so that we followed the traditional high-altitude routes rather than the projected course of the road, which they thought was unsuitable. But the Chinese insisted, saying that if we went that way there would be no facilities. So we went on. It is something of a miracle that more than three people were not killed. Those that died were innocent, young Chinese soldiers from among those made to stand joined together along the side of the track to shield us from avalanches. I felt so sorry for these people. They had no choice. Several mules also fell over a precipice, bursting their guts.

Then one evening, General Chiang Chin-wu, who was also present, came to my tent and explained that the going tomorrow would be even worse. We would have to dismount and walk. Therefore, in his capacity as representative of the Central People's Government, he would personally link arms and escort me along the way. As he said this, it occurred to me that the General was under the impression that not only could he exert his power over my two Prime Ministers, but he could also bully Nature.

I duly spent the next day entwined with Chiang. He was much older than me and very unfit, so it was quite a tiresome arrangement. Moreover, I was concerned that the rocks which continually crashed on to the road from above might not be able to discriminate between us in the event that the General's time had come!

Throughout the journey, each time we stopped, we did so at military outposts manned by the PLA and bedecked with red flags. Chinese soldiers would then come over and offer us tea. On one occasion, I was so thirsty that I accepted some without bothering to find my own drinking vessel. After I had quenched my thirst, I noticed that the mug I was drinking from was disgustingly dirty with scraps of food and dried saliva on the sides. This rather revolted me. I remembered how particular I had been as a small child, though now, whenever I think of the incident, I cannot help laughing.

After about two weeks we reached a small town called Demo, where we camped by a stream for the night. The weather was perfect and I remember being enchanted at the sight of the river-banks, which were adrift with yellow buttercups and mauve-pink primulas. Ten days later we reached the Poyul region. From now on the road was motorable and the party travelled by jeep and truck. This was a great relief as I had begun to be very sore from riding, though I was not the only one. I shall never forget the sight of one of my officials. His backside was so painful that he rode sitting diagonally across his saddle. In this way, he contrived to rest first one cheek and then the other.

At this distance from Lhasa, the Chinese were in much more effective control of the country. Already they had built many barracks for their soldiers and houses for their officials. And in every town and village there were loudspeakers which played Chinese martial music and exhortations to the people to work and work harder 'for the glory of the Motherland'.

Soon, we reached Chamdo, the capital of Kham, where a large reception awaited me. Here, because the Chinese administered the place directly, the proceedings had a very curious flavour. Military bands played hymns of praise to Chairman Mao and to the Revolution and Tibetans stood waving red flags.

From Chamdo, I was taken by jeep to Chengdu, the first town in China proper. On the way, we crossed the hill at a place called Dhar Tse-dho, which marks the historic border between Tibet and China. As we descended to the plains on the other side, I remarked to myself how different the countryside was. Might the Chinese people prove to be as different from my own people as their countryside was from ours?

I did not see much of Chengdu as I caught a fever on arrival and was confined to my bed for several days. As soon as I was sufficiently recovered, I and the most senior members of my entourage were taken to Shingang, where I was joined by the Panchen Lama, who had set off from Shigatse some months before. We were then flown to Xian.

The craft in which we flew was very old and even I could tell that it had seen better days. Inside, the seats were very uncomfortable steel frames without any sort of upholstery. But I was so excited at the prospect of getting airborne that I was able to overlook the obvious defects and felt no fear at all, although since then I have developed a much more cautious attitude to flying. Nowadays I don't like it much and am a rather poor seat companion. I much prefer saying prayers to holding conversations.

In Xian, we changed forms of transport again and completed the last leg of the journey by train. This was another wonderful experience. The carriages reserved for the Panchen Lama and myself were equipped with every facility imaginable, from beds and bathrooms to an elaborate dining-car. The only thing that marred the journey for me was a growing sense of apprehension the closer we drew to the Chinese capital. When at last we arrived at Peking railway station, I felt extremely nervous, though this abated a little when I saw huge crowds of young people gathered to welcome us. But it did not take long for me to realise that their smiles and cheers were entirely false, and that they were acting under orders, whereupon my anxiety returned.

As we stepped off the train, we were greeted by Chou En-lai, the Prime Minister, and Chu Teh, Vice-Chairman of the People's Republic, both of whom seemed quite friendly. With them was the same middle-aged Tibetan I had seen with General Tan Kuan-sen at Lhasa. After courtesies had been exchanged, this man, whose name was Phuntsog Wangyal, accompanied me to my quarters, which was a bungalow with a beautiful garden that had previously belonged to the Japanese diplomatic mission, where he explained the agenda for the next few days.

In due course I became firm friends with Phuntsog Wangyal. He had been converted to the Communist cause many years back. Before coming to China, he had acted as an agent for the Communists whilst teaching at a school run by the Chinese Mission in Lhasa. When the Mission was closed down following the expulsion of its members in 1949, he and his wife, who happened to be a Tibetan Muslim, left too. He himself was from Kham. As a child he had attended a Christian Missionary School at Bathang, his home town, where he learned some English. By the time of our acquaintance he had acquired an excellent command of Chinese too and made a brilliant interpreter between Chairman Mao and myself.

Phuntsog Wangyal turned out to be a very able man, calm and wise; a good thinker too. He was also very sincere and honest, and I enjoyed his company a great deal. Evidently, he felt very happy in his assignment as my official interpreter, not least because of the access it gave him to Chairman Mao, whom he idolized. However, his feelings towards me were equally strong. Once, when we were talking about Tibet, he said that he was full of optimism for the future as he considered that I was very open-minded. He told me how many years ago he had been to a public audience at the Norbulingka and seen a small boy on a throne. 'And now you are a small boy no longer, here with me in Peking.' This thought moved him very much and he wept openly. After several minutes he continued, now speaking as a true Communist. He told me that the Dalai Lama should not rely on astrology as a tool with which to govern the country. He also said that religion was not a reliable thing to base one's life on. Because of his obvious sincerity, I listened carefully. On the subject of what he called superstitious practices, I explained the Buddha's own emphasis on the need for thorough investigation before accepting something as true or false. I also told him that I was convinced that religion is essential, especially for those engaged in politics. At the end of our conversation I felt that we had a high regard for one another. Such differences as we had were personal matters, so there was no basis for conflict. In the final analysis, we were both Tibetans thinking deeply about the future of our country.

A day or two after our arrival, I was told that all members of the Tibetan delegation were invited to a banquet. That afternoon we were taken through a dress rehearsal of the evening's activities. It turned out that our hosts were very particular about protocol (which I later discovered to be a general characteristic of officials of the People's Republic) and our liaison officers worked themselves up into a frantic pitch of anxiety. They were terrified that we would bungle the affair and make them look foolish, so they gave us all strict and detailed instructions about what to do, even down to the number of paces to take and after how many to turn left or right. It was like a military parade. There was a precise order in which everyone was to appear. I was to go in first, followed by the Panchen Lama, then my two Tutors, the *Kalons* (the four members of the *Kashag*), each in order of seniority, and then everyone else, according to rank. All of us were to bear gifts and again these had to match the status of the person carrying them. The whole procedure seemed very complicated, even to us Tibetans whose aristocracy is also known for its love of etiquette. But the trepidation of our hosts was infectious and soon we were all in a dither, save for Ling Rinpoché, who disliked all formality. He would have nothing to do with it.

Next day, so far as I can remember, I had my inaugural encounter with Chairman Mao. This was at a public meeting, with a format similar to the banquet, all of us filing in according to rank. As we entered the hall, the first thing I noticed was an array of spotlights that had been erected for a whole army of official photographers. Beneath these stood Mao himself, looking very calm and relaxed. He did not have the aura of a particularly intelligent man. However, as we shook hands I felt as if I was in the presence of a strong magnetic force. He came across as being very friendly and spontaneous, despite the formality of the occasion. It began to look as if the apprehension I had felt was unfounded.

In all, I had at least a dozen meetings with Mao, most of which were at large gatherings, but a few of which were held in private with no one but Phuntsog Wangyal in attendance. Whatever the occasion, whether it was a banquet or a conference, he always made me sit next to him and on one occasion he even served me my food. This worried me somewhat as I had heard a rumour that he was suffering from tuberculosis.

I found him a most impressive man. Physically he was extraordinary. His complexion was very dark, but at the same time his skin seemed shiny. It was as if he used some kind of ointment; his hands were very beautiful with perfect fingers and an exquisitely formed thumb, which had the same curious sheen as well.

I also noticed that he did seem to have some difficulty with breathing and he panted a great deal. This may have had an effect on his speech, which was always very slow and precise. He was given to using short sentences, perhaps for the same reason. His movements and mannerisms were similarly slow. If he moved his head from left to right it would take several seconds, which gave him an air of dignity and assurance.

In contrast to the distinction of his manner were his clothes, which looked completely worn out. His shirts were always thread-bare at the cuff and the jackets he wore were shabby. These were identical to those worn by everyone else, save for the colour, which was a slightly different shade of drab. The only part of his attire that looked well kept were his shoes, which were always well polished. But he did not need luxurious clothes. In spite of looking down-at-heel, he had a very emphatic air of authority and sincerity. His mere presence commanded respect. I felt, too, that he was completely genuine as well as very decisive.

During the first few weeks of our stay in China, the main topic of conversation amongst all of us Tibetans was naturally how we could best reconcile our needs with China's desires. I myself acted as mediator between the *Kashag* and the Communist leadership. There were several preliminary meetings, which went very well. The discussions were given further impetus when I had my first private meeting with Mao. During the course of it, he told me that he had come to the conclusion that it was too early to implement all of the clauses of the Seventeen-Point 'Agreement'. One of them in particular he felt could safely be ignored for the time being. This was the one that concerned the establishment of a Military Affairs Commission in Tibet whereby the country would be governed effectively by the PLA. 'It would be better to establish a Preparatory Committee for the "Autonomous Region" of Tibet,' he said. This organisation would see to it that the pace of reform was dictated by the wishes of the Tibetan people themselves. He was most insistent that the terms of the 'Agreement' were put into effect as slowly as we ourselves judged necessary. When I reported this news back to the *Kashag*, they were highly relieved. It really began to look as if we might be able to achieve a workable compromise now that we were dealing directly with the highest in the land.

At a later private meeting with Mao, he told me how glad he was that I had come to Peking. He went on to say that the whole purpose of China's presence in Tibet was to help us. 'Tibet is a great country,' he said. 'You have a marvellous history. Long ago you even conquered a lot of China. But now you have fallen behind and we want to help you. In twenty years' time you could be ahead of us and then it will be your turn to help China.' I could hardly believe my ears, but he seemed to be speaking out of conviction and not just for effect.

I began to get very enthusiastic about the possibilities of association with the People's Republic of China. The more I looked at Marxism, the more I liked it. Here was a system based on equality and justice for everyone, which claimed to be a panacea for all the world's ills. From a theoretical standpoint, its only drawback as far as I could see was its insistence on a purely materialistic view of human existence. This I could not agree with. I was also concerned at the methods used by the Chinese in pursuit of their ideals. I received a strong impression of rigidity. But I expressed a wish to become a Party member all the same. I felt sure, as I still do, that it would be possible to work out a synthesis of Buddhist and pure Marxist doctrines that really would prove to be an effective way of conducting politics.

At the same time I started to learn Chinese and also at the suggestion of my new Chinese security officer – a delightful man and a veteran of the Korean War – began to do some physical exercises. He used to come and supervise me every morning. However, he was not at all used to getting up early and could not understand why I rose before five o'clock to pray. Often he would appear tousle-haired and unwashed. As for the regime, it did seem to have some effect. My chest, which up until then had been rather boney and narrow, began to flatten out considerably.

In all, I spent around ten weeks in Peking after our arrival. Much of the time was taken up by attending political meetings and conferences, not to mention innumerable banquets. The food at these enormous meals I found to be quite good on the whole, although I still shudder at the thought of the hundred-year-old eggs which are considered to be such a delicacy. Their smell was overpowering. It lingered too, so that when you had done with eating them you could not tell whether you were still tasting them in your mouth or whether it was simply the smell: they completely overwhelmed your senses. Some European cheeses have a similar effect, I have noticed. These banquets were considered to be very important by our hosts, who seemed to be of the opinion that genuine friendships could develop just by people sitting together at the dining-table. This is quite wrong, of course.

When the First Assembly of the Communist Party took place at around this time, I was made a Vice-President of the Steering Committee of the People's Republic of China. This was a nominal appointment that carried some prestige, if not actually any political power. (The Steering Committee discussed policy before it was put up to the Politburo, where the real power lay.)

The political meetings and conferences of the Steering Committee were a much more useful experience than the banquets, although they tended to go on for ever. Sometimes the speaker would talk for five, six or even seven hours at a stretch, which was extremely boring. I spent the time sipping hot water and yearning for the end. However, the meetings that were attended by Mao were a different matter. He was spellbinding. Best of all, when he had done with speaking, he would canvass his audience for their opinions. He was always trying to sound out people's deepest feelings on any given matter and was open to anything that might be said. He even went so far as to criticise himself on a number of occasions and once, when he was not getting the results he wanted, he produced a letter that had been sent to him from his own village complaining about the behaviour of the local Party authorities. This was altogether impressive but as time went on I began to realise how artificial the majority of these meetings were. People were afraid to speak their minds, especially the non-Party members, who were always desperate to please the Party members and be polite to them.

Gradually, it began to dawn on me that political life in China was full of contradictions, although I could not exactly decide on what was the cause of this. Every time I saw Mao, he inspired me again. I remember one occasion when he presented himself without warning at my residence. He wanted to speak to me privately on some matter, I forget what exactly, but during the course of our conversation he surprised me very much by speaking favourably of the Lord Buddha. He praised him for being 'anti-caste, anti-corruption and anti-exploitation'. He also mentioned the goddess Tara, a well-known female Buddha. Suddenly he seemed quite pro-religion.

On another occasion I sat facing the Great Helmsman, as he was known, at a long table, at either end of which were two generals. He pointed both men out to me, saying that he was posting them to Tibet. Then he looked at me hard and said, 'I am sending these men to serve you. If they don't listen to what you tell them, you are to let me know and I shall recall them.' Yet at the same time as receiving these favourable impressions, I could see for myself the paranoia with which the great majority of Party officials went about their daily tasks. They were in constant fear of their jobs, if not their lives.

As well as spending time with Mao, I saw quite a lot of Chou En-lai and Lu Shao-chi as well. The latter was a man of few words and little laughter. In short, he was very tough. On one occasion

I was present at a meeting between Lu and U Nu, the Prime Minister of Burma. Before it began, each person present was briefed on the subject they were to take care of. Mine was religion: if the Burmese leader wanted to talk about religion, I was to answer. This seemed unlikely and was, in fact, very far from what U Nu had in mind. Instead, he wanted to ask Lu about China's support for Communist insurgents in his country. But when he spoke, adding that the guerrillas were creating trouble for his Government, Lu simply looked away. He refused to be drawn and U Nu's question went unanswered. I was shocked, but consoled myself with the thought that at least Lu did not lie or attempt deceit. Chou En-lai would undoubtedly have said something clever at this point.

Chou was a very different sort of person and, where Lu was steady and rather grave, he was full of smiles and charm and swift intelligence. In fact he was over-polite, which is invariably a sign of someone not to be trusted. He was also very sharp-eyed. I remember that at one particular banquet I attended, he was escorting some foreign dignitary to the table when suddenly his guest tripped on a small stair. Chou had a dysfunctional arm but, as the man stumbled, his good one was already out, waiting to catch him. He did not even stop chatting.

His tongue was sharp too. After U Nu's visit to Peking, Chou addressed a meeting of over a thousand officials, during which he openly made derogatory remarks about the Burmese Prime Minister. I found this very strange as publicly he had always been exceedingly polite and courteous to the man.

Whilst in Peking I was asked to give teachings to some Chinese Buddhists. My translator on this occasion was a Chinese monk who, I was told, had studied in Tibet and received teachings from a Tibetan lama. (In former times, many Chinese monks had been to study in Tibet, particularly in the field of dialectics.) I was highly impressed by him: he struck me as being a very devoted and sincere practitioner of his faith.

Some of the Communists I met were also extremely nice people, totally selfless in their service to others and, personally, very helpful to me. I learned a great deal from them. One such was a high official at the Office of Minorities, called Liu Ka-ping, who was appointed to give me lessons on Marxism and the Chinese Revolution. He was, in fact, a Muslim and I used to tease him by asking him whether he ever ate pork. He also had one finger missing, I remember, and was a delightful person. We became very good friends. His wife, who was so much younger than him that she could have been his daughter, became equally good friends with my mother and elder sister. When I came to leave China, he cried like a child.

I remained in Peking until after the October celebrations. That year marked the fifth anniversary of the founding of the People's Republic and a number of foreign dignitaries were expected in the capital at that time. Amongst these were Khrushchev and Bulganin, both of whom I was introduced to. Neither man made much of an impression on me, certainly nothing compared with Pandit Nehru, who also visited Peking whilst I was there. He was guest of honour at a banquet presided over by Chou En-lai and, as usual, all the other guests filed past him to be introduced. From a distance he seemed very affable and had no trouble finding a few words for everyone as they came to him. However, when it was my turn and I stood shaking him by the hand, he seemed to get stuck. His eyes remained fixed in front of him and he was completely speechless. I felt rather embarrassed at this and broke the ice by saying how pleased I was to meet him and that I had heard a great deal about him, despite Tibet being such a remote country. At last he spoke, but only in the most perfunctory manner.

I was very disappointed, as I had particularly wanted to be able to speak with him and ask him about his country's attitude to Tibet. It was altogether a very odd meeting.

Later on I did get to talk to the Indian Ambassador, at his request, but this was almost as much of a failure as my meeting with Nehru. Although I had with me an official who spoke excellent English, the Chinese insisted that I take along with me one of their interpreters instead. This meant that what the Indian Ambassador said in English had to be laboriously translated into Chinese and then into Tibetan. It was a very uncomfortable session. There were certain things that I had wanted to discuss that no longer could be brought up on account of the Chinese presence. Much the best part of the afternoon came when a servant started to pour tea for us all and knocked over a large bowl of exotic fruits that must have been procured at great expense. At the sight of all these apricots, peaches and plums rolling about on the floor, my very grave Chinese interpreter and his assistant (no official ever went alone) got down on their hands and knees and started crawling about on the carpet to pick them up. It was all I could do to stop myself laughing.

I had a much better time with the Russian Ambassador, whom I sat next to at a banquet. In those days, Russia and China were firm friends so there was no danger of interference here. The Ambassador was very amicable and showed some interest in finding out my impressions of Socialism. When I replied that I saw great possibilities in it, he said that I ought to come and visit the Soviet Union. This sounded an excellent idea and I immediately developed a strong desire to undertake a trip to his country – preferably as an ordinary member of a delegation. That way, wherever this imaginary delegation went I would go too, but, not having any responsibilities, I could spend the whole time minding my own business and just looking around. Sadly the idea came to nothing. It was over twenty years before I was able to realise my ambition of visiting the USSR. And, needless to say, the circumstances were very different from those I had fondly imagined.

On the whole the Chinese authorities were very reluctant to let me meet with foreigners. I suppose that I must have been something of an embarrassment to them. At the time of Tibet's invasion there had been widespread condemnation of the Communists from many countries around the world. This was a source of irritation to them and they were busy doing all they could to improve their image and show how their occupation of Tibet was justifiable both historically and in terms of a great nation helping a weaker one. But I could not help noticing how completely differently our hosts behaved when foreign visitors were present. Whereas habitually they were arrogant in their attitude towards foreigners, in their presence they were very meek and subdued.

Quite a few visitors to Peking expressed an interest to meet me, however, including a Hungarian dance troupe, whose members all wanted my autograph – which I gave them. Also, several thousand Mongolians came to the Chinese capital hoping to see me and the Panchen Lama. This did not please the Chinese authorities, perhaps because the notion of Tibetans and Mongolians together was an uncomfortable reminder of how different things had been in the past. Not only had Tibetan forces extracted tribute from the Chinese in the eighth century, but Mongolia had actually ruled China from 1279 until 1368 AD, following the successful invasion of Kublai Khan, the Mongolian warlord.

At this time, there was an interesting historical incident. Kublai Khan became a Buddhist and had a Tibetan *guru*. This lama persuaded the Mongolian leader to stop his practice of controlling the Chinese population increase by drowning thousands of them in the sea. In so doing, the Tibetan saved many Chinese lives.

During the winter of 1954 I went on an extensive tour of China, together with my complete entourage, including both my mother and Tenzin Choegyal, my youngest brother, to see the marvels of industrial and material progress. I enjoyed this a great deal, but many of my Tibetan officials were completely uninterested in what was on offer and would heave a sigh of relief whenever it was announced that there was to be no 'sightseeing' on that particular day. My mother, especially, did not enjoy her time in China. Her unhappiness increased when, during an excursion, she contracted a fever which developed into quite a serious case of flu. Luckily my personal physician, the 'fat doctor' of my childhood, was with us. He was a very learned man and a great friend of my mother's. He duly prescribed some medicine for her which she took at once. Unfortunately, she misunderstood his directions and took in one go what should have been two separate daily draughts.

This produced a strong reaction, which, on top of her fever, made her very ill indeed. For several days she was extremely weak and I became concerned for her. But after a week she began to recover and, in fact, went on to live for more than twenty-five years. Ling Rinpoché also fell severely ill, but he did not make such a good recovery and it was not until after coming into exile that he fully regained his strength.

Tenzin Choegyal, who is twelve years my junior, was a constant source of delight and terror to everyone, including the Chinese, who were very fond of him. Being extremely intelligent, he picked up fluent Mandarin in a matter of months, which was both an advantage and a disadvantage. He loved to see the grown-ups embarrassed. If ever my mother or anyone made a disparaging remark about one of our hosts, my little brother would pass it on without hesitation. We all had to be very careful of what we said in front of him. Even then, he could always sense when someone was being vague or evasive. But he was so delightful that Trijang Rinpoché, my Junior Tutor, was the only person who succeeded in being reserved towards him, mainly I think because Tenzin Choegyal used to jump all over the furniture and he was worried about having to explain to the Chinese how it came to be broken. Ling Rinpoché was, on the other hand, an enthusiastic playmate for him. Personally I did not see a great deal of my brother, although recently he reminded me of an occasion when I found that he had fished all the carp out of an ornamental pond and laid them out neatly on the grass beside it. He tells me that I boxed his ears hard.

Although my interest in China's material development was not shared by many of my officials, I was much impressed with what the Communists had managed to achieve in the field of heavy industry. I was eager for my own country to make similar progress. I was particularly taken with a hydro-electric power station that we were taken to see in Manchuria. It did not take much imagination to see that there were endless possibilities for this type of power generation in Tibet. But what made this particular trip so memorable was the expression on the face of the official who was showing me over the project when I asked him some pertinent questions about electrical power. Thanks to my work on that old diesel generator in Lhasa, I had quite a good grasp of the basic principles involved. I suppose it must have seemed very incongruous for a young foreigner in monk's robes to be asking about kilowatt hours and turbine size.

The highlight of this excursion came when I was taken on board an old warship, also in Manchuria. I was fascinated. No matter that it was so ancient and that I could not make head or tail of any of the instruments or dials. Just to be on board this giant, grey, metal structure with its peculiar smell of oil and sea water was enough for me.

On the negative side, I came to realise that the Chinese authorities had no intention of allowing me contact with ordinary Chinese people. Every time I wanted to break away from the programme or even just get out to see places for myself, I was prevented from doing so by the officials sent to look after me, always on the pretext of 'security, security': my safety was their perpetual excuse. Yet it was not only I who was kept isolated from the common people; so were all the Chinese from Peking. They too were forbidden to do anything independently.

However, Serkon Rinpoché, one of my *tsenshap*, always managed to get out and about. He never listened to anything the Chinese said to him and simply did what he thought was proper. And, perhaps because he was lame and quite inconspicuous, no one thought to try to stop him. He was thus the only one who managed to get an intimate picture of what life was like in the brave, new People's Republic. I learned a good deal from him. He painted a very sombre picture of great poverty and fear amongst the population.

I did, however, have one very interesting conversation with a hotel porter whilst visiting an industrial zone. He told me that he had seen photographs of my departure from Lhasa and was pleased to know that my people had been so happy about my visit to China. When I told him that this was far from being the case, he was surprised. 'But it said so in the newspaper,' he said, to which

I replied that the situation must have been misrepresented as the truth was that the majority of my people had been utterly distraught. At this, my friend expressed shock and amazement. I, for my part, realised for the first time to what extent things were distorted in the Communist press: it seemed as if telling lies was in the blood of the authorities.

Whilst on this journey around China, I went over the border into Mongolia, where I travelled accompanied by Serkon Rinpoché and some others. It was a very moving experience, which made me realise how closely related is that country to my own.

We arrived back in Peking in late January 1955, just in time to celebrate *Losar*, the Tibetan New Year. As a mark of its importance, I decided to host a banquet, to which I would invite Chairman Mao and the other members of the 'Big Four', that is, Chou En-lai, Chu Teh and Lu Shao-chi. They all accepted. During the course of the evening Mao was very friendly. At one point he leaned over and asked me what I was doing as I threw a pinch of *tsampa* up into the air. I explained that this was a symbolic offering, whereupon he took some between his own fingers and did the same. Then he took another lot and, with a mischievous look on his face, threw it on to the floor.

This slightly sarcastic gesture was the only thing that spoiled an otherwise memorable evening, which seemed to hold out a promise of genuine fraternity between our two countries. Certainly that was how the Chinese portrayed the event. To this end they had organised the usual battery of photographers, who were to record the scene for posterity. Some of the photographs were published in the newspaper a day or two later with glowing reports, emphasising the speeches that were made. These pictures must also have been syndicated to Tibet because, when I was back in Lhasa, I saw one of them reproduced in a Chinese-run local newspaper. It depicted Chairman Mao and myself sitting together with my head turned towards him and my hands making some inexplicable gesture. The Tibetan picture editor of the newspaper had made up his own mind about what was going on and ran a caption to the effect that this was a photograph of His Holiness the Dalai Lama explaining to the Great Helmsman how to make *khabse* (*Losar* cookies)!

The day before I was due to leave China to return to Tibet, that is during the spring of 1955, I was attending a meeting of the Steering Committee. Lu Rau-chi, who was presiding over it, was halfway through an oration when suddenly my security officer burst in and came running over to me. 'Chairman Mao wants to see you at once. He is waiting for you,' he said. I did not know what to say. I couldn't just get up and leave the meeting, and Lu showed no sign of drawing breath. 'In that case,' I replied, 'you will have to go and have me excused.' This he did straight away.

We went directly to Mao's office, where he was indeed waiting for me. It was to be our last meeting. He announced that he wanted to give me some advice about government before I went back to Tibet, and proceeded to explain how to organise meetings, how to draw out people's opinions and then how to decide on the key issues. It was all excellent information and I sat busily taking notes, as I always did whenever we met. He went on to tell me that communications were a vital ingredient in any form of material progress and stressed the importance of seeing to it that as many young Tibetans as possible were trained up in this field. He added that whenever he passed anything on to me, he wanted to be able to do so through a Tibetan. Finally, he drew closer to me and said, 'Your attitude is good, you know. Religion is poison. Firstly it reduces the population, because monks and nuns must stay celibate, and secondly it neglects material progress.' At this I felt a violent burning sensation all over my face and I was suddenly very afraid. 'So,' I thought, 'you are the destroyer of the *Dharma* after all.'

It was by now late in the evening. As Mao spoke those fateful words I leaned forward as if to write something, half hiding my face. I hoped that he would not sense the horror I felt: it might have broken his trust in me. Luckily, Phuntsog Wangyal was not, for some reason, interpreting between us on this occasion. Had he done so, I am sure that he would have discovered my thoughts

– especially as we invariably discussed everything together afterwards.

Even so, I could not have concealed my feelings for much longer. Fortunately, Mao ended the interview after only a few more minutes. I felt a tremendous sense of relief when he stood up to shake my hand. Amazingly, his eyes were full of life and he was completely alert, despite the late hour. We went outside together, into the night-time quiet. My car was waiting. He opened and closed the door for me. As the vehicle began to move I turned to wave. My last sight of Mao was of him standing out in the cold with neither hat nor coat, waving.

Fear and amazement gave way to confusion. How could he have misjudged me so? How could he have thought that I was not religious to the core of my being? What had caused him to think otherwise? Every move I made was recorded, that I knew: how many hours sleep I took, how many bowls of rice I ate, what I said at every meeting. No doubt a weekly report on my behaviour was sent for analysis and then submitted to Mao. That being so, he surely could not have failed to notice that every day I spent at least four hours in prayer and meditation and that furthermore, all the time I was in China, I was receiving religious instruction from my tutors. He must have known too that I was working hard towards my final monastic examinations, which now could not be very many years away, six or seven at the most. I was perplexed.

The only possible explanation was that he had misinterpreted my great interest in scientific matters and material progress. It was true that I wanted to modernise Tibet in line with the People's Republic and true also that my cast of mind is basically scientific. So it could only be that, in his ignorance of Buddhist philosophy, Mao had ignored the Buddha's instruction that anyone who practises the *Dharma* should test for themselves its validity. For this reason I have always been open to the discoveries and truths of modern science. Perhaps this was what tricked Mao into thinking that my religious practices were nothing more to me than a prop or convention. Whatever his reasoning, I now knew that he had misjudged me completely.

Next day, I left Peking for the return journey to Tibet. Progress was faster than it had been the previous year now that the Qinghai highway had been completed. On the way, I took the opportunity to stop for two or three days at a time in different places so that I could meet with as many of my countrymen as possible and tell them something of my experiences in China and what hope I had for the future. In spite of having had to revise my opinion of Mao, I still felt that he was a great leader and above all a sincere person. He was not deceitful. Therefore, I was convinced that so long as his officials in Tibet carried out his instructions, and provided he kept a firm control of them, there was good reason to be optimistic. Besides, as far as I was concerned, a positive approach was the only sensible one to take. There was no point in being negative: that only makes a bad situation worse. Not that my optimism was shared by many of my entourage. Few of them had gained a good impression of China and they were afraid that the rigid methods of the Communists would lead to oppression in Tibet. They were further disturbed by a story then circulating about a high official in the Chinese Government, called Gan Kung. It was whispered that he had been critical of Lu Shao-chi and for this had been murdered in a most horrible way.

It was not long before I began to have fresh doubts of my own. When I visited Tashikiel in far eastern Tibet, there was a huge turn-out of people. Many thousands had travelled to be able to see me and pay their respects. I was deeply moved by their great devotion. However, I was devastated to hear, some time later, that the Chinese authorities had misled people into believing that I would arrive a week later than I actually did. They lied about the date in order to prevent people from seeing me. As a result, thousands more turned up after I left.

A further cause for unhappiness was the paranoia of the Chinese concerning my personal safety. When I visited my home village, they insisted that I should not accept food from anyone but my own cooks. This meant that I could not receive any of the offerings brought to me by my people, even though some of them were from my own family who still lived in Taktser. As if any one of these simple, devout, humble people would ever take it into their heads to try to poison the Dalai Lama. My mother was deeply upset. She did not know what to tell them. And when I spoke to Tibetans there, asking about their living conditions, they replied that, 'Thanks to Chairman Mao, to Communism and the People's Republic of China, we are very happy' – but with tears in their eyes.

Throughout my journey back to Lhasa, I received as many people as possible. Unlike China, this was not difficult. Thousands came, bringing their sick and old, just to catch a glimpse of me. A lot of Chinese attended these gatherings as well. This gave me the opportunity to express the need for them to understand the Tibetan mentality. In doing so, I took the trouble to find out which were Party members and which were not. Experience had taught me that the former were, on the whole, more straightforward.

The attitude of the Chinese authorities in Tibet towards me was very interesting. On one occasion, an official said, 'The Chinese people do not love Chairman Mao so much as Tibetans love the Dalai Lama.' On another, a guard, who was throwing his weight around in a very brutal manner, came over to my jeep and demanded to know where the Dalai Lama was. At the reply of 'Here', he took off his hat and asked for a blessing. And when I had left Chengdu, many of the Chinese officials who accompanied me throughout my visit wept to see me go. I had similarly warm feelings towards them: despite our differences of opinion, we had developed a strong, personal relationship.

Seeing the country people of Tibet after so many months allowed me to look afresh at the differences between them and their Chinese counterparts. For a start, you could tell just by comparing their faces that the Tibetans were much happier. This was due to a number of cultural factors I feel. Firstly, the relationship between landlord and serf was much milder in Tibet than in China and conditions for the poor were much less harsh. Secondly, in Tibet there was never anything like the barbarisms of foot-binding or castration, which until recently had been widespread throughout China. However, I think that these points were lost on the Chinese, who looked on our feudal system as a replica of their own.

Shortly before reaching Lhasa, I met up with Chou En-lai, who had flown to a place in Kham that had just suffered an earthquake. It was a curious encounter in which he said some positive things about religion. I still wonder why, as this was very much out of character. Perhaps he was speaking on Mao's instructions, trying to repair the damage done at our final meeting.

○ CHAPTER SIX ○

Mr Nehru Regrets

○

WHEN I ARRIVED back in Lhasa in June 1955, I was greeted as usual by many thousands of people. My long absence had caused much sorrow amongst Tibetans and it was a relief that they now had the Dalai Lama back in their midst. It was a relief for me as well. Evidently, the Chinese were behaving with more restraint here than in eastern Tibet. On the return journey from China I had received, in addition to many ordinary people, numerous deputations from local chieftains begging that I ask our new masters to change their policies in those rural areas. They saw that the Chinese directly threatened the Tibetan way of life and were very afraid.

In the city itself, I found things were relatively normal, except that there were now many cars and trucks bringing noise and pollution to the city for the first time in history. The food shortages had eased and active displays of anger had given way to resentment mixed with passive resistance. Now that I was back, there was even a resurgence of optimism. For my part, I felt that my status amongst the local Chinese authorities must be enhanced by Mao's public show of confidence in me and I remained cautiously optimistic for the future.

Yet I was conscious that outside Tibet the world had turned its back on us. Worse, India, our nearest neighbour and spiritual mentor, had tacitly accepted Peking's claims to Tibet. In April 1954, Nehru had signed a new Sino–Indian treaty which included a memorandum known as Panch Sheel, whereby it was agreed that India and China would under no circumstances interfere with one another's 'internal' affairs. According to this treaty, Tibet was part of China.

The summer of 1955 was undoubtedly the best we were to experience during the decade of uneasy coexistence between the Chinese authorities and my own Tibetan administration. But summer in Tibet is a short season and it was not many weeks before disturbing news began to reach my ears about the activities of the Chinese authorities in Kham and Amdo. Far from leaving the people be, they had begun to press ahead unilaterally with all kinds of 'reform'. New taxes were imposed on houses, land and cattle, and, to add insult to injury, the contents of monasteries were also assessed for tax. Large estates were confiscated and the land redistributed by the local Chinese cadres in accordance with their own political ideology. Landowners were publicly arraigned and punished for 'crimes against the people'; to my horror some were even put to death. Simultaneously, the Chinese authorities began to round up the many thousands of nomad farmers who roamed these fertile regions. To our new masters, nomadism was repugnant as it smacked of barbarism. (In fact, *mantze*, a common Chinese word for 'Tibetan', literally means 'barbarian'.)

Also disturbing was the news that the work of the monasteries was being grossly interfered with and the local population had begun to be indoctrinated against religion. Monks and nuns were subject to severe harassment and publicly humiliated. For example, they were forced to join in extermination programmes of insects, rats, birds and all types of vermin, even though the Chinese authorities knew that taking any form of life is contrary to Buddhist teaching. If they refused, they were beaten. Meanwhile, the Chinese in Lhasa carried on as if nothing was amiss. By not interfering with religion here in the capital, they were clearly hoping that I would be lulled into a false sense of security whilst they did as they pleased elsewhere.

Towards the end of 1955, preparations were put in hand for the inauguration of the Preparatory Committee for the Autonomous Region of Tibet (PCART), Mao's alternative to rule by military commission. But as autumn progressed to winter, the news from the east became worse. The Khampas, who were not used to outside interference, did not take kindly to Chinese methods: of all their possessions, the one they valued above all others was their personal weapon. So when the local cadres began to confiscate these, the Khampas reacted with violence. Throughout the winter months the situation deteriorated rapidly. As it did so, refugees from Chinese oppression began to arrive in Lhasa, bringing with them horrifying stories of brutality and degradation. The Chinese dealt viciously with Khampa resistance: not only were public beatings and executions carried out, but often these were done by the victim's own child. Public criticism was also introduced. This is a method especially favoured by the Chinese Communists. The 'offender' is trussed up with a rope in such a way that the shoulders are dislocated. Then, when the person is utterly helpless and crying out in pain, members of the public – including women and children – are called forward to inflict further injury. Apparently, the Chinese felt that this was all it took to make people change their minds, and that it aided in the process of political re-education.

At the beginning of 1956, during *Losar*, I had a very interesting encounter with the Nechung oracle, who announced that the 'light of the Wish-Fulfilling Jewel [one of the names by which the Dalai Lama is known to Tibetans] will shine in the West'. I took this to indicate that I would travel that year to India, though I now see that the prophecy had a deeper implication.

A more pressing concern were the many refugees from Kham and Amdo who had recently arrived in Lhasa. The city was simmering. For the first time, there was an overtly political flavour to the New Year festivities. Posters denouncing the Chinese went up all over the capital and leaflets were distributed. The people held public meetings and elected popular leaders. Never before had Tibet witnessed such a thing. Naturally, the Chinese were furious. They quickly arrested three men who, they said, were responsible for inciting anti-democratic crimes. But this did nothing to curtail popular reaction to their rule.

During the *Monlam* festival, leading Amdowa and Khampa businessmen began to collect money for a ceremony of *Se-tri Chenmo* to be performed later in the year. This involves an offering to the protector divinities of Tibet, beseeching them to grant the Dalai Lama long life and prosperity. So successful was their fund-raising that the occasion was marked by the donation to me of an immense, jewel-studded, golden throne. However, as I later discovered, this activity had another aspect. It also marked the formation of an alliance called *Chushi Gangdruk*, meaning 'Four rivers, six ranges', the traditional collective name for the two provinces of Kham and Amdo. This organisation subsequently co-ordinated a widespread guerrilla resistance movement.

After *Monlam*, preparations for the forthcoming inauguration of PCART, of which I was to be chairman, continued apace. Within a few short months the Chinese, using Tibetan labour, built three large public buildings: a guest-house for visiting Chinese officials, a bathing house and a municipal hall. This last was a modern, two-storeyed building with a corrugated iron roof, capable of seating about twelve hundred people in front of a raised platform and a further three hundred in a gallery above. It stood directly in front of the Potala.

In April 1956, Marshal Chen Yi, deputy Prime Minister and Foreign Minister of the People's Republic of China, arrived with his wife and a large delegation from Peking to represent Chairman Mao. I remembered Chen Yi from my visit to China. Personally he was a very nice man, although his reputation as a speaker was formidable. He once made a speech lasting a full seven hours. The Marshal appeared in Lhasa wearing a tie, of which he was very proud, though he did not seem to know how to wear it. And the shirt he wore could barely contain his paunch. None of this bothered him, however: he was jovial, fond of luxury and not lacking in self-confidence. His arrival in Lhasa signalled the start of an impressive show. The Chinese had laid on extravagant entertainments for him and there were many banquets and speeches held in his honour. When PCART was formally inaugurated at a meeting in the new municipal hall, the place was decorated with many flags and banners depicting Chairman Mao and his chief colleagues. A Chinese military band played and Communist songs were sung. It was all very festive. Chen Yi then made a (comparatively short) speech in which he announced that 'necessary reforms' would be introduced 'to rid Tibet of its backward situation', explaining that this was necessary to bring the Tibetans up to the level of the 'advanced' Chinese nationality. There followed a succession of adulatory speeches made by Chinese and Tibetans alike, all praising Socialism and the Party and welcoming the presence of the Chinese in Tibet. I even had to make one myself, pointedly adding that I was sure that the Chinese would honour all their undertakings to introduce reform at the pace the people wanted and to permit freedom of worship.

The constitution of PCART provided for the creation of various new government departments to administer, for example, finance, education, agriculture, communications, medicine, religion and security. These were to be run mostly by Tibetans. Also the administration of Chamdo was to return to Lhasa. Together they comprised the so-called Tibet Autonomous Region. However, the rest of Kham and all of Amdo were to remain under the direct control of Peking. The Committee itself was to be comprised of fifty-one regional delegates. Only five were Chinese. At the same time, the *Kashag* and the National Assembly were to remain, although it was clear that the Chinese intended to marginalise and eventually to do away with all traces of traditional government.

Whilst on paper PCART promised to mark an important advance towards autonomy, the reality was very different. When Chen Yi announced the appointments, it turned out that of these fifty-one delegates (none of whom was elected), all but a handful owed their positions to the Chinese: they were allowed to keep their power and property so long as they did not voice any opposition. In other words, it was all a sham.

Nevertheless, there were a few surprises. One of these was Lobsang Samten's appointment as a member of the newly created security department. Being such a kind and gentle person, there can have been no one less suited to the job than he. I shall never forget the look on his face when he returned from a meeting with his Chinese opposite number. All had gone well until the man turned to Lobsang Samten (who spoke some Chinese) and asked him what was the Tibetan for 'Kill him'. Up to that moment my brother had thought this new official to be quite pleasant and straightforward, but this question left him dumbfounded. The idea of killing even an insect was so far from his mind that he was lost for words. When he arrived at the Norbulingka that same evening, his face was full of bewilderment. 'What *am* I to do?' he asked. This story is another illustration of the differences between Chinese and Tibetan attitudes. To one, the killing of human beings was a fact of life; to the other, it was unthinkable.

Shortly after the inauguration of PCART, I heard that the Chinese authorities in Kham made an attempt to win over all the local leaders. This they did by calling them all together and asking them to vote on the introduction of the 'democratic reforms', meaning, specifically, the establishment of several thousand agri-cultural co-operatives which were to comprise more than 100,000 households in the area that included Gar-chu and Karze. Of the 350 people they assembled, about two hundred agreed to go along with the reforms when I and my Cabinet consented to them. Forty said that they were prepared to accept them straight away, and the remainder said that they never wanted these so-called reforms. After that, they were allowed home.

A month later, the dissenters were summoned once more, this time to a fort called Jomdha Dzong, which lay to the north-east of Chamdo. As soon as they were inside, the building was sur-rounded by 5,000 PLA troops and the captives were told that they would not be released until they agreed to accept the reforms and promise that they would help carry them out. After two weeks of imprisonment, the Khampas gave in. There seemed to be no alternative. However, that night the guard on the fort was reduced. Seeing their opportunity, every one of them escaped and took to the hills. At a stroke, the Chinese had created a nucleus of outlaws, which in the years to come caused them many difficulties.

The incident at Jomdha Dzong occurred at around the same time as I was given a copy of a newspaper, published by the Chinese authorities at Karze in Kham. In disbelief, I saw that it contained a photograph of a row of severed heads. The caption said something to the effect that they had belonged to 'reactionary criminals'. This was the first concrete evidence of Chinese atrocity that I had seen. Thereafter, I knew that every terrible thing I heard about our new masters' behaviour was true. The Chinese, for their part, realising the bad effect that this newspaper was having on the people, tried to call it back – even offering to buy copies.

With this new information, coupled with the realisation that PCART was nothing but *tzuma* (eye-wash), I began to wonder whether there could be any hope for the future. My predecessor's prophecy was beginning to be proved entirely accurate. I was sick at heart. Outwardly, however, my life continued much as usual. I prayed, meditated and studied hard under my tutors. I also continued as usual to take part in all the religious festivals and ceremonies and to give and receive teachings from time to time. Occasionally, I used my authority to travel and left Lhasa to visit various monasteries. One such excursion was to Reting monastery, seat of the former Regent, which lay a few days' journey to the north of Lhasa. Shortly before leaving, I received a letter sent from an important Tibetan already living in exile. The situation in Lhasa had become so grave that even I began to feel suspicious and rather than open it, I kept it on my person, at night placing it carefully under my pillow until after I left for Reting.

It was such a relief to get out of the city and away from the madness of trying simultaneously to work with the Chinese authorities and to limit the damage they caused. As ever, I travelled as unostentatiously as possible and tried to remain incognito. In this way I was able to meet with the local people and hear what they had to say. On one particular occasion, not far from Reting, I fell into conversation with a herdsman. 'Who are you?' he asked. He was a tall, sturdy man with long, shaggy hair like a yak's. 'A servant of the Dalai Lama,' I replied. We talked about his life out here in the countryside and about his hopes and fears for the future. He knew little about the Chinese and had never been to Lhasa. He was too busy coaxing a living from the earth, with its thin, bitter soil, to worry about what was going on in the cities and beyond.

Yet for all his simplicity, I was delighted to find that he had a deep religious conviction and that the Buddha *Dharma* was thriving even in this remote region. He lived the life of peasants everywhere, in tune with Nature and the environment, but with little interest in the world that lay beyond his immediate horizon. I questioned him about his experiences with local government officials. He told me that they were mostly fair, though a few were officious. I greatly enjoyed our talk, which gave me many useful insights. Above all I learned that, despite this man's total lack of education, he was content and that, although he had not the slightest material comfort, he was secure in the knowledge that life for him was just as it had been for countless generations of his forebears and doubtless would continue the same for his children and their children. At the same time, I realised that this world view was no longer appropriate, that Tibet could no longer exist in elected peaceful isolation, no matter what the outcome with the Communist Chinese. When we finally parted company, we did so as the best of friends.

But the story continues. It so happened that the following day I was called upon to address the people of the next village that lay along our route and give them my blessing. A makeshift throne was put out for me and several hundred people gathered. All went well at first but then, looking around, I saw my friend of the day before standing amongst the audience with a look of abject bewilderment on his face. He could not believe his eyes. I smiled at him, but he stared blankly back. I felt quite sorry to have duped him.

When I actually arrived at Reting monastery, and came to pay my respects before its most important statue, I remember that, for no particular reason, I became very emotional. I felt a powerful sense of having in some way been long connected with the place. Since then, I have often thought of building a hermitage at Reting and spending the rest of my life there.

*

During the summer of 1956, an incident occurred which brought me more unhappiness than at almost any time before or since. The Khampa/Amdowa freedom-fighters' alliance began to have considerable success. By May/June, numerous sections of the Chinese military road had been destroyed along with a great many bridges. As a result, the PLA drafted in 40,000 troop reinforcements. This was exactly what I had feared. No matter how successful the resistance was, the Chinese would overcome it in the end by sheer force of numbers and superior fire-power. But I could not have predicted the aerial bombing of the monastery at Lithang in Kham. When I heard of it, I cried. I could not believe that human beings were capable of such cruelty to each other.

This bombardment was followed by the merciless torture and execution of women and children whose fathers and husbands had joined the resistance movement and, incredibly, by the disgusting abuse of monks and nuns. After arrest, these simple, religious people were forced – in public – to break their vows of celibacy with one another and even to kill people. I did not know what to do, but do something I must. I immediately demanded a meeting with General Chiang Kuo-ha, whom I informed that I was intending to write personally to Chairman Mao. 'How are Tibetans supposed to trust the Chinese if this is how you behave?' I demanded. I told him point-blank that it was wrong for them to have done such a thing. But this only started an argument. My criticisms were an insult to the Motherland, which wanted only to protect and assist my people. If some of my countrymen did not want reforms – reforms which would benefit the masses because they would prevent their exploitation – then they could expect to be punished. His reasoning was lunatic. I told him that this could in no way justify the torture of innocent people, still less bombing them from the air.

It was a useless exercise, of course. The General stood his ground. My only hope was that Chairman Mao would see that his subordinates were disobeying his instructions.

I dispatched a letter straight away. There was no reply. So I sent another, again via the official channel. At the same time, I persuaded Phuntsog Wangyal to deliver a third letter personally to Mao. But this also went unacknowledged. As the weeks went by and I had still heard nothing from Peking, I began for the first time really to doubt the intentions of the Chinese leadership. This shook me. After my visit to China, and despite the many negative impressions I had received, my attitude towards the Communists was still basically positive. Now, however, I began to see Chairman Mao's words as being like a rainbow – beautiful, but without substance.

Phuntsog Wangyal had arrived in Lhasa at the time of the inauguration of PCART. I was very glad to see him again. He was as committed as ever to Communism. After the April festivities, he accompanied some important Chinese officials on a tour of the outlying districts. On his return, he told me an amusing story. One of the Chinese high officials had asked a peasant living in some remote farming community what he thought of the new regime. The man replied that he was quite happy. 'Except for one thing. This new tax.' 'What new tax?' the official asked. 'The clapping tax. Every time a Chinese comes to visit, we all have to turn out and clap.'

I always felt that so long as Phuntsog Wangyal retained the confidence of Chairman Mao, there was hope for Tibet. After he had left for Peking once more, I therefore submitted a request to General Chiang Chin-wu that he be posted to Tibet as Party Secretary. At first the idea was accepted in principle, but there was a long gap before I heard anything more.

At the end of 1957, a Chinese official informed me that Phuntsog Wangyal would no longer be coming to Tibet because he was a dangerous man. I was amazed to hear this, as I knew that Chairman Mao thought highly of him. The official explained that there were several reasons, the first and foremost being that when he had lived in Kham, before coming to Lhasa, Phuntsog Wangyal had organised a separate Tibetan Communist Party which was not open to membership by Chinese nationals. For this crime he had been demoted and prevented from returning to Tibet. I was sorry to hear this – and even more sad when I heard, the following year, that my old friend had been stripped of office and detained. Eventually, he went to jail, where he remained, officially designated a 'non-person', until the late 1970s. All this despite his being a sincere and dedicated Communist, as anyone could see. It made me realise that the Chinese leadership was not truly Marxist, dedicated to a better world for all, but really highly nationalistic. Actually, these people were nothing but Chinese chauvinists posing as Communists: a collection of narrow-minded fanatics.

Phuntsog Wangyal is still alive, though very old now. I would very much like to see him once more before he dies. I continue to have a high regard for him as an old, experienced Tibetan Communist. The present authorities in China are aware of this and I still have hopes that we might meet again.

One very welcome guest to Lhasa during the spring of 1956 was the Maharaj Kumar of Sikkim, Crown Prince of the tiny state which lay along part of our border with India not far beyond Dromo. He was a delightful man: tall, quiet, gentle and calm, with large ears. With him he brought wonderful news contained in the form of a letter from the Indian Maha Bodhi society, of which he was President. This organisation, which represents Buddhists throughout the sub-continent, was inviting me to attend the Buddha Jyanti celebrations to mark the 2,500th birth anniversary of the Lord Buddha.

I was ecstatic. For us Tibetans, India is *Aryabhumi*, the Land of the Holy. All my life I had longed to make a pilgrimage there: it was the place that I most wanted to visit. Furthermore, an expedition to India might provide me with the opportunity to speak with Pandit Nehru and other heirs of Mahatma Gandhi. I desperately wanted to be able to make contact with the Indian Government, if only to see the way that a democracy worked. Of course, there was a chance that the Chinese would not let me go, but I had to try. So I took the letter to General Fan Ming.

Unfortunately, Fan Ming was by far the most disagreeable of the local Chinese authorities. He received me politely enough. But when I explained the reason for my call he grew evasive. He did not think it sounded like a good idea. There were many reactionaries in India. It was a dangerous place. Besides, the Preparatory Committee was very busy and he doubted whether I could be spared. 'Anyway,' he said, 'it's only an invitation from a religious society. It's not as if it was from the Indian Government itself. So don't worry, you don't have to accept.' I was devastated. It was obvious that the Chinese authorities intended even to prevent me from carrying out my religious duties.

A period of several months went by during which nothing more was said about Buddha Jyanti. Then, sometime about the middle of October, Fan Ming contacted me to ask who I wanted to nominate as leader of the delegation: the Indians needed to know. I replied that I would send Trijang Rinpoché, my Junior Tutor, adding that the delegation was ready to go as soon as he gave final clearance. Another two weeks went by and I gradually began to put the whole thing out of my mind when suddenly Chiang Chin-wu, who had just arrived back from Peking, came to tell me that the Chinese Government had decided that it would be all right for me to go after all. I could hardly believe my ears, so happy was I. 'But be careful,' he warned me. 'There are many reactionary elements and spies in India. If you try to do anything with them, I want you to realise that what happened in Hungary and Poland will happen in Tibet.' (He was referring to the brutal Russian response to rebellion in those countries.) When he had finished speaking, I realised that I should conceal my great joy and instead do my best to appear to be very anxious. I indicated that I was genuinely surprised and concerned at his information about imperialists and reactionaries. This reassured Chiang and he adopted a more conciliatory tone. 'Don't worry too much,' he said. 'If you have any difficulties, our Ambassador will always be there to help you.' With that our meeting ended. The General stood up and, with his customary formality, took leave of me. As soon as he was gone, I rushed off, smiling as if my mouth would reach my ears, to tell my personal attendants the news.

In the few days that remained before our departure, I heard an interesting story about this sudden about face by the Chinese authorities. It transpired that the Indian Consulate in Lhasa had asked my officials whether I would in fact be going to India to attend the celebrations. On being given a negative answer, the Indians relayed this message to their own Government – with the result that Mr Nehru had personally intervened on my behalf. However, the Chinese authorities still did not want to let me go. It was not until General Chiang arrived back in Lhasa and discovered that the Indian Consul had told a number of people about Nehru's communication that, under threat of harm to Sino–Indian relations, the Chinese were forced to change their minds.

I finally left Lhasa towards the end of November 1956, full of joy at the prospect of being able to move about freely without the constant supervision of some Chinese official or other. My entourage was quite small and, thanks to the military roads that now ran north and south, east and west linking all of Tibet with China, we were able to travel almost the whole way to Sikkim by car. At Shigatse we paused to pick up the Panchen Lama and then continued on to Chumbithang, the last settlement before the Nathu pass, where the border lay. There we exchanged cars for horses and I bade farewell to General Tin Ming-yi, who had accompanied us from Lhasa. He seemed genuinely sorry to see me go. I think that he was convinced that my life was in danger from foreign imperialists, spies, revanchists and all the other demons in the Communist pantheon. He gave me another warning along the lines of General Chiang's and urged me to be careful, adding that I must explain to any foreign reactionaries I met all about Tibet's great progress since 'Liberation'. If they didn't believe me, he said, they could come to Tibet and see for themselves. I assured him that I would do my best. With that I turned to mount my pony and began the long trek up into the mists.

At the top of the Nathu pass there stood a large cairn set about with colourful prayer-flags. As is the custom, we each added a stone to the cairn and shouted out, *'Lha Gyal Lo!'* ('Victory to the gods!'), at the top of our voices before beginning the descent into the Kingdom of Sikkim.

On the other side, just below the pass, we were met in the mist by a welcoming party consisting of a military band, which played both the Tibetan and Indian national anthems, and several officials. One of these was Mr Apa B. Pant, formerly Indian Consul in Lhasa and now Political Officer in Sikkim. Also present was Sonam Topgyal Kazi, a Sikkimese who was to be my translator throughout the visit. And, of course, my friend Thondup Namgyal, the Maharaj Kumar, was there too.

From the border, I was escorted down to a small settlement on the edge of Lake Tsongo, where we were to spend the night. It was by now very dark and cold and snow lay deep on the ground. On arrival, I received a wonderful surprise – both Taktser Rinpoché and Gyalo Thondup, neither of whom I had seen for several years now, were there to greet me. Lobsang Samten and little Tenzin Choegyal had both travelled with me, so, for the first time in our lives, all five brothers were together.

The following day, we travelled to Gangtok, capital of Sikkim, first by pony, then by jeep and then, for the final leg of the journey, by saloon. At this point, I was met by the Maharajah of Sikkim, Sir Tashi Namgyal, whose car it was. There followed an amusing, but telling incident. Just as we were entering Gangtok, the convoy paused amongst a large crowd of people that had gathered. Thousands of people, including many joyful schoolchildren, pressed in from all sides, throwing *katas* and flowers, and prevented us from moving, when suddenly, an anonymous, young Chinese appeared from nowhere. Without a word, he tore down the Tibetan flag that flew from one wing of the car, opposite the Sikkimese state flag, and replaced it with a Chinese pennant.

We spent one night in Gangtok before leaving very early the next morning for Bagdogra airport. It was an unpleasant journey, I recall. I was very tired from having travelled all the way from Lhasa and, moreover, there had been a state banquet the night before. On top of that, I was, to my dismay, given noodles for breakfast, and then the heat in the car as we descended to the Indian plains was stifling.

The aeroplane that was waiting for us was much more comfortable than the one I had flown in in China. It took us to Allahabad, where we stopped for lunch, and then to Palam airport in New Delhi. As we sped along, thousands of feet above the teeming Indian towns and countryside, I reflected on how different India felt from China. I had been there for no time at all, but already I was aware of an immense gulf between the way of life of the two countries. Somehow, India seemed so much more open and at ease with herself.

This impression was reinforced when we landed at the Indian capital. A large guard of honour awaited us, along with Mr Nehru, the Prime Minister, and Dr Radhakrishnan, the Vice-President. There was more show and ceremony than anything I had seen in China but, at the same time, every word that was spoken, whether in greeting by the Prime Minister or in private by a minor official, had an undertone of sincerity. People expressed their real feelings and did not say just what they thought they ought to say. There was no artifice.

From the airport I was taken directly to Rashtrapathi Bhavan to meet the President of India, Dr Rajendra Prasad. I found him to be quite an old man, slow and very humble. He contrasted hugely with his aide-de-camp, a tall, splendid man in an impressive uniform, and with his very grand, ceremonial bodyguards.

The following day, I made a pilgrimage to Rajghat on the banks of the Jamuna river, where Mahatma Gandhi was cremated. It was a calm and beautiful spot and I felt very grateful to be there, the guest of a people who, like mine, had endured foreign domination; grateful also to be in the country that had adopted *Ahimsa*, the Mahatma's doctrine of non-violence. As I stood praying, I experienced simultaneously great sadness at not being able to meet Gandhi in person and great joy at the magnificent example of his life. To me, he was – and is – the consummate politician, a man who put his belief in altruism above any personal considerations. I was convinced too that his devotion to the cause of non-violence was the only way to conduct politics.

The next few days were taken up with the Buddha Jyanti celebrations. During these, I spoke of my belief that the teachings of the Lord Buddha could lead not only to peace in the lives of individuals, but also to peace between nations. I also took the opportunity to have discussions with many Gandhians about how India had achieved independence through non-violence.

One of my main discoveries about India at this point was that, although the banquets and receptions to which I was frequently invited were considerably less elaborate than those I had attended in China, the prevailing atmosphere of sincerity meant that there was an opportunity for genuine friendship to develop. This was in direct contrast to my experience in the People's Republic, where the received opinion was that you can change people's minds by bullying them. I could now make comparisons and see for myself that this was faulty thinking. Only through the development of mutual respect, and in a spirit of truth, can friendship come about. By these means it is possible to move human minds, but never by force.

As a result of these observations, and mindful of an old Tibetan saying that a prisoner who once manages to escape should not go back, I began to consider remaining in India. I made up my mind to explore the possibility of seeking political asylum when I met with Pandit Nehru, which I did soon after.

In fact, I met with the Prime Minister on several occasions. He was a tall, good-looking man, whose Nordic features were emphasised by his small Gandhi cap. Compared with Mao, he appeared to have less self-assurance, but then there was nothing dictatorial about him. He seemed honest – which was why he was later deceived by Chou En-lai. The first time we met, I took the opportunity to explain in detail the full story of how the Chinese had invaded our peaceful land, of how unprepared we were to meet an enemy and of how hard I had tried to accommodate the Chinese as soon as I was aware that no one in the outside world was prepared to acknowledge our rightful claim to independence.

At first he listened and nodded politely. But I suppose that my passionate speech must have been too long for him and after a while he appeared to lose concentration, as if he was about to nod off. Finally, he looked up at me and said that he understood what I was saying. 'But you must realise,' he went on somewhat impatiently, 'that India cannot support you.' As he spoke in clear, beautiful English, his long lower lip quivered as if vibrating in sympathy with the sound of his voice.

This was bad, but not entirely unexpected news. And although Nehru had now made his position clear, I continued by saying that I was considering seeking exile in India. Again he demurred. 'You must go back to your country and try to work with the Chinese on the basis of the Seventeen-Point "Agreement".' I protested that I had already tried my utmost to do so, adding that every time I thought I had reached an understanding with the Chinese authorities, they broke my trust. And now the situation in eastern Tibet was so bad that I feared a massive, violent reprisal which could end up destroying the whole nation. How could I possibly believe that the Seventeen-Point 'Agreement' was workable any longer? Finally, Nehru said that he would speak on the subject personally to Chou En-lai, who was due in Delhi the very next day en route to Europe. He would also arrange for me to meet the Chinese Minister.

Nehru was as good as his word and, the following morning, I went with him to Palam airport where he arranged for me to see Chou that evening. When we met again I found my old friend just as I remembered him: full of charm, smiles and deceit. But I did not respond to his artful manners. Instead, I told him quite straightforwardly of my concern about how the Chinese authorities were behaving in eastern Tibet. I also pointed out the marked difference I had noticed between the Indian Parliament and the Chinese system of government: the freedom of people in India to express themselves as they really felt and to criticise the Government if they thought it necessary. As usual, Chou listened carefully before replying with words that positively caressed the ear. 'You were present in China only at the time of the First Assembly,' he said. 'Since then, the Second Assembly has met and everything has changed immeasurably for the better.' I did not believe him, but it was useless to argue. Then he said that he had heard a rumour that I was considering staying in India. It would be a mistake, he warned. My country needed me. That was perhaps true, but I left feeling that we had resolved nothing.

My two brothers, Taktser Rinpoché and Gyalo Thondup, also met with Chou, or 'Chew and Lie' as one Indian newspaper called him, whilst he was in Delhi. They were even more forthright than I was and told him that they had no intention of returning to Lhasa, despite his entreaties with them to do so. Meanwhile, I began at last my pilgrimage to the holy places of India, during which I tried to put politics out of my mind. Unfortunately, I found it almost impossible to shake off anxious thoughts about the fate of my country. The Panchen Lama, who accompanied me everywhere, was a constant reminder of our terrible situation. No longer was he the kind and humble boy I had known before: the constant pressure put upon his adolescent mind by the Chinese had had an inevitable effect.

Still, I found a few moments when I was able to give myself wholly to deep feelings of joy and veneration as I journeyed across the country from Sanchi to Ajanta, then to Bodh Gaya and Sarnath: I felt that I had returned to my spiritual home. Everything seemed somehow familiar.

In Bihar, I visited Nalanda, site of the greatest and most famous Buddhist university which had lain in ruins for hundreds of years. Many Tibetan scholars had studied there and now, as I looked at the pitiful piles of rubble that marked the birthplace of some of the most profound Buddhist thought, I saw again how true is the doctrine of Impermanence.

Finally, I reached Bodh Gaya. I was deeply moved to be at the very place where the Lord Buddha had attained Enlightenment. But my happiness did not last long. Whilst there, I received a message from my Chinese escorts saying that Chou En-lai was returning to Delhi and wanted to see me. Then in Sarnath, I received a telegram from General Chiang Chin-wu requesting that I return to Lhasa forthwith. Subversive reactionaries and imperialist collaborators were planning a revolt and my presence was required urgently, it said.

I returned to Delhi by train and was met by the Chinese

Ambassador at the station. To the alarm of my Lord Chamberlain and my bodyguard, he insisted that I travel with him in his car to the Embassy, where I met with Chou En-lai. The two men feared that I might be kidnapped and when they reached the Embassy were uncertain whether I was really there or not, so they asked someone there to take a sweater up to me to see what their reaction was. Meanwhile, I was having a frank discussion with Chou. He told me that the situation in Tibet had deteriorated, indicating that the Chinese authorities were ready to use force to crush any popular uprising.

At this point I restated bluntly my concern at the way the Chinese were behaving in Tibet, forcing on us unwanted reforms, despite explicit reassurances that they would do no such thing. Again he replied with great charm, saying that Chairman Mao had announced that no reform should be introduced in Tibet for at least the next six years. And if after that we were still not ready, they could be postponed for fifty years if necessary: China was only there to help us. Still I was not convinced. Chou continued, saying he understood that I was planning to pay a visit to Kalimpong. This was true. I had been asked to deliver teachings to the large Tibetan population that lived there. He strongly advised me not to do so as it was 'full of spies and reactionary elements'. He added that I should be careful of which Indian officials I trusted: that some were good, but that others were dangerous. Then he changed the subject. Would I, he asked, be prepared to return to Nalanda and, in my capacity as a representative of the People's Republic of China, present to the organisation there a cheque and a relic of Tang s'en, the Chinese spiritual master? Knowing that Pandit Nehru would be present at this function, I accepted.

When I saw him next, the Indian Prime Minister had with him a copy of the Seventeen-Point 'Agreement'. Again, he urged me to return to Tibet and to work with the Chinese on the basis of the 'Agreement'. There was no alternative, he said, adding that he must make it clear that India could be of no assistance to Tibet. He also told me that I should do as Chou En-lai said and return to Lhasa without stopping at Kalimpong. But when I pressed him on this point, he suddenly changed his mind. 'India is a free country, after all,' he said. 'You would not be breaking any of her laws.' He then undertook to make all the necessary arrangements for the visit.

It was February 1957 when I journeyed by train with my small entourage to Calcutta. On the way, I remember that my mother, unaware of any restrictions and feeling totally unrestrained, brought out a small stove and cooked a most delicious *thugpa* (traditional Tibetan noodle soup). After our arrival in the capital of West Bengal, we remained a few days before flying north to Bagdogra, where the foothills of the Himalayas begin their craggy ascent from the hot immensity of the Indian plains. For the final leg of the journey we travelled by jeep. When we reached Kalimpong I went to stay in the same house, owned by a Bhutanese family, that my predecessor had stayed in once during his period of exile in India. They gave me the very same room that he had used. It was a strange feeling to be there under such similar circumstances. The family of this very friendly household was that of the Bhutanese Prime Minister, who was later assassinated. There were three young sons, the smallest of which took a great interest in their guest. He kept coming up to my room as if to check up on me. Then, laughing, he would slide down the banisters.

Not long after my arrival I was met by Lukhangwa, my former Prime Minister, who had recently arrived from Lhasa, ostensibly on a pilgrimage. I was very pleased to see him, although I quickly discovered that he was utterly opposed to my returning home. My two brothers, who had likewise travelled to Kalimpong, agreed with him and now began to try to persuade me to stay. The three of them also begged the *Kashag* not to let me return. Whilst in Bodh Gaya, my brothers had made contact with a number of sympathetic Indian politicians, one of whom – Jaya Prakash Narayan – had promised on some future appropriate occasion to raise India's voice in support of Tibetan freedom. My brothers, Lukhangwa and one or two others were certain that when this happened, Nehru would be forced to support Tibetan independence. After all, it did not benefit India to have Chinese troops on her northern border. But I was not convinced. I asked Ngabo Ngawang Jigme (the leader of the delegation which had been forced to sign the Seventeen-Point 'Agreement'), who was also in my entourage, what he thought. His advice was that if it were possible to come up with a definite plan, then it might be worthwhile to consider staying. But in the absence of anything concrete, he felt that I had no alternative but to return.

I consulted the oracle. There are three principal oracles whose advice the Dalai Lama can seek. Two of them, Nechung and Gadong, were present. Both said that I should return. Lukhangwa came in during one of these consultations, at which the oracle grew angry, telling him to remain outside. It was as if the oracle knew that Lukhangwa had made up his mind. But Lukhangwa ignored him and sat down all the same. Afterwards he came up to me and said, 'When men become desperate they consult the gods. And when the gods become desperate, they tell lies'!

My two brothers were adamant that I should not return to Tibet. Like Lukhangwa, they were both powerful and persuasive men. Neither could understand my hesitation. They believed that with the very existence of the Tibetan people under threat, it was essential to confront the Chinese in any way possible. The best way to do this, they felt, was for me to remain in India. It would then be possible to seek foreign support, which they were sure would be easy to obtain. They were convinced that America would help us.

Although there was no talk at this time of an armed struggle against the Chinese, my brothers, unbeknown to me, had already made contact with the American Central Intelligence Agency. Apparently, the Americans felt that it was worthwhile to provide limited assistance to the Tibetan freedom fighters, not because they cared about Tibetan independence, but as part of their worldwide efforts to destabilise all Communist governments. To this end they undertook to supply a limited amount of simple weaponry to the freedom fighters by air-drop. They also made plans for the CIA to train some of them in techniques of guerrilla warfare and then parachute them back into Tibet. Naturally, my brothers judged it wise to keep this information from me. They knew what my reaction would have been.

When I explained that, although I could see the logic of their arguments, I could not accept them, Gyalo Thondup began to show signs of agitation. He was – and still is – the most fiercely patriotic of my brothers He has a very strong character and a tendency to be single-minded to the point of stubbornness. But his heart is good and, of all of us, he was the most affected when our mother died. He cried a great deal. Taktser Rinpoché is milder mannered than Gyalo Thondup, but underneath his calm and jovial exterior there lies a tough and unyielding core. He is good in a crisis, but on this occasion he too showed signs of exasperation. In the end, neither prevailed and I made up my mind to return to Tibet to give the Chinese one last try, in accordance both with the advice of Nehru and the assurances of Chou En-lai.

After leaving Kalimpong, I was compelled to remain in Gangtok for a full month before being able to cross the Nathu pass once more. But I did not regret this at all and I took the opportunity to give teachings to the local population.

Finally, and with a heavy heart, I set out for the return journey to Lhasa towards the end of March 1957. My sadness was increased by Lobsang Samten's last-minute decision to remain in India due to his poor physical condition following a recent operation for appendicitis. When I reached the border and bade farewell to the last of my Indian friends – all of whom wept – my spirits sank even lower. Fluttering amongst the colourful Tibetan prayer-flags were at least a dozen blood-red banners proclaiming the People's Republic of China. It was no consolation at all that General Chin Rhawo-rhen had come to meet me. For, although he was a good and sincere man, I could not help thinking of him in terms of the military uniform that he wore, rather than in terms of 'liberation'.

Escape into Exile

o

ONCE OVER THE Tibetan border, I drove back to Lhasa via Dromo, Gyantse and Shigatse. At each place I addressed large public gatherings, to which I invited both Tibetan and Chinese officials. As usual, I gave a short, spiritual teaching combined with what I had to say about temporal matters. In doing so, I laid great emphasis on the obligation of all Tibetans to deal honestly and justly with the Chinese authorities. I insisted that it was the duty of everyone to right wrongs whenever they saw them, no matter who had committed them. I also urged my people to adhere strictly to the principles of the Seventeen-Point 'Agreement'. I told them of my talks with Nehru and Chou En-lai and of how, during the first week of February that year, Chairman Mao himself had publicly acknowledged that Tibet was not yet ready for reform. Finally, I reminded them of the Chinese claim that they were in Tibet to help Tibetans. If any of the authorities failed to be co-operative, they were acting against Communist Party policy. I added that others could be left to sing praises, but we, according to Chairman Mao's own directive, should be self-critical. At this, the Chinese present became clearly uncomfortable.

In this way I tried to assure my people that I was doing all I could for them and to send warning to our new, foreign masters that, from now on, there would be no hesitation in pointing out malpractices whenever necessary. However, at every stage along the journey, my forced optimism was dealt fresh blows by the news and reports of widespread fighting in the east. Then one day, General Tan Kuan-sen, the Political Commissar, came to meet me and asked that I send a representative to ask the freedom fighters to lay down their arms. Since this was my own wish, I agreed to do so and sent a lama to talk with them. But they did not, and by the time I reached Lhasa on 1 April 1957, I knew that the situation throughout Tibet was rapidly slipping not only from Chinese control, but also from my own.

In midsummer there was open warfare throughout Kham and Amdo. The freedom fighters, under the command of a man named Gompo Tashi, were increasing their numbers on a daily basis and becoming ever more audacious in their raids. The Chinese, for their part, showed no restraint. As well as using aircraft to bomb towns and villages, whole areas were laid waste by artillery barrage. The result was that thousands of people from Kham and Amdo fled to Lhasa and were now camped on the plains outside the city. Some of the stories they brought with them were so horrifying that I did not really believe them for many years. The methods that the Chinese used to intimidate the population were so abhorrent that they were almost beyond the capacity of my imagination. It was not until I read the report published in 1959 by the International Commission of Jurists that I fully accepted what I had heard: crucifixion, vivisection, disembowelling and dismemberment of victims was commonplace. So too were beheading, burning, beating to death and burying alive, not to mention dragging people behind galloping horses until they died or hanging them upside down or throwing them bound hand and foot into icy water. And, in order to prevent them shouting out, 'Long live the Dalai Lama', on the way to execution, they tore out their tongues with meat hooks.

Realising that disaster was in the offing, I announced that I would present myself for my final monastic examinations during the *Monlam* festival of 1959, eighteen months from now. I felt that I must graduate as soon as possible, lest time run out. At the same time, I began very much to look forward to the arrival in Lhasa of Pandit Nehru, who had accepted my invitation (warmly approved by the Chinese Ambassador) to visit Tibet the following year. I hoped that his presence would compel the Chinese authorities to start behaving in a civilised way.

Meanwhile, life in the capital continued much as it always had since the Chinese first arrived six years before, although they themselves became significantly more aggressive. From now on, whenever the Generals came to see me, they were armed. They did not wear their guns openly, however, but concealed them under their clothes. This forced them to adopt very awkward positions when they sat down, and even then the barrels were clearly visible. When they spoke, they continued to offer me the usual assurances, but their faces betrayed their real feelings by turning the colour of radishes.

Also, the Preparatory Committee continued to meet on a regular basis to discuss meaningless policy amendments. It was extraordinary to what lengths the Chinese authorities went to provide a façade behind which they could carry out their abominations elsewhere in the country. I felt powerless. Yet I was certain that if I resigned (which I did consider doing) or opposed the Chinese directly, the consequences would be devastating. And I could not allow Lhasa and those areas of Tibet that were not so far engulfed in bloodshed to succumb as well. Already there were at least eight divisions of the PLA operating in the east: over 150,000 trained men with sophisticated battlefield technology confronting an irregular band of horsemen and mountain warriors. The more I thought about the future, the less hope I felt. It seemed that no matter what I or any of my people did, sooner or later all of Tibet would be turned into a mere vassal state in the new Chinese Empire, without religious or cultural freedoms, let alone those of free speech.

Life at the Norbulingka, where I stayed permanently now, also continued much as ever. The thousands of gilded Buddhas that stood flickering in the gentle light of countless butter lamps were a pointed reminder that we live in a world of Impermanence and Illusion. My routine was much the same as it always had been, although now I got up earlier, usually before five o'clock, to pray and study texts alone for the first part of the morning. Later on, one of my tutors would come to discuss the texts I was reading.

Then we would be joined by my *tsenshap*, of whom there were now four, and I spent much of the rest of the day debating – for this was how I would be examined. And, as usual, I would, on certain days of the calendar, preside over a *puja* in one of the many palace shrine-rooms.

Lhasa itself had changed considerably since the Chinese invasion, however. A whole new district had sprung up to accommodate the Communist officials and their dependents. Already there was evidence of a modern Chinese city which would one day swamp the ancient capital. They had built a hospital and a new school – although I regret to say that these were of little benefit to the Tibetan population – and several new barracks. Also, in view of the deteriorating situation, the military had begun to dig trenches around their quarters and fortify them with sandbags. And now when they went out, whereas before they had felt secure enough to go in pairs (though never alone), they did so only in convoys. But my contact with this world was slight and most of my information about it came from the dismal reports brought to me by my sweepers and various officials.

In the spring of 1958, I moved into a new palace at the Norbulingka, it being the tradition for each successive Dalai Lama to found his own building within the Jewel Park. Like the others, mine was quite small and designed to be used as no more than my own personal living quarters. What made it special, however, were the modern fittings and appliances with which it was furnished. I had a modern, iron bed in place of my old wooden box; and there was a bathroom complete with running water. There was plumbing for heating it too, but unfortunately my tenure at the Norbulingka was interrupted before it could be got to work properly. Electric lighting was also fitted throughout, on both floors. In my audience-room I had chairs and tables rather than the traditional Tibetan cushions (for the benefit of foreign visitors), as well as a large radio, a gift from the Indian Government, if I remember correctly. It was the perfect home. Outside, there was a small pond and a beautiful rockery and a garden whose planting I personally supervised. Everything grows well in Lhasa and it was soon electric with colour. Altogether, I was extremely happy there, but not for long.

The fighting throughout Kham and Amdo and now central Tibet continued to gain momentum. By early summer several tens of thousands of freedom fighters had joined forces and were pressing home their raids closer and closer to Lhasa, despite being poorly supplied with small arms and ammunition. Some of what they had was captured from the Chinese, some of it had come from a raid on a Tibetan Government ammunition dump near Tashilhunpo, and a small amount of it had duly materialised courtesy of the CIA, but they were still hopelessly ill-equipped.

When I went into exile, I heard stories of how weapons and money were dropped into Tibet by aircraft. However, these missions caused almost more harm to the Tibetans than to the Chinese forces. Because the Americans did not want their assistance to be attributable, they took care not to supply US-manufactured equipment. Instead, they dropped only a few badly made bazookas and some ancient British rifles which had once been in general service throughout India and Pakistan and thus could not be traced to source in the event of capture. But the mishandling they received whilst being air-dropped rendered them almost useless.

Naturally, I never saw any of the fighting but, during the 1970s, an old lama who had recently escaped from Tibet told me of how he had once observed a skirmish from his hermitage cell high up in the mountains in a remote part of Amdo. A small posse of six horsemen had attacked a PLA encampment several hundred strong, just near the bend of a river. The result was chaos. The Chinese panicked and started shooting wildly in all directions, killing large numbers of their own troops. Meanwhile the horsemen, having escaped across the river, turned back and, approaching from a different direction, attacked again from the flank before disappearing into the hills. I was very moved to hear of such bravery.

The inevitable crisis point was finally reached during the second half of 1958, when members of *Chushi Gangdruk*, the freedom-fighters' alliance, besieged a major PLA garrison at Tsethang, hardly more than two days' travel from the gates of Lhasa itself.

At this point, I began to see more and more of General Tan Kuan-sen. He looked like a peasant and had yellow teeth and close-cropped hair, and he now came on an almost weekly basis, accompanied by very arrogant interpreters, to urge, cajole and abuse me. Previously his visits had rarely been more than once a month. As a result, I grew to loathe my new audience-room at the Norbulingka. Its very atmosphere was tainted by the tension of our interviews and I began to dread going in there.

At first the General demanded that I mobilise the Tibetan army against the 'rebels'. It was my duty to do so, he said. He was furious when I pointed out that if I did, he could be sure that the soldiers would take it as an opportunity to go over to the side of the freedom fighters. After this he confined himself to railing against the ungratefulness of Tibetans and saying that it would all end badly for us. Finally, he identified Taktser Rinpoché and Gyalo Thondup and several of my ex-officials (each of whom was out of the country) as culprits and ordered me to revoke their Tibetan citizenship. This I did, thinking that firstly they were abroad and therefore safe, and secondly that for the time being it was better to acquiesce than provoke the Chinese into open military confrontation within Lhasa itself. I wanted to avoid this by almost any means. I felt that if the people of Lhasa became involved in fighting, there could be no hope of restoring peace.

Meanwhile, the freedom fighters were in no mood to compromise. They even tried to secure my approval for what they were doing. Alas I could not give it, even though as a young man and a patriot I had some thought now to do so. I was still pinning hope on Nehru's impending visit, but at the last moment the Chinese authorities cancelled it. General Tan Kuan-sen announced that he could not guarantee the Indian Prime Minister's safety and the invitation would have to be withdrawn. This was a disaster, I felt.

At the end of summer 1958, I went to Drepung, followed by Sera monastery, for the initial part of my final monastic examination. This involved several days of debates with the most outstanding scholars of these two centres of learning. The first day at

Drepung began with the wonderfully harmonious chanting of several thousand monks in the public assembly hall. Their praise of the Buddha, his saints and successors (many of them Indian sages and teachers), moved me to tears.

Before leaving Drepung, I went, as per tradition, to the top of the tallest mountain behind the monastery, from which it was possible to obtain a panoramic view over literally hundreds of miles. It was so high that even for Tibetans there was a danger of altitude sickness – but not too high for the beautiful birds that nested far above the plateau, nor the profusion of wild flowers known in Tibetan as *upel*. These spectacular plants were light blue in colour, tall and thorny, and shaped like a delphinium.

Unfortunately, these pleasant observations were marred by the fact that it was necessary to deploy Tibetan soldiers in the mountains to protect me. For just in front of Drepung, there was a Chinese military garrison, set about with barbed wire and bunkers, within whose perimeter could be heard troops practising with small arms and artillery every day.

When I returned to Lhasa after my examinations were over, I learned that, so far, I had passed very well. One of the abbots, a most learned monk named Pema Gyaltsen, told me that if I had had the same opportunities for study as an ordinary monk, my performance would have been unsurpassed. So I felt very happy that this lazy student did not in the end disgrace himself.

Back in the capital, after this short interlude of sanity, I found the situation considerably worse than when I left. Thousands more refugees from Chinese atrocity outside Lhasa had arrived and were bivouacked on its outskirts. By now, the Tibetan population of the city must have been about double the usual number. Yet still there was an uneasy truce and no fighting actually took place. All the same, when, during the autumn, I went to Ganden to continue my debates, I was encouraged by some of my advisors to take the opportunity to head south, where much of the country was in the hands of the 'defenders of the Buddha *Dharma*'. The tentative plan was that I should then repudiate the Seventeen-Point 'Agreement' and reinstate my own Government as the rightful

administration of Tibet. I gave serious thought to their proposition, but I was again forced to conclude that to do so would
achieve nothing positive. Such a declaration would only provoke
the Chinese into launching a full-scale attack.

So I returned to Lhasa to continue my studies throughout the
long, cold, winter months. I had one final examination to take
during *Monlam* at the beginning of the following year. It was hard
to concentrate on my work. Almost every day I heard new reports
of Chinese outrages against the non-combatant population. Sometimes the news was favourable to Tibet – but this gave me no
comfort. Only the thought of my responsibility to the six million
Tibetans kept me going. That and my faith. Early every morning,
as I sat in prayer in my room before the ancient altar with its
clutter of statuettes standing in silent benediction, I concentrated
hard on developing compassion for all sentient beings. I reminded
myself constantly of the Buddha's teaching that our enemy is in a
sense our greatest teacher. And if this was sometimes hard to do,
I never really doubted that it was so.

At last the new year came upon us and I left the Norbulingka
to take up residence at the Jokhang for the *Monlam* festival, after
which came my final examination. Just before I did so, I received
General Chiang Chin-wu, who came, as was his custom, with a
New Year message. He also announced the arrival in Lhasa of a
new dance troupe from China. Might I be interested to see them?
I replied that I would be. He then said that they could perform
anywhere, but since there was a proper stage with footlights at the
Chinese military headquarters, it might be better if I could go
there. This made sense as there were no such facilities at the
Norbulingka, so I indicated that I would be happy to do so.

When I arrived at the Jokhang, I found, as I had expected, more
people thronging the temple than ever before. In addition to the
laity drawn from the furthest reaches of Tibet, there must have
been 25–30,000 monks mingled with the huge crowd.

Each day, the *Barkhor* and *Lingkhor* were packed with devotees
earnestly circumambulating. Some went, prayer-wheel in hand,
chanting the sacred words '*Om Mani Padme Hum*', almost our

national *mantra*. Others silently clasped their hands to forehead, to throat and to heart before prostrating themselves full-length on the ground. The market-place in front of the temple was also bursting with people: women, in floor-length dresses decorated with colourful aprons; jaunty Khampas, their long hair tied with bright red braid and rifles slung across their shoulders; wizened nomads from the hills; and everywhere gleeful children.

Never had I seen such bustle as I squinted through the curtains of my apartment windows. Only this year there was an air of expectancy that even I, secluded as I was, could not fail to notice. It was as if everyone knew that something momentous was about to happen.

Shortly after the main *Monlam* ceremony was over (the one involving a long recital), two junior Chinese officials came unannounced to renew General Chiang Chin-wu's invitation to see the dance troupe. They also asked for a date when I could attend. I replied that I would be pleased to go after the festival was over. But for the moment I had rather more important things to think about, namely my final examination, which was soon to take place.

The night beforehand I prayed earnestly and, as I did so, felt more deeply than ever before the awesome, unending responsibility that my office entails. Then, next morning, I presented myself for the debates which were to be held before an audience of many thousands of people. Before noon the subject was logic and epistemology, and my opponents were undergraduates like myself. In the middle of the day, the topics were *Madhyamika* and *Prajnaparamita*, again debated with undergraduates. Then in the evening, all five major subjects were hurled at me, this time by graduates, all of them considerably older and more experienced than myself.

At last, at around seven o'clock in the evening, it was all over. I felt exhausted – but relieved and delighted that the panel of judges had unanimously agreed that I was worthy to receive my degree and with it the title of *geshe*, or Doctor of Buddhist Studies.

On 5 March, I left the Jokhang to return to the Norbulingka, as usual in a splendid procession. For the last time, the full

pageantry of more than a thousand years of uninterrupted civilisa-
tion was on display. My bodyguard, dressed in their brightly
coloured ceremonial uniforms, surrounded the palanquin in which
I rode. Beyond them were the members of the *Kashag* and nobles
of Lhasa sumptuously clad in silk and flowing robes, their horses
stepping high as if they knew that the bits in their mouths were
made of gold. Behind them came the most eminent abbots and
lamas in the land, some lean and ascetic, others looking more like
prosperous merchants than the highly evolved spiritual masters
they were.

Finally, thousands upon thousands of citizens lined the route,
and the road was packed with eager spectators along the full
four-mile distance between the two buildings. The only people
missing were the Chinese who, for the first time since their arrival,
had neglected to send a contingent. This did nothing to reassure
either my bodyguard or the army. The latter had posted men up
in the hills nearby, ostensibly to 'protect' me from the freedom
fighters. But in reality they had a very different enemy in mind. My
bodyguards had a similar fear. Several of them openly established a
position and kept their Bren gun pointing at the Chinese military
headquarters.

It was not until two days later that I again had indirect communication with the Chinese authorities. They wanted to know for
definite when I would be free to attend the theatrical show. I
replied that the 10th of March would be convenient. Two days
later, the day before the performance, some Chinese called on the
Kusun Depon, commander of my bodyguard, at home, saying that
they had been told to take him to the headquarters of Brigadier
Fu, the military advisor. He wanted to brief him about arrangements for my visit the following evening.

The Brigadier began by telling him that the Chinese authorities
wanted us to dispense with the usual formality and ceremony of
my visits. Pointedly, he insisted that no Tibetan soldiers accompany me, only two or three unarmed bodyguards if absolutely
necessary, adding that they wanted the whole affair to be conducted in absolute secrecy. These all seemed strange requests and

there was much discussion about them amongst my advisors afterwards. Nevertheless, all agreed that I could not refuse without causing a severe breach of diplomacy which might have very negative consequences. So I agreed to go with a minimum of fuss and to take along only a handful of staff.

Tenzin Choegyal, my younger brother, was also invited. He was by this time studying at Drepung monastery, so he was to travel independently. In the meantime, word went out that on the following day there were to be traffic restrictions in the vicinity of the stone bridge that led over the river adjacent to the Chinese headquarters.

Of course, it was completely impossible for my movements to be kept secret and the very fact that the Chinese wanted to do so shocked my people, who were already greatly concerned about my safety. The news spread like flames on dry grass.

The result was catastrophic. Next morning, after my prayers and then breakfast, I went outside in the quiet early morning light for a walk in the garden. Suddenly, I was startled by shouting in the distance. I hurried back inside and instructed some attendants to find out what the noise was all about. When they came back, they explained that people were pouring out of Lhasa and heading in our direction. They had decided to come and protect me from the Chinese. All morning their numbers grew. Some remained in groups at each entrance to the Jewel Park, others began to circumambulate it. By noon an estimated thirty thousand people had gathered. And during the morning, three members of the *Kashag* had difficulty getting past the crowds at the front entrance. The people were showing hostility to anyone they thought guilty of collaboration with the Chinese. One senior official, who was accompanied in his car by a bodyguard, was stoned and badly injured because people thought he was a traitor. They were mistaken. (During the 1980s, his son, who was a member of the delegation forced to sign the Seventeen-Point 'Agreement', came to India, where he wrote a detailed account of what really happened. But later, someone was actually killed.

I was appalled at this news. Something had to be done to defuse the situation. It sounded to me as though, in a fit of anger, the crowd might even be tempted to attack the Chinese garrison. A number of popular leaders had been spontaneously elected and were calling for the Chinese to leave Tibet to the Tibetans. I prayed for calm. At the same time I realised that whatever my own personal feelings might be, there was no question of my going over to the Chinese headquarters that evening. Accordingly, my Lord Chamberlain telephoned to pass on my regrets, adding, on my instructions, that I hoped normality would be restored very soon and that the crowds could be persuaded to disperse.

However, the crowd at the gates of the Norbulingka was determined not to move. As far as the people and their leaders were concerned, the life of the Dalai Lama was in danger from the Chinese and they would not leave until I gave a personal assurance that I would not go to the Chinese military headquarters that night. This I did, via one of my officials. But it was not enough. They then demanded that I should never go to the camp. Again they were given my assurance, at which point most of the leaders left and went into the city, where further demonstrations were held; but many of the people outside the Norbulingka remained. Unfortunately, they did not realise that their continued presence constituted a far greater threat than if they had gone away.

That same day, I sent three of my most senior ministers to meet with General Tan Kuan-sen. When eventually they reached his headquarters, they found that Ngabo Ngawang Jigme was already there. At first the Chinese were polite. But when the General arrived he was in an ill-concealed rage. He and two other senior officers harangued the Tibetans for several hours about the treachery of the 'imperialist rebels', adding the accusation that the Tibetan Government had been secretly organising agitation against the Chinese authorities. Furthermore, it had defied the orders of the Chinese and refused to disarm the 'rebels' in Lhasa. They could now expect drastic measures to be taken to crush this opposition.

When they reported back to me that evening in my audience-room at the Norbulingka, I realised that the Chinese were issuing an ultimatum. Meanwhile, at about six o'clock, around seventy junior government officials, together with the remaining popular leaders and members of my personal bodyguard, held a meeting outside the Jewel Park and endorsed a declaration denouncing the Seventeen-Point 'Agreement', adding that Tibet no longer recognised Chinese authority. When I heard of this, I sent a message saying that it was the duty of the leaders to reduce the existing tension and not to aggravate it. But my advice seemed to fall on ears that could not hear.

Later that same evening a letter arrived from General Tan Kuan-sen suggesting, in suspiciously moderate tones, that I move to his headquarters for my own safety. I was amazed at his effrontery. There was no question of doing any such thing. However, in order to try to buy time, I wrote him a conciliatory reply.

The next day, 11 March, the crowd leaders announced to the Government that they would post guards outside the Cabinet office, which was situated within the outer wall of the Norbulingka. This was to prevent any ministers from leaving the palace grounds. They feared that if they did not take the law into their own hands the Government might be forced into a compromise by the Chinese authorities. The *Kashag* in turn held a meeting with these leaders and requested them to call off the demonstration as it was in danger of precipitating an open confrontation.

At first, the leaders showed willingness to listen, but then two more letters arrived from General Tan Kuan-sen. One of these was addressed to me, the other to the *Kashag*. To the former, which was similar to the first, I again replied politely, agreeing that there were dangerous elements within the crowd which sought to undermine relations between Tibet and China. I also agreed that it might be a good idea if, for my safety, I went to his headquarters. (But then again it might not.)

In his other letter, the General ordered the ministers to instruct the crowd to take down the barricades that had been erected on the road outside Lhasa that led to China. Unfortunately, this had a calamitous effect. It seemed to the crowd leaders that, by saying they wanted these removed, the Chinese were making a clear indication that they planned to bring in reinforcements which would be used to attack the Dalai Lama. They refused.

On hearing this, I decided that I must speak to these men myself. I did so, explaining that there was a serious danger that Chinese troops would use force to dispel the crowd if people did not leave very soon. Evidently my entreaty was partially successful, as afterwards they announced that they would move to Shöl, the village at the foot of the Potala, where many angry demonstrations were subsequently held. But the majority of the people outside the Norbulingka remained.

It was at around this point that I consulted the Nechung oracle, which was hurriedly summoned. Should I stay or should I try to escape? What was I to do? The oracle made it clear that I should stay and keep open the dialogue with the Chinese. For once, I was unsure of whether this really was the best course of action. I was reminded of Lukhangwa's remark about the gods lying when they too became desperate. So I spent the afternoon performing *Mo*, another form of divination. The result was identical.

The next days passed in a dizzying, frightening blur. I began to receive reports of a Chinese military build-up and the mood of the crowd grew almost hysterical. I consulted the oracle a second time, but his advice was the same as before. Then, on the 16th, I received a third and final letter from the General, together with an enclosure from Ngabo. General Tan's letter was much along the lines of his last two. Ngabo's, on the other hand, made clear what I and everyone else had dimly concluded, namely that the Chinese were planning to attack the crowd and shell the Norbulingka. He wanted me to indicate on a map where I would be – so that the artillery men could be briefed to aim off whichever building I marked. It was a horrifying moment as the truth sank in. Not only was my own life in danger, but the lives of thousands upon thousands of my people now seemed certain to be lost. If only they could be persuaded to go away, to return to their homes. Surely they could see that they had demonstrated to the Chinese the strength of their feelings? But it was no use. They were in such a pitch of fury against these unwelcome foreigners with their brutal methods that nothing could move them. They would stay till the end and die keeping guard over their Precious Protector.

Reluctantly, I set about replying to Ngabo and General Tan, saying something along the lines that I was dismayed by the disgraceful behaviour of reactionary elements amongst the population of Lhasa. I assured them that I still thought it a good idea that I should move to the sanctuary of the Chinese headquarters, but that it was very difficult just at the moment; and that I hoped they too would have the patience to sit out the disturbances. Anything to buy time! After all, the crowd could not stay put indefinitely. I took care not to say where I was in the hope that this lack of knowledge would cause uncertainty and delay.

Having dispatched my replies, I was at a loss as to what to do next. The following day, I again sought the counsel of the oracle. To my astonishment, he shouted, 'Go! Go! Tonight!' The medium, still in his trance, then staggered forward and, snatching up some paper and a pen, wrote down, quite clearly and explicitly, the route that I should take out of the Norbulingka, down to the last Tibetan town on the Indian border. His directions were not what might have been expected. That done, the medium, a young monk named Lobsang Jigme, collapsed in a faint, signifying that Dorje Drakden had left his body. Just then, as if to reinforce the oracle's instructions, two mortar shells exploded in the marsh outside the northern gate of the Jewel Park.

Looking back on this event at a distance of more than thirty-one years, I am certain that Dorje Drakden had known all along that I must leave Lhasa on the 17th, but he did not say so for fear of word getting out. If no plans were made, nobody could find out about them.

I did not begin preparations for my escape immediately, however. First I wanted to confirm the oracle's decision, which I did by performing *Mo* once more. The answer agreed with the oracle, even though the odds against making a successful break seemed terrifyingly high. Not only was the crowd refusing to let anyone into or out of the palace grounds without first searching and interrogating them, but also Ngabo's letter made it clear that the

Chinese had already considered the possibility that I might try to escape. They must have taken precautions. Yet the supernatural counsels fitted in with my own reasoning: I was convinced that leaving was the only thing I could do to make the crowd disperse. If I was no longer inside, there could be no reason for people to remain. I therefore decided to accept the advice.

Because the situation was so desperate, I realised that I should tell as few people as possible of my decision and at first informed only my Lord Chamberlain and the *Chikyab Kenpo*. They then had the task of making preparations for a party to leave the palace that night, but without anyone knowing who would be amongst it. At the same time as we discussed how they were to go about this, we decided on the composition of the escape party. I would take with me only my closest advisors, including my two tutors, and those members of my immediate family who were present.

Later that afternoon, my tutors and the four members of the *Kashag* left the palace hidden under a tarpaulin in the back of a lorry; in the evening, my mother, Tenzin Choegyal and Tsering Dolma went out, disguised, on the pretext of going to a nunnery on the south side of the Kyichu river. I then summoned the popular leaders and told them of my plan, stressing the need not only for maximum co-operation (which I knew was assured), but also for absolute secrecy. I was certain that the Chinese would have spies amongst the crowd. When these men had gone, I wrote them a letter explaining my reasons for leaving and begging them not to open fire except in self-defence, trusting that they would relay this message to the people. It was to be delivered next day.

At nightfall, I went for the last time to the shrine dedicated to Mahakala, my personal protector divinity. As I entered the room through its heavy, creaking door, I paused for a moment to take in what I saw before me. A number of monks sat chanting prayers at the base of a large statue of the Protector. There was no electric light in the room, only the glow of dozens of votive butter lamps set in rows of golden and silver dishes. Numerous frescoes covered the walls. A small offering of *tsampa* sat on a plate on the altar. A server, his face half in shadow, was bending over a large urn from which he was ladling out butter for the lamps. No one looked up, although I knew that my presence must have been noticed. To my right, one of the monks took up his cymbals, whilst another put a horn to this lips and blew a long, mournful note. The cymbals clashed together and were held, vibrating. Its sound was comforting.

I went forward and presented a *kata*, a length of white silk, to the divinity. This is the traditional Tibetan gesture on departure and signifies not only propitiation, but also implies the intention of return. For a moment I lingered in silent prayer. The monks would now suspect that I was going, but I was assured of their silence. Before leaving the room, I sat down for a few minutes and read from the Buddha's *sutras*, stopping at the one which talks of the need to 'develop confidence and courage'.

On leaving, I instructed someone to dim the lights throughout the remainder of the building before going downstairs, where I found one of my dogs. I patted it and was glad that it had never been very friendly with me. Our parting was not too difficult. I was much more sad to be leaving behind my bodyguards and sweepers. I then went outside into the chill March air. At the main entrance to the building was a landing with steps running off either side down to the ground. I walked round it, pausing on the far side to visualise reaching India safely. On coming back to the door, I visualised returning to Tibet.

At a few minutes before ten o'clock, now wearing unfamiliar trousers and a long, black coat, I threw a rifle over my right shoulder and, rolled up, an old *thangka* that had belonged to the Second Dalai Lama over my left. Then, slipping my glasses into my pocket, I stepped outside. I was very frightened. I was joined by two soldiers, who silently escorted me to the gate in the inner wall, where I was met by the *Kusun Depon*. With them, I groped my way across the park, hardly able to see a thing. On reaching the outer wall, we joined up with *Chikyab Kenpo*, who, I could just make out, was armed with a sword. He spoke to me in a low, reassuring voice. I was to keep by him at all costs. Going through the gate, he announced boldly to the people gathered there that he was undertaking a routine tour of inspection. With that, we were allowed to pass through. No further words were spoken.

I could sense the presence of a great mass of humanity as I stumbled on, but they did not take any notice of us and, after a few minutes' walk, we were once more alone. We had successfully negotiated our way through the crowd, but now there were the Chinese to deal with. The thought of being captured terrified me. For the first time in my life I was truly afraid – not so much for myself but for the millions of people who put their faith in me. If I was caught, all would be lost. There was also some danger that we could be mistaken for Chinese soldiers by freedom fighters unaware of what was happening.

Our first obstacle was the tributary of the Kyichu river that I used to visit as a small child, until forbidden to do so by Tathag Rinpoché. To cross it, we had to use stepping-stones, which I found extremely difficult to negotiate without my glasses. More than once I almost lost my balance. We then made our way to the banks of the Kyichu itself. Just before reaching it, we came across a large group of people. The Lord Chamberlain spoke briefly with their leaders and then we passed on to the river-bank. Several coracles were waiting for us, together with a small party of ferry-men.

The crossing went smoothly, although I was certain that every splash of oars would draw down machine-gun fire on to us. There were many tens of thousands of PLA stationed in and around Lhasa at that time and it was inconceivable that they would not have patrols out. On the other side, we met up with a party of freedom fighters who were waiting with some ponies. Here we were also joined by my mother, my brother and sister and my tutors. We then paused to wait for my senior officials, who were following, to join us. Whilst we did so, we took the opportunity to exchange, in highly charged whispers, remarks about the iniquitous behaviour of the Chinese which had driven us to this pass. I also put my glasses back on – I could bear sightlessness no longer – but then almost wished I hadn't as I could now make out the torchlight of PLA sentries guarding the garrison that lay only a few hundred yards from where we stood. Fortunately, the moon was obscured by low cloud and visibility was poor.

As soon as the others arrived, we set off towards the hill and the mountain pass, called Che-La, that separates the Lhasa valley from the Tsangpo valley. At around three o'clock in the morning, we stopped at a simple farm house, the first of many to provide us with shelter over the next few weeks. But we did not remain long and after only a little while left to continue the trek up to the pass, which we reached at around eight o'clock. Not long before we reached it, the first light of day dawned and we saw to our amusement the result of our haste. There had been a mix-up with the ponies, their harnesses and their riders. Because the monastery that had provided the animals had had almost no warning, and because of the dark, the best of them had been fitted with the worst saddles and given to the wrong people, whereas some of the oldest and shaggiest mules wore the finest harnesses and were being ridden by the most senior officials!

At the top of the 16,000-foot pass – Che-La means Sandy Pass – the groom who was leading my pony stopped and turned it round, telling me that this was the last opportunity on the journey for a look at Lhasa. The ancient city looked serene as ever as it lay spread out far below. I prayed for a few minutes before dismounting and running on foot down the sandy slopes that gave the place its name. We then rested again for a short while before pushing on towards the banks of the Tsangpo, which we reached finally not long before noon. There was only one place to cross it, by ferry, and we had to hope that the PLA had not reached it first. They had not.

On the far side, we stopped in a small village whose inhabitants turned out to greet me, many weeping. We were now on the fringes of some of Tibet's most difficult country: an area with only a few remote settlements. It was a region that the freedom fighters had made their own. From here on, I knew we were invisibly surrounded by hundreds of guerrilla warriors who had been warned of our impending arrival and whose job it was to protect us as we travelled.

It would have been difficult for the Chinese to follow us, but if they had information on our whereabouts it was possible that they might calculate our intended route and mobilise forces ahead to try to intercept us. So for our immediate protection an escort of about three hundred and fifty Tibetan soldiers had been assembled, along with a further fifty or so irregulars. The escape party itself had by now grown to about one hundred people.

Almost everyone but myself was heavily armed, including even the man appointed as my personal cook, who carried an enormous bazooka and wore a belt hung with its deadly shells. He was one of the young men trained by the CIA. So eager was he to use his magnificent and terrible-looking weapon that, at one point, he lay down and fired off several shots at what he claimed looked like an enemy position. But it took such a long time to reload that I felt sure he would have been made short work of by a real enemy. Altogether, it was not an impressive performance.

There was another of these CIA operatives amongst the party, a radio operator who was apparently in touch with his headquarters throughout the journey. Exactly whom he was in contact with, I do not know to this day. I only know that he was equipped with a Morse-key transmitter.

That night we stopped at a monastery called Ra-Me, where I wrote a hurried letter to the Panchen Lama telling him of my escape and advising him to join me in India if he could. I had not heard from him since the middle of winter, when he had written to offer his good wishes for the year ahead. In a separate, secret note he had also said he thought that, with the situation deteriorating throughout the country, we needed to formulate a strategy for the future. This was the first indication he had given of being no longer in the thrall of our Chinese masters. Unfortunately, my message never reached him and he remained in Tibet.

The next pass was called Sabo-La, which we reached two or three days later. At the top, it was very cold and snowing a blizzard. I began to be deeply worried about some of my companions. Although I was young and fit, some of the older ones amongst my entourage found the going very difficult. But we dared not slacken the pace as we were still in grave danger of being intercepted by Chinese forces. Particularly we were in danger of being caught in a pincer movement by troops stationed at Gyantse and in the Kongpo region.

At first, it was my intention to halt at Lhuntse Dzong, not far from the Indian border, where I would repudiate the Seventeen-Point 'Agreement', re-establish my Government as the rightful administration of all Tibet, and try to open negotiations with the Chinese. However, on about the fifth day, we were overtaken by a posse of horsemen who brought terrible news. Just over forty-eight hours after my departure, the Chinese had begun to shell the Norbulingka and to machine-gun the defenceless crowd, which was still in place. My worst fears had come true. I realised that it would be impossible to negotiate with people who behaved in this cruel and criminal fashion. There was nothing for it now but for us to get as far away as possible, though India still lay many days' journey distant, with several more high mountain passes in between.

When eventually we reached Lhuntse Dzong, after more than a week's travel, we paused for only two nights, just long enough for me formally to repudiate the Seventeen-Point 'Agreement' and to announce the formation of my own Government, the only legally constituted authority in the land. Over a thousand people attended the ceremony of consecration. I wanted very much to stay longer, but reports informed us that there were Chinese troop movements not far away. So reluctantly we prepared to move on to the Indian border, which now lay just sixty miles away in a straight line, though actually about double that on the ground. There was still another range of mountains to cross and it would take several more days to cover the distance, especially as our ponies were already worn out and there was very little fodder to give them. They would need frequent halts to conserve their energy. Before we left, I sent on a small party of the fittest men, who were to reach India as quickly as possible, find the nearest officials and warn them that I was planning to seek asylum there.

From Lhuntse Dzong we passed to the small village of Jhora and from there to the Karpo pass, the last before the border. Just as we were nearing the highest point of the track we received a bad shock. Out of nowhere, an aeroplane appeared and flew directly overhead. It passed quickly – too quickly for anyone to be able to see what markings it had – but not so fast that the people on board could have missed spotting us. This was not a good sign. If it was Chinese, as it probably was, there was a good chance that they now knew where we were. With this information they could return to attack us from the air, against which we had no protection. Whatever the identity of the aircraft, it was a forceful reminder that I was not safe anywhere in Tibet. Any misgivings I had about going into exile vanished with this realisation: India was our only hope.

A little later, the men I had sent on from Lhuntse Dzong returned with the news that the Indian Government had signalled its willingness to receive me. I was very relieved to hear this, as I had not wanted to set foot in India without permission.

I spent my last night in Tibet at a tiny village called Mangmang. No sooner had we reached this final outpost of the Land of Snows than it began to rain. This was on top of a week of appalling weather, which threw blizzards and snow glare at us by turns as we straggled along. We were all exhausted and it was the last thing that we needed, but it continued torrentially throughout the night. To make matters worse, my tent leaked and no matter where I dragged my bedding I could not escape the water which ran in rivulets down the inside. The result was that the fever I had been fighting off for the past few days developed overnight into a case of full-blown dysentery.

The following morning, I was too ill to continue, so we remained where we were. My companions moved me to a small house nearby, but it provided little more protection than my tent. Moreover, I was oppressed by the stench of cows that rose from the ground floor to where I lay above. That day, I heard on the small portable radio we had with us a report on All-India Radio saying that I was en route to India, but that I had fallen off my horse and was badly injured. This cheered me up rather, as it was one misfortune that I had managed to avoid, though I knew my friends would be concerned.

Next day, I decided to move on. I now had the difficult task of saying goodbye to the soldiers and freedom fighters who had escorted me all the way from Lhasa, and who were now about to turn and face the Chinese. There was one official too who decided to remain. He said that he did not think that he could be of much use in India, therefore it would be better to stay and fight. I really admired his determination and courage.

After bidding these people a tearful farewell, I was helped on to the broad back of a *dzomo*, for I was still too ill to ride a horse. And it was on this humble form of transport that I left my native land.

A Desperate Year

o

WE MUST HAVE BEEN a pitiful sight to the handful of Indian guards that met us at the border – eighty travellers, physically exhausted and mentally wretched from our ordeal. I was delighted, however, that an official I knew from my visit two years earlier was there to rendezvous with us. He explained that his orders were to escort me to Bomdila, a large town that lay a further week's travel away, for rest.

We finally reached it some three weeks after leaving Lhasa, though it seemed like an aeon. On arrival, I was greeted by my old liaison officer and interpreter, Mr Menon and Sonam Topgyal Kazi respectively, one of whom handed me a telegram from the Prime Minister:

> 'My colleagues and I welcome you and send greetings on your safe arrival in India. We shall be happy to afford the necessary facilities to you, your family and entourage to reside in India. The people of India, who hold you in great veneration, will no doubt accord their traditional respect to your personage. Kind regards to you. Nehru.'

I remained in Bomdila, where I was looked after very well by the family of the local District Commissioner, for about ten days. At the end of which, I was fully recovered from my dysentery. Then, early on 18 April 1959, I was taken by jeep to a road camp called Foothills, where a small guard of honour was formed up on either side of a makeshift carpet of canvas leading to the camp overseer's house, my base for the morning. Inside, I was given a breakfast that included fresh bananas – of which I ate too many, with unfortunate consequences to my digestive system – and briefed by Mr Menon about the arrangements that had been made by the Indian Government on my behalf.

That afternoon, I was to be taken to Tezpur, and from there began the journey to Mussoorie, a hill station not far from Delhi, where a house had been procured for me. A special train to take us the 1,500-mile distance had already been laid on.

As I left the building at Foothills, and climbed into a big red car for the thirty-mile drive to the railway station, I noticed large numbers of cameramen. It was explained to me that these were representatives of the international press. They had come to report on the 'story of the century'. I should expect to see many more of them on arrival in the city.

When we reached Tezpur I was taken directly to the Circuit House, where many hundreds of messages, telegrams and letters awaited me, all sending greetings and good wishes from people the world over. For a few moments I was lost in gratitude, but the exigencies of the present were almost overwhelming. The most pressing requirement, I felt, was to prepare a short statement to give to the many people waiting for some word from me to send back to their newspapers. In it, I gave an outline in straightforward and carefully moderate terms of the history I have related in these chapters. That done, and after a light lunch, we left for our train, which was due to depart at one o'clock.

On the way, hundreds if not thousands of people pressed around my convoy, waving and shouting greetings. This continued to happen throughout the whole journey to Mussoorie. At some points, the tracks themselves had to be cleared of well-wishers. News travels swiftly amongst rural communities and it seemed that no one was unaware of my presence on board that train. Thousands upon thousands of people turned out and shouted their welcome: '*Dalai Lama Ki Jai! Dalai Lama Zinda-bad!*' ('Hail to the Dalai Lama! Long live the Dalai Lama!') It was very moving. At three major cities en route, Siliguri, Benares and Lucknow, I was obliged to leave my carriage and address huge, impromptu meetings of flower-throwing well-wishers. The whole journey was like an extraordinary dream. Thinking back on it, I am immensely grateful to the people of India for their effusive demonstration of goodwill at that time.

The train finally pulled in at Dehra Dun station after several days of travel. Again, there was a large welcome for me. From there we drove up to Mussoorie, which was about an hour's drive. I was then taken to Birla House, a residence of one of India's leading industrial families, which had been requisitioned for my use by the Indian Government. There I was to stay until long-term plans could be made. As things turned out, it became my home for a year.

A day or so after my arrival, I heard of a New China News Agency report suggesting that because my Tezpur statement had been written in the third person it could not have been true. It went on to assert that I had been blatantly abducted and put under duress by 'rebels', and referred to my statement as 'a crude document, lame in reasoning, full of lies and loopholes'. This Chinese version of the story described the Tibetan people's uprising as having been organised by 'a reactionary upper-strata clique'. However, they explained, 'with the aid of the patriotic Tibetan monks and laymen, the People's Liberation Army completely crushed the rebellion. Primarily, this is because the Tibetan people are patrio- tic, support the Central People's Government, ardently love the People's Liberation Army and oppose the imperialists and traitors.' I therefore issued another brief communiqué confirming that the initial statement had been authorised by me.

On 24 April, Pandit Nehru himself arrived in Mussoorie. We talked together for over four hours, assisted by a single interpreter. I began by telling him everything that had happened since I had returned to Tibet – largely, as I reminded him, at his insistence. I went on to say that I had done just as he had suggested and dealt fairly and honestly with the Chinese, criticising them where necessary and trying hard to keep to the terms of the Seventeen-Point 'Agreement'. I then explained that I had not originally intended to seek India's hospitality but that I had wanted to establish my Government at Lhuntse Dzong. Only the news from

Lhasa had changed my mind. At this point he became rather irritated. 'The Indian Government could not have recognised it even if you had,' he said. I began to get the impression that Nehru thought of me as a young person who needed to be scolded from time to time.

During other parts of our conversation he banged the table. 'How can this be?' he asked indignantly once or twice. However, I went on in spite of the growing evidence that he could be a bit of a bully. Finally, I told him very firmly that my main concern was twofold: 'I am determined to win independence for Tibet, but the immediate requirement is to put a stop to the bloodshed.' At this he could restrain himself no longer. 'That is not possible!' he said in a voice charged with emotion. 'You say you want independence and in the same breath you say you do not want bloodshed. Impossible!' His lower lip quivered with anger as he spoke.

I began to realise that the Prime Minister found himself in an extremely delicate and embarrassing position. In the Indian Parliament, another tense debate on the Tibetan question had followed the news of my escape from Lhasa. For years now, he had been criticised by many politicians over his handling of the situation. And now, it seemed to me, he was showing signs of a guilty conscience at having been so insistent that I return to Tibet in 1957.

Yet at the same time it was clear that Nehru wanted to protect India's friendly relations with China and was determined to adhere to the principles of the Panch Sheel memorandum, despite the Indian politician Acharya Kripalani's description of it as having been 'born in sin to put the seal of our approval on the destruction of an ancient nation'. He made it quite clear that the Government of India still could not contemplate taking issue with the Chinese over the question of Tibetan rights. For now, I should rest and not make any plans for the immediate future. We would have the opportunity for further discussions on other occasions. Hearing this, I began to realise that my future, and that of my people, was far less certain than I had imagined. Our meeting ended cordially enough but, as the Prime Minister left, I experienced a profound feeling of disappointment.

It quickly became clear, however, that we were faced with more immediate problems than the question of Tibetan independence. No sooner had we arrived in Mussoorie than we started to receive reports of large numbers of refugees arriving not only in India but also in Bhutan. Immediately, I sent some of my officials to receive them at the camps hastily opened by the Indian Government.

From these new arrivals I learnt that, after their initial bombardment of the Norbulingka, the Chinese had turned their guns on to the Potala and the Jokhang, slaughtering and wounding thousands. Both buildings were badly damaged. The Chakpori Medical School was totally destroyed. No one knows how many people were killed during this onslaught, but a PLA document captured by Tibetan freedom fighters during the 1960s stated that between March 1959 and September 1960, 87,000 deaths through military action were recorded. (This figure does not include all those who died as a result of suicide, torture and starvation.)

As a result, countless thousands of my people tried to leave Tibet. Many died, either directly at the hands of the Chinese, or from wounds, malnutrition, cold and disease. Those who managed to escape across the border did so in a state of abject dereliction. And although there was food and shelter for them on arrival, the relentless Indian sun began to exact a pitiless toll from them. There were two main transit camps, one at Missamari, close to Tezpur, the other at Buxa Duar, a former British prisoner-of-war camp located close to the Bhutanese border in the north-east.

Both places were much lower than Mussoorie's elevation of 6,000 feet, so the heat was unmitigated. For although it can get quite hot in Tibet during summer, the air at the high altitude people were used to was extremely dry, whereas on the Indian plains the heat is accompanied by high levels of humidity. This was not just uncomfortable for the refugees but all too often fatal. Diseases which were unknown to Tibetans proliferated in this new environment. Thus, on top of the danger of death from injuries sustained whilst escaping from Tibet, there was also danger of death from heat stroke and illnesses such as tuberculosis, which flourished under these conditions. Many succumbed.

Those of us who lived in Mussoorie were considerably more fortunate than the majority of our fellow countrymen and women. And because there were fans installed at Birla House, I suffered perhaps least of all – though the fans themselves did cause their own difficulties, I found. The tendency was to leave them on at night, which caused digestive problems. I was reminded of a proverb of one of my sweepers at the Potala: 'In the winter it is cold and you wrap up at night. But in the summer it is warm and you forget.'

Another small observation I made at this time was that hot weather encourages fruit eating, whereas when it is cold there is no such desire.

I had limited personal experience of the discomfort due to heat suffered by my fellow exiles on those occasions when I had cause to go down to the plains during those summer months. The first of these was in June, when I travelled to Delhi to call on the Prime Minister for discussions about the growing refugee population. Already there were 20,000 and the numbers were increasing on a daily basis.

I began by pleading for the new arrivals to be moved somewhere that the climate was less damaging than at Tezpur and Buxa Duar. They had arrived wearing long robes and heavy boots, completely ignorant of the imminent hot season. And although the first few thousand refugees to escape from the murderous hands of Tibet's 'liberators' were mostly men, many from Lhasa and surrounding districts, later whole families began to arrive. These people came principally from the border areas, where Chinese control was not yet absolute.

I impressed upon Nehru my conviction that the majority would die if they were left there. At first, he showed some signs of irritation. He said that I was asking too much. I must remember that India was a poor, developing country. But quickly his humanitarian instincts won him over. Already the *Kashag* had held discussions with Indian officials about a plan to employ the refugees on road camps in northern India and now Nehru said that he would see to it that the arrangements were made as quickly as possible. This would then allow them to earn their keep and, at the same time, to be taken to a more suitable climate.

He then began to talk about the future education of the refugee children, quickly warming to the subject, so that in the end he was showing such interest that it was as if he considered the matter to be his own personal responsibility. He said that, since as far as he was concerned we would be guests of India for the foreseeable future, our children were our most precious resource. They should be well educated. And, in order to preserve Tibetan culture, it would be necessary to have separate schools for them. There should therefore be an independent Society for Tibetan Education within the Indian Ministry of Education. He added that the Indian Government would bear all the expenses for setting up the schools. (To this day, it continues to fund the greater part of our education programme.)

Finally, he cautioned me that, whilst it was very important that the children should be brought up with a thorough knowledge of their own history and culture, it was vital that they should be conversant with the ways of the modern world. I agreed whole-heartedly. For that reason, he said, we would be wise to use English as our medium of instruction, for 'it is the international language of the future'.

Our meeting was followed by lunch, at which point Nehru said he would call Dr Shrimali, the Education Minister. This gave us the opportunity to continue our discussion. Then, that same afternoon, the Prime Minister told me that the Government would announce the formation of the Society that very day. I was highly impressed with such a rapid response.

Over the years now, the people and Government of India have given an extraordinary amount to us Tibetan refugees, both in terms of financial assistance and in many other ways – this despite their own enormous economic difficulties. I doubt whether any other refugees have been so well treated by their hosts. It is always in my mind whenever the Tibetans have been compelled to ask for more money that, in the meantime, hundreds of thousands of India's own children lack even basic education.

Yet in a way, it is only right that India should come to our aid. For Buddhism came to Tibet from India, along with many other important cultural influences. There is no doubt in my mind that she has a better claim on Tibet than China, whose influence was only ever slight. I often compare the relationship between India and Tibet with that between a teacher and a pupil. When the pupil gets him or herself into difficulty, it is the responsibility of the teacher to come to the pupil's assistance.

Not far behind the generosity of the Indian people has been that of many foreign relief organisations. Much of their assistance has been of a practical nature, especially in the fields of health and education. Also important has been their help in establishing handicraft and other work centres, which have provided meaningful employment for many people. The first were carpet-weaving workshops set up in Darjeeling, the tea-producing town high up on the border with Nepal, and at Dalhousie, not far from Dharamsala. Both were founded by the Indian Government towards the end of 1959. These then provided the model for several other such centres set up with assistance from the overseas agencies – some of whom continue their support to this day. Now, many years later, each of those organisations which were involved at the beginning of our exile have expressed full satisfaction with the progress made by the refugees under their guidance.

The positive way in which Tibetans have responded to the help given them is the best way for us to express our enormous gratitude. This is important, not least because I am conscious that much of the money donated to these agencies often comes from the pockets of people with quite limited resources themselves.

On returning to Mussoorie after this visit to Delhi, I felt that the time was now ripe for me to break my elected silence and, on 20 June, I held a press conference. There were still a great number of newspapermen in Mussoorie waiting to hear something from me. Although the 'story' was by now over two months old, a total of 130 reporters attended, representing countries the world over.

I began by formally repudiating once more the Seventeen-Point 'Agreement'. I explained that, since China herself had broken the terms of her own 'Agreement', there could no longer be any legal basis for recognising it. I then elaborated on my original short statement and detailed some of the the atrocities committed against the Tibetans. I was sure that people would realise that my story was nearer the truth than the incredible fiction put about by the Chinese. But although my latest statement received wide coverage, I had underestimated the power of an efficiently conducted public relations campaign such as the Chinese Government was able to carry out. Or perhaps I overestimated the willingness of mankind to face the truth about itself. I believe that it took first the evidence of the Cultural Revolution, then the sight of the 1989 Tiananmen Square Massacre on its television screens before the world fully accepted the mendacity and barbarity of the Communist Chinese.

That same evening, a communiqué was issued on behalf of the Indian Government saying that it did not recognise the Dalai Lama's Government in Exile. I was at first a little surprised and hurt by this. I knew perfectly well that it did not support us politically, but such distancing seemed unnecessary. However, my wounded feelings quickly gave way to a sense of enormous gratitude as I saw, really for the first time, the true meaning of the word 'democracy'. The Indian Government vehemently opposed my point of view, but it did nothing to try to prevent me from expressing it, much less from holding it.

Likewise, there was no interference from Delhi over how I and the growing numbers of Tibetans conducted our lives. In accordance with popular requests, I had begun to give weekly audiences in the grounds of Birla House. This gave me the opportunity to meet a variety of people and tell them about the real situation in Tibet. It also helped me begin the process of removing the protocol which did so much to separate the Dalai Lama from his people. I had a strong feeling that we should not cling to old practices that were no longer appropriate. As I often reminded people, we were now refugees.

To this end, I insisted that all formality should be deliberately reduced and made clear that I no longer wanted people to perform the old courtesies. I felt this was especially important when dealing with foreigners. They would be much more likely to respond to genuine worth if they found it. It is very easy to put others off by remaining aloof. So I was determined to be entirely open, to show everything and not to hide behind etiquette. In this way I hoped that people would relate to me as one human being to another.

I also stipulated that whenever I received anybody, he or she should sit on a chair of equal height, rather than one lower than mine as was customary. At first, even I found this rather difficult as I did not have much self-confidence, but it grew from then on. And despite the misgivings of some of my older advisors, I think the only people who were discomfited by these principles were occasional new arrivals from Tibet who did not know that the Dalai Lama no longer lived the way they were used to.

Life at Birla House was hardly conducive to formality anyway. It was neither especially grand nor large and at times it became quite crowded. I shared it with my mother as well as my household, and the remainder of my officials lived very close by. This was the first time in my life that I had seen so much of my mother. I very much enjoyed her company.

In addition to reducing formality, our tragedy also gave me the opportunity greatly to simplify my own personal life. In Lhasa I had had many possessions which were of little use, but it was very difficult to give them away. Now, I possessed almost nothing and I found it much easier to pass on things that were given to me if they could be of use to my fellow refugees.

In the field of administration, too, I was able to make radical changes. For example, I saw at this time to the creation of various new Tibetan government departments. These included Offices of Information, Education, Rehabilitation, Security, Religious Affairs and Economic Affairs. I also particularly encouraged women to take part in government. I reminded people that selection for important positions should never be based on the question of gender, only on the quality and aptitude of the candidate. As I have already mentioned, women always played an important part in Tibetan society and today there are many who hold key posts in the Tibetan Government in Exile.

I returned to Delhi during September. By this time, I was somewhat easier in my mind about the refugees. Their numbers had by now grown to almost thirty thousand, but Nehru was true to his word and already many had been removed to road camps in the hills of northern India. My main aim now was to do what I could to have the question of Tibet's right to independence raised at the United Nations. Once again I began my visit by calling on the Prime Minister. We spent some time discussing a proposal to transfer some of the new arrivals to the south of India. He had already written to the heads of several Indian states asking whether any would be prepared to make land over to us Tibetans.

After expressing great satisfaction to hear that more than one offer had been made, I mentioned my plan to try to have a hearing at the UN. At this, Nehru began to show signs of exa eration. Since neither Tibet nor China were member states, he said, it was highly unlikely that I would succeed. And even if I did, it would not have much effect. I replied that I was aware of the difficulties, but that I simply wanted the world to keep Tibet in mind. It was vital that my people were not forgotten in their misery. 'The way to keep the Tibetan question alive is not through the UN, but through the proper education of your children. But it's up to you. You live in a free country,' he said.

I had already written to the Governments of many countries and now I had meetings with the Ambassadors of several. I found this a very trying ordeal. I was still only twenty-four, and my experience of dealing with high-ranking officials was limited to what I had gained during my visit to China and my few talks with Nehru and his colleagues. Nevertheless, it paid off to the extent that some were very sympathetic and gave me advice on how to proceed, and all promised to inform their Governments of my requests for support. In the end, the Federation of Malaysia and the Republic of Ireland sponsored a draft resolution which was debated by the UN General Assembly during October. It was passed in our favour in a vote split forty-five for and nine against, with twenty-six abstentions. India was one of the abstainers.

Also during this particular visit to the capital, I had meetings with a number of sympathetic Indian politicians, including Jaya Prakash Naryan who, true to his commitment back in 1957, had set up a Tibet Support Committee. There was now, he felt, a good chance of persuading the Government to change its stance on Tibet. His enthusiasm was infectious and deeply moving, though instinctively I knew that Pandit Nehru would never change his mind. Another welcome development was news that the International Commission of Jurists, an independent organisation dedicated to upholding justice around the world, had recently published a report on the legal status of Tibet that vindicated our position entirely. The Commission, which had taken up our case early in the year, was now planning to conduct a full-scale enquiry.

A month later, after returning to Mussoorie, I received a welcome boost to morale when the Afro–Asian Committee met in Delhi. It devoted almost the whole of its business to discussing the Tibetan issue. The majority of its delegates were from countries that had themselves suffered from colonial oppression, so naturally they were well disposed towards Tibet. They saw us in the same position as they themselves had been before they won their independence. I received reports of their unanimous support with feelings of great joy and optimism and began to feel that something positive must surely come of all this. But alas, deep down it was clear to me that the Prime Minister was right. We Tibetans must not think in terms of an early return to our country. Instead we must concentrate on building a strong community in exile so that when the time eventually came, we would be able to resume our lives back home transformed by our experience.

The offers of land Nehru had mentioned seemed to hold the best prospect of allowing us to do this. Three thousand acres near to Mysore in southern India were immediately available if we wanted them, but, generous though this was, I was at first hesitant to accept. I had visited the area whilst on pilgrimage during my first visit to the country, and knew it to be quiet and lightly populated. However, it is considerably hotter there than it is in the north and I felt that the conditions would likely be too harsh. Furthermore, with my administration located in Dharamsala, I feared the distance was too great.

On the other hand, given our present situation, I realised it was necessary to think in terms of settling semi-permanently in India. Only then would it be possible to begin an education programme and take steps to ensure the cultural continuity of the Tibetan people. In the end, I concluded that these considerations out-weighed the geographical and psychological problems, and I grate-fully accepted the land. A first batch of 666 settlers would leave in the New Year of 1960 to begin the work of making it habitable. On the basis of one acre per refugee, the eventual aim was to establish a community for 3,000.

Towards the end of 1959 came news of two organisations, the Central Relief Committee, headed by Acharya Kripalani, and the American Emergency Committee for Tibetan Refugees, that had been set up specifically to help us. These were later followed by other similarly dedicated agencies in other countries which, between them, provided invaluable assistance.

Meanwhile, I began to receive visits from a number of interest-ing people. One of these was the same Indian monk that I had met in Dromo when he was travelling with a relic of the Lord Buddha. I was delighted to see him again. He was very scholarly and had a particular interest in socio-economics. In the time since we had last met, he had expended much time and energy in trying to synthesise Marxist ideology with the spiritual principles of Buddhism. This interested me greatly. I was convinced that, because so much of Asia, from the Thai border up to Siberia, whose native faith was Buddhism, was now suffering terribly as a result of Marxism's hostility to religion, such work was vital.

Also at around this time, I received a visit from a left-leaning Sinhalese monk. At the end of his stay in Mussoorie, my new friend invited me to Sri Lanka. This was somewhere I very much wanted to go to, not least because it would give me the opportunity to see the most important of all relics, the Buddha's tooth. However, some months later, when the time approached for me to make the journey, I received a forceful indication of how uncertain is the status of a refugee. The Sri Lankan Government sent a communication regretting that my visit would have to be indefinitely postponed as there had been 'unforeseen developments'. These turned out to have originated from Peking. Again I was reminded of the power of brothers and sisters in high places to stop even religious activities if they chose to.

The urgency of opening a meaningful dialogue with the Chinese was brought home to me when I received a deputation from some other victims of Communist expansionism. They were from East Turkestan, which had been overrun by China in 1949. We had much to talk about and spent many hours relating our experiences to one another. It transpired that the East Turkestani refugees were considerably more numerous than us and one of their leaders was a lawyer. This was at a time when there was not a single practitioner of allopathic medicine amongst the entire Tibetan population, let alone a qualified lawyer. We discussed at length the various ways we could carry on the struggle for freedom in our countries. Finally, we agreed to keep in close touch, which we do to this day, although somehow the Tibetan cause has always attracted more publicity than theirs.

In December, I made the six-hour journey down to Delhi once more, this time as the first leg of a new pilgrimage. I wanted to spend more time at the places I had visited at the beginning of 1957. On my way I called on the Prime Minister once more. I was somewhat anxious of what he might have to say to me on account of the UN resolution and I half expected him to be annoyed. In fact, he congratulated me warmly. I began to see that, despite his occasional heavy-handedness, he was a man of great magnanimity. And once again, I was reminded of the meaning of the word 'democracy'. Even though I had rejected his opinion, there was no change whatever in his attitude towards the Tibetans. As a result, I felt more disposed than ever to listen to him. This was exactly contrary to my experience in China. Nehru did not smile much. He would sit quietly listening with that tremulous lower lip protruding slightly, before making his reply, which would always be frank and honest. Above all, he gave me complete freedom to follow my own conscience. The Chinese, on the other hand, had always been full of smiles and deceit.

I also saw the Indian President, Dr Rajendra Prasad, once more. I was his guest at Rastrapathi Bhavan, along with a Jain, Acharya Tulsi, towards whom I developed strong feelings of respect. As I had been on our first meeting back in 1956, I was deeply impressed by the President's humility. His demeanour was something quite extraordinary and I was actually moved to tears. He seemed to me like a true Bodhisattva. The last time I saw him was in the garden of his residence. I went down very early in the morning for a walk and found that he was outside too, an old man, hunched and magnificent, in a large, black wheelchair.

From Delhi I proceeded to Bodh Gaya. Whilst there, I received a deputation of sixty or more Tibetan refugees who were also making a pilgrimage. A very moving moment followed when their leaders came to me and pledged their lives in the continuing struggle for a free Tibet. After that, for the first time in this life, I ordained a group of 162 young Tibetan novices as *bikshus*. I felt greatly privileged to be able to do this at the Tibetan monastery which stands within sight of the Mahabodhi temple, next to the Bodhi Tree under which the Buddha finally attained Enlightenment.

I then travelled to Sarnath and the Deer Park, where the Buddha had preached his first sermon. With me I had a small retinue of staff, including Ling Rinpoché, Trijang Rinpoché and, of course, my Masters of the Robes, the Ritual and the Kitchen. On arrival, I found that something like two thousand Tibetan refugees, newly arrived through Nepal, had assembled, knowing that I planned to give a teaching. They were in very poor condition, but I could see that they were facing their hardship with great spirit. Tibetans are indefatigable traders and already they had set up stalls. Some were selling a few valuables they had managed to bring with them, others were selling old clothes. Many sold just tea. I was much encouraged by their vigour in the face of such suffering. Each person could have told a tale of desperate hardship and cruelty, yet here they were making the best of what little life had to offer them.

This first week-long teaching in the Deer Park was a wonderful event for me. It meant a great deal to be able to give it in the very place where the Buddha himself had taught 2,500 years before. During the course of it, I concentrated on the positive aspects of our ordeal. I reminded everyone of the Buddha's own words when he said that suffering is the first step towards liberation. There is an old Tibetan saying, too, that 'pain is what you measure pleasure by'.

Shortly after returning to Mussoorie, I learned that the Indian Government had plans to move me to permanent accommodation at a place called Dharamsala. This was unexpected news and quite alarming. I found Dharamsala on the map and discovered that it was another hill station, like Mussoorie, but in a considerably more remote location. On further investigation I was told that, unlike Mussoorie, which was only a few hours from Delhi, Dharamsala was a whole day's journey from the capital. I began to have some suspicion that the Indian Government was now trying to hide us away somewhere without good communications in the hope that we Tibetans would disappear from the sight of the outside world.

I therefore requested that I be allowed to send a Tibetan Government official to Dharamsala to see whether it was really suitable for our needs. My plea was heard and I sent a member of the *Kashag*, J. T. Kundeling, to reconnoitre the spot. When he came back after a week's absence, he announced that 'Dharamsala water is better than Mussoorie milk'. So we made preparations to shift camp without delay.

In the meantime, I made the first of many visits to the northern provinces, where thousands of my people were now engaged on road building. I was heartbroken when I saw them. Children, women and men were all working side by side in gangs: former nuns, farmers, monks, officials, all thrown together. They had to endure a full day's hard physical toil under a mighty sun, followed by nights crammed into tiny tents. Nobody was yet properly acclimatised to the conditions and even though it was a bit cooler than in the transit camps, heat and humidity still exacted a frightening toll. The air was fetid and thick with mosquitoes. As a result, sickness was universal and often fatal, thanks to the already weakened state of people's constitutions. Worse still, the work itself was quite risky. Much of it was done on steep mountain-sides and the dynamite they used claimed its own share of casualties.

Even today, quite a few old people carry scars from this terrible labour and are maimed and crippled. And although now the fruit of their labours is clearly visible, at the time there were moments when the whole venture seemed pointless. It took only one fierce downpour of rain to wash away their efforts in a slick of red mud. Yet for all this, despite their desperate situation, the refugees showed me deep, personal respect and listened closely when I said that it was vital for us to remain optimistic. I was very moved.

These first visits to the road camps made me aware of a new problem, however. The children of the roadworkers were suffering badly from malnutrition and their mortality rate was very high. So I contacted the Indian Government, which hurriedly organised a new transit camp dedicated specifically to their needs. At the same time, an initial batch of fifty children was sent to Mussoorie, where the first of our schools had been set up.

On 1 February 1960, the first settlers arrived at Bylakuppe in Mysore state. I heard later that when they saw the land, many of the refugees broke down and cried. The task before them seemed so immense. They had been supplied with tents and basic equipment, but apart from this, their only resource was such determination as they could bring to bear.

Just over a month later, on 10 March, just before leaving for Dharamsala with the eighty or so officials who comprised the Tibetan Government in Exile, I began what is now a tradition by making a statement on the anniversary of the Tibetan People's Uprising. On this first occasion, I stressed the need for my people to take a long-term view of the situation in Tibet. For those of us in exile, I said that our priority must be resettlement and the continuity of our cultural traditions. As to the future, I stated my belief that, with Truth, Justice and Courage as our weapons, we Tibetans would eventually prevail in regaining freedom for Tibet.

CHAPTER NINE

100,000 Refugees

○

THE JOURNEY to Dharamsala was by a combination of overnight train and motorcade. Together with my entourage, I left Mussoorie on 29 April 1960 and arrived at Pathankot station in Himachal Pradesh the following day. I well remember the drive that followed our train ride. After about an hour on the road I saw white peaks towering high up in the far distance. We were headed straight for them. On the way we passed through some of the most beautiful countryside in India – lush green fields dotted with trees and everywhere flowers wild with colour. After three hours we pulled into the centre of Dharamsala, and I exchanged my limousine for a jeep to ride the final few miles to my house, which was situated just above the village of McLeod Ganj, over-looking a broad valley.

It was a steep and rather hair-raising climb and I was reminded of some of the journeys around Lhasa where, from the edge of the road, you could sometimes look down thousands of feet. When we arrived at McLeod Ganj, we found that a new bamboo gate had been erected for us, with a sign saying 'Welcome' painted in gold letters across the top. From there it was a matter of only one more mile to my new home, Swarg Ashram, formerly Highcroft House and residence of the Divisional Commissioner in the days of the British Raj. It was a smallish house, set in woodland and surrounded by a compound of outbuildings, one of which was the kitchen. A further three houses had been requisitioned for my officials. Although it had good potential for expansion, this was less room than we had been used to, but I was grateful that we could now settle down.

MAJOR TIBETAN
SETTLEMENTS IN INDIA

PAKISTAN

HIMACHAL
PRADESH
•Dalhousie
Dharamsala •Kulu
Simla•
PUNJAB •Mussoorie
•Rajpur

HIMALAYAS

TIBET

NEPAL

Delhi

UTTAR
PRADESH

BHUTAN
Tezpur
Darjeeling Kalimpong

Kanpur
Sarnath •Buxa
Benares Bodh Gaya

BANGLA-
DESH

Mainpat

Calcutta•

I N D I A

•Bandhara

Bombay•

Ganjam

BAY OF

BENGAL

ARABIAN SEA

•Mundgood

Bangalore
Cauvery Valley •Hunsur
Bylakuppe
•Kollegal

•Madras

KERALA

N

Trivandrum•

SRI LANKA

It was quite late when we arrived so I was not able to see much, but the following morning, when I woke, the first thing I heard was the distinctive call of a bird which I later discovered is peculiar to this place. '*Kara-chok, Kara-chok,*' it seemed to say. I looked out of the window to see where it was, but could not find it. Instead, my eyes were greeted by a view of magnificent mountains.

On the whole, our experience at Dharamsala has been quite happy, although I note that Kundeling rediscovered his taste for Mussoorie milk and retired back there some years ago. The only real drawback of the Dharamsala region is its rainfall, which is the second highest in the Indian sub-continent. At first there were less than a hundred Tibetans all told. But today the refugee population has grown to more than five thousand. Only once or twice has there been any serious thought of moving. The last time was a few years ago when a severe earthquake caused damage to several buildings. People began to say that it was too dangerous to remain. We did not leave, however, mainly because whilst there is quite often seismic activity in the area, it is normally only slight. The last serious disturbance occurred in 1905, during the time that the British used the place as a summer retreat. On that occasion, the spire of their parish church was knocked down. So it seems reasonable to assume that large-scale tremors are very infrequent. Besides which, for practical reasons, it would be very difficult to move.

As at Birla House, I shared my new home with my mother – and also a couple of Lhasa Apso dogs which had recently been presented to me. These animals were a continual source of amusement to everyone. They both had very distinctive characters. The larger of the two was called Sangye. I often thought that he must have been a monk in his previous life, perhaps one of those who died of starvation in Tibet, as many did. I say this because on the one hand he showed no interest in the opposite sex, but on the other, he was most enthusiastic about food: even when he must have been completely full, he could always find room for more. Also, he was extremely loyal to me.

Tashi, the other, was very different. Despite being smaller, he was much the braver of the two. He was given to me by Tenzin Norgay, the Everest mountaineer, so that may have had something to do with it. I well remember a time when he got ill and had to be given injections. After the first of these, he became very frightened. So on succeeding occasions when the vet came, he had to be caught up by two people and held down whilst the drugs were administered. Meanwhile, Tashi would growl and snarl at his persecutor who, when he had completed his work, had quickly to leave the house. Only then was it safe to let the little dog go, whereupon he would go racing off, sniffing all over the house in search of the poor man. But if he seemed rather ferocious, his bark was much worse than his bite: his jaw overlapped in such a way that he could not actually sink his teeth into anything.

When I moved to Dharamsala, I went with an Indian Government liaison officer, Mr Nair, and a number of Indian army bodyguards. I had an excellent relationship with Mr Nair, who volunteered to teach me English. Realising its importance, I had already arranged for Tenzin Choegyal to be sent to North Point, an English school in Darjeeling, and had started taking language lessons whilst at Mussoorie. Very generously, the Indian Government had provided someone to give me regular coaching, perhaps two or three times a week. But I was not at that time a very willing pupil and quickly found excuses to avoid them. So far I had made little progress. However, I enjoyed working with my new liaison officer and progressed well under his tuition, though I could not get enthusiastic about the mass of writing he gave me to do. I was sorry when he was posted elsewhere after two years.

From then on, my instruction in English was much less formal. Various other people helped me, including some Tibetans, but I doubt whether my command of the language is much better now than it was twenty-five years ago. I am always painfully reminded of this when I go abroad. I am often embarrassed at the terrible mistakes I make and regret that I did not work harder when I had the opportunity.

In addition to learning English during those first years of living in Dharamsala, I also rededicated myself to religious study. I began by reviewing a number of Tibetan texts I had first looked at as a teenager. At the same time, I took teachings from some of the spiritual masters of different traditions who had come into exile. And although the realisation of *Bodhichitta* (the aspiration to achieve Buddhahood for the benefit of all sentient beings) still seemed a long way off, I found that now there was no compulsion to work, the idea of it was not so unpleasant and I began to get a lot done. Unfortunately, lack of time quickly became a major obstacle to advancement in this sphere. But I can say that, insofar as I have achieved anything spiritually, it is out of all proportion to the amount of effort I have managed to put in.

Within a fortnight of our arrival in Dharamsala, I was able to open the first nursery for Tibetan refugee children. This was established in a small, previously derelict building rented for us by the Indian Government to house the growing number of orphans amongst the new arrivals. I appointed my elder sister, Tsering Dolma, to run it. There was not much room for them when the initial consignment of fifty children arrived. But they lived in luxury compared with later on, for, by the end of the year, their numbers had multiplied tenfold, with no end to the increase in sight. At one point, 120 shared a single bedroom. They had to sleep five or six to a bed, lying across it so that they could all fit on. But although conditions were harsh, I could not help feeling joy every time I went to visit my sister and her new extended family. For, parentless as they were, these destitutes were so full of laughter and joy that they seemed to make a mockery of their hardship.

My sister proved to be an excellent leader, who never gave in to despair. She was a powerful woman and quite strict, having inherited the family temper in full measure. At heart though, she was a very kind person with a good sense of humour. Her contribution in those difficult times was invaluable. As a simple village girl, she had had no education whatever and much of her early life was spent helping my mother run the family house. She had an enormous capacity for hard work. This, coupled with her rather fierce nature, made her an excellent leader.

However, it soon became apparent that neither we nor the Indian Government had sufficient resources to cope with all our orphans, and I came to the conclusion that it was necessary to have at least some of them adopted overseas, if that were possible. I therefore contacted a Swiss friend, Dr Aeschmann, and asked him to look into the possibility. Switzerland seemed to me an ideal place, given the fact that it is a relatively small country with excellent communications and, as a bonus, mountains which are reminiscent of home.

The Swiss Government was co-operative from the start and said it was willing to take 200 children immediately. Furthermore, it agreed to take steps to help ensure that, although the children were to be adopted into ordinary Swiss families, as far as possible there would be opportunities for them to pursue their own unique Tibetan culture and identity.

This first batch of children was followed by others, and later there was also a scheme not only for some older students to study in Switzerland but also for the resettlement of 1,000 adult refugees. As our situation improved, we no longer needed to call on the generosity of the Swiss nation. But I continue to be tremendously grateful to them for all they have done for my people.

Soon after arriving in Dharamsala, I came into personal contact with members of the International Commission of Jurists, whose work the previous year had done so much to encourage us. They invited me to give evidence to the Commission's Legal Inquiry Committee, which I gladly did. The results of these investigations were published in Geneva during August 1960. Once again, the Jurists entirely vindicated the Tibetan viewpoint: China, it reported, had violated sixteen articles of the Universal Declaration of Human Rights and was guilty of genocide in Tibet. They also detailed some of the vile atrocities I have already mentioned.

On a practical level, I learned one very useful thing from my discussions with the Commission. One of its members, an Englishman I think, asked me whether we had someone monitoring Peking's radio broadcasts. No, I replied, we did not. He was a little shocked at this and explained in some detail the necessity of listening carefully to what they said. It is a comment on our lack of sophistication that this had not occurred to us. As far as we were concerned, Radio Peking did nothing but disseminate lies and propaganda. We did not see the value of listening to it for an indication of what was going on in the Chinese mind. However, I could see the logic of doing so and immediately instructed the *Kashag* to organise a monitoring team – whose successors carry on their work to this day.

Throughout 1960, I continued to work at reforming the Tibetan Administration and, together with the *Kashag* and others, I began the difficult process of full democratisation. On 2 September, I inaugurated the Commission of Tibetan People's Deputies. Membership of this organisation, the highest legislative body of the Government, was open to freely elected representatives of the three regions of Tibet, U-Tsang, Amdo and Kham. Each of the main traditions within Tibetan Buddhism likewise had seats. Later, followers of the old Bon religion were also included. The Commission, now known as the Assembly of Tibetan People's Deputies, or *Bhoe Mimang Chetui Lhenkhang*, functions much like a house of parliament. Its members meet with the *Kashag* and the secretaries of the different Departments, or *Lhenkhangs*, for discussions once a month. On specific occasions, it meets with the full National Working Committee, or *Gyunle*, which comprises the heads of the *Lhenkhangs* and members of the *Kashag* (whose members are today no longer appointed by me but elected). Anything put to the vote by the People's Deputy must be carried out according to the result.

To begin with, these new arrangements were not very satisfactory. Because the changes were so radical to Tibetans, some people even suggested that the Government in Dharamsala was practising *true* Communism! Three decades later, we are still faced with many problems, but things are changing and improving all the time. Certainly we are far ahead of our brothers and sisters in China, who could learn a great deal from us. At the time of writing, the Tibetan Government in Exile is in the process of implementing new measures to promote democracy further.

Some of the older officials who had come into exile found these changes hard to accept at first. But, on the whole, they saw the need for reform of our system and worked hard and enthusiastically to achieve it. I shall always think fondly of them. In the early years, although I was able to live in some degree of comfort, the same was by no means true for the majority of government officials. Many of them, even quite elderly men, were compelled to live under very poor conditions – some taking shelter in cowsheds, for example. But this they did cheerfully and without complaint, even though they had often lived extremely well throughout their lives in Tibet. And even if some of them disagreed in their hearts with the direction in which I was heading, due to their conservatism, each and every one contributed something during those dark days. They faced the difficulties we shared with great joy and determination and did all they could to help rebuild the shattered lives of our people, entirely without thought of personal gain. Their salary in those days was not above 75 rupees, or £3, a month, even though they could have done much better for themselves elsewhere, thanks to their education.

None of which is to say that the business of administration at that time was easy. Naturally, there were some personal differences between people and a fair amount of petty squabbling. That is only human nature. But overall, everyone expended their energies enthusiastically and unselfishly for the good of others.

My other main preoccupation right from the start was the preservation and continuation of our religion. Without it, I knew that the well-spring of our culture would dry up. Initially, the Government of India agreed to provide for a scholastic community of 300 monks to be established at the old prisoner-of-war camp at Buxa Duar, near the Bhutanese border. But, by explaining that Buddhism depends upon a high standard of scholarship, we managed eventually to persuade them to increase the commitment to funding for 1,500 of all traditions. This figure represented the youngest and most able of the 6,000-odd monks who had escaped into exile, and as many experienced teachers as had survived.

Unfortunately, conditions at Buxa Duar remained very bad.

The climate there was especially hot and humid and disease was rampant. These problems were exacerbated by the fact that food rations had to be sent in from far away. When they arrived, they were often in an extremely bad state. Within months, several hundred of these scholar monks had developed tuberculosis. Nevertheless, they worked and studied hard until they could be moved. To my sorrow, I was unable to visit the site but, meanwhile, I tried to sustain them with letters and taped messages. Evidently this paid off to some degree for, although the camp never overcame its terrible problems, the survivors became the nucleus of a vigorous monastic community.

Of course, one of the greatest difficulties we faced during those early years was lack of money. This was not a problem so far as our educational and resettlement programmes were concerned, thanks to the enormous generosity of the Indian Government and the various voluntary agencies overseas, which funded many projects. But I did not feel that it was appropriate to ask for assistance with things like the Administration. The small amount of revenue raised by the imposition of a voluntary freedom tax of 2 rupees per person per month, combined with a similarly voluntary monthly income tax of two per cent for salaried workers, did not go far. However, we had a lifeline in the form of the treasure, which Kenrap Tenzin had deposited in Sikkim with such foresight back in 1950. It was still there.

At first, I had it in mind to sell the treasure directly to the Indian Government, a plan proposed by Nehru himself. But my advisors were adamant that the treasure should be sold on the open market. They were certain we could get more for it that way. So it was finally disposed of in Calcutta, where it fetched what seemed to me an enormous sum, equivalent then to $8 million.

A number of enterprises were invested in with this money. There was a plant to manufacture iron pipes and a business connected with a paper mill, amongst other supposedly guaranteed money-spinning projects. Unfortunately, it was not long before each of these attempts to make our precious capital work for us failed. Sadly, we were not well served by a number of people who were ostensibly helping us. It seems they were more interested in helping themselves, and we lost the majority of the funds. The vision of the *Chikyab Kenpo* turned out to have been largely wasted.

Less than an eighth of the original total was salvaged to form what came to be known as His Holiness the Dalai Lama's Charitable Trust, which was set up in 1964. However, if there is some sadness in this episode, I myself do not regret very much the way things turned out. In retrospect, it is clear that the treasure belonged to all the people of Tibet, not just the few who had escaped into exile. We did not, therefore, have an exclusive right to it, no *Karmic* right. I was reminded of the example set by Ling Rinpoché, who left his favourite watch behind on the night that we left Lhasa. He felt that by going into exile he was forfeiting his right to it. I now see that this was the correct view.

As to my own personal finances, whereas in the old days there were two offices to look after the financial affairs of the Dalai Lama, since 1959 there has been only one. This is the Private Office, which handles all my income and expenditure, including my own allowance, which is paid in the form of a stipend by the Indian Government at the (unchanged) rate of 20 rupees a day: slightly more than a dollar, rather less than a pound. Theoretically, it pays for my food and clothing. As in former times, I have nothing directly to do with money, which is probably just as well as I have a suspicion that mine is a free-spending nature, although at the same time I know from my childhood that I can be very stingy over small amounts. However, I am of course able to direct how such funds as I personally receive are spent (for example, the Nobel Peace Prize money).

During that first summer in Dharamsala, I found time for some relaxation and took to playing badminton most evenings. (I often did not wear monk's robes.) Then, during the winter, which was very severe, we all enjoyed playing in the snow. My elder sister and my mother were particularly enthusiastic participants in snowball fights, despite their age.

A more serious form of recreation was trekking in the nearby

Dhauladar Range, whose highest mountain reaches to over seventeen thousand feet. I have always loved mountains. On one occasion, I climbed to a great height with a party consisting of my Tibetan bodyguards. At the top, we were all extremely tired, so I suggested we stop for some moments' rest. As we sat breathlessly admiring the beautiful view, I noticed that we were being watched from a distance by one of the mountain dwellers native to the area: a small, dark-skinned, rather furtive-looking man. He stood staring at us for a few minutes, then suddenly sat down on what looked like a small piece of wood and slid at great speed down the side of the mountain. I looked on fascinated as he disappeared into a speck thousands of feet below. I suggested we try his method of descent.

Someone produced a rope and all ten of us joined ourselves together with it. Then we all did as our silent friend had done and sat either on pieces of wood or flat rocks and sped off down the slope. It was great fun, if rather dangerous. There was much bumping and subsequent bruising as we slammed into one another in a whoosh of streaming snow. Luckily no one was hurt, but thereafter I noticed a certain reluctance on the part of many of my attendants to venture beyond our base-camps. My bodyguards in particular showed great hesitation whenever I announced a new expedition.

One other spare-time activity during this early period was my work with David Howarth, an English writer, on a book, *My Land and My People*, in which I gave a first account of my life.

In 1961, the Government published a synopsis of a Draft Constitution of Tibet. All members of the Tibetan population were invited to submit comments and criticisms. There were plenty of these. Mainly they referred to the important clause relating to the office of Dalai Lama. As a principal means of formalising the move away from theocracy to full democracy, I made provision for the National Assembly to be able to remove the incumbent from office given a two-thirds majority in favour. Unfortunately, the thought that the Dalai Lama could be deposed flabbergasted many Tibetans. I had to explain that democracy is very much in keeping with Buddhist principles and, somewhat autocratically perhaps, insisted that the clause be left in.

During the early part of that year, in addition to visiting the road gangs again, I paid my first visit to the new settlement at Bylakuppe. On arrival, I found the settlers all to be very dark and thin. I saw immediately why they had been so pessimistic. The camp consisted of nothing but a few tents on the edge of a forest and, although the countryside was just as beautiful as I remembered it from my pilgrimage, the land itself did not look promising. Moreover, the heat from burning debris, combined with the heat of the sun, was almost unbearable.

The settlers had made a special tent for me with bamboo walls and a canvas roof. But even though it was well made, it was no proof at all against the terrible dust thrown up by the clearing process. Every day, a thick cloud of smoke and soot hung over the whole area. At night it would settle slowly, penetrating every tiny opening, so that in the morning you woke covered in a fine layer of powder. Because of these conditions, morale was very low. Yet there was not much I could do save give these pioneers every encouragement. I told them that we must not give up hope and assured them, hardly believing it myself, that in time we would be prosperous once more. I promised them that we would prevail. Fortunately, they believed every word I said and sure enough, little by little, their situation was transformed.

Thanks to the generosity of several Indian states, we were able, during the early 1960s, to establish over twenty settlements, gradually taking people off the roads, so that today there are only a few hundred, out of the present total of over 100,000 refugees, who are still making their living in road camps. And now it is of their own free will.

Because nearly half of the land given to us was situated in southern India, where the climate is considerably hotter than in the north, I stipulated that only the strongest should be sent in the early stages. Nevertheless, the death toll from sunstroke and heat exhaustion was at times so high that I wondered whether I had been right to accept land in the tropics. Yet, I was certain that, eventually, my people would learn to adapt. Just as they had faith in me, I had faith in them.

Often I had to console the refugees in their sadness when I visited these camps. The thought of being so far from home and with no prospect of seeing ice or snow, let alone our beloved mountains, was hard for them to bear. I tried to take their minds off the past. Instead, I told them that the future of Tibet depended on us refugees. If we wanted to preserve our culture and way of life, the only way to do so was by building strong communities. I spoke too of the importance of education and even of the significance of the institution of marriage. Although it was not really a proper thing for a monk to advise, I told the women that wherever possible they should marry Tibetan men so that the children they bore would be Tibetans too.

The majority of the settlements were begun between 1960 and 1965. I visited them all as often as I could over this period. Although I never entertained thoughts of failure, there were moments when our problems seemed insurmountable. At Band-hara in Maharashtra state, for example, the first batch of settlers went in spring, just before the start of the hot season. Within a matter of weeks, a hundred (that is, a fifth) of them had died from the heat. When I visited them for the first time, they came to me with tears in their eyes and begged to be evacuated to a cooler place. I could do nothing other than explain to them that their arrival had been badly timed but that the worst was now certainly over. They should therefore learn to adopt the ways of the natives and see whether they couldn't make the best of the situation. I urged them to try for one more year. If they could not make a success of the place by the time I returned the following winter, then I promised to have them moved.

As it turned out, things went well from then on. Twelve months later I went back and found the settlers beginning to prosper. 'So you're not all dead!' I said when I met the camp leaders. They laughed and replied that everything had happened just as I said it would. However, I must add that, although this particular community has since become quite successful, it proved impossible to attract more than 700-odd settlers, due to the heat problem. As at Bylakuppe, we were given 3,000 acres of land on the basis of one acre per settler. But because of the small number who arrived we forfeited the remaining 2,300 acres, which were made over to some other refugees – though they did not last long either.

One of the great difficulties of the resettlement programme was that whilst we were able to foresee many of the obstacles before they arose, there were some that took us completely by surprise. At one place, for example, great difficulties were experienced as a result of wild boars and elephants straying on to the land. Not only did they destroy the crops, but they stampeded from time to time, knocking down several huts and killing a number of people.

I remember one old lama who lived there asking me to pray for their protection, but using the Sanskrit term *hathi* for elephant. It means, literally, precious creature and refers to the mythological elephants which symbolise charity. I knew precisely what he meant, but I was very surprised to hear the word used in this way. I suppose the monk had expected real elephants to be benevolent animals.

As it happened, many years later, whilst on a trip to Switzerland, I was on a tour of inspection at a farm where I was shown some electric fencing. Much to the surprise of my guide, I asked him whether he thought that this could deter elephants. He said that if the voltage were turned up sufficiently, he did not see why not. So I arranged for a batch to be sent out to the settlement in question.

Not all our problems were practical, however. At times, our culture has made it difficult for us Tibetans to adapt to new conditions. On that first visit to Bylakuppe, I well remember the settlers being very concerned that the burning they were having to carry out to clear the land was causing the death of innumerable small creatures and insects. For Buddhists, this was a terrible thing to be doing, since we believe that all life, not just human life, is sacred. Several of the refugees even came up to me and suggested that the work should be stopped.

A few of the projects set up with the assistance of the overseas aid agencies failed for similar reasons. For example, all attempts to found poultry farms and piggeries have been unsuccessful. Even in their reduced circumstances, Tibetans have shown themselves unwilling to become involved in animal production for food. This has given rise to a certain amount of sarcasm on the part of some foreigners, who point out the anomaly between Tibetans' willingness to eat meat and their disinclination to provide it for themselves.

That said, the majority of projects undertaken with the help of these organisations have succeeded very well and our friends have been overjoyed at the positive results.

These experiences of support, freely given by people from the industrially advanced nations, have confirmed my basic belief in what I call Universal Responsibility. It seems to me to be the key to human development. Without such a sense of Universal Responsibility, there can be only unequal development in the world. The more people come to realise that we do not live on this planet of ours in isolation – that ultimately we are all brothers and sisters – the more likely is progress for all humankind, rather than for just parts of it.

Some of the people who came from overseas and gave their lives to the refugees stand out. One of these was Maurice Friedmann, a Jew from Poland. I met him for the first time in 1956, together with Uma Devi, a painter friend of his, also Polish. They had both settled (independently) on the sub-continent to pursue the Indian way of life. When we came into exile, they were amongst the very first people to offer their assistance.

Friedmann, who was quite old by this time, was in poor physical condition. He had a permanent stoop and thick spectacles which betrayed his failing sight, yet he had the most piercing blue eyes and an extremely sharp brain. He could be exasperating at times: he would argue stubbornly in favour of projects which were completely impossible. But on the whole, the advice he gave, especially in regard to the establishment of children's homes, was invaluable. Uma Devi, who was more spiritually inclined than

Friedmann, but similarly oldish, also devoted the rest of her life to working on behalf of my people.

Another important character was Mr Luthi, who worked for the Swiss Red Cross. *Pala* ('Papa' in Tibetan), as he was known, was a man of tremendous zeal and energy, a real leader, who drove the people under him extremely hard. The habitually easy-going Tibetans found him quite difficult to take and I know there was a certain amount of grumbling about his methods, but in reality he was well-loved by all. I cherish his memory, and that of others like him, who worked so hard and so selflessly for my people.

For us Tibetan refugees, one significant event during the early 1960s was the Sino–Indian War of 1962. Naturally, I was extremely sad when the fighting began, but it was a sadness tinged with fear. At that time, the resettlement process was still in its earliest stage. Several of the road camps were situated perilously close to where the fighting took place, in Ladakh and NEFA, with the result that they were forced to close. Some of my people thus became refugees a second time. What made the whole experience even sadder for us was the spectacle of our saviours, the Indians, being humiliated by Chinese soldiers stationed on Tibetan soil.

Mercifully, it was a short war, although at the end of it there were many dead on both sides for no obvious gain to either. Reflecting on his China policy, Nehru was forced to state that India had been 'living in a fool's paradise of our own making'. All his life, he had dreamed of a free Asia, in which every country would coexist in harmony. Now Panch Sheel was shown to be an empty vessel, less than a decade after it had been signed and despite everything that this most humane man had done to preserve it.

I remained in contact with Pandit Nehru right up to his death in 1964. He himself continued to take a close interest in the plight of the Tibetan refugees, especially the children whose education he always held to be of the greatest importance. Many people say that the Sino–Indian War broke his spirit. I think they may be right. I saw him for the last time in May of that year. As I entered his room, I sensed that he was in a state of deep mental shock. He had just suffered a stroke and was very weak and haggard-looking, propped up in an armchair with pillows under each arm. As well as obvious signs of acute physical discomfort, I also noticed indications of intense mental strain in him. Our meeting was short and I left with a heavy heart.

Later that same day he left to go to Dehra Dun, and I went to bid him farewell at the airport. When I got there, I happened to see Indira Gandhi, his daughter, whom I had come to know well over the years since I first met her when she accompanied her father to Peking in 1954 (I had at first been under the impression that she was his wife). I told her how sorry I was to find her father in such poor health. I went on to say that I feared I had seen him for the last time.

As it turned out I was right, for within less than a week he was dead. Unfortunately, I was unable to attend his cremation. Instead, I participated in the scattering of his ashes at the confluence of the three rivers in Allahabad. This was a great honour for me, as it made me feel close to his family. One of its members that I saw there was Indira. Sometime after the ceremony, she came up to me and, looking straight into my eyes, said, 'You knew.'

CHAPTER TEN

A Wolf in Monk's Robes

○

TSERING DOLMA also died in 1964. Her work was taken over by Jetsun Pema, our younger sister, who has shown similar courage and determination. Today, the nursery thrives as part of the Tibetan Children's Village (TCV) in Dharamsala.

The TCV, which has many branches throughout the settlements, today houses and educates more than six thousand children in all, around fifteen hundred of them at Dharamsala. Although most of the initial funding was by the Indian Government, much of the expense is now met by the charity SOS International. Thirty years on, it is pleasing to see the results of our efforts in the field of education. Presently, more than two thousand refugee children have graduated from schools of higher education – most of them in India, but a growing number in the West. Throughout this time I have taken a close interest in our education programme, always mindful of Nehru's remark about children being our most precious resource.

In those early days, these schools were nothing more than dilapidated buildings where Indian teachers taught very diverse groups of children. Now, we have a healthy number of qualified Tibetan staff. But still there are considerable numbers of Indian educators involved. To these men and women, and their predecessors, I wish to offer my deepest thanks. I cannot adequately express the gratitude I feel for the many who have so freely devoted much of their lives to the service of my people, often in very poor conditions and in remote areas.

On the negative side, it is unfortunately the case that many children do not finish their education, especially girls. This is sometimes due to their own disinclination, sometimes to their parents' shortsightedness. Whenever I have the opportunity, and it is appropriate, I tell parents that they have a great responsibility not to use their children's small hands for their own short-term benefit. Otherwise, there is a danger of producing semi-educated children, who see the colourful opportunities of life but, because of their lack of education, are not equipped to grasp them. This can result in dissatisfaction and even greed.

The man who succeeded Pandit Nehru as Prime Minister of India was Lal Bahadur Shastri. Despite his being in power for less than three years, I met him quite a number of times and grew to respect him very much. Like Nehru before him, Shastri was a great friend of the Tibetan refugees. Even more than Nehru, however, he was also a political ally.

In autumn 1965, Tibet was discussed at the United Nations once more, thanks to a draft resolution submitted by Thailand, the Philippines, Malta, Ireland, Malaysia, Nicaragua and El Salvador. On this occasion India, at Shastri's insistence, voted in favour of Tibet. During his tenure of office, it began to look as if the new Indian Government might even recognise the Tibetan Government in Exile. But sadly, the Prime Minister did not live long. In the meantime, India went to war once more, this time with Pakistan. Fighting broke out on 1 September 1965.

Because Dharamsala lies less than a hundred miles from the Indo–Pakistan border, I was able to see at first hand the tragic effects of battle. Not long after the fighting had begun, I left home for one of my frequent visits to the settlements in the south. It was night and there was a total blackout in force. We were compelled to drive the three hours to Pathankot railway station without headlights. The only other traffic on the road was military and I remember thinking that it is a very sad state of affairs when ordinary citizens are forced into hiding and the 'defence forces' are called forward. In reality, of course, these are the same people – human beings like myself.

When at last we reached the station, after a difficult journey, I could hear the heavy shelling of Pathankot airport in the near distance. At one point, I heard jets shrieking overhead and then, moments later, the luminous stutter of anti-aircraft tracers spat up into the sky. The noise was terrifying and I was quite frightened, though I am pleased to say that I was not the only one. I have never been on a train that pulled out of a station as fast as ours did that night!

On arrival in the south, I went first to Bylakuppe, where I saw the original refugee settlement, reaching it on 10 September. By now it was home to more than 3,200 people. There was also permanent housing, each building being constructed of brick and roofed with local tiles, and work on the drilling of wells and cutting down of trees was completed. According to the original plan, agricultural work was now beginning in earnest. Each person had been given nominal ownership of one acre of land, though really it was farmed co-operatively, with a small proportion kept over for private kitchen gardens which produced seasonal fruits and vegetables. The main crops were to be rice, maize and *ragi* (millet). I was very happy to see such progress. It confirmed my belief in the tremendous power of a positive outlook when coupled with great determination.

Overall, I found the situation considerably improved. No longer did I have to confront people who were on the edge of despair. Nor did I have to make promises of future prosperity which I myself could hardly believe. But although there were signs that their tenacity was paying off, the life of the settlers was still extremely hard.

In the earliest days of planning the resettlement programme with the Indian Government, we had hoped that the refugees would be self-sufficient within five years. Thereafter, it was intended that the Tibetans would begin to contribute to India's economy by raising an agricultural surplus which could then be sold. However, our optimism failed fully to acknowledge that the workforce was completely untrained. Few of the people who worked on the land had any knowledge of farming. Former tradesmen, monks, soldiers, nomads and simple villagers who knew nothing were all pitched into this new enterprise, regardless. And of course, agriculture in the Indian tropics is a very different proposition from agriculture at Tibet's high altitudes. So even those who did know something about it had to learn entirely new methods, from working with bullocks to using and maintaining tractors. Thus, even after almost five years, conditions in the camps were still very primitive.

Yet, looking back, I see that in some ways the mid-1960s were a high point in the Tibetan resettlement programme: the majority of the necessary land clearance had been done, most of the refugees had access to basic medical attention, courtesy of the International Red Cross and others – and the farm machinery was still fairly new, whereas today it is old and in great need of replacement.

On this occasion in 1965, I remained for a week or ten days at Bylakuppe, after which I took the opportunity to visit Mysore, Ootamacund and Madras by road before proceeding to Trivandrum, capital of Kerala, India's most literate state. I was invited to reside with the Governor. In the end, my stay turned out to be one of several weeks on account of the war in the north, which continued to look very dangerous: two bombs had already fallen on Dharamsala. However, the time was not wasted.

It so happened that my room in the Rajbhavan, the Governor's residence, looked directly on to the kitchens opposite. One day I chanced to see the slaughter of a chicken, which was subsequently served up for lunch; as it was having its neck wrung, I thought of how much suffering the poor creature was enduring. The realisation filled me with remorse and I decided it was time to become a vegetarian. As I have already mentioned, Tibetans are not, as a rule, vegetarians, because in Tibet vegetables are often scarce and meat forms a large part of the staple diet. Nevertheless, according to some *Mahayana* texts, monks and nuns should really be vegetarians.

To check my resolve, I had the food sent in to me. When it arrived, I looked at it very carefully. The chicken had been cooked in the English style, with onions and gravy; it smelled delicious. But I had no difficulty refusing it. From that moment on, I adhered minutely to the vegetarian rule and, in addition to abstaining from meat, ate neither fish nor eggs.

This new regime suited me well and I was very contented; I felt a sense of fulfilment from a strict interpretation of the rule. Back in 1954, in Peking, I had discussed the subject of vegetarianism with Chou En-lai and another politician at a banquet. This other man claimed to be vegetarian, yet he was eating eggs. I questioned this and argued that because chickens come from eggs, eggs could not be considered to be vegetarian food. We disagreed quite strongly – at least until Chou brought the discussion to a diplomatic close.

The war with Pakistan ended on 10 January 1966. But with this happy event came bad news: the death of Prime Minister Shastri in Tashkent, where he had gone to negotiate a settlement with the Pakistani President, Ayub Khan. He passed away within a few hours of signing the peace treaty.

Lal Bahadur Shastri has left a powerful impression on my memory for, although he was a small, rather weak and ineffectual-looking man, he had a powerful mind and spirit. Despite his frail appearance, he was an outstanding leader. Unlike so many people who hold positions of great responsibility, he was bold and decisive: he did not allow events to carry him along, but did his best to direct them.

Shortly after, I was invited to attend the cremation, which I did on my way back home from Trivandrum. It was a sorrowful affair, particularly as it was the first time in my life that I had seen a dead body from close up – even though as a Buddhist I visualise death every day. I remember looking at his inert form lying on top of the funeral pyre and recalling all his mannerisms and the little bits of personal information he had shared with me. He himself was a strict vegetarian, he had told me, because as a young schoolboy he had once chased a wounded pigeon round and round until it died of exhaustion. He was so horrified at what he had done that he vowed never to eat another living creature. So not only had India lost one of her finest politicians, not only had the world lost an enlightened leader, but mankind had lost a genuinely compassionate spirit.

After paying my final respects to the late Prime Minister, I returned to Dharamsala, but not before visiting some of the hospitals in Delhi containing casualties from the war. Most of those that I saw were officers. Many were in great pain and enduring terrible hardship. As I walked between the rows of beds, amongst sobbing family members of the wounded, I thought to myself that this was the only real result of war: tremendous human suffering. Anything else that might arise from conflict could just as easily be brought about by peaceful means. It was small consolation to realise that the people in this hospital were being well looked after: many of those who had been caught up in the struggle would not have the benefit of such good facilities.

A fortnight later, Indira Gandhi was sworn in as Prime Minister of India. Because I had seen her practically every time I saw her father, I already felt quite close to her. I have reason to believe that she felt quite close to me too. More than once she took me into her confidence about people and things that were causing her trouble. And for my part, I considered that I knew her well enough to be able to remind her, on one occasion towards the end of her first administration, that it is vital for a leader to keep in touch with the common people.

I myself had learned at an early age that anyone who wishes to lead must remain close to the common people. Otherwise, it is all too easy to be misled by advisors and officials and others around you who, for reasons of their own, might wish to prevent you from seeing things clearly.

As with each of India's Prime Ministers, I owe a great debt of gratitude to Indira Gandhi for her warm support of the Tibetan refugees. From its inception, she was a member of the Tibetan Homes Foundation based in Mussoorie and was particularly helpful in the field of education. She had her father's vision when it came to the importance of schooling. And although much strong language was used to denounce her after the Emergency, with some people even calling her a dictator, I note that she relinquished power quite gracefully when the electorate delivered its verdict in March 1977. To me that was a wonderful example of democracy in action: though there was much conflict both within Parliament and without, when the moment came for her to leave, she did so without fuss. I remember thinking the same about President Nixon. So often a change of leadership is taken as a cue for blood-letting. It is a sign of a truly civilised country when parliamentary procedure triumphs over personal interest.

The People's Republic of China presented a very different picture of domestic politics at this time. From the mid-1960s until Mao's death in 1976, the country, together with its colonies, endured a series of bloody and violent upheavals. Many years passed before a true picture of the so-called Cultural Revolution began to emerge. It turned out that not only was this a period of aimless madness, but the behaviour of Chiang Ching, Mao's wife, resembled that of an Empress. At the same time, I realised that the Communist leaders, who at first I had thought of as having a single mind inhabiting their different bodies, were all at each other's throats.

Then, however, it was not possible to do more than guess at the extent of the turmoil. Along with many Tibetans I realised that terrible things were happening in our beloved homeland. But communications had dried up entirely. Our only sources of news were individual Nepalese traders who were occasionally allowed over the border. However, such information as they were able to give us was scant and invariably outdated. For example, it was not until over a year later that I learned of a large-scale revolt that took place in several different parts of Tibet during 1969. According to some reports, even more people were killed during the reprisals that followed than in 1959.

We know now that many such outbreaks of unrest occurred. Of course, I had no direct contact with the leaders in Peking who, at this time, began to refer to me as the 'wolf in monk's robes'. I became the focus of the Chinese Government's bile and was regularly denounced in Lhasa as someone who merely posed as a religious leader. In reality, the Chinese said, I was a thief, a murderer and a rapist. They also suggested that I performed certain quite surprising sexual services for Mrs Gandhi!

Thus, for almost fifteen years, the Tibetan refugees entered a period of darkness. The prospect of returning to our homeland seemed further off then than when we had first come into exile. But of course night is the time for regeneration and during these years the resettlement programme was brought to fruition. Gradually, more and more people were taken off the roads and put into the new settlements around India. Also, a few of the refugees left India to found small communities around the world. At the time of writing, there are approximately 1,200 spread throughout Canada and the United States (in equal proportions), some 2,000 in Switzerland, 100 in Great Britain, and a handful in almost every other European country, including one young family in Ireland.

In tandem with this second wave of resettlement, the Tibetan Government in Exile opened offices in several countries overseas. The first of these was in Kathmandu, the second in New York, followed by Zurich, Tokyo, London and Washington respectively. As well as looking after the interests of Tibetans living in these countries, the Offices of Tibet also do what they can to disseminate information about our country, culture, history and way of life both in exile and at home.

In 1968, I made plans to move from Swarg Ashram, my home for eight years, into a small house called Bryn Cottage. The building itself was no bigger than the last one, but it had the advantage of a newly constructed compound, which housed the Private Office and the Indian Security Office, along with an audience-room and an office for myself. The Tibetan Government in Exile had grown to be an organisation several hundred strong, and most of them were now moved into a complex of offices some distance away. At the same time as this reorganisation was taking place, my mother also moved to a new house, Kashmir Cottage (thought not very willingly at first), enabling me to live a truly monastic life once more.

Shortly after moving to Bryn Cottage, I was able to refound

Namgyal monastery, whose monks were previously living in a small house above Swarg Ashram. Today it occupies a building not far from my own residence. A little later, in 1970, work was also completed on a new temple, the Tsuglakhang. This meant that I now had the opportunity to take part in the various ceremonies of the traditional Tibetan calendar in an appropriate setting. Today, adjacent to the buildings at Namgyal, is housed the School of Buddhist Dialectics, which helps to keep alive the art of debating within our monastic community. Most afternoons, the courtyard outside the temple is now full of young monks in maroon robes clapping their hands and shaking their heads and laughing as they practise for their examinations.

In 1963, I had called a meeting of all heads of the different traditions, together with representatives of the Bon religion. We discussed our common difficulties and strategies for overcoming them in order to preserve and propagate the different aspects of our Tibetan Buddhist culture. At the end of several days, I was satisfied that, if we could only provide ourselves with the right facilities, our religion would survive. And now, soon after reinaugurating my own monastery, I re-established Ganden, Drepung and Sera, in the southern state of Karnataka, initially with a complement of 1,300 monks – the survivors from Buxa Duar.

Today, as we begin our fourth decade in exile, there is a thriving monastic community over six thousand strong. I would even go so far as to say that we have too many monks: after all, it is the quality and dedication of these people that counts, not their numbers.

Another cultural enterprise begun towards the end of the 1960s was the Library of Tibetan Works and Archives, which not only contains more than forty thousand original Tibetan volumes but is also involved in publishing both English-language and Tibetan books. During 1990, it published its 200th English title. The Library building is constructed in traditional Tibetan style and, besides housing literature, also contains a museum that is stocked with many items brought to India by the refugees. Of the few possessions that people were able to bring with them, a lot took *thangkas*, books of scripture and other religious artefacts. Many of these they characteristically offered to the Dalai Lama. I in turn passed items on to these organisations.

Just before actually moving in to Bryn Cottage, I became very ill for a number of weeks. On returning to Dharamsala in early 1966, after the cessation of conflict between India and Pakistan, I had taken enthusiastically to my new, vegetarian diet. Unfortunately, there are few dishes in Tibetan cuisine that do not use meat and it was some time before the cooks learned how to make them taste good without it. But eventually they succeeded and began to produce delicious meals. I felt really well on them. Meanwhile, several Indian friends told me of the importance of supplementing my diet with plenty of milk and different kinds of nuts. I followed this advice faithfully – with the result that after twenty months I contracted a severe case of jaundice.

On the first day, I vomited a great deal. Thereafter, I lost my appetite completely for two or three weeks, and fell into a state of utter exhaustion. To move at all required tremendous effort. On top of this, my skin turned bright yellow. I looked like the Buddha himself! Some people used to say that the Dalai Lama lives as a prisoner in a golden cage: on this occasion, I was golden-bodied too.

Eventually the illness, which turned out to be Hepatitis B, cleared up, but not before I had consumed large quantities of Tibetan medicine (about which I shall say more in a later chapter). As soon as I began once more to take an interest in eating, I was instructed by my doctors that not only must I take less greasy food, cut out nuts and reduce my consumption of milk, but also I must start eating meat again. They were very much afraid that the illness had caused permanent damage to my liver and were of the opinion that, as a result, my life has probably been shortened. A number of Indian doctors I consulted were of the same opinion, so reluctantly I returned to being non-vegetarian. Today, I eat meat except on special occasions required by my spiritual practice.

The same is true for a number of Tibetans who followed my example and suffered a similar fate.

From the start, I was very happy in my new home. Like Swarg Ashram, the house was originally built by the British and stands at the top of a hill in a small garden of its own, surrounded by trees. It has a fine view both of the Dhauladar mountain range and of the valley, in which lies Dharamsala itself. Apart from having sufficient space just outside to address over a thousand people, its main attraction for me is the garden. I set to work on it immediately and planted many different types of fruit trees and flowers. This I did with my own hands: gardening is one of my great joys. Sadly, few of the trees did well and they produce rather poor, bitter fruit, but I took consolation from the great variety of animals, and particularly birds, that came to visit.

I enjoy watching wildlife even more than gardening. For this purpose, I constructed a bird table just outside my study window. It is surrounded by wire and netting to keep out the larger birds and birds of prey, which tend to scare off their smaller brethren. This is not always sufficient to keep them away, however. Occasionally I am compelled to take out one of the air guns that I acquired shortly after arriving in India, in order to discipline these fat, greedy trespassers. Having spent a great deal of time as a child at the Norbulingka practising with the Thirteenth's old air rifle, I am quite a good shot. Of course, I never kill them. My intention is only to inflict a measure of pain in order to teach a lesson.

My days at Bryn Cottage were taken up in much the same way as before. Each winter I toured the refugee settlements, and from time to time I gave teachings. I also continued my religious studies. In addition, I began to try to learn something about Western thought, particularly in the fields of science, astronomy and philosophy. And in my spare moments, I rediscovered my old enthusiasm for photography. As a thirteen or fourteen year old, I had acquired my first box camera through the good offices of Serkon Rinpoché, the lame *tsenshap*.

At first, I entrusted the exposed films to him for development. He then pretended that the films were his own (to save me from embarrassment if I had photographed anything that might be considered unworthy of the Dalai Lama) and took them to a merchant. They were then processed in India. This procedure always caused him anxiety – because if my subject matter really had been unsuitable, he would have had to take responsibility! Later on though, I constructed a darkroom at the Norbulingka and, from Jigme Taring, one of my officials, learned how to do this work myself.

Another hobby that I resumed after moving to my new home was that of mending watches. Having more space than before, I was able to set aside a room as a workshop, for which I acquired a proper set of tools. For as long as I can remember, I have been fascinated by watches and rosaries, a facet of character that I share with the Thirteenth Dalai Lama. Often, when I look at our differences in nature, I think that it is not possible that I am his reincarnation. But considering our interest in watches and rosaries, I realise that of course I must be!

When I was very young, I carried my predecessor's pocket-watch. But what I always longed for was a wrist-watch – although some people advised me against them. As soon as I was old enough to convince Serkon Rinpoché that I needed them, I arranged for him to buy me a Rolex and an Omega from the Lhasa market. Incredible as it may seem, even in those far off days before the Chinese had arrived to civilise us, it was possible to buy Swiss watches in Lhasa. In fact, there were few things that you could not buy from the market – everything from Marmite and Yardley's soap from England to last month's edition of *Life* magazine were quite easily obtainable.

Needless to say, the first thing I did with my latest acquisitions was take them apart. When I first saw the tiny pieces that comprised the mechanism, I regretted my haste. But it did not take me long to put them back together again or to learn how to slow them down and speed them up. So I was delighted when I was finally able to have a proper workshop to do these things. I repaired quite a few apparently hopeless cases for family and friends and still to this day like to keep my tools handy, although I no longer have time to do very much of this work. Besides, so many watches that are made today are impossible to open without scratching. I fear that I have disappointed a number of people whose timepieces have been returned to them in full working order, but in less than pristine condition.

That said, I have managed more or less to keep up with modern technology, although, of course, digital watches are outside my scope. I need admit only to a couple of failures. One of these was the beautiful, gold Patek Philippe sent to me as a gift by President Roosevelt. With separate movements for the second hand and date, it was beyond me – and beyond the professional repairers I sent it to as well. It was not until I took it personally to the manufacturers whilst on a visit to Switzerland a few years ago that anyone has succeeded in getting it to run properly. Fortunately, it was in the hands of an Indian repairer at the time of my escape from Lhasa. Another failure was a watch belonging to a member of my Government: I regret to say that I had to send it back in an envelope – in pieces.

At this point I can perhaps mention the three cats which I have owned whilst in India. The first of them joined my household towards the end of the 1960s. It was a black-and-white spotted female called Tsering, who had many good points, amongst which was her friendliness. I have few rules for any creature that joins my household, other than that they are compelled to be monks and nuns, but Tsering had one major failing which I, as a Buddhist, could not tolerate: she was unable to resist chasing mice. I frequently had to discipline her for this. It was on one of these occasions that I regret to say she met her end. I caught her in the very act of killing a mouse inside my house. When I shouted at her, she ran to the top of a curtain, where she suddenly lost her grip, fell to the ground and was mortally wounded. Despite all the attention and care I could give her, she did not recover and died within a few days.

Not long afterwards, however, I discovered a small kitten in the garden, which had apparently been abandoned by its mother. I picked it up and noticed that its hind legs were crippled in just the same way as Tsering's were when she died. I took this creature into my house and looked after it until eventually it was able to walk. Like Tsering, she was also female, but very beautiful and even more gentle. She also got along very well with the two dogs, particularly Sangye, against whose furry chest she liked to lie.

When she in her turn died, after both dogs, I decided against having any more pets. As my Senior Tutor, Ling Rinpoché, himself a great animal lover, had once said, 'Pets are in the end only an extra source of anxiety to their owners.' Besides, from the Buddhist point of view, it is not enough to be thinking and caring about only one or two animals when all sentient beings are in need of your thoughts and prayers.

However, during the winter of 1988, I happened to notice a sick kitten with its mother in the kitchens opposite the front entrance to my house. I took her into my care. To my surprise, I found that she too was crippled, just as her two predecessors had been. So I fed her with Tibetan medicine and milk from a pipette until she was strong enough to be able to look after herself, and she has now joined my household. At the time of writing, she does not yet have a name: that will come in due course. In the meantime, she has proved herself to be a very lively individual and very curious. Whenever I have a visitor to the house, she invariably comes to inspect them. So far she is quite well behaved as regards chasing other creatures, though she is not above helping herself to food from my table if the opportunity arises.

One observation about animals I have is that, even as pets and despite having all facilities, they tend to run away, given the chance. This reinforces my belief that the desire for freedom is fundamental to all living beings.

To me, one of the most important aspects of my thirty-one years in exile has been my meetings with people from all walks of life. Thanks to India being a free country, there has been no restriction on who I am permitted to see. On occasion, I have had the good fortune to welcome some truly remarkable people. Sometimes, though, I also receive people who are quite sick, even mentally disturbed. But mostly, those that I see are ordinary men and women.

Whenever I do meet people, my aim is to help in any way that I can, and also to learn what I can.

Infrequently, these audiences are awkward in some way, but in every case that I can recall, I have parted on friendly terms with all who have come to visit. I believe that this has been possible by always having the same motivation of sincerity.

Especially, I enjoy meeting men and women from varied backgrounds, including some from different religious traditions. One famous example was J. Krishnamurti. I found him to be an impressive person, with a sharp mind and considerable learning. Although he had a gentle appearance, he had very clear-cut views about life and its meaning. Subsequently, I have also met many followers of his who have derived much benefit from his teachings.

One of my happiest memories of this time is the occasion when I was fortunate enough to receive a visit from Father Thomas Merton, the American Trappist monk. He came to Dharamsala in November 1968, just a few weeks before his tragic death in Thailand. We met on three consecutive days, for two hours at a time. Merton was a well-built man of medium height, with even less hair than me, though that was not because his head was shaved as mine is. He had big boots and wore a thick leather belt round the middle of his heavy, white cassock. But more striking than his outward appearance, which was memorable in itself, was the inner life that he manifested. I could see he was a truly humble and deeply spiritual man. This was the first time that I had been struck by such a feeling of spirituality in anyone who professed Christianity. Since then, I have come across others with similar qualities, but it was Merton who introduced me to the real meaning of the word 'Christian'.

Our meetings were conducted in a very pleasant atmosphere. Merton was both humorous and well informed. I called him a Catholic *geshe*. We talked about intellectual and spiritual matters that were of mutual interest and exchanged information about monasticism. I was keen to learn all that I could about the monastic tradition in the West. He told me a number of things that surprised me, notably that Christian practitioners of meditation do not adopt any particular physical position when they meditate. According to my understanding, position and even breathing are vital. We also discussed the vows taken by Christian monks and nuns.

For his part, Merton wanted to know all he could about the Bodhisattva ideal. He also hoped to meet a teacher who could introduce him to Tantrism. Altogether, it was a most useful exchange – not least because I discovered from it that there are many similarities between Buddhism and Catholicism. So I was extremely sad to hear of his sudden death. Merton acted as a strong bridge between our two very different religious traditions. Above all, he helped me to realise that every major religion, with its teaching of love and compassion, can produce good human beings.

Since my meeting with Father Thomas Merton, I have had considerable contact with other Christians. On my visits to Europe, I have visited monasteries in a number of different countries and, on each occasion, have been very impressed with what I have seen. The monks that I have met have shown a devotion to their calling of which I am quite envious. Although they are comparatively few in number, I have the impression that their quality and dedication are very high. Conversely, we Tibetans, even in exile, have a very large number of monks – four or five per cent of the exile population. Yet there is not always the same degree of dedication.

I am also very impressed with the practical work of Christians of all denominations through charitable organisations dedicated to health and education. There are many wonderful examples of these in India. This is one area where we can learn from our Christian brothers and sisters: it would be very useful if Buddhists could make a similar contribution to society. I feel that Buddhist monks and nuns tend to talk a great deal about compassion without doing much about it. On several occasions, I have discussed this matter with Tibetans as well as other Buddhists and am actively encouraging the setting up of similar organisations. However, if it is true that we can learn from Christians, I also feel that they could learn from us. For example, the techniques we have developed for meditation and one-pointed concentration of the mind might well help them in other areas of the religious life.

The end of the 1960s coincided with the first signs that my dream of resettling all 100,000 Tibetan exiles in India, Nepal and Bhutan could be achieved. So although the little news I heard from Tibet was very depressing, I looked forward to the future with a sense of real and well-founded optimism. However, two series of events outside my direct control reminded me of just how precarious our position was.

The first of these concerned approximately four thousand refugees who had settled in Bhutan. The Kingdom of Bhutan is a remote country lying on the far eastern border of India, due south of U-Tsang, the central province of Tibet. Like Tibet, it is a land of majestic mountains and is home to a devoutly religious people who follow the same Buddhism as we do. Unlike Tibet, it is a full member of the United Nations.

The late King of Bhutan was very kind to the Tibetans who sought exile in his country and, with assistance from the Indian Government, he provided land and transport and helped to set up agricultural settlements for my people.

All went well to begin with, and the Tibetans were very happy. When I met with a group of them at the first *Kalachakra* initiation ceremony that I gave in Bodh Gaya in 1974, I was pleased to learn that they were doing well. They were full of praise for their hosts, and especially for the new king, Jigme Wangchuk, who had recently ascended the throne. He impressed everyone with his maturity in handling affairs of state. But only a few months later, matters took a turn for the worse. Twenty-two prominent members of the Tibetan community were arrested, tortured and thrown, without trial, into jail in Timphu, the capital. My personal representative, Lhading (a relation of the late king), was amongst them. I was deeply distressed at this news and felt that there should be a thorough investigation (though I did not believe the allegations of conspiracy levelled against these people). This did not happen and the true position never became clear. Eventually, I realised that these Tibetans were being used as scapegoats in an internal affair of the Bhutanese Government.

After this unfortunate occurrence, many of the refugees decided to leave Bhutan. But those who remained have since continued to live peacefully, despite there still being some suspicion and resentment against them, I believe. In any case, I am grateful to the Bhutanese people and Government for all they have done for my people and am certain that in the future our traditional friendly relations will be fully restored.

The other sad episode concerned the guerrillas, trained and equipped by the CIA, who continued their struggle to regain Tibetan freedom by violent means. On more than one occasion, I tried to discover detailed information about these operations from Gyalo Thondup and others, but I have never heard the full story. I do know, however, that in 1960 a guerrilla base was established in Mustang, an area which lay in the most remote northern region of Nepal, right on the border with Tibet. A force several thousand strong drawn from the exile population was assembled there (though only a small proportion actually received training from the Americans). Unfortunately, the logistics of this camp were not well planned. As a result, the would-be insurgents endured many difficulties, though of course nothing compared with the dangers faced by the many extraordinarily brave freedom fighters who carried on the struggle from inside Tibet itself.

When the base finally became operational, the guerrillas harassed the Chinese on a number of occasions and once managed to destroy a convoy. It was this raid which captured the document recording the 87,000 deaths in Lhasa during the period March 1959–September 1960. These successes had some positive result in that they boosted morale. But the fact that there was no consistent, effective follow-up probably only resulted in more suffering for the people of Tibet. Worse, these activities gave the Chinese Government the opportunity to blame the efforts of those seeking to regain Tibetan independence on the activities of foreign powers – whereas, of course, it was an entirely Tibetan initiative.

In the end, the Americans discontinued their backing for the guerrillas following their recognition of the Chinese Government in the 1970s – which indicates that their assistance had been a reflection of their anti-Communist policies rather than genuine support for the restoration of Tibetan independence.

The guerrillas, however, were determined to fight on. This caused the Chinese Government (who must have been considerably troubled by their activities) to demand that Nepal disarm the forces in Mustang, even though there must have been some arrangement between these Tibetans and the Nepalese Government. But when they tried to do so, the guerrillas refused, saying that they were determined to carry on even if it meant that they must now fight the Nepalese army as well.

Although I had always admired the determination of the guerrillas, I had never been in favour of their activities and now I realised that I must intervene. I knew that the only way I could hope to make an impression on them was by making a personal appeal. Accordingly, I instructed former *Kusun Depon* P. T. Takla to take a taped message to their leaders. In it, I said that it would be senseless to fight the Nepalese, not least because there were several thousand Tibetan refugees settled in Nepal who would also suffer if they did. Instead they ought to be grateful to the Nepalese Government. They should therefore lay down their arms and themselves settle peacefully. The Tibetan struggle needed a long-term approach.

Afterwards, P. T. Takla told me that many of the men felt that they had been betrayed – a few of their leaders actually cut their own throats rather than leave. I was distraught to hear this. Naturally, I had had mixed feelings about appealing to the freedom fighters. It seemed wrong in a way to challenge such courage, such loyalty and such love for Tibet, though I knew in my heart that it was the right thing to do.

The great majority of the guerrillas did put down their weapons.

But some of them, less than a hundred, ignored my plea, with the result that they were pursued by the Nepalese army as they crossed from one side of the border to the other. Finally, they were caught in an ambush and met the violent deaths they must have been expecting. Thus ended one of the saddest episodes in the history of the Tibetan diaspora.

CHAPTER ELEVEN

From East to West

○

I MADE my first journey outside India during the autumn of 1967, when I went to Japan and Thailand. Since then, I have travelled with increasing frequency – this despite the difficulties often imposed by my brothers and sisters in China. Unfortunately, although the great majority of my journeys overseas are entirely private (generally at the invitation of one of the Tibetan or Buddhist communities abroad), the Chinese always consider them to be political, and anyone who meets me is seen by the authorities in Peking to be making a political statement. For this reason, there have been times when leading public figures have been prevented from making my acquaintance for fear of incurring their government's or China's displeasure.

At the time of those first visits, the Vietnam War was at its height. I recall that at one point on the flight out, as we cruised at high altitude, I noticed another, larger aircraft climbing past us. I recognised it as a B-52 bomber. With great sorrow I realised that this plane must be about to shed its load not harmlessly over the sea but on to other human beings like myself. I was further dismayed to see that, even at 30,000 feet above the earth's surface, it is not possible to escape evidence of man's inhumanity to man.

On landing in Tokyo, I was pleased to find signs of man's better nature. The first thing I noticed was an extraordinary tidiness. Everything was far cleaner than I had ever seen before. I soon discovered that this emphasis on outward orderliness extended even to the food, which was always exquisitely presented. It seemed to me that according to Japanese sensibilities, its arrangement on the plate was considered to be of greater importance than the taste. Another thing that struck me immediately was the huge number of cars and trucks that plied their way up and down the city streets, transporting people and goods throughout the day and night. Seeing this impressed on me the tremendous potential for good of modern technology. I was particularly interested to find that, although Japan has achieved great material advancement, she has done so without losing sight of her traditional culture and values.

Whilst in Japan, I was very happy to see a number of young Tibetan students studying there. I was also glad to meet some Japanese who spoke Tibetan and had a good knowledge of my homeland. As recently as the time of the Thirteenth Dalai Lama, Japanese scholars had come to Tibet to study. So it was a pleasure to re-establish, albeit as a refugee, links between our two countries.

My impressions of Thailand were quite different. I found the people there wonderfully easy-going. This was in contrast to Japan, where even the waiters struck me as formal. That said, there are certain rules of etiquette to be observed in Thailand which I found distinctly difficult. According to Thai custom, the laity should always show respect for the *Sangha*, as Buddhist monasticism is properly known. However, it is considered entirely wrong for a monk to acknowledge such reverence, even when a person prostrates him or herself. I found this extremely hard to get used to. Under normal circumstances, I always try to return greetings. And whilst I did my best to restrain myself, I often found my hand behaving independently!

Visiting Thailand on a subsequent occasion, this tradition presented me with an interesting problem when I was invited to lunch with the King. Should I or should I not shake his hand? He might consider it unseemly for me to do so. Nobody was quite sure. In the event, he came forward and shook my hand warmly.

My only other difficulty in that country was the heat which, even more than in southern India, was stunning. That and the mosquitoes. Together they made sleeping very difficult. On the positive side, some of the senior monks I was privileged to meet were deeply impressive. As in Japan, there was much to discuss as our different traditions share many common practices – which helped me see that Buddhism in the Tibetan tradition is a very complete form of Buddhism.

In 1973, I made my first trip to Europe and Scandinavia. It lasted for over six weeks and took in eleven countries. By the end, I was completely exhausted. Yet I was exhilarated to have had the opportunity of seeing so many new places and of meeting so many new people. I was also pleased to renew some old acquaintances. It was especially good to see Heinrich Harrer once more. He was his usual, jovial self and his sense of humour was as coarse and earthy as ever. He had been to Dharamsala once, but it was many years since I had last seen him, and his yellow hair, about which I had always teased him when I was a boy, was now very grey. Otherwise, the years had not changed him much. His strong mountaineer's fingers still captivated me and, although he had collected even more injuries than when I knew him last, thanks to an accident whilst leading an expedition in New Guinea, he was altogether very full of himself.

My first stop was Rome, where I met His Holiness the Pope. As the aircraft came in to land, I was very curious to see whether the landscape offered any indications of the tremendous differences that are supposed to exist between East and West. Even though I had seen countless photographs of European cities, particularly in my collection of books about the First and Second World Wars, I was still not quite sure what to expect. So it was with relief that I saw the same trees and vegetation and the same signs of human habitation that I knew from the East. Things were obviously not so different, after all.

On landing, I went straight to Vatican City, where I found St Peter's Basilica in some ways reminiscent of the Potala, at least in terms of its size and great antiquity. On the other hand, the Swiss guards, in their very colourful uniforms, seemed quite comical. They looked almost like decorations. My talk with Pope Paul VI was very brief, but I took the opportunity to express to him my belief in the importance of spiritual values for all humanity, no matter what the particular creed. He was in complete agreement with me and we parted on very good terms.

The following day I flew to Switzerland for a week, where I met some of the 200 children who had been adopted into Swiss families. I found them very shy and awkward in their behaviour towards me. Sadly, most of them had completely lost the ability to speak their native language. (However, on a subsequent visit, in 1979, I found the situation much improved. The children had taken lessons and spoke to me in broken Tibetan, rather like my own broken English.) Remembering their sad state six years previously, I was delighted to see their smiling faces and to discover that, as I had hoped, the people of Switzerland had greeted them with open arms. It was obvious that they had grown up in an atmosphere of love and kindness.

From Switzerland, I travelled to Holland, where one of the people I met was a rabbi. This was a particularly moving experience. Because of the language difficulties, we hardly exchanged any words, but there was no need. In his eyes I clearly saw all the terrible suffering of his people, and wept.

I spent only two days in the Netherlands and a few hours in Belgium before flying on to Ireland, then Norway, Sweden and Denmark, each for only a day or two. Time was far too short to gain more than the slightest impression of these places. But everywhere I went, I found the same kindness and hospitality and thirst for information about Tibet. It became clear to me that my country holds a special fascination for many people around the world. One of the particular joys of this energetic trip was the opportunity it gave me of thanking in person some of the many people who had organised aid to the Tibetan refugees. In Norway, Denmark and Sweden, for example, I visited the organisations which had made it possible for forty young Tibetan men and women to be trained as mechanics and agriculturalists.

The country in which I spent the most amount of time was the United Kingdom. I stayed for ten days and was pleased to find confirmation of my belief that, of all western countries, Britain has the closest links with Tibet. To my surprise, I met a number of very old people who were actually able to speak to me in Tibetan. It turned out that they, or, in some cases, their parents, had been stationed in Tibet as officials at one time or another. One of these was Hugh Richardson, whom I had last seen about ten years previously when he came to Dharamsala.

While in Britain I met Sir Harold Macmillan, who impressed me very much. He seemed extraordinarily nice and had an air of authority combined with humility that was very striking. He also showed an interest in spiritual values. Another person whose acquaintance I made and who has since become a valued friend was Edward Carpenter, then Dean of Westminster, whose wife now always calls me 'My boy'.

Although in 1960 I saw an Indian newspaper report saying that President Eisenhower had indicated that he would receive the Dalai Lama if I went to America, an enquiry into the possibility of my going there in 1972 suggested that there might be some difficulty in obtaining a visa. Naturally, I was very curious to see the country that is said to be both the richest and freest nation on earth, but it was not until 1979 that I was able to do so.

On arrival in New York, where I went first, I was immediately impressed by an atmosphere of liberty. The people I met seemed very friendly and open and relaxed. But at the same time, I could not help noticing how dirty and untidy some parts of the city were. I was also very sorry to see so many tramps and homeless people taking shelter in doorways. It amazed me that there could be any beggars in this vastly rich and prosperous land. I was reminded of what my Communist friends had told me about the injustices of the 'American Imperialist Paper Tiger', how it exploits the poor for the benefit of the rich. Another surprise was to discover that although, like many Easterners, I held the view that the US was the champion of freedom, actually very few people had any knowledge of the fate of Tibet. Now, as I have come to know the country better, I have begun to see that, in some ways, the American political system does not live up to its own ideals.

None of this is to say that I did not hugely enjoy that first visit, nor that I did not see much that impressed me. I particularly enjoyed addressing many student audiences, where I found continual expressions of goodwill. No matter how badly I expressed myself in English, the response I had was always warm, whether people understood everything or not. This helped me to overcome my shyness of speaking in public using this foreign language and helped me to grow in confidence, for which I am very grateful. However, I now wonder whether this kindness did not contribute in some way to a loss of determination on my part to improve my English further. For although I now made up my mind to do so, as soon as I returned to Dharamsala, I found that my resolve had vanished entirely! The result is that I continue on the whole to prefer talking to German and French and other European people, many of whom speak English as I do, ungrammatically and with a heavy accent. Least of all do I enjoy speaking it with the English themselves, many of whom strike me as very reserved and formal.

Since those first visits to different parts of the world, I have been back many times. Especially, I welcome the opportunity offered by travel to meet and talk with people from different walks of life – some poor, some rich, some well educated, some ill educated, some who are religious, many who are not. So far, I have received only support for my belief that wherever you go, people everywhere are basically the same, despite certain superficial differences. They all, like myself, seek happiness: no one wants suffering. Furthermore, everyone appreciates affection and at the same time has the potential for showing affection to others. With this in mind, I have found that friendship and understanding can develop.

Overall I have found much that is impressive about western society. In particular, I admire its energy and creativity and hunger for knowledge. On the other hand, a number of things about the western way of life cause me concern. One thing I have noticed is an inclination for people to think in terms of 'black and white' and 'either, or', which ignores the facts of interdependence and relativity. They have a tendency to lose sight of the grey areas which inevitably exist between two points of view.

Another observation is that there are a lot of people in the West who live very comfortably in large cities, but virtually isolated from the broad mass of humanity. I find this very strange – that under the circumstance of such material well-being and with thousands of brothers and sisters for neighbours, so many people appear able to show their true feelings only to their cats and dogs. This indicates a lack of spiritual values, I feel. Part of the problem here is perhaps the intense competitiveness of life in these countries, which seems to breed fear and a deep sense of insecurity.

For me, this sense of alienation is symbolised by something I once saw at the home of a very rich man whose guest I was on one of my trips abroad. It was a very large private house, obviously designed expressly for convenience and comfort, and fitted with every kind of appliance. However, when I went into the bathroom, I could not help noticing two large bottles of pills on the shelf above the hand basin. One contained tranquillisers, the other sleeping pills. This was proof, too, that material prosperity alone cannot bring about lasting happiness.

As I have already said, I usually go abroad at the invitation of others. Very often, I am also asked to address groups of people. When this happens, my approach is threefold. Firstly, as a human being, I talk about what I have termed Universal Responsibility. By this I mean the responsibility that we all have for each other and for all sentient beings and also for all of Nature.

Secondly, as a Buddhist monk I try to contribute what I can towards better harmony and understanding between different religions. As I have said, it is my firm belief that all religions aim at making people better human beings and that, despite philosophical differences, some of them fundamental, they all aim at helping humanity to find happiness. This does not mean that I advocate any sort of world religion or 'super religion'. Rather, I look on religion as medicine. For different complaints, doctors will prescribe different remedies. Therefore, because not everyone's spiritual 'illness' is the same, different spiritual medicines are required.

Finally, as a Tibetan, and furthermore as the Dalai Lama, I talk about my own country, people and culture whenever anyone shows interest in these matters. However, although I am greatly encouraged when people do show concern for my homeland and my suffering fellow countrymen and women in occupied Tibet, and although it gives fuel to my determination to continue the fight for justice, I do not consider those who support our cause to be 'pro-Tibet'. Instead, I consider them to be pro-Justice.

One of the things that I have noticed whilst travelling is the amount of interest shown by young people in the things that I talk about. This enthusiasm could, I suppose, be due to the fact that my insistence on absolute informality appeals to them. For my own part, I greatly value exchanges with younger audiences. They ask all sorts of questions concerning everything from the Buddhist theory of Emptiness, through my ideas about cosmology and modern physics, to sex and morality. Those questions which are unexpected and complicated are the ones I appreciate most. They can help me a great deal as I am compelled to take an interest in something that might not otherwise have occurred to me. It becomes a bit like debating.

Another observation is that many of the people I talk to, especially in the West, have a highly sceptical cast of mind. This can be very positive, I feel, but with the proviso that it is used as the basis for further enquiry.

Perhaps the most sceptical of all are the journalists and reporters with whom, because of my position as the Dalai Lama, I inevitably have a great deal of contact, especially when I travel. However, although it is often said that these men and women from the world's free press are very tough and aggressive, I have found that in general this is not so. The majority turn out to be friendly, even if the atmosphere is sometimes a little tense at first. Just occasionally, a question and answer session will turn into a serious argument. If this happens, I usually stop when it comes to politics, which I try to avoid. People have a right to their own opinions and I do not see it as my role to try to change their minds.

On a recent trip abroad, exactly this happened. After the press conference was over, some people felt that the Dalai Lama had not given good answers. However, I was not concerned. People must decide for themselves whether or not the Tibetan cause is a just one.

Much worse than the odd unsatisfactory encounter with newspaper people have been a couple of incidents involving television appearances. On one occasion, when I was in France, I was invited to speak on a live news programme. It was explained that the presenter would speak to me directly in French. What he was saying would be simultaneously translated into English for me, via a small earphone. But in the event, I was unable to understand a word of what came out.

On another occasion, when I was in Washington, I was asked to do a similar thing, only this time I was alone in the studio. The interviewer spoke to me from New York. I was told to look directly at a screen showing not his face, but my own. This completely unsettled me. I found it so disconcerting to be talking to myself that I was lost for words!

Whenever I go abroad, I try to contact as many other religious practitioners as possible, with a view to fostering inter-faith dialogue. On one of my foreign visits, I met some Christians with a similar desire. This led to a monastic exchange whereby for a few weeks some Tibetan monks went to a Christian monastery, whilst a similar number of Christian monks came out to India. It proved to be an extremely useful exercise for both parties. In particular, it enabled us to gain a deeper understanding of other people's way of thinking.

Amongst the many religious personalities that I have met, I will single out a few notable Christians (though I should add that I have been fortunate enough to meet wonderful people from a great variety of religious backgrounds). The present Pope is a man I hold in high regard. To begin with, our somewhat similar backgrounds give us an immediate common ground. The first time we met, he struck me as a very practical sort of person, very broad-minded and open. I have no doubt that he is a great spiritual leader. Any man who can call out 'Brother' to his would-be assassin, as Pope John Paul did, must be a highly evolved spiritual practitioner.

Mother Teresa, whom I met at Delhi airport on my way back from a conference at Oxford, England, during 1988 (which she had also attended), is someone for whom I have the deepest respect. I was at once struck by her demeanour of absolute humility. From the Buddhist point of view she could be considered to be a Bodhisattva.

Another person whom I think of as a highly evolved spiritual master is a Catholic monk I met at his hermitage near Monserrat in Spain. He had spent a great many years there, just like an Eastern sage, surviving off nothing more than bread and water and a little tea. He spoke very little English – even less than me – but from his eyes I could see that I was in the presence of an extraordinary person, a true practitioner of religion. When I asked him what his meditations were about, he answered simply, 'Love'. Since then, I have always thought of him as a modern Milarepa, after the Tibetan master of that name who spent much of his life hidden away in a cave, meditating and composing spiritual verses.

One religious leader with whom I have had several good conversations is the outgoing Archbishop of Canterbury, Dr Robert Runcie (whose courageous emissary, Terry Waite, I always remember in my prayers). We share the view that religion and politics do mix and both agree that it is the clear duty of religion to serve humanity, that it must not ignore reality. It is not sufficient for religious people to be involved with prayer. Rather, they are morally obliged to contribute all they can to solving the world's problems.

I remember once an Indian politician taking me to task over this view. He said to me, quite humbly, 'Oh, but we are politicians, not religious people. Our first concern is with serving people through politics,' to which I replied, 'Politicians need religion even more than a hermit on retreat. If a hermit acts out of bad motivation, he harms no one but himself. But if someone who can directly influence the whole of society acts with bad motivation, then a great number of people will be adversely affected.' I find no contradiction at all between politics and religion. For what is religion? As far as I am concerned, any deed done with good motivation is a religious act. On the other hand, a gathering of people in a temple or church who do not have good motivation are not performing a religious act when they pray together.

Although I do not seek them out, I have also made the acquaintance of a number of politicians whilst on my travels. One of these was Edward Heath, the former Prime Minister of Great Britain, whom I have met four times. Like Nehru, on the occasion of our first private meeting, I found that he seemed to have some difficulty concentrating on what I had to say. However, on the last three occasions, we had long and frank discussions about Tibet and China, during which Mr Heath expressed his enthusiasm for Chinese successes in agriculture. As someone who has visited Tibet more recently than I have, he also said that I should realise that many changes have taken place in my homeland – particularly with regard to support for the Dalai Lama. In his opinion, it is fast vanishing, especially amongst the younger generation.

This was a very interesting point of view to hear from such a senior politician, moreover one who has had extensive dealings with Peking. Nevertheless, I explained that my concern was not for the Dalai Lama's position but for the rights of the six million who live in occupied Tibet. Having said this, I told him that as far as I was aware, support for the Dalai Lama amongst young people in Tibet was at its highest level ever and that my exile had united the Tibetan people in a way that had never been possible before.

We still keep in touch, despite our differences of opinion, and I continue to value Mr Heath as a man with great knowledge of world affairs. Yet at the same time, I am highly impressed at the effectiveness of Chinese disinformation and deception even on such an experienced person as he is.

An interesting phenomenon of the past two decades or so has been the rapid growth of interest in Buddhism amongst western nations. I see no special significance in this, although of course I am very happy that there should now be more than five hundred centres of Tibetan Buddhism worldwide, many of them in Europe and North America. I am always glad if someone derives benefit from adopting Buddhist practices. However, when it actually comes to people changing their religion, I usually advise them to think the matter through very carefully. Rushing into a new religion can give rise to mental conflict and is nearly always difficult.

Nevertheless, even in those places where Buddhism is quite new, I have, for the benefit of those wishing to participate, performed ceremonies on a few occasions. For example, I have given the *Kalachakra* initiation in more than one country outside India – my motive for doing so being not only to give some insight into the Tibetan way of life and thinking, but also to make an effort, on an inner level, in favour of world peace.

Whilst on the subject of the spread of Buddhism in the West, I want to say that I have noticed some tendency towards sectarianism amongst new practitioners. This is absolutely wrong. Religion should never become a source of conflict, a further factor of division within the human community. For my own part, I have even, on the basis of my deep respect for the contribution that other faiths can make towards human happiness, participated in the ceremonies of other religions. And, following the example of a great many Tibetan lamas both ancient and modern, I continue to take teachings from as many different traditions as possible. For whilst it is true that some schools of thought felt it desirable for a practitioner to stay within his or her own tradition, people have always been free to do as they think fit. Furthermore, Tibetan society has always been highly tolerant of other people's beliefs. Not only was there a flourishing Muslim community in Tibet, but also there were a number of Christian missions which were admitted without hindrance. I am therefore firmly in favour of a liberal approach. Sectarianism is poison.

As for my own religious practice, I try to live my life pursuing what I call the Bodhisattva ideal. According to Buddhist thought, a Bodhisattva is someone on the path to Buddhahood who dedicates themselves entirely to helping all other sentient beings towards release from suffering. The word Bodhisattva can best be understood by translating the *Bodhi* and *Sattva* separately: *Bodhi* means the understanding or wisdom of the ultimate nature of reality, and a *Sattva* is someone who is motivated by universal compassion.

The Bodhisattva ideal is thus the aspiration to practise infinite compassion with infinite wisdom. As a means of helping myself in this quest, I choose to be a Buddhist monk. There are 253 rules of Tibetan monasticism (364 for nuns) and by observing them as closely as I can, I free myself from many of the distractions and worries of life. Some of these rules mainly deal with etiquette, such as the physical distance a monk should walk behind the abbot of his monastery; others are concerned with behaviour. The four root vows concern simple prohibitions: namely that a monk must not kill, steal or lie about his spiritual attainment. He must also be strictly celibate. If he breaks any one of these, he is no longer a monk.

I am sometimes asked whether this vow of celibacy is really desirable and indeed whether it is really possible. Suffice to say that its practice is not simply a matter of suppressing sexual desires. On the contrary, it is necessary fully to accept the existence of these desires and to transcend them by the power of reasoning. When successful, the result on the mind can be very beneficial. The trouble with sexual desire is that it is a blind desire. To say 'I want to have sex with this person' is to express a desire which is not intellectually directed in the way that 'I want to eradicate poverty in the world' is an intellectually directed desire. Furthermore, the gratification of sexual desire can only ever give temporary satisfaction. Thus as Nagarjuna, the great Indian scholar, said:

'When you have an itch, you scratch.
But not to itch at all
Is better than any amount of scratching.'

Regarding my actual daily practice, I spend, at the very least, five and a half hours per day in prayer, meditation and study. On top of this, I also pray whenever I can during odd moments of the day, for example over meals and whilst travelling. In this last case, I have three main reasons for doing so: firstly, it contributes towards fulfilment of my daily duty; secondly, it helps to pass the time productively; thirdly, it assuages fear! More seriously though, as a Buddhist, I see no distinction between religious practice and daily life. Religious practice is a twenty-four-hour occupation. In fact, there are prayers prescribed for every activity from waking to washing, eating and even sleeping. For Tantric practitioners, those exercises which are undertaken during deep sleep and in the dream state are the most important preparation for death.

However, for myself, early morning is the best time for practice. The mind is at its freshest and sharpest then. I therefore get up at around four o'clock. On waking, I begin the day with the recitation of *mantras*. I then drink hot water and take my medicine before making prostrations in salutation of the Buddhas for about half an hour. The purpose of this is twofold. Firstly, it increases one's own merit (assuming proper motivation) and secondly, it is good exercise. After my prostrations, I wash – saying prayers as I do so. Then I generally go outside for a walk, during which I make further recitations, until breakfast at around 5.15 am. I allow about half an hour for this meal (which is quite substantial) and whilst eating read scriptures.

From 5.45 am until around 8.00 am, I meditate, pausing only to listen to the 6.30 news bulletin of the BBC World Service. Then, from 8.00 am until noon, I study Buddhist philosophy. Between then and lunch at 12.30, I might read either official papers or newspapers, but during the meal itself I again read scripture. At 1 pm I go to my office, where I deal with government and other matters and give audiences until 5.00 pm. This is followed by another short period of prayer and meditation as soon as I get back home. If there is anything worthwhile on television, I watch it now before having tea at 6.00 pm. Finally, after tea, during which I read scripture once more, I say prayers until 8.30 or 9.00 pm, when I go to bed. Then follows very sound sleep.

Of course, there are variations to this routine. Sometimes during the morning I will participate in a *puja* or, in the afternoon, I will deliver a teaching. But, all the same, I very rarely have to modify my daily practice – that is my morning and evening prayers and meditation.

The rationale behind this practice is quite simple. During the first part of it when I make prostrations, I am 'taking refuge' in the Buddha, the *Dharma* and the *Sangha*. The next stage is to develop *Bodhichitta* or a Good Heart. This is done firstly by recognising the impermanence of all things and secondly by realising the true nature of being which is suffering. On the basis of these two considerations, it is possible to generate altruism.

To engender altruism, or compassion, in myself, I practise certain mental exercises which promote love towards all sentient beings, including especially my so-called enemies. For example, I remind myself that it is the actions of human beings rather than human beings themselves that make them my enemy. Given a change of behaviour, that same person could easily become a good friend.

The remainder of my meditation is concerned with *Sunya* or Emptiness, during which I concentrate on the most subtle meaning of Interdependence. Part of this practice involves what is termed 'deity yoga', *lhai naljor*, during which I use different *mandalas* to visualise myself as a succession of different 'deities'. (This should not, however, be taken to imply belief in independent external beings.) In so doing, I focus my mind to the point where it is no longer preoccupied with the data produced by the senses. This is not a trance, as my mind remains fully alert; rather it is an exercise in pure consciousness. What exactly I mean by this is hard to explain: just as it is difficult for a scientist to explain in words what is meant by the term 'space-time'. Neither language nor every-day experience can really communicate the experience of 'pure mind'. Suffice to say that it is not an easy practice. It takes many years to master.

One important aspect of my daily practice is its concern with the idea of death. To my mind, there are two things that, in life, you can do about death. Either you can choose to ignore it, in which case you may have some success in making the idea of it go away for a limited period of time, or you can confront the prospect of your own death and try to analyse it and, in so doing, try to minimise some of the inevitable suffering that it causes. Neither way can you actually overcome it. However, as a Buddhist, I view death as a normal process of life, I accept it as a reality that will occur whilst I am in *Samsara*. Knowing that I cannot escape it, I see no point in worrying about it. I hold the view that death is rather like changing one's clothes when they are torn and old. It is not an end in itself. Yet death is unpredictable – you do not know when and how it will take place. So it is only sensible to take certain precautions before it actually happens.

As a Buddhist, I further believe that the actual experience of death is very important. It is then that the most profound and beneficial experiences can come about. For this reason, many of the great spiritual masters take release from earthly existence – that is, they die – whilst meditating. When this happens, it is often the case that their bodies do not begin to decay until long after they are clinically dead.

My spiritual 'routine' changes only when I undertake a retreat. On these occasions, in addition to my normal daily practice, I also perform special meditations. This takes the place of my usual period of meditation and of my study of Buddhist philosophy between breakfast and noon. These I shift to the afternoon. After tea, there is no change. However, there are no hard and fast rules. Sometimes, because of external pressures, I am compelled to deal with official matters, or even to give audiences whilst on retreat. In that case, I may sacrifice some sleep in order to be able to fit everything in.

The purpose of undertaking a retreat is to enable a person to concentrate fully on inner development. As a rule, my opportunities for doing so are very limited. I am lucky if I can find two periods of a week in any given year, although occasionally I have managed a month or so. In 1973, I had a strong desire to undertake a three-year retreat, but unfortunately circumstances did not permit. I would still like very much to do this one day. In the meantime, I have to make do with just short battery-charging sessions, as I call them. A week is not long enough to make any actual progress or to develop in any way, but it is just sufficient to allow me to recharge myself. It takes much longer periods actually to train the mind to any extent. This is one of the reasons why I consider myself to be very much in the primary grade of spiritual development.

Of course, one of the main reasons I have so little time for retreats is the amount of travelling that I do nowadays, though I do not regret this. By travelling, I am able to share my experiences and hope with many more people than would otherwise be possible. And if, when I do so, it is always from the viewpoint of my being a Buddhist monk, this does not mean I believe that it is only by practising Buddhism that people can bring happiness to themselves and others. On the contrary, I believe that this is possible even for people who have no religion at all. I only use Buddhism as an example because everything in life has confirmed my belief in its validity. Besides, as a monk since the age of six, I have some knowledge in this field!

CHAPTER TWELVE

Of 'Magic and Mystery'

○

I AM OFTEN asked questions about the so-called magical aspects of Tibetan Buddhism. Many westerners want to know whether the books on Tibet by people like Lobsang Rampa and some others, in which they speak about occult practices, are true. They also ask me whether Shambala (a legendary country referred to by certain scriptures and supposed to lie hidden among the northern wastes of Tibet) really exists. Then there was the letter I received from an eminent scientist, during the early 1960s, saying he had heard that certain high lamas were capable of performing supernatural feats and asking whether he could conduct experiments to determine whether this was so.

In reply to the first two questions, I usually say that most of these books are works of imagination and that Shambala exists, yes, but not in any conventional sense. At the same time, it would be wrong to deny that some Tantric practices do genuinely give rise to mysterious phenomena. For this reason I half considered writing to the scientist to say that what he had heard was correct and, further, that I was in favour of experimentation; but I regretted to have to inform him that the person on whom these experiments could be performed had not yet been born! Actually, there were at that time various practical reasons why it was not possible to participate in enquiries of this sort.

Since then, however, I have agreed to a number of scientific investigations into the nature of certain specific practices. The first of these was carried out by Dr Herbert Benson, who is presently head of the Department of Behavioural Medicine at Harvard Medical School in America. When we met during my

1979 visit, he told me that he was working on an analysis of what he terms the 'relaxation response', a physiological phenomenon encountered when a person enters a meditative state. He felt that it would further understanding of this process if he were able to conduct experiments on highly advanced practitioners of meditation.

As a strong believer in the value of modern science, I decided to let him proceed, though not without some hesitation. I knew that many Tibetans were uneasy about the idea. They felt that the practices in question should be kept confidential because they derive from secret doctrines. Against this consideration I set the possibility that the results of such an investigation might benefit not only science but also religious practitioners and could therefore be of some general benefit to humankind.

In the event, Dr Benson was satisfied that he had found something extraordinary. (His findings were published in several books and scientific journals, including *Nature*.) He came out to India with two assistants and several pieces of sophisticated equipment and conducted experiments on some monks in hermitages near to Dharamsala and in Ladakh and Sikkim, further north.

The monks in question were practitioners of *Tum-mo* yoga, which is designed to demonstrate proficiency in particular Tantric disciplines. By meditating on the *chakras* (energy centres) and the *nadis* (energy channels), the practitioner is able to control and prevent temporarily the activity of the grosser levels of consciousness, permitting him or her to experience the subtler levels. According to Buddhist thought, there are many levels of consciousness. The grosser pertain to ordinary perception – touch, sight, smell and so forth – whilst the subtlest are those which are apprehended at the point of death. One of the aims of *Tantra* is to enable the practitioner to 'experience' death, for it is then that the most powerful spiritual realisations can come about.

When the grosser levels of consciousness are suppressed, physiological phenomena can be observed. In Dr Benson's experiments, these included the raising of body temperatures (as measured

internally by rectal thermometer and externally by skin thermometer) by up to 18° Fahrenheit (10 Centigrade). These increases allowed the monks to dry out sheets, soaked in cold water
and draped round them, even though the ambient temperature
was well below freezing. Dr Benson also witnessed, and took
similar measurements from, monks sitting naked on snow. He
found they could remain still throughout the night without any
loss of body temperature. During these sessions, he also noted
that the practitioner's oxygen intake decreased to around seven
breaths per minute.

Our knowledge of the human body and how it works is not yet
sufficient to offer an explanation of what is happening here. Dr
Benson believes that the mental processes involved may enable the
meditator to burn 'brown fat' deposits in the body – a phenomenon
previously thought to be confined to hibernating animals. But
whatever mechanisms are at work, what interests me most is the
clear indication that there are things about which modern science
could learn from Tibetan culture. What is more, I believe that
there are several other areas of our experience which could usefully
be investigated. For example, I hope one day to organise some
sort of scientific enquiry into the phenomenon of oracles, which
remain an important part of the Tibetan way of life.

Before I speak about them in detail, however, I must stress that
the purpose of oracles is not, as might be supposed, simply to
foretell the future. This is only part of what they do. In addition,
they can be called upon as protectors and in some cases they are
used as healers. But their principal function is to assist people in
their practice of the *Dharma*. Another point to remember is that
the word 'oracle' is itself misleading. It implies that there are
people who possess oracular powers. This is wrong. In the Tibetan
tradition there are merely certain men and women who act as
mediums between the natural and the spiritual realms, the name
for them being *kuten*, which means, literally, 'the physical basis'.
Also, I should point out that whilst it is usual to speak of oracles
as if they were people, this is done for convenience. More accu-
rately, they can be described as 'spirits' which are associated with

particular things (for example a statue), people and places. This should not be taken to imply belief in the existence of external independent entities, however.

In former times there must have been many hundred oracles throughout Tibet. Few survive, but the most important – those used by the Tibetan Government – still exist. Of these, the principal one is known as the Nechung oracle. Through him manifests Dorje Drakden, one of the protector divinities of the Dalai Lama.

Nechung originally came to Tibet with a descendant of the Indian sage Dharmapala, settling at a place in Central Asia called Bata Hor. During the reign of King Trisong Dretsen in the eighth century AD, he was appointed protector of Samye monastery by the Indian Tantric master and supreme spiritual guardian of Tibet, Padmasambhava. (Samye was in fact the first Buddhist monastery to be built in Tibet and was founded by another Indian scholar, the abbot Shantarakshita.) Subsequently, the second Dalai Lama developed a close relationship with Nechung – who had by this time become closely associated with Drepung monastery – and thereafter Dorje Drakden was appointed personal protector of succeeding Dalai Lamas.

For hundreds of years now, it has been traditional for the Dalai Lama, and the Government, to consult Nechung during the New Year festivals. In addition, he might well be called upon at other times if either have specific queries. I myself have dealings with him several times a year. This may sound far-fetched to twentieth-century western readers. Even some Tibetans, mostly those who consider themselves 'progressive', have misgivings about my continued use of this ancient method of intelligence gathering. But I do so for the simple reason that as I look back over the many occasions when I have asked questions of the oracle, on each one of them time has proved that his answer was correct. This is not to say that I rely solely on the oracle's advice. I do not. I seek his opinion in the same way as I seek the opinion of my Cabinet and just as I seek the opinion of my own conscience. I consider the gods to be my 'upper house'. The Kashag constitutes my lower house. Like any other leader, I consult both before making a decision on affairs of state. And sometimes, in addition to Nechung's counsel, I also take into consideration certain prophecies.

In one respect, the responsibility of Nechung and the responsibility of the Dalai Lama towards Tibet are the same, though we act in different ways. My task, that of leadership, is peaceful. His, in his capacity as protector and defender, is wrathful. However, although our functions are similar, my relationship with Nechung is that of commander to lieutenant: I never bow down to him. It is for Nechung to bow to the Dalai Lama. Yet we are also very close, friends almost. When I was small, it was touching. Nechung liked me a lot and always took great care of me. For example, if he noticed that I had dressed carelessly or improperly, he would come over and rearrange my shirt, adjust my robe and so on.

But despite this sort of familiarity, Nechung has always shown respect for me. Even when his relations with the Government have deteriorated, as they did during the last few years of the Regency, he invariably responds enthusiastically whenever asked anything about me. At the same time, his replies to questions about government policy can be crushing. Sometimes he just responds with a burst of sarcastic laughter. I well remember a particular incident that occurred when I was about fourteen. Nechung was asked a question about China. Rather than answer it directly, the *kuten* turned towards the East and began bending forward violently. It was frightening to watch, knowing that this movement combined with the weight of the massive helmet he wore on his head would be enough to snap his neck. He did it at least fifteen times, leaving no one in any doubt about where the danger lay.

Dealing with Nechung is by no means easy. It takes time and patience during each encounter before he will open up. He is very reserved and austere, just as you would imagine a grand old man of ancient times to be. Nor does he bother with minor matters: his interest is only in the larger issues, so it pays to frame questions accordingly. He also has definite likes and dislikes, but he does not show them very readily.

Nechung has his own monastery in Dharamsala, but usually he comes to me. On formal occasions, the *kuten* is dressed in an elaborate costume consisting of several layers of clothing topped by a highly ornate robe of golden silk brocade, which is covered with ancient designs in red and blue and green and yellow. On his chest he wears a circular mirror which is surrounded by clusters of turquoise and amethyst, its polished steel flashing with the Sanskrit *mantra* corresponding to Dorje Drakden. Before the proceedings begin, he also puts on a sort of harness, which supports four flags and three victory banners. Altogether, this outfit weighs more than seventy pounds and the medium, when not in trance, can hardly walk in it.

The ceremony begins with chanted invocations and prayers, accompanied by the urgings of horns, cymbals and drums. After a short while, the *kuten* enters his trance, having been supported until then by his assistants, who now help him over to a small stool set before my throne. Then, as the first prayer cycle concludes and the second begins, his trance begins to deepen. At this point, a huge helmet is placed on his head. This item weighs approximately thirty pounds, though in former times it weighed over eighty.

Now the *kuten*'s face transforms, becoming rather wild before puffing up to give him an altogether strange appearance, with bulging eyes and swollen cheeks. His breathing begins to shorten and he starts to hiss violently. Then, momentarily, his respiration stops. At this point the helmet is tied in place with a knot so tight that it would undoubtedly strangle the *kuten* if something very real were not happening. The possession is now complete and the mortal frame of the medium expands visibly.

Next, he leaps up with a start and, grabbing a ritual sword from one of his attendants, begins to dance with slow, dignified, yet somehow menacing, steps. He then comes in front of me and either prostrates fully or bows deeply from the waist until his helmet touches the ground before springing back up, the weight of his regalia counting for nothing. The volcanic energy of the deity can barely be contained within the earthly frailty of the *kuten*, who moves and gestures as if his body were made of rubber and driven by a coiled spring of enormous power.

There follows an interchange between Nechung and myself, where he makes ritual offerings to me. I then ask any personal questions I have for him. After replying, he returns to his stool and listens to questions put by members of the Government. Before giving answers to these the *kuten* begins to dance again, thrashing his sword above his head. He looks like a magnificent, fierce Tibetan warrior chieftain of old.

As soon as Dorje Drakden has finished speaking, the *kuten* makes a final offering before collapsing, a rigid and lifeless form, signifying the end of the possession. Simultaneously, the knot holding his helmet in place is untied in a great hurry by his assistants, who then carry him out to recover whilst the ceremony continues.

Surprising as it may seem, the oracle's replies to questions are rarely vague. As in the case of my escape from Lhasa, he is often very specific. But I suppose that it would be difficult for any scientific investigation either to prove or disprove conclusively the validity of his pronouncements. The same would surely be true of other areas of Tibetan experience, for example the matter of *tulkus*. Nevertheless, I hope one day that some sort of enquiry into both phenomena will be made.

Actually, the business of identifying *tulkus* is more logical than it may at first appear. Given the Buddhist belief that the principle of rebirth is fact, and given that the whole purpose of reincarnation is to enable a being to continue its efforts on behalf of all suffering sentient beings, it stands to reason that it should be possible to identify individual cases. This enables them to be educated and placed in the world so that they can continue their work as soon as possible.

Mistakes in this identification process can certainly be made, but the lives of the great majority of *tulkus* (of whom there are presently a few hundred known, although in Tibet before the Chinese invasion there were probably a few thousand) are adequate testimony of its efficacy.

As I have said, the whole purpose of reincarnation is to facilitate the continuity of a being's work. This fact has great implications when it comes to searching for the successor of a particular person. For example, whilst my efforts in general are directed towards helping all sentient beings, in particular they are directed towards helping my fellow Tibetans. Therefore, if I die before Tibetans regain their freedom, it is only logical to assume that I will be born outside Tibet. Of course, it could be that by then my people will have no use for a Dalai Lama, in which case they will not bother to search for me. So I might take rebirth as an insect, or an animal – whatever would be of most value to the largest number of sentient beings.

The way that the identification process is carried out is also less mysterious than might be imagined. It begins as a simple process of elimination. Say, for instance, we are looking for the reincarnation of a particular monk. First it must be established when and where that monk died. Then, considering that the new incarnation will usually be conceived a year or so after the death of its predecessor – these lengths of time we know from experience – a timetable is drawn up. Thus, if Lama X dies in year Y, his next incarnation will probably be born around eighteen months to two years later. In the year Y plus five, the child is likely to be between three and four years old: the field has narrowed already.

Next, the most likely place for the reincarnation to appear is established. This is usually quite easy. First, will it be inside or outside Tibet? If outside, there are a limited number of places where it is likely – the Tibetan communities of India, Nepal or Switzerland, for example. After that, it must be decided in which town the child is most likely to be found. Generally this is done by referring to the life of the previous incarnation.

Having narrowed the options and established parameters in the way I have shown, the next step is usually to assemble a search party. This need not necessarily mean that a group of people is sent out as if they were looking for treasure. Usually it is sufficient to ask various people in the community to look out for a child of between three and four who might be a candidate. Often there are helpful clues, such as unusual phenomena at the time of the child's birth; or the child may exhibit peculiar characteristics.

Sometimes two or three or more possibilities will emerge at this stage. Occasionally, a search party is not required at all because the previous incarnation has left detailed information right down to the name of his successor and the name of his successor's parents. But this is rare. Other times, the monk's followers may have clear dreams or visions about where to find his successor. On the other hand, one high lama recently directed that there should be no search for his own rebirth. He said that whoever seemed likely to serve the Buddha *Dharma* and his community best should be installed as his successor, rather than for anyone to worry about an accurate identification. There are no hard and fast rules.

If it happens that several children are put forward as candidates, it is usual for someone well known to the previous incarnation to conduct a final examination. Frequently, this person will be recognised by one of the children, which is strong evidence of proof, but sometimes marks on the body are also taken into consideration.

In some cases, the identification process involves consulting one of the oracles or someone who has powers of *ngon shé* (clairvoyance). One of the methods that these people use is *Ta*, whereby the practitioner looks into a mirror in which he or she might see the actual child, or a building, or perhaps a written name. I call this 'ancient television'. It corresponds to the visions that people had at Lake Lhamoi Lhatso, where Reting Rinpoché saw the letters *Ah*, *Ka* and *Ma* and the views of a monastery and a house when he began the search for me.

Sometimes, I myself am called upon to direct the search for a reincarnation. In these circumstances it is my responsibility to make the final decision on whether a given candidate has been correctly chosen. I should say here that I have no powers of clairvoyance. I have had neither the time nor the opportunity to develop them, although I have reason to believe that the Thirteenth Dalai Lama did have some ability in this sphere.

As an example of how I do this, I will relate the story of Ling

Rinpoché, my Senior Tutor. I always had the greatest respect for Ling Rinpoché, although when I was a child I only had to see his servant to become afraid – and whenever I heard his familiar footsteps, my heart missed a beat. But, in time, I came to value him as one of my greatest and closest friends. When he died not long ago, I felt that life without him at my side would be very difficult. He had become a rock on which I could lean.

I was in Switzerland, in the late summer of 1983, when I first heard of his final illness: he had suffered a stroke and become paralysed. This news disturbed me very much. Yet, as a Buddhist, I knew there was not much use in worrying. As soon as I could, I returned to Dharamsala, where I found him still alive, but in a bad physical state. Yet his mind was as sharp as ever, thanks to a lifetime of assiduous mental training. His condition remained stable for several months before deteriorating quite suddenly. He entered a coma from which he never emerged and died on 25 December 1983. But, as if any further evidence of his being a remarkable person were needed, his body did not begin to decay until thirteen days after he was pronounced dead, despite the hot climate. It was as if he still inhabited his body, even though clinically it was without life.

When I look back at the manner of his demise, I am quite certain that Ling Rinpoché's illness, drawn out as it was over a long period, was entirely deliberate, in order to help me get used to being without him. However, that is only half the story. Because we are speaking of Tibetans, the tale continues happily. Ling Rinpoché's reincarnation has since been found, and he is presently a very bright and naughty boy of three. His discovery was one of those where the child clearly recognises a member of the search party. Despite his being only eighteen months old, he actually called the person by name and went forward to him, smiling. Subsequently he correctly identified several other of his predecessor's acquaintances.

When I met the boy for the first time, I had no doubts about his identity. He behaved in a way that made it obvious he knew me, though he also showed the utmost respect. On that first occasion, I gave little Ling Rinpoché a large bar of chocolate. He stood impassively holding on to it, arm extended and head bowed all the time he was in my presence. I hardly think any other infant would have kept something sweet untasted and remained standing so formally. Then, when I received the boy at my residence and he was brought to the door, he acted just as his predecessor had done. It was plain that he remembered his way round. Moreover, when he came into my study, he showed immediate familiarity with one of my attendants, who was at the time recovering from a broken leg. First, this tiny person gravely presented him with a *kata* and then, full of laughter and childish giggles, he picked up one of Lobsang Gawa's crutches and ran round and round carrying it as if it were a flagpole.

Another impressive story about the boy concerns the time he was taken, at the age of only two, to Bodh Gaya, where I was due to give teachings. Without anyone telling him of its whereabouts, he found my bedroom, having scrambled on his hands and knees up the stairs, and laid a *kata* on my bed. Today, Ling Rinpoché is already reciting scriptures, though it remains to be seen whether, when he has learned to read, he will turn out to be like some of the young *tulkus* who memorise texts at astonishing speed, as if they were simply picking up where they had left off. I have known a number of small children who could declaim many pages with ease.

Certainly there is an element of mystery in this process of identifying incarnations. But suffice to say that, as a Buddhist, I do not believe that people like Mao or Lincoln or Churchill just 'happen'.

Another area of Tibetan experience that I would like very much to be scientifically investigated is the Tibetan medical system. Although it dates back more than two thousand years and is derived from a variety of sources, including ancient Persia, today its principles are wholly Buddhist. This gives it an entirely different complexion from western medicine. For example, it holds that the root causes of disease are Ignorance, Desire or Hatred.

According to Tibetan medicine, the body is dominated by three main *nopa*, meaning literally 'harmers' but more often translated as 'humours'. These *nopa* are considered to be ever present within an organism. This means that it can never be entirely free from disease, or at least from its potential. But provided they are kept in a state of equilibrium, the body remains healthy. However, an imbalance brought about by one or more of the three root causes will manifest as illness, which is generally diagnosed by feeling a patient's pulse and checking his or her urine. Altogether, there are twelve principal places on the hands and wrists where the pulse is checked. The urine is similarly assessed in a variety of different ways (for colour, smell and so forth).

As regards treatment, the first line of approach concerns behaviour and diet. Medicine forms the second line; acupuncture and moxibustion (a specific heat treatment) the third; surgery the fourth. The medicines themselves are made from organic materials, sometimes combined with metal oxides and certain minerals (including, for example, crushed diamonds).

So far, there has been little clinical research into the value of the Tibetan medical system, although one of my former physicians, Dr Yeshe Dhonden, did participate in a series of laboratory experiments at the University of Virginia, USA. I understand that he had some surprisingly good results in curing white mice of cancer. But much more work needs to be done before any definite conclusions can be reached. In the meantime, I can only say that, in my personal experience, I have found Tibetan medicine to be very effective. I take it regularly, not just as a cure but also as a preventative against illness. I have found that it helps to strengthen the constitution, whilst its side effects are negligible. The result is that, despite my long days and intensive periods of meditation, I almost never experience feelings of tiredness.

Yet another area where I believe that there is scope for dialogue between modern science and Tibetan culture concerns theoretical rather than experiential knowledge. Some of the latest discoveries of particle physics seem to point towards the non-duality of mind and matter. For example, it has been found that if a vacuum (that is to say empty space) is compressed, particles appear where there were none before, matter being apparently inherent in some way. These findings would appear to offer an area of convergence between science and the Buddhist *Madhyamika* theory of Emptiness. Essentially this states that mind and matter exist separately, but interdependently.

I am well aware, however, of the danger of tying spiritual belief to any scientific system. For whilst Buddhism continues to be relevant two and a half millennia after its inception, the absolutes of science tend to have a relatively short life. This is not to say that I consider things like the oracle and the ability of monks to survive nights spent out in freezing conditions to be evidence of magical powers. Yet I cannot agree with our Chinese brothers and sisters, who hold that Tibetan acceptance of these phenomena is evidence of our backwardness and barbarity. Even from the most rigorous scientific viewpoint, this is not an objective attitude.

At the same time, even if a principle is accepted, it does not mean that everything connected with it is valid. By way of analogy, it would be ludicrous to follow slavishly and without discrimination every utterance of Marx and Lenin in the face of clear evidence that Communism is an imperfect system. Great vigilance must be maintained at all times when dealing in areas about which we do not have great understanding. This, of course, is where science can help. After all, we consider things to be mysterious only when we do not understand them.

So far, the results of the enquiries I have described have been beneficial to all parties. But I realise that these are only ever as accurate as the experiments employed to achieve them. Furthermore, I am aware that not finding something does not mean that it does not exist. It only proves that the experiment was incapable of finding it. (If I have a non-metallic object in my pocket which is not picked up by a metal detector, it does not mean that my pocket is empty.) This is why we must be careful in our investigations, especially when dealing in an area where scientific experience is slight. It is also important to keep in mind the limitations imposed by nature itself. For example, whilst scientific enquiry cannot apprehend my thoughts, not only does this not mean that they are non-existent, but also that some other method of investigation cannot discover something about them – which is where Tibetan experience comes in. Through mental training, we have developed techniques to do things which science cannot yet adequately explain. This, then, is the basis of the supposed 'magic and mystery' of Tibetan Buddhism.

CHAPTER THIRTEEN

The News from Tibet

○

IN early 1959, as tension began to mount towards the final cataclysm, I heard of a PLA memorandum sent to Chairman Mao. It reported that the Tibetans were unhappy with the continued presence of the PLA, adding that there was so much disobedience that all the prisons were now full. Mao supposedly replied that there was no need to worry. The feelings of the Tibetans could be disregarded: they were irrelevant. As to the disobedience, the authorities must be prepared to put the whole population in prison if need be. Therefore, room would have to be made. I remember being horrified at hearing this. What a contrast from the old days when I could recognise every prisoner in Lhasa and considered each to be my friend.

Another story from around this time concerned Mao's reaction to a report sent him after the March uprising, saying that order had been restored. 'And what about the Dalai Lama?' he is said to have asked. When told that I had escaped, he replied, 'In that case we have lost the battle.' After that, all my information concerning the Great Helmsman came from reading newspapers and listening to the BBC World Service news broadcasts. I had no contact whatever with Peking; nor did the Tibetan Government in Exile, until after Mao's death in September 1976.

At that time I was in Ladakh, part of the remote northern Indian province of Jammu and Kashmir, where I was conducting a *Kalachakra* initiation. On the second of the ceremony's three days, Mao died. On the third day, it rained all morning. But, in the afternoon, there appeared one of the most beautiful rainbows I have ever seen. I was certain that it must be a good omen. However, despite this auspicious sign, I did not expect the dramatic pace of change that followed in Peking. Almost immediately, the Gang of Four, led by Mao's wife, Chiang Ching, was arrested. It quickly became apparent that it was they who had effectively ruled China behind the ailing Chairman's back for the past several years, pursuing viciously radical policies and supporting a continuation of the Cultural Revolution.

Then, in 1977, Li Xiannian, at that time President of the People's Republic of China, was reported as saying that although it had achieved much, the Cultural Revolution had simultaneously caused some damage. This was the first sign that the Chinese leadership had at last begun to face reality. It was followed by a conciliatory statement about Tibet when, in April of that year, Ngabo Ngawang Jigme (by now a high ranking member of the administration in Peking), publicly announced that China would welcome the return of the Dalai Lama 'and his followers who fled to India'. Since the 1960s, the Chinese had been calling for all who had left Tibet to return, saying that they would be welcomed with open arms.

This statement marked the start of an intensive propaganda campaign to try to entice people back. We began to hear more and more about the 'unprecedented happiness in Tibet today'. Soon afterwards, Hua Guofeng, Mao's designated successor, called for the full restoration of Tibetan customs and, for the first time in twenty years, elderly people were permitted to circumambulate the Jokhang once more and national dress was allowed. This seemed very promising, and it proved not to be the last hopeful sign.

On 25 February 1978, to my great joy and surprise, the Panchen Lama was suddenly released after almost a decade in jail. And soon afterwards, Hu Yaobang, then in the ascendant, revised President Li Xiannian's pronouncement on the Cultural Revolution and stated that it had been an entirely negative experience, which had not benefited China in any way.

This sounded like a remarkable advance. But still, I felt that if the Chinese had really had a change of heart, this would best be signalled by genuine openness as regards Tibet. In my 10 March speech (marking the nineteenth anniversary of the Tibetan people's national uprising), I therefore called on the Chinese authorities to allow unrestricted access to Tibet for foreigners. I also suggested that they should permit Tibetans in occupied Tibet to visit their families in exile, and vice versa. I felt that if the six million Tibetans really were happy and prosperous as never before, as was now being suggested, we had no reason to argue otherwise. But it was only right that we should have the opportunity to find out the truth of these statements.

To my surprise, it seemed that my suggestions were taken note of. For, not long after, the first foreign visitors were admitted to Tibet. And, in accordance with my wishes, provision was made for Tibetans both inside and outside Tibet to be able to make visits, although in neither case were these new permissions unrestricted.

The upheavals in China occurred at a time when India was going through important changes too. In 1977, Mrs Gandhi lost the election she called after a period of Emergency. She was followed in office by Mr Moraji Desai, whose Janata party succeeded in toppling the Congress party for the first time since Independence. It was not long before Mrs Gandhi regained power, but in the meantime I came to deepen my acquaintance with Mr Desai, whom I had first met in 1956 and already knew and liked.

At the time of writing, he is still alive, though now a very old man, and I continue to regard him as a close friend. He is a remarkable person with a wonderful face, full of life and free of worries. By this, I do not mean he is without his faults. But as with Mahatma Gandhi, his daily life is very austere. He is a strict vegetarian; he does not touch alcohol or tobacco. He is also utterly straightforward in his dealings with others. I sometimes wonder if he is not too straightforward. However, if this is one of his failings, in my eyes it is more than made up for by his friendship towards the Tibetan people. He once wrote to me saying that Indian culture and Tibetan culture are different branches of the same Bodhi Tree. This is quite true. As I have already made clear, the relationship between our countries goes very deep. Many

Indians consider Tibet to be a manifestation of Heaven on Earth – a land of gods and holy places. Both Mount Kailash and Lake Mansarova, in south and south-western Tibet respectively, are important places of pilgrimage to devout Indians. Similarly, we Tibetans consider India to be *Aryabhumi*, the Land of the Holy.

Towards the end of 1978, there was a further encouraging development when Deng Xiao-ping emerged as paramount authority in Peking. As leader of a more moderate faction, his ascendancy seemed to signal real hope for the future. I had always felt that Deng might one day do great things for his country. When I was in China during 1954-5, I met him a number of times and had been very impressed by him. We never had any long conversations but I heard much about him – particularly that he was a man of great ability and very decisive too.

The last time I saw him I remember him sitting, a very small man in a large armchair, slowly and methodically peeling an orange. He did not talk much, but it was clear that he was listening intently to all that was being said. He struck me as a powerful man. Now it began to look as if, in addition to these qualities, he was also quite wise. He came up with a number of impressive catch phrases, such as 'It is important to seek truth from facts', 'So long as it catches mice, it doesn't matter whether it's black or white' and 'If your face is ugly, there is no use trying to pretend otherwise.' Furthermore, as regards policy, he appeared more concerned with the economy and education than with political doctrine and the usual empty slogans.

Then, in November 1978, thirty-four prisoners, mostly elderly members of my own administration, were publicly released with great ceremony in Lhasa. These men were purportedly the last of the 'rebel leaders'. Chinese newspapers stated that, after being taken on a month-long tour of the 'New Tibet', they were to be assisted in finding jobs and even in going abroad if that was what they desired.

The arrival of the New Year brought no let-up in this spate of extraordinary developments. On 1 February 1979, coincidentally

the day that the People's Republic of China was formally recognised by the US, the Panchen Lama, in his first public appearance for fourteen years, added his voice to those calling for the
Dalai Lama and his fellow exiles to return. 'If the Dalai Lama is
genuinely interested in the happiness and welfare of the Tibetan
masses, he need have no doubts about it,' he said. 'I can guarantee
that the present standard of living of the Tibetan people in Tibet
is many times better than that of the "old society".' A week later,
this invitation was repeated by Radio Lhasa as it announced the
formation of a special welcoming committee to receive Tibetans
from abroad.

This was followed just a week later by the unexpected arrival of
Gyalo Thondup in Kanpur (Uttar Pradesh) where I was attending
a religious conference. To my surprise, he announced that he had
heard through some old and trusted friends of his in Hong Kong
(where he now lives) that *Xinhua*, the New China News Agency,
which constitutes China's official legation to the British colony,
wanted to make contact with him. Following this, he had met a
personal emissary of Deng Xiao–ping, who explained that the
Chinese leader wanted to open communications with the Dalai
Lama. As a mark of his goodwill, Deng wanted to invite Gyalo
Thondup to Peking for talks. My brother had refused as he wanted
to seek my opinion first.

This was totally unexpected, and I did not reply immediately.
The developments of the past two years all looked very promising.
However, as the ancient Indian saying goes, 'When you have
once been bitten by a snake, you become cautious even of rope.'
And unfortunately, all my experience of the Chinese leadership
suggested that it was untrustworthy. Not only did the authorities
in question lie, but worse, when these lies were exposed they were
not the least bit ashamed. The Cultural Revolution had been a
'tremendous success' whilst it was going on; now it was a failure
– but there was no sense of humility in this admission. Nor
was there anything to suggest that these people ever kept their
promises. Despite the concrete undertaking of clause thirteen of
the Seventeen-Point 'Agreement' that the Chinese would 'not

arbitrarily take a needle or thread' from the Tibetans, they had ransacked the whole country. On top of this, through countless atrocities, they had shown a total disrespect for human rights. It seemed that to the Chinese mind, perhaps because of the huge size of their own population, human life is considered to be a cheap commodity – and Tibetan lives to be of still less value. I therefore felt it necessary to exercise extreme caution.

On the other hand, my basic belief is that human problems can only be solved through human contact. So there could be no harm in hearing what the Chinese had to say. Hopefully we could simultaneously explain our own views. We certainly had nothing to hide. Also, if the authorities in Peking were in earnest, we might even be able to send some fact-finding missions to discover for ourselves the real situation.

With these considerations in mind, and knowing that our cause was 100 per cent just and in accordance with the wishes of the entire population of Tibet, I told my brother he was free to go. After he had seen the Chinese leaders, we would consider the next step. At the same time, I sent word to Peking via the Chinese Embassy in India, proposing that a fact-finding mission from Dharamsala should be permitted to visit Tibet with a view to discovering the real situation there and reporting back to me. I also suggested to my brother that he should see whether this might be feasible.

Soon afterwards, I received another exciting piece of news from an entirely different quarter. This came in the form of an invitation to visit the Buddhist communities of the Republic of Mongolia and of the USSR. I realised that to go might not please my friends in Peking, but, on the other hand, I felt that as a Buddhist monk and furthermore as the Dalai Lama, I had a responsibility to serve my co-religionists. Besides, how could I refuse the very people who gave me my title! And moreover, since I had not been able to fulfil my dream of visiting Russia when I was a high Chinese official (albeit one whose movements were severely restricted), I did not wish to miss the opportunity of going as a Tibetan refugee. I therefore accepted joyfully.

In the event, there were no negative repercussions and, when Gyalo Thondup returned to Dharamsala at the end of March, he announced that the Chinese had accepted my proposal to send a fact-finding mission to Tibet. This encouraged me enormously. It appeared that China was at last trying to find a peaceful solution to the Tibetan question. A date in August was set for the departure of the delegation.

Meanwhile, I left for Moscow en route to Mongolia in early June. On arrival I felt as if I was back in a familiar world. I recognised at once the same repressive atmosphere that I had come to know so well in China. But it did not put me off, for I could see that the people I met were essentially good and kind – and surprisingly naïve. This last observation was brought home to me when a journalist from one of the Russian daily newspapers came to interview me. All his questions were clearly designed to extract compliments. If I said anything that was not supportive of the Government or if my answers were not exactly what he was looking for, he gave me angry looks. On another occasion, a journalist, having come to the end of his prepared list of questions, became quite humble and said with total simplicity, 'What do you think I should ask you now?'

Wherever I went in Moscow, I saw this same charm beneath surface conformity. It was further confirmation of my belief that nobody anywhere in the world consciously wants suffering. At the same time, I was reminded of the importance of contact with people on a personal level: I could see for myself that the Russians were not monsters any more than the Chinese or the British or the Americans are. I was particularly touched by the warmth of my reception by members of the Russian Orthodox Church.

From Moscow I journeyed to the Buryat Republic, where I spent a day at a Buddhist monastery. Although I was unable to communicate directly with anyone, I found I could understand their prayers as these were said in Tibetan, rather as Catholics all over the world use Latin. The monks also wrote in Tibetan. On top of this, I discovered that we could converse very well with our eyes. As I entered the monastery, I noticed that many of the monks and lay people in the congregation were in tears. This was just the sort of spontaneous expression that Tibetans are prone to and I felt immediate kinship.

The monastery in Ulan Ude, the capital of Buryat, was one of the most remarkable things I saw in the USSR. It had been built in 1945, when Stalin was at the height of his power. I did not see how this could be, but it helped me to realise that spirituality is so deeply rooted in the human mind that it is very difficult, if not totally impossible, to eradicate. Like my own countrymen and women, the people of Buryat had suffered horribly for their faith, and for an even longer period of time. Yet everywhere I went, I found clear evidence that, given the slightest opportunity, their spiritual life flourished.

This deepened my conviction that it is vital for there to be dialogue between Buddhism and Marxism, where it survives, as indeed there must be between all religions and any form of materialist ideology. The two approaches to life are so obviously complementary. It is sad that people tend to think of them as being in opposition. If materialism and technology really are the answer to all of humanity's problems, the most advanced industrial societies would by now be full of smiling faces. But they are not. Equally, if people were meant only to be concerned with matters of spirituality, we would all be living joyously according to their religious beliefs. But then there would be no progress. Both material and spiritual development are required. And humanity must not stagnate, for that is a kind of death.

From Ulan Ude, I flew to Ulan Bator, the capital of the Republic of Mongolia, where I was met by a group of monks who gave me an emotional welcome. However, the joy and spontaneity with which I was greeted were evidently not approved of by the authorities. On that first day, people pressed in from all sides, trying to touch me. But next morning, I found everyone behaving as if they were statues and I noticed tears in their eyes. No one came near me when I visited the house where my predecessor had stayed at the beginning of this century. Later, though, one person did manage secretly to defy officialdom. As I left a museum, I felt something very curious in the handshake of a man standing at the gate. On looking down, I realised that he was pressing a small rosary into my hand for blessing. Seeing this, I felt simultaneously great sorrow and compassion.

It was in this museum that I happened to notice a picture showing a monk with a huge mouth into which nomads were walking with their cattle. It was obviously intended as anti-religious propaganda. I moved over to take a closer look, but my guide nervously tried to steer me away from this embarrassing example of Communist propaganda. So I said there was no need to hide anything from me. There was a certain amount of truth in what the picture was saying. Such facts should not be shied away from. Every religion has the capacity to do harm, to exploit people as this image suggested. This is not the fault of the religion itself, but the fault of the people who practise it.

A further amusing incident concerned another exhibit which was a model of the *Kalachakra mandala*. I noticed that there were some inaccuracies in the way it was laid out, so when one young woman staff member began to explain its meaning to me, I said, 'Look! I'm the expert in these matters, why don't you let me explain it to you?' and began to point out the inaccuracies in the *mandala*. I found this quite satisfying.

As I got to know the Mongolians, I began to realise just how strong are the links between our two countries. For a start, the religion of Mongolia is the same as ours. As I have already mentioned, in the past, many Mongolian scholars visited Tibet, where they contributed a great deal to our culture and religion. Tibetans also use many religious texts which were written by Mongolians. Furthermore, we share many customs, for example the giving of *katas*. (One slight difference is that whereas Tibetan ones are white, Mongolian *katas* are pale blue or slate grey.) Thinking along these lines, it occurred to me that, historically speaking, Mongolia has a similar relationship with Tibet as Tibet has with India. With this in mind, I arranged for an exchange between students from our respective communities, thereby reviving an ancient link between our two countries.

When I came to leave, I had gained many favourable impressions of both the USSR and of Mongolia. Some of these concerned the material progress I had seen, particularly in the latter country where considerable advances had been made in the fields of industry, agriculture and animal husbandry. I have been back to Russia once since then (in 1987), when I was pleased to find that the atmosphere had changed dramatically for the better. This was tangible evidence that political liberty has a direct bearing on the way people feel about themselves. Now that they were able to express their true feelings, they clearly felt much happier.

On 2 August 1979, a delegation comprised of five members of the Tibetan Government in Exile left New Delhi en route to Tibet via Peking. I had chosen them carefully. Because it was important that they should be as objective as possible, I selected men who not only knew Tibet as it was before the Chinese invasion, but were familiar with the modern world as well. I also ensured that there was a representative of each of the three different provinces.

My brother Lobsang Samten was one of their number. He had long since renounced his monastic vows, leaving me as the only member of the family in the *Sangha*, and was at that time going through a very modern phase in terms of dress and appearance. He wore his hair long and had a thick, droopy moustache. His clothes were very casual too. I was a little worried that he might not be recognised by those in Tibet who should remember him.

More than ten years later, I still do not quite know what impression the leadership in Peking expected the delegation to have of the 'new' Tibet. But I think they were convinced that they would find such content and prosperity throughout their homeland that they would see no point in remaining in exile. (And in fact, fearing that the delegation might be physically attacked by a right-thinking local population, the Chinese authorities actually briefed Tibetans to show courtesy to the delegates!) I also suspect that the Dalai Lama and the existence of the Tibetan Government in Exile were a great embarrassment to China, which was becoming anxious about world opinion. Therefore, any means to lure us back was acceptable.

It was fortunate they were so certain of themselves. For, whilst the first delegation was in Peking, the Chinese authorities accepted my proposal that this mission should be followed by three more.

My five representatives spent two weeks in Peking holding meetings and planning their route which, over a period of four months, was to take them across the length and breadth of Tibet. However, as soon as they arrived in Amdo, things started to go wrong for the Chinese. The delegates were mobbed by crowds of thousands of people wherever they went, especially by young people, all asking for blessings and for news about myself. This outraged the Chinese, who frantically signalled ahead to Lhasa to alert the authorities there of what might be in store for them. A reply came back saying, 'Thanks to the high standard of political training in the capital, there is no possibility of embarrassment.'

Yet, every step of the way, the welcome the five exiles received was ecstatic. And, on arrival in Lhasa, they were greeted by an immense crowd – the photographs brought back by them show the streets to be dense with thousands and thousands of well-wishers – who disobeyed an explicit warning to stay away. Whilst in the city, one of the delegates overheard a senior Chinese cadre turn to a colleague and say, 'The efforts of the last twenty years have been wasted in a single day.'

Although there is often a gap between the leadership and the people in countries where there is an authoritarian government, here it seemed that the Chinese had made an altogether extraordinary miscalculation. Even though they had a highly efficient intelligence system designed to prevent this sort of thing, their assessment was entirely wrong. But what I find still more surprising is that despite these experiences, the Chinese continue to persevere with the system. So, for example, when Hu Yaobang, then General Secretary of the Chinese Communist Party and Deng's heir apparent, visited Tibet the following year, he was taken to the Chinese equivalent of a Potemkin village and completely misled. Similarly, in 1988, I was told that when a prominent Chinese leader visited

Lhasa, he asked an old woman directly what she felt about the present situation in Tibet. She, of course, faithfully repeated the Party line and he duly took this to be the true feelings of a Tibetan. It is as if the Chinese authorities actually want to fool themselves. Yet surely anyone who was half sensible would realise that a person under threat of violent punishment would not reveal any negative thoughts?

Fortunately, Hu Yaobang was not entirely deceived. He publicly expressed shock at the living conditions of Tibetans and even asked whether all the money sent to Tibet had been thrown in the river. He went on to promise the withdrawal of eighty-five per cent of the Chinese cadres stationed in occupied Tibet.

Little more was heard about these proposed measures. Hu Yaobang's ascendancy did not last long and he was eventually forced to resign as General Secretary of the Chinese Communist Party. Nevertheless, I am very grateful to his memory for the great courage he displayed in admitting China's mistakes in Tibet. The fact that he did so is clear evidence that not everyone, even amongst the leadership in China, supports the Government's repressive policies abroad. But if Hu Yaobang's admission did not have a lasting impact on Tibetan affairs, the report prepared by the first delegation, after its return to Dharamsala in late December, most certainly did.

When I arrived back from two long journeys of my own (to Russia, Mongolia, Greece, Switzerland and finally the United States) in October 1979, the five members of the delegation returned. With them they brought hundreds of rolls of film, many hours of recorded conversations and enough general information to occupy many months of collation, distillation and analysis. They also brought back more than seven thousand letters from Tibetans to their families in exile – the first time that mail had left Tibet for more than twenty years.

Unfortunately, their impressions of the 'new' Tibet had been strongly negative. At the same time as being mobbed by tearful Tibetans wherever they went, they saw abundant evidence of the way that the Chinese authorities had ruthlessly and systematically tried to destroy our ancient culture. Moreover, they were regaled with numberless accounts of years of famine, mass starvation, public execution and gross and disgusting violations of human rights, the least of which included the abduction of children either into forced labour gangs or for 'education' in China, the imprisonment of innocent citizens, and the deaths of thousands of monks and nuns in concentration camps. It was a horrific litany, graphically illuminated by dozens of photographs of monasteries and nunneries reduced to piles of rubble, or turned into grain stores or factories or cattle pens.

However, in the face of this information, the Chinese authorities made it clear that they would not hear any criticism either from the delegates or any other Tibetan from the exile community. So long as we remained outside, we had no right to criticise what went on inside, they said. When Lobsang Samten told me this, I was reminded of an incident that took place during the 1950s. A Tibetan official was asked by a Chinese Party member what was his opinion of Chinese rule in Tibet. 'First let me leave the country,' the Tibetan replied, 'and then I will tell you.'

Yet it is true to say that the delegation did bring back some hopeful pieces of news. For example, when they were in Peking, they met a number of young students who were being educated as Communist Party cadres. But instead of them all being blindly Marxist and pro-Chinese policy, they turned out to be fully committed to the cause of Tibetan freedom. And, judging by the numerous instances when ordinary Tibetans openly defied Chinese authority to express their love and respect for the Dalai Lama, the spirit of the people was far from broken. In fact, it seemed that these desperate experiences had only served to strengthen their resolve.

Another positive event for the first delegation was its meeting, in Peking, with the Panchen Lama. He had been treated with great cruelty by the Chinese authorities and showed his five compatriots permanent marks on his body that had been inflicted during torture. He explained that after my flight into exile, his own monastery at Tashilhunpo had been left unharmed by the

PLA. But after he had begun to criticise our new masters, troops were sent in. Then, during 1962, he was told to take my place as Chairman of the Preparatory Committee. He refused and instead sent to Chairman Mao a 70,000-character-long memorandum of complaints. Subsequently, he was stripped of office (although Mao shamelessly assured him that his observations would be heeded), and the handful of elderly caretaker monks that had found their way back to Tashilhunpo were arrested, accused of criminal activities and subjected to abuse in front of the people of Shigatse.

At the beginning of 1964, the Panchen Lama was given the opportunity of rehabilitation. He was invited to make a speech to the people of Lhasa during the *Monlam* festival, which was to be revived for a single day. He agreed to do so. However, to the amazement of the Chinese authorities, he announced to the assembled crowd that the Dalai Lama was indeed the true leader of the Tibetan people. He ended his speech with a rousing cry of 'Long live the Dalai Lama!' He was duly arrested and, after a secret trial lasting seventeen days, he disappeared from view. Many people feared that he too had been killed. But now it turned out that he had at first been put under house arrest before eventually being imprisoned in China's maximum security jail, where he was subjected to intensive torture and political 're-education'. Conditions there were so harsh that he attempted suicide more than once.

So, the Panchen Lama was alive and comparatively well. But the delegates saw that the health of Tibet itself was very poor. True, the country's economy had been transformed and there was more of everything. Yet this was of zero benefit to the Tibetans as all commodities were in the hands of the occupying Chinese. For example, there were now factories where there had been none before, but all that they produced went to China. And the factories themselves were sited with no regard for anything other than utility, with predictably detrimental results to the environment. The same was true of the hydro-electric power stations. Furthermore, the Chinese quarter of every town and city was flooded with light but, even in Lhasa, in the Tibetan district one bulb of

15 to 20 watts was the most that could be found in any room. These often failed, especially in winter when electric power resources were diverted to accommodate heavier use throughout the rest of the city.

As to agriculture, the Chinese had insisted that winter wheat be sown in place of the traditional barley crop. This was because the Chinese eat wheat rather than barley. Consequently, thanks to new intensive farming methods, one or two bumper crops were produced – followed by years of famine. The changes had caused the rapid erosion of Tibet's thin, fragile layer of fertile topsoil, leaving miles of desert.

Other land resources, such as forestry, had been similarly exploited. Since 1955, it was estimated that nearly fifty million trees had been felled and many millions of acres all but cleared of vegetation. Animal husbandry had improved dramatically: in some places there were ten times the number of animals feeding off the same amount of pasture as in former times. But in other places, over-exploitation meant the environment could no longer support any kind of grazing. As a result, whole ecologies have been lost. The once ubiquitous herds of deer, *kyang* and *drong* have now all but disappeared and the huge flocks of ducks and geese that were such a familiar sight are no longer to be seen.

Regarding health care, it now became clear that there were indeed a considerable number of hospitals, just as the Chinese had said. But these practised open discrimination on behalf of the immigrant population. And whenever a Chinese required blood in a transfusion, this would be taken from Tibetan 'volunteers'.

There were also far more schools than there had ever been. But again, the education programme had been perverted to benefit the Chinese. For example, the first delegation heard stories of how, in order to obtain funds from the central administration, the local Chinese authorities claimed that they were improving facilities for the Tibetans. The money was then used to benefit their own children. As to the education the Chinese provided for Tibetans, most of it was conducted in Chinese. It had been promised that the Tibetan language itself would be eradicated 'within fifteen years'. In reality, many of the schools were nothing more than labour camps for children. The only ones who really received proper schooling were the fifteen hundred or so most intellectually promising ones, who were forcibly sent to establishments in China, on the grounds that it would foster 'unity'.

The delegates also found that communications throughout Tibet had been transformed dramatically. There were roads criss-crossing it and linking almost every settlement. There were thousands of vehicles too, mainly heavy trucks – but all belonging to the Chinese Government. For ordinary Tibetans, however, movement was impossible without permission. Granted, the rules had recently been relaxed somewhat, but very few could afford to take advantage of this.

Similarly, although consumer goods were certainly available, none but a tiny handful of Tibetans could afford them. The great majority lived in a state of abject and pitiful poverty. The delegates heard how until only recently food rationing had been so tight that the quota for thirty days could only be eked out for twenty. After that, people were reduced to eating leaves or grass. A month's butter ration, for example, which would in former times have been used in a single serving of tea, could only be used to smear the lips. And, everywhere they went, the delegates found the local people stunted in growth from malnutrition and dressed literally in rags. Gone, needless to say, were the gay ornaments and pieces of jewellery – earrings and so forth – which even the least exalted Tibetan would have had in former times.

On top of this extraordinary hardship, people were taxed unbelievably, though of course the charges were not called taxes: it was 'rent', or whatever. Even nomads were forced to pay for the privileges of their precarious livelihood. All in all, China's economic programme for Tibet was itself a form of torture.

As if this were not enough, with regard to Tibetan culture the delegates found that it had been brutally suppressed. For example, the only songs allowed were political paeans sung to Chinese tunes. Religion was banned. Thousands of monasteries and nunneries had been desecrated. They heard how this had been systematically carried out from the late 1950s onwards. Each building was visited first by clerks who documented the contents. They were followed by teams of workers who loaded everything of immediate value on to trucks which went straight back to China, where the booty was either melted down for bullion or sold on the international art market in exchange for hard currency. Next, more workers would be sent in to remove any other materials that could be useful, including the roof tiles and timber. Finally, members of the local population would be forced to 'show their contempt' for the old society and the 'corrupt' monks. Within a matter of weeks, there would be nothing left but piles of rubble.

The contents of these monasteries represented the real disposable wealth of Tibet. For hundreds of years, they had amassed the donations of succeeding generations of families who always gave the best they could afford. Now, all this had vanished into the insatiable stomach of the Chinese nation.

Still not content with this, the Chinese authorities had also determined to control the Tibetan population. A limit of two children per couple had been imposed in Tibet (and not just in China itself, as was claimed). Those who exceeded this quota were sent to medical facilities like the one known simply as 'the butchery' in Gyantse, where pregnant women had their foetuses forcibly aborted prior to sterilisation. Indeed, many women were involuntarily forced into using birth control, as we now know from recent arrivals from Tibet who were discovered to have been fitted with crude copper intra-uterine devices.

And when the people rose in revolt, which they did on several different occasions after 1959, whole villages were razed, their inhabitants murdered, whilst tens of thousands of the remaining population were put into prison. There they were kept under the most vile conditions, with forced labour by day, *thamzing* sessions until late at night, and only starvation rations to nourish them. I myself have since spoken to a number of people who were prisoners of the Chinese. One of them was Dr Tenzin Choedrak, who had been appointed my junior personal physician in the late 1950s. When the first fact-finding mission went to Peking, I requested that they ask the authorities there that he be released and allowed to join me in exile.

Nothing came of this at first, but a year later he was finally freed and, at the end of 1980, he came to Dharamsala. The stories of cruelty and degradation he brought with him were almost unbelievable. Many times over the twenty years of his incarceration he had been close to death from starvation. He told me of how he and his fellow prisoners were forced to consume their own clothing for food and how one inmate, with whom he was in hospital at one time, was so desperate that when he passed a worm in his meagre stool, he washed it and ate it.

I do not repeat any of this information gratuitously. I write as a Buddhist monk not to antagonise my Chinese brothers and sisters but because I want to educate people. There are undoubtedly many good Chinese people who are unaware of the true situation in Tibet. Nor do I relate such grim facts out of bitterness. On the contrary, these things have happened, so there is nothing to be done except look to the future.

Since the return of the first fact-finding delegation, more than ten years ago now, its findings have been confirmed from numerous other sources, including further Tibetan delegations and foreign journalists and tourists, as well as a few sympathetic Chinese. Unfortunately, in the interval, although there has been some further material progress, the picture has in many ways worsened.

We now know that more than 300,000 Chinese troops are stationed in Tibet, many of them along the still-disputed border with India, but also at least 50,000 based within a day's journey from Lhasa. On top of this, China maintains at least one-third of its nuclear weaponry on Tibetan soil. And because Tibet contains one of the world's richest deposits of uranium, the Chinese are likely to render large areas of the country hazardous from radioactive waste through their mining activities. In Amdo, the northeastern province where I was born, there exists the largest gulag known to man – big enough, by some estimates, to cater for the internment of up to ten million prisoners.

And following a massive immigration programme, the population of Chinese in Tibet now comfortably exceeds that of Tibetans. My countrymen and women are today in grave danger of becoming nothing more than a tourist attraction in their own country.

O CHAPTER FOURTEEN O

Initiatives for Peace

O

THE SECOND and third fact-finding missions both left India for Tibet during May 1980. One was comprised of younger people, the other of educators. In the first instance, I wanted to try to gain an impression of how the situation in Tibet appeared to people whose perspective had the freshness of youth. In the second, I wanted to know what were the prospects for the youth of Tibet itself.

Unfortunately, the young people's mission was unable to complete its investigations. When Tibetans began turning out in force to greet the exiles and to denounce the Chinese presence, the authorities accused the delegates of inciting the masses to acts of defiance and expelled the delegation from Tibet for endangering the 'unity of the Motherland'. Naturally, I was disturbed by this turn of events. Far from 'seeking truth from facts', it seemed that the Chinese were determined to ignore facts altogether. But, at least this expulsion showed that they were taking some notice of the feelings of Tibetans.

The third delegation, which was led by my sister Jetsun Pema, was permitted to stay, however. Returning to Dharamsala in October 1980, its findings made clear that although there had been a slight improvement in the general standard of education over the past twenty years, this was not much of a blessing, for it seemed that, to the Chinese, the real value of reading was to enable children to study the thoughts of Chairman Mao and of writing to enable them to produce 'confessions'.

Overall, the information gathered by the fact-finding missions revealed not only the full extent of China's rape of Tibet, but also that living conditions for Tibetans continued to be wretched. And although, compared with the suffering of the previous twenty years, the situation had undoubtedly improved, it was evident that the Chinese authorities still considered Tibetans to be 'backward, ignorant, cruel and barbaric', as they put it.

In 1981, my mother died after a short period of illness following a stroke. All her long life (she was as old as the century) she had enjoyed good health, so to be bedridden was a new experience for her. It meant that for the first time she was dependent on others. Previously, my mother had always taken care of herself. For example, although she liked to get up very early, she never imposed this on her servants, always fetching her own tea in the morning, despite an injured wrist which made it difficult for her to manage.

During the last months of her life, Tenzin Choegyal, who at that time lived with her, asked her quite candidly which one of her children was her favourite. I think he was hoping that he would receive the citation. But no, she replied that it was Lobsang Samten. I tell this story not just because, when my younger brother related it to me, I too thought for a moment that I might be a candidate, but also because, as it turned out, Lobsang Samten was the only one of her children present at her passing. I myself saw her shortly beforehand, when I walked down to her cottage, but at the actual time I was away at Bodh Gaya.

As soon as I heard the news, I began to say prayers asking that she should have a good rebirth. I was joined in this by every Tibetan present; it was very touching to see the depth of feeling shown by all these other people. Naturally, the Government sent a letter of condolence too. This was addressed to Ling Rinpoché, who was supposed to break the news. But for some reason it was delivered directly to me. An amusing incident followed. Having read the letter, I passed it on to him. When he in turn had read it, he came up to me puzzled and, scratching his head, said: 'I see that I was supposed to convey this letter to you, not the other way round. Now what am I to do?' It was the only time I ever saw Ling Rinpoché lost for words.

Of course, I was very sad at my mother's death. I had seen less and less of her as the years went by and the pressure of my work and duties increased. Yet we remained spiritually close, so I experienced a great sense of loss – just as I always do when any old member of my entourage dies. Of course, with time, the older generation is gradually passing away, as it must. More and more I am surrounded by people who are younger than me. In fact, the average age of my administration is under thirty-five. This, I feel, is good in many ways. The challenges presented by the situation in Tibet today require modern minds. Also, it is hard for people who grew up in the old Tibet to comprehend what is happening there. It is better that those who address these problems should not have to bear the burden of memory. Besides, it is for our children that the struggle to regain Tibet's rightful independence is being waged and it is they who must carry on that fight, if they still want to.

At the beginning of April 1982, a three-member team of negotiators from Dharamsala flew to Peking for discussions on the future of Tibet. It was led by Juchen Thubten Namgyal, then senior member of the *Kashag*. With him were Phuntsog Tashi Takla, my former *Kusun Depon*, who was one of the interpreters for Ngabo Ngawang Jigme in 1951, and Lodi Gyaltsen Gyari, Chairman of the *Chetui Lhenkhang*, the Tibetan People's Assembly. Whilst there, they met senior members of the Chinese Government with a view to both sides clarifying their position.

Among the points put forward for discussion by the Tibetans were, firstly, the historical facts concerning our homeland. They reminded the Chinese that, historically speaking, Tibet has always been separate from China, a fact that was implicitly recognised when Peking imposed the Seventeen-Point 'Agreement'. Secondly, the negotiators put it to the Chinese that, despite the 'progress' in Tibet, loudly publicised with outrageous exaggeration, in reality the Tibetan people were totally dissatisfied. On the basis of these facts, they suggested, it was up to China to find a new approach which acknowledged reality.

One of the negotiators also asked whether Tibetans, in view of their different race, should not have the same rights, if not more, than the Chinese Government had said it was prepared to grant its own people in Taiwan. He was told that these offers were being made to Taiwan because it had not yet been 'liberated'. 'But Tibet is already on the glorious road to Socialism.'

Unfortunately it turned out that, for their part, the Chinese did not have anything of substance to say. They lectured the delegates and accused us of using the evidence of the fact-finding missions to distort the truth. All that they really wanted to discuss was the return of the Dalai Lama. To this end, they produced the following list of five points regarding my future status:

1 The Dalai Lama should be confident that China has entered a new stage of long-term political stability, steady economic growth and mutual help among all nationalities.

2 The Dalai Lama and his representatives should be frank and sincere with the Central Government, not beat about the bush. There should be no more quibbling over the events of 1959.

3 The central authorities would sincerely welcome back the Dalai Lama and his followers. This is based on the hope that they will contribute to upholding China's unity, to promoting solidarity between the Han and Tibetan nationalities and among all nationalities, and to promoting the modernisation programme.

4 The Dalai Lama will enjoy the same political status and living conditions as he had before 1959. It is suggested that he need not go to live in Tibet or hold local posts there. Of course, he may go back to Tibet from time to time. His followers need not worry about their jobs and living conditions. These will only be better than before.

5 When the Dalai Lama wishes to come back, he can issue a brief statement to the press. It is up to him to decide what he would like to say in the statement.

Then after the delegates had returned to Dharamsala, the Chinese Government published a heavily slanted version of the proceedings, which referred to our viewpoint as being 'splittist', 'reactionary' and 'opposed by the Chinese people and most strenuously by the Tibetans'. It began to look as if China's 'new' policy regarding Tibet was much less than the developments of the late 1970s had suggested. As an old Tibetan saying goes, 'Before your eyes they show you brown sugar, but in your mouth they put sealing wax.'

As regards the five points concerning myself, I do not know quite why the Chinese thought that my personal status was of much importance to me. Throughout our struggle I have not been concerned for myself but for the rights, welfare and freedom of my six million fellow countrymen and women. My reason for this is not simply a concern with borders and so forth. It is because I believe that the most important thing for humankind is its own creativity. I further believe that, in order to be able to exercise this creativity, people need to be free. I have freedom in exile. And, as a refugee for over thirty-one years, I have learned something of its value. Therefore, it would be wrong for me to return to Tibet before all Tibetans enjoy similar liberty in their own country.

Nevertheless, despite the unproductive nature of these discussions with the Chinese administration, I decided I would make a short trip to Tibet, if that were acceptable to Peking. I wanted to talk with my people and find out for myself what the situation really was. The response was favourable, and preparations were put in hand for an advance party to go over in 1984 prior to my own visit the following year.

In the meantime, owing to the lifting of travel restrictions, a considerable number of Tibetans began to arrive in India. They continue to do so, though less and less. At the time of writing, about 10,000 have made the journey and more than half, mostly young people who want to take advantage of the education offered by our schools and monastic universities, have remained. Of those who returned, most did so for compelling reasons.

I try to greet all these visitors and new arrivals from Tibet in person. Invariably, our meetings are very emotional: most are such sad, innocent people, ragged and destitute. I always ask them about their own lives and families. And always there are tears when they reply – some breaking down entirely as they relate their pitiful stories.

Also during this period I began to meet growing numbers of tourists who had been to Tibet. For the first time in history, foreigners (mostly western) were being given limited access to the Land of Snows. Unfortunately, the Chinese authorities imposed severe restrictions from the start. Except during the initial period of the open-door policy, entry was virtually impossible unless as a member of a group with a planned itinerary. And once inside, the number of places open to visitors was strictly limited. Furthermore, contact with Tibetans was minimal, since the great majority of accommodation available was Chinese-owned and run. The few Tibetans working in these establishments were in menial jobs as servants and cleaners.

All of this was – and continues to be – a drawback. Worse, the Chinese tour guides inevitably only show people those monasteries and buildings which have been or are being rebuilt. They do not see the thousands still in ruins. It is true, especially in and around Lhasa, that much restoration work has been under way for the past ten years or so. But it is not cynicism which prompts me to say that this is largely for the benefit of the tour groups. Since the monks allowed into these revived buildings are, we know, carefully screened by the authorities, and since, rather than study, they must carry out the restoration work themselves (with money provided mainly by private individuals), it is the only possible conclusion.

Thanks to the carefully trained guides, few tourists ever realise this. And if they ask why so much restoration work is necessary, they are told that, regrettably, the excesses of the Cultural Revolution reached even into Tibet but that the Chinese people, who are truly sorry for what happened under the rule of the Gang of Four, are taking all steps necessary to put right those terrible wrongs. It is never said that the majority of the destruction was carried out long before the Cultural Revolution.

Sadly, to many visitors, Tibet is probably little more than an exotic destination, another stamp in the passport. They see enough monasteries to satisfy their curiosity, and enough colourfully dressed pilgrims visiting them to allay any suspicions they may have. However, if this is true of most, it is not true of all. And this is where the real benefit of tourism in Tibet lies. It has nothing to do with economics or statistics, but rather with the small percentage of visitors who have real imagination and curiosity. They are the ones who take the opportunity to slip away from their chaperones and look where they are not supposed to look and, more importantly, hear information that they are not supposed to hear.

Between 1981 and 1987, the number of visitors to Tibet rose from 1,500 to 43,000 per year. From those who subsequently contacted us in exile, we learned that there was little substance to China's supposed 'liberalism'. Tibetans were still denied free speech. And although in private people made clear their opposition to China's occupation of our country, they dared not do so in public. Furthermore, their access to information was strictly controlled, as was the practice of religion. It took little objectivity to see that Tibet was a police state where people were terrorised into submission. Thus they continued to live in fear, despite the promises of genuine reform in the immediate aftermath of Mao's death. And now they had to contend with the increasing influx of Chinese immigrants who threatened to swamp them.

Many of the visitors that I met subsequently said they had basically been pro-China before they went, only to have their ideas overturned by what they saw. Similarly, a lot said that, although they were basically uninterested in politics, they now felt compelled to change their stance. I remember in particular a Norwegian man who told me that initially he had admired the Chinese for their destruction of religion. But now that he had been back to Lhasa for a second time, he had seen what was really happening. Was there anything, he asked, that he could do to help my people? I replied to him, as I reply to all those who have been to Tibet and ask this question, that the best thing he could do was tell the truth of what he had seen to as many people as possible. That way, the world's knowledge of Tibet's plight is gradually increased.

Following what I learned both from the new arrivals and those tourists I met, I was not greatly surprised to hear, in September 1983, of a new bout of repression in China and Tibet. Executions were reported in Lhasa, Shigatse and Gyantse, with further arrests in Chamdo and Karze. Ostensibly, the crack-down (which covered China as well) was aimed at 'criminal and anti-social elements' but this clearly meant dissidents. However, although this seemed to indicate a hardening in the attitude of the Chinese authorities, there was a positive aspect to the news. For the first time, information about China's activities in Tibet was disseminated by the international press, which had recently been permitted to send correspondents to Tibet.

Feeling that this new terror must signal a return to the old, harsh methods of the Mao era, the refugee population reacted strongly. Mass demonstrations of protest were held in Delhi and throughout the settlements in India. For my own part, I felt it was too soon to tell whether this brutality merely represented a backlash by conservatives against Deng Xiao-ping's regime, or whether Tibet was re-entering a period of darkness. But it was evident that the advance party to my visit could not now take place. Subsequently my own did not materialise.

By May 1984, it had become clear that China's policy with regard to Tibet had indeed undergone a major shift. In direct contradiction to Hu Yaobang's pledge to reduce by eighty-five per cent the number of Chinese officials in Tibet, a massive effort to encourage immigration began. In the name of 'development', 60,000 skilled and unskilled workers were recruited to start the process and given financial guarantees, housing assistance and the promise of home-leave entitlements. Simultaneously, due to the relaxation of travel restrictions within China itself, many others followed as private individuals, lured by the prospect of finding work. Thus, in accordance with the Tibetan saying that where there is one Chinese, ten will follow, a huge influx ensued – and continues unabated.

In late autumn that same year, Mrs Gandhi was assassinated and the Tibetan refugees lost a true friend. I was very shocked when I heard the news, en route to Delhi from London – not least because I was due to have lunch with her and J. Krishnamurti that very day. She was succeeded in office by her son Rajiv, who, as a young leader, had great determination to do something for his country and whatever he could for the Tibetan exile community.

Rajiv Gandhi is a man with a friendly, gentle nature and a very good heart. I well remember the first time I saw him. During my 1956 visit to India, I was invited to lunch at the residence of his grandfather, Pandit Nehru. When the Prime Minister showed me into the garden, I noticed two small boys playing around a tent with a large firework that they were trying unsuccessfully to launch into space. This was Rajiv and his younger brother Sanjay. Recently, Rajiv reminded me that I had tied them both inside the tent, much to their amusement.

Less than a year later, Tibet lost one of its very greatest supporters when Lobsang Samten died. He was only fifty-four. In a way, despite my profound sorrow, I was not much surprised by this. His experiences as a member of the first fact-finding mission had affected him profoundly. He could make no sense of Chinese indifference to Tibet in the face of such obvious suffering and unhappiness. And whereas previously he had always been full of jokes and fun (he had a highly developed and very vulgar sense of humour), subsequently he fell into long periods of depression. I do not think it an exaggeration to say that he died of a broken heart.

I deeply regretted Lobsang Samten's death, not only because we were so close, but also because I was unable to be with him during his fatal illness. The last time I saw him was on a visit to Delhi, where he was attending to some business connected with his work as director of the Tibetan Medical Institute. Rather than return to Dharamsala by bus with his wife, he had decided to remain an extra day to carry on with his work. He would then travel back with me. But on arrival at the train station, he had a change of heart. His business was not quite finished so, despite the opportunity of a lift home, he felt that really he ought to stay. This was typical of him. He never put himself first. A day later he went down with 'flu for no apparent reason. This progressed to pneumonia complicated by jaundice and he was dead within three weeks.

Whenever I think about Lobsang Samten today, I am struck by his humility. He always paid me the same respect as an ordinary Tibetan, and did not really treat me as a brother. For example, whenever I arrived home or left to travel somewhere, he invariably lined up with the people at the gate to my residence to greet me or wish me a safe journey. And not only was he humble, but he was also very compassionate. I recall once mentioning to him something about the leper colony at Orissa in eastern India. Like me, he was deeply impressed with any kind of work dedicated to relieving the suffering of others. So when I told him that I was wondering whether the Tibetan community in exile could do anything to help them, he burst into tears and said that he personally was ready to do anything he could.

Following my visits to America in 1979, 1981 and 1984, many people in that country had expressed a desire to do something for Tibet. As a direct result of this, in July 1985, ninety-one members of the US Congress signed a letter to the then President of the People's Assembly in Peking, Li Xiannian, expressing support for direct talks between the Chinese Government and my representatives. The letter urged the Chinese to 'grant the very reasonable and justified aspirations of His Holiness the Dalai Lama and his people every consideration'.

For the first time, Tibet had formal political support – something I took as an encouraging sign that the justice of our cause was finally beginning to be recognised internationally. Further evidence of this was a surge of interest among people in other countries, who started to take similar steps.

Then, in early 1987, I received an invitation to address the Human Rights Caucus of the US Congress in Washington DC. I accepted gladly. A date was fixed for a visit during the autumn. In the meantime, a number of my old friends suggested that I should use this opportunity to put forward some definite goals for the Tibetan cause with which supporters of justice round the world could identify. This struck me as good advice and I began to formalise some of the ideas that I had had in mind over the past few years.

Just before I was due to leave for America, Congress published a new report on human rights violations in Tibet. In this, it was noted that its 1985 letter to President Li Xiannian had been ignored: 'there has been no evidence of any consideration [of the Dalai Lama's very reasonable and justified aspirations] being granted by the People's Republic of China'.

After arriving in America, I delivered my address on Capitol Hill on 21 September 1987. The proposals that I outlined have since become known as the Five-Point Peace Plan. It is comprised of the following points:

1 The transformation of the whole of Tibet into a zone of peace.

2 Abandonment of China's population transfer policy which threatens the very existence of the Tibetans as a people.

3 Respect for the Tibetan people's fundamental human rights and democratic freedoms.

4 Restoration and protection of Tibet's natural environment and the abandonment of China's use of Tibet for the production of nuclear weapons and dumping of nuclear waste.

5 Commencement of earnest negotiations on the future status of Tibet and of relations between Tibetan and Chinese peoples.

After briefly putting forward these suggestions, I invited questions from the audience. As I did so, I noticed a number of people who looked as though they might be Chinese. I asked them whether they were. There was a moment's hesitation before they replied that, yes, they were from *Xinhua*, the New China News Agency. Since then, I have noticed that Peking now invariably sends monitors whenever I speak in public abroad. Often, these men and women show personal friendliness towards me and only occasionally have they been negative and sarcastic, their faces distorted with guilt.

I would like to explain in general terms the Five-Point Peace Plan. Its first component, my proposal that the whole of Tibet, including the eastern provinces of Kham and Amdo, be transformed into a zone of *Ahimsa* (a Hindi term meaning a state of peace and non-violence) is in keeping with Tibet's position as a peaceful Buddhist nation. It is also in keeping with Nepal's similar move to proclaim itself a peace zone, something that has already drawn China's support. If implemented, it would allow Tibet to resume its historical role of acting as a neutral buffer state separating the continent's great powers.

The following are key elements of the proposed Zone of *Ahimsa*:

-   The entire Tibetan plateau would be demilitarised.

-   The manufacture, testing and stockpiling of nuclear weapons and other armaments on the Tibetan plateau would be prohibited.

-   The Tibetan plateau would be transformed into the world's largest natural park or biosphere. Strict laws would be enforced to protect wildlife and plant life; the exploitation of natural resources would be carefully regulated so as not to damage relevant ecosystems; and a policy of sustainable development would be adopted in populated areas.

- The manufacture and use of nuclear power and other technologies which produce hazardous waste would be prohibited.
- National resources and policy would be directed towards the active promotion of peace and environmental protection. Organisations dedicated to the furtherance of peace and to the protection of all forms of life would find a hospitable home in Tibet.

- The establishment of international and regional organisations for the promotion and protection of human rights would be encouraged in Tibet.

When established, the Zone of *Ahimsa* would enable India to withdraw her troops and military installations from the Himalayan regions bordering Tibet. This would be achieved under an international agreement which would satisfy China's legitimate security needs and build trust among the Tibetan, Chinese, Indian and other peoples of the region. This is in everyone's best interest, particularly that of China and India, as it would enhance their security, at the same time reducing the economic burden of maintaining high troop concentrations on the disputed Himalayan border. Historically, relations between China and India were never strained. It was only when Chinese armies marched into Tibet, creating for the first time a common border, that tensions arose between these two powers, ultimately leading to the 1962 war. Since then, numerous dangerous incidents have continued to occur.

A restoration of good relations between the world's two most populous countries would be greatly facilitated if they were separated – as they have been throughout history – by a large and friendly intermediary region.

To improve relations between the Tibetan people and the Chinese, the first requirement is the creation of trust. After the holocaust of the last three decades, during which, incredibly, almost one and a quarter million Tibetans lost their lives from starvation, execution, torture and suicide, and tens of thousands lingered in prison camps, only a withdrawal of Chinese troops could start a genuine process of reconciliation. The vast occupation force in Tibet is a daily reminder to Tibetans of the oppression and suffering they have experienced. A troop withdrawal would be an essential signal that in future a meaningful relationship might be established with the Chinese, based on friendship and trust.

Unfortunately, Peking read this first part of my proposal as a move towards separation, though it is not so to my mind. All that I meant by it is the logical conclusion that if there is to be genuine harmony between our two peoples, then one side or the other must make a concession or at least some conciliatory gesture. And since Tibet is the aggrieved party, because we Tibetans have lost everything, we have nothing to offer the Chinese. Therefore, it is reasonable that, in order to bring about an atmosphere of mutual trust, those people who carry rifles (whether these rifles be hidden or not) should be withdrawn. That is what I mean by a zone of peace: simply an area where no one carries weapons. Not only will this help to create trust between the two sides, but it will also give the Chinese an important economic boost. Their expenditure on maintaining large standing armies in Tibet is an enormous drain on their resources as a developing country.

The second component of my Five-Point Peace Plan concerns what amounts to the greatest threat to the continuation of Tibetans as a distinct race, namely the population transfer of Chinese into Tibet. By the mid-1980s, it had become clear that the Government in Peking is pursuing a deliberate policy of Sinocisation: what some people have called a 'final solution' by stealth. They are doing this by reducing the native Tibetan population to an insignificant and disenfranchised minority in its own homeland. This must be stopped. Such a massive transfer of Chinese civilians into Tibet is in direct contravention of the Fourth Geneva Convention. As a result of it, in the eastern parts of our country the Chinese now greatly outnumber Tibetans. For example, in Qinghai Province which today comprises Amdo, where I was born, there are, according to Chinese statistics, 2.5 million Chinese and only

750,000 Tibetans. Even in the so-called Tibet Autonomous Region (that is to say, central and western Tibet), the Chinese already outnumber Tibetans, according to our information.

This population transfer policy is not new. China has systematically applied it to other areas. Not long ago, the Manchus were a distinct race with their own culture and traditions. Today, only two to three million Manchurians are left in Manchuria, where 75 million Chinese have settled. In Eastern Turkestan, which the Chinese now call Xinjang, the Chinese population has grown from 200,000 in 1949 to over seven million today: more than half the total population. In the wake of the Chinese colonisation of Inner Mongolia, the Chinese number 8.5 million, Mongolians only 2.5 million. At present, in the whole of Tibet, we estimate that there are already 7.5 million Chinese, outnumbering the Tibetan population of around six million.

For the Tibetans to survive as a people, it is imperative that population transfer is stopped and that Chinese settlers be allowed to return to China. Otherwise, Tibetans will soon be no more than a tourist attraction and relic of a noble past. At present it seems that it is mainly economic incentive which keeps them there; they certainly find the conditions difficult: altitude sickness is reported to be endemic amongst the Chinese population.

The third component of my proposal concerns human rights in Tibet. These must be respected. The Tibetan people must once again be free to develop culturally, intellectually, economically and spiritually and to be able to exercise basic democratic freedoms. Human rights violations in Tibet are amongst the most serious in the world. This is attested to by Amnesty International and other such organisations. Discrimination is practised in Tibet under a policy of outright apartheid which the Chinese call 'segregation and assimilation'. In reality Tibetans are, at best, second-class citizens in their own country. Deprived of all basic democratic rights and freedoms, they exist under a colonial administration of occupation in which all real power is wielded by Chinese officials of the Communist Party and the PLA. Although the Chinese Government allows Tibetans to rebuild some Buddhist monasteries and to worship in them, it forbids all serious study and teaching of religion. Thus, while Tibetans in exile have the opportunity to exercise their democratic rights under the draft constitution promulgated by myself in 1963, thousands and thousands of my countrymen continue to suffer in prisons and labour camps for their belief in freedom. For in Tibet a Tibetan who shows loyalty to China is called 'progressive', but anyone who shows loyalty to his or her own country is branded a 'criminal' and incarcerated.

My fourth proposal calls for serious efforts to be made to restore the natural environment of Tibet. Tibet should not be used for the production of nuclear weapons and the dumping of nuclear waste. Tibetans have a great respect for all forms of life. This inherent feeling is enhanced by our Buddhist faith which prohibits the harming of all sentient beings, whether human or animal. Prior to the Chinese invasion, Tibet was a fresh, beautiful, unspoiled wilderness sanctuary in a unique natural environment.

Sadly, during the past few decades, the wildlife of Tibet has been almost totally destroyed and, in many places, irreparable damage has been done to its forests. The overall effect on Tibet's delicate environment has been devastating – particularly since the country's altitude and aridity mean that the process of restoring vegetation will take much longer than in lower, wetter regions. For this reason, what little is left must be protected and efforts made to reverse the effects of China's iniquitous and wanton destruction of the Tibetan environment.

In doing so, the first priority will be to halt the production of nuclear weaponry and, even more importantly, to prevent the dumping of nuclear waste. Apparently, China plans not only to dispose of its own but also to import other countries' waste, in exchange for hard currency. The danger this represents is obvious. Not only living generations, but future generations are threatened. Furthermore, the inevitable problems this would cause locally could so easily turn into a catastrophe of global proportions. Giving waste to China, which might have access to large areas of lightly populated land but has only crude technology, will likely prove only a short-term solution to the problem.

In my call for negotiations on the future status of Tibet, I expressed my wish to approach the subject in a spirit of frankness and conciliation, with a view to finding a solution that is in the long-term interest of everyone – the Tibetans, the Chinese and ultimately all people on earth – my motivation in all this being the possibility of contributing to world peace through regional peace. I said nothing merely to criticise the Chinese. On the contrary, I want to help the Chinese in any way that I can. I hoped that my suggestions would be useful to them. Unfortunately, they chose only to see them as a call for separatism (although, with regard to the future of Tibet, I nowhere spoke of sovereignty) and Peking moved swiftly to denounce my speech in strong terms.

This did not much surprise me. Nor was I greatly surprised at the reaction of the people of Tibet – though I did not expect it. A few days after I had spoken in Washington, there came reports of huge demonstrations in Lhasa.

Universal Responsibility and the Good Heart

o

I LATER DISCOVERED that the demonstrations of September and October 1987 followed directly Peking's denunciation of my Five-Point Peace Plan. Lhasans in their thousands turned out to call for a restoration of Tibetan independence. Predictably, the Chinese authorities reacted with violence and cruelty. Armed police moved in to break up the demonstrations, opening fire indiscriminately and killing at least nineteen people. Many more were wounded.

At first the Chinese denied that any shots had been fired. Six months later they admitted that some members of the security forces had fired warning shots into the air above the heads of the crowd. But, they suggested, some of these rounds must have struck the crowd, instead of falling harmlessly. (When I heard this, I wondered whether perhaps they were referring to some new secret weapon: a Tibetan blood-seeking bullet.)

News of the demonstrations and the merciless and bloody crackdown flashed around the world and, for the first time since 1959, Tibet was headline news. However, it was not until some time afterwards that I heard the full details of what happened. And for this I was indebted to the handful of western tourists who happened to be in the capital at that time.

Forty of them subsequently formed a group and submitted a report on the atrocities they had seen. From this I learned that the pattern of both demonstrations was the same. Initially, a handful of monks had gathered in front of the Jokhang, shouting,

'*Bö rangzen*': 'Independence for Tibet'. They were quickly joined by hundreds, then thousands, of lay people who echoed these calls for freedom. Suddenly a battalion of security men appeared. Without warning, about sixty monks and lay people were arrested and hustled into the police station, which today lies immediately opposite the Jokhang. Before being taken inside, they were viciously beaten. Meanwhile, people pleaded with officials for the release of the demonstrators. But suddenly dozens of security men arrived with video cameras and began filming the crowd. Fearing subsequent identification, several people began throwing stones at the police as they filmed. A few Tibetans panicked and began overturning police vehicles and setting them alight, whereupon armed members of the security forces started shooting. Most people showed great restraint, however, and when some of the police ran away, dropping their guns, they gathered up the weapons and broke them on the ground.

During the disturbances of 1 October 1987, the police station itself was, regrettably, set on fire by the demonstrators, who, in a desperate attempt to release their companions, tried to burn down the door. Until then, members of the security forces had repeatedly come running out of the building to drag people inside, where they were horribly beaten.

When eventually the crowd dispersed, at least a dozen Tibetans, including several children, lay dead. That night and on subsequent nights, hundreds were seized from their homes. In the end, more than two thousand were imprisoned. Of these, most were subjected to beatings and torture, and one report spoke of forty executions.

Before going further, I wish to express my deep appreciation to those foreigners who, despite their having no obligation to do so, selflessly risked their lives to help their suffering fellow human beings. Such spontaneous expressions of humanity represent the only hope for the future of mankind. Some of these men and women repeatedly risked their lives trying to help the many seriously wounded Tibetans. They also witnessed, and took photographs of, numerous acts of Chinese barbarity.

Although the Chinese authorities hurriedly expelled not only those journalists present in Tibet but also all foreigners, their atrocities received worldwide coverage. As a result, several western Governments called on the Chinese to respect human rights in Tibet and to release all political prisoners there. The Government in Peking replied by saying that the disturbances were an internal matter for themselves and rejected any criticism of their actions.

Because Tibet was now closed to the outside world, I heard little more information for several months. But I now know that, in the immediate aftermath of the demonstrations, the Chinese began a massive programme of political 're-education'. They even tried to organise a counter-demonstration in late October, offering potential participants the equivalent of a week's wages. But it had to be called off: no one came forward. Also, in order to try to prevent any more news leaking out, the PLA did its best to seal Tibet's borders, while the Government in Peking actually succeeded in pressuring a sovereign state, namely the Kingdom of Nepal, into arresting and handing over twenty-six Tibetans who managed to slip through the net. But it was during this period that I was informed by a Chinese source (motivated, like the tourists, by compassion and outrage) that an order to open fire on the demonstrators had most certainly been given.

At the beginning of 1988, the Chinese authorities in Lhasa instructed the monastic community to hold the *Monlam* prayer festival as usual. (It had been revived after twenty years in 1986.) However, the monks felt this would be inappropriate while so many people remained in prison and they resisted the edict. The Central People's Government in Peking then ordered that the celebrations must go ahead as planned, hoping to show the outside world that the situation in Tibet was normal. So the monks were forced to proceed. But evidently the Chinese feared more disturbances. On 28 February, the BBC reported that

'Thousands of Chinese security forces have been moved into the Lhasa area – road blocks are in force all over the city. Long convoys of armoured vehicles patrol the streets at night, and people are advised through loud-speaker announcements to stay at home. One message said bluntly, "If you misbehave, we will kill you."'

Then, a week before *Monlam*, a Reuters dispatch from Peking stated that fifty military vehicles and more than a thousand Chinese police, many in riot gear, rehearsed their manoeuvres in front of the Jokhang.

The festival began with tensions running high. A large military presence accompanied the opening ceremonies and there were at least ten security personnel to every monk present. In addition, many plain-clothes police mingled with the crowd, some again armed with video cameras. It also appears that members of the security forces disguised themselves, some by shaving their heads, others by wearing wigs, to give the impression either that they were monks or that they were from outside Lhasa.

At first, peace prevailed; but, on 5 March, some monks began shouting for the release of a *tulku* named Yulu Dawa Tsering, one of the many protestors to have been imprisoned without charge since the previous October. Next, the crowd that had assembled for the last part of the prayer festival, when a statue of Maitreya is taken round the *Barkhor*, began to denounce the Chinese presence in Tibet and to throw stones at the police who paraded provocatively nearby. To this, the security forces responded first by repeatedly charging into the crowd with clubs and electric cattle prods. Then the military opened fire, not indiscriminately this time. With precision they singled out and shot several protestors. There followed running battles which caused hundreds of Tibetan casualties. At around noon, police stormed the Jokhang and murdered at least twelve monks. One they beat severely, before tearing both his eyes out and hurling him from the roof. Tibet's holiest shrine became like a butcher's shop.

The whole Tibetan quarter of Lhasa was now in uproar and, during the night, about twenty Chinese shops, whose owners had repeatedly expressed a negative attitude towards Tibetans, were burned down. At the same time, the security forces made frequent assaults, dragging away hundreds of men, women and children.

Because there was only a handful of westerners in the city at the time, none of them journalists, little news escaped the media blackout and it was several weeks before I heard any details. In the meantime, it quickly became apparent that this latest disturbance exceeded in both scale and severity those of the previous autumn. As a result, a two-week curfew was imposed, during which at least 2,500 arrests were made and the entire Tibetan population of Lhasa was ruthlessly intimidated.

Once again, I was not greatly surprised by this expression of the Tibetan people's desperation, but I was nevertheless profoundly shocked to hear of China's violent response. World opinion was equally outraged and for the second time in six months there was wide coverage of the disturbances in the international press, despite the small amount of information available. Meanwhile, China's official reaction was the same as before: this was an internal matter for the Peking Government and they denounced the demonstrations as the work of a handful of 'reactionary splittists' and called me a dangerous criminal. The Dalai Lama, they suggested, had deliberately incited riots and sent in agents to Tibet to carry them out. This was predictable, though I was disturbed that the Chinese were now openly accusing foreigners of having played a leading part in both disturbances.

I received the first full report of the *Monlam* demonstration from the British politician, Lord Ennals, who arrived in Lhasa less than a month later. As leader of an independent delegation sanctioned by the Peking Government, Lord Ennals's aim was to investigate the human rights situation in Tibet. Along with the other members of his team, he was shocked to find that gross violations continued to be committed against the Tibetan people. The delegates also came across irrefutable evidence of torture and physical abuse of prisoners following the demonstrations, about which they heard complete details from numerous eyewitnesses. Their report, published by International Alert, spoke of a 'crisis which demands a rapid and positive response'.

At the time that this fact-finding mission was in Tibet, I myself was in Britain, where I had gone at the invitation of a number of groups interested in Tibetan Buddhism. Whilst there, I was impressed to find intense and sympathetic media interest in the plight of the Tibetan people. Also, I was pleased to receive an invitation to speak to a group of concerned politicians at the European Parliament later in 1988. This coincided with several western leaders calling on China to open negotiations with myself on the future of Tibet.

Thinking that this invitation offered an opportunity to restate the Five-Point Peace Plan and, in particular, to expand on its fifth component, I gladly accepted. In my speech, which I delivered in Strasbourg in June 1988, I mentioned my opinion that, under certain special circumstances, it could be possible for the whole of Tibet to exist in association with the People's Republic of China, with foreign affairs and limited defence directed from Peking until a regional peace conference takes place, after which the whole of Tibet would be designated a zone of peace. I also made plain that the Tibetan Government in Exile was ready to negotiate with the Chinese authorities whenever they were ready. But I insisted that this was only a proposal and any decisions would have to be made by the Tibetan people, not by me.

Again, the response from Peking was negative. My speech was denounced and the European Parliament was severely criticised for having permitted me to speak. However, during the autumn of 1988, in a very promising development, the Chinese indicated that they wished to discuss the future of Tibet with the Dalai Lama. For the first time, they professed themselves willing not merely to discuss the Dalai Lama's status, but the matter of Tibet itself. It was left to me to choose a venue. Immediately, I nominated a team of negotiators and proposed that the two sides meet in Geneva during January 1989. My reason for this choice was to enable me to participate personally in the talks as soon as it became apparent that my presence was required.

Unfortunately, no sooner had they agreed in principle to talks, than the Chinese began to put up conditions and objections. At first, they expressed a preference for Peking as the venue; then they made a condition that no foreigner could be a member of the negotiating team; next they said that they could not accept anyone who was a member of the Tibetan Government in Exile, because they did not recognise it; then they said they could not talk to anyone who had ever called for Tibetan independence. Finally, they said they would only talk to me. This was very disappointing. Having professed a clear willingness to talk, the Chinese had then made it virtually impossible for the talks ever to begin. And whilst I am by no means averse to meeting the Chinese personally, it is only sensible that there are preliminary discussions with my representatives first. So, although Geneva was finally agreed to as a venue, January 1989 came and went with nothing accomplished.

On 28 January 1989, news came that the Panchen Lama had died whilst on a rare visit to Tibet from Peking, where he lived. He was only fifty-three, and naturally I was deeply saddened. I felt that Tibet had lost a true freedom fighter. It cannot be denied that some Tibetans see him as a controversial character. Indeed, during the early 1950s, when he was still very young, I have a suspicion that, by siding with the Chinese, he thought he could use the situation to his own advantage. But his patriotism was real, I believe. And even though the Chinese used him as a puppet after releasing him from jail in 1978, he continued to oppose them until the end. Just before he died, he made a speech, reported by *Xinhua*, that was highly critical of the 'many mistakes' made in Tibet by the Chinese authorities. It was a courageous last act.

Two days later, he made his final appearance at Tashilhunpo monastery, where, shortly after consecrating the tombs of his predecessors, he apparently suffered a fatal heart attack. Many felt that the Panchen Lama's death in his own monastery was symbolic, the deliberate gesture of a true spiritual master.

Although I was not able to see him before he died, I did speak with the Panchen Lama on the telephone three times. Twice I spoke to him at his office in Peking, where he had been appointed to the National Assembly, and once whilst he was abroad. Inevitably, his conversations in Peking were monitored. I know this because, some weeks after the second of them, a carefully edited transcript of our conversation was published in the Chinese press. However, while he was in Australia, he managed to give his escort the slip at a prearranged time and I spoke to him from West Germany. We were not able to speak for long, but it was enough to assure me that in his heart the Panchen Lama remained true to his religion, to his people and to his country. So I was not too concerned when I heard bad reports of him from Lhasa, where he was criticised for having extensive business interests. It was also said that he had taken a wife.

Following his death, I received an invitation from the Buddhist Society of China to attend his funeral in Peking. This amounted to an official invitation to visit China. Personally, I wanted to go but hesitated, as inevitably there would be some discussion about Tibet if I went. Had the Geneva talks taken place as planned, this might have been opportune. However, under the circumstances, I felt it would be inappropriate to go and regretfully refused.

Meanwhile, China's procrastination produced its inevitable result. On 5 March 1989, there began three more days of demonstrations in Lhasa. In some of the most vigorous expressions of discontent since March 1959, many tens of thousands took to the streets. Changing their tactics, the Chinese security forces remained on the sidelines throughout the first day, merely filming scenes which they showed on television that night. Then, on the following days, they reacted with repeated baton charges and indiscriminate shooting. Witnesses reported seeing them firing automatic weapons into Tibetan homes killing whole families.

Unfortunately, Tibetans reacted to this not only by attacking the police and security forces, but also, in a few instances, innocent Chinese civilians. This made me very sad. It makes no sense whatever for Tibetans to resort to violence. If they wanted to, with a thousand million people against our six million, China could forcefully erase the entire Tibetan race from the face of the earth. It would be much more constructive if people tried to understand their supposed enemies. Learning to forgive is much more useful than merely picking up a stone and throwing it at the object of one's anger, the more so when the provocation is extreme.

For it is under the greatest adversity that there exists the greatest potential for doing good, both for oneself and others.

Yet, in truth, I realise that for most people such words are unrealistic. It is too much to ask. It is not right for me to expect Tibetans, who live their daily lives under such terrible hardship, to be able to love the Chinese. So whilst I will never condone it, I accept that some violence is inevitable.

Actually, I greatly admire and respect the courage of my people. Many of those who joined in the demonstrations were women, children and old people: hundreds of men were arrested on the first evening, so it was mostly their families who continued to express their feelings so vividly on the second and third days. Many of them are now probably dead. Even more are still in prison, being tortured and beaten on a daily basis.

Thanks to the presence of a few brave foreigners, some of whom experienced personal harassment, reports of this latest outrage were quickly transmitted to the outside world. As before, there was overwhelming support for the Tibetan people: the United States, France and the European Parliament condemned China's reprisals, which caused the deaths of at least two hundred and fifty unarmed Tibetans, not to mention the wounding of countless others. Many other Governments expressed their 'grave concern', and the subsequent imposition of martial law on 8 March drew widespread criticism.

The idea of China imposing martial law in Lhasa was terrifying, for, in reality, the city had been under military rule ever since 26 October 1951, when the first PLA troops arrived. It looked as if the Chinese must be about to turn the place into a slaughter-house, a Himalayan killing fields. Two days later, on the thirtieth anniversary of the Tibetan People's Uprising, I therefore sent an appeal to Deng Xiao-ping, asking that he intervene personally to lift martial law and end the repression of innocent Tibetans. He did not reply.

Within only a few weeks of the protests in Lhasa came the uprising in China. I followed events there with a mixture of disbelief and horror, becoming especially anxious when some of the demonstrators began a hunger strike. The students were obviously so bright, so sincere, so innocent, with their whole lives to live. Against them, they had a Government that remained totally stubborn and cruel and indifferent. At the same time, I could not help feeling a certain admiration for the Chinese leadership, those decrepit, foolish old men who clung so fiercely and determinedly to their ideas. In spite of clear evidence that their system was breaking down and that Communism was failing throughout the world, and in spite of a million protestors outside their front door, they held to their faith.

Naturally, I was appalled when the military was finally deployed to break up the demonstration. But considered politically, I feel it denoted no more than a temporary setback for the democracy movement. By resorting to violence, the authorities can only have helped develop a favourable attitude towards the students amongst ordinary Chinese people. In so doing, they shortened by half to two-thirds the life of Communism in China. Also, they showed the world the truth about their methods: scepticism of Tibetans' claims about Chinese human rights abuse is no longer possible.

On a personal level, I feel somewhat sorry for Deng Xiao-ping. His name is now irreparably damaged, whereas without the massacre in 1989 he would have gone down in history as a great leader of his country. I also feel sympathy for his co-leaders who, in their ignorance, destroyed China's reputation abroad after a decade of assiduous image-building. It seems that, although they failed to propagandise the people, they succeeded only too well with themselves.

In cruel counterpoint to the many wonderful happenings elsewhere in the world, martial law prevailed in Lhasa throughout 1989. Never was I more conscious of this sad fact than when, on a visit to the US that autumn, I learned that I had won the Nobel Prize for Peace. Although the news did not matter much to me personally, I realised that it would mean a great deal to the people of Tibet, for it was they who were the real 'winners' of the prize.

My own satisfaction derived from what I saw as international recognition of the value of compassion, forgiveness and love. Moreover, I was pleased that at that moment the people of many countries were discovering for themselves that peaceful change was not impossible. In the past, the idea of non-violent revolution had seemed perhaps idealistic, and I drew great comfort from this overwhelming proof to the contrary.

Chairman Mao once said that political power comes from the barrel of a gun. He was only partly right: power that comes from the barrel of a gun can be effective only for a short time. In the end, people's love for truth, justice, freedom and democracy will triumph. No matter what governments do, the human spirit will always prevail.

I had direct experience of this truth right at the end of 1989, when I visited Berlin on the very day that Egon Kranz was toppled. Thanks to the co-operation of the East German authorities, I was able to go up to the Wall itself. As I stood there, in full view of a still-manned security post, an old lady silently handed me a red candle. With some emotion, I lit it and held it up. For a moment the tiny dancing flame threatened to go out, but it held and, while a crowd pressed round me, touching my hands, I prayed that the light of compassion and awareness would fill the world and dispel the darkness of fear and oppression. It was a moment I shall always remember.

Something similar happened when I went to Czechoslovakia a few weeks later as the guest of President Havel, who, fresh from a jail sentence for his political activities, was now President of his country. On arrival, I was greeted by an emotional crowd. Many people had tears in their eyes as they waved and gave the victory sign. And I saw at once that, despite the years of totalitarianism, these men and women were full of life and exultant in their newly won freedom.

I felt greatly honoured to be invited to Czechoslovakia, not only by a head of state – for the first time – but also by a man who has consistently shown such devotion to truth. I found the new President to be very gentle and full of honesty, humility – and humour. At dinner that evening, as he sat drinking a glass of beer and holding a cigarette, he told me he identified strongly with the Sixth Dalai Lama, who had a reputation for worldliness. This prompted me to look forward to a second revolution in Czechoslovakia: that of less smoking at mealtimes! But what really impressed me about President Havel was his lack of pretence. He seemed quite unaffected by his new position, and his looks and talk suggested great sensitivity.

Another person I met in early 1990, who made a vivid impression on me, was Baba Amte, a man who founded a village in southern India. On what was previously barren earth he has brought into existence a thriving community surrounded by trees, a rose garden and a vegetable garden, and provided with a small hospital, an old people's home, schools and workshops. This alone is a great achievement, but what makes the place remarkable is that it was built entirely by handicapped people.

As I walked round it, I saw nothing to suggest any concessions to disability. At one point I went into a shed where a worker was repairing a bicycle wheel. In what remained of his leprous hands, he held a chisel and a hammer, which he was wielding with such vigour that I couldn't help feeling he was showing off. But his exuberant self-confidence made it clear to me that, given enthusiasm and proper organisation, even those people with crucial disadvantages can gain dignity and come to be recognised as productive members of society.

Baba Amte is an extraordinary person. After a long, vigorous life, during which he has suffered great physical hardship, he is himself virtually a cripple and, because of damage to his spine, he can now only stand straight or lie down. Yet he remains so full of energy that I could not do his work, even though I am much fitter. As I sat on his bed holding his hand, and he lay talking to me, I could not help feeling that here was someone who was truly compassionate. I told him that whereas my compassion is just so much talk, his shone through everything he did. In turn, Baba Amte told me the story of how he had made the decision to dedicate his life to helping others. One day, he had seen a leper with worms in the place where his eyes had been. That was all it took.

Such examples of humanity as this give me the conviction that one day there will be an end to my people's suffering at the hands of the People's Republic of China, for there are many hundreds of millions of Chinese, and whilst maybe several thousand are participating in acts of cruelty at any one moment, I believe there must be several million performing acts of kindness.

That said, I cannot forget the present situation in Tibet, where neither discontent nor repression are confined to Lhasa. Between the end of September 1987 and May 1990, more than eighty separate demonstrations have been reported. Many have involved no more than a handful of protestors, and not all have ended in bloodshed. But as a result, my fellow countrymen and women are enduring a new reign of terror. In the capital itself, where Chinese now far outnumber Tibetans, tanks have recently been sighted while recent reports by organisations such as Amnesty International and Asia Watch make clear that brutal repression continues throughout Tibet. Arrests without justification, beatings and torture, prison sentences and even execution without trial, characterise the behaviour of the Chinese authorities.

To this unhappy list must be added the testimonies of several Tibetans who, having been imprisoned and pitifully ill-treated following one or more of the demonstrations, have since succeeded in escaping to India. One, who must remain nameless for fear of reprisals against his family, described to human rights investigators how he was kept naked and handcuffed in his cell for prolonged periods, during which he was abused physically and verbally. On occasions, drunken guards came into his cell and beat him. One night his head was repeatedly struck against the wall until his nose bled, although he remained conscious. He also described being used as a target for martial arts' practice by guards 'smelling of alcohol'. In between periods of interrogation trying to force him to confess that he had taken part in the protests, he was sometimes left alone for days without food or bedding in a bitterly cold cell.

On the fifth day of detention this person was woken after dawn and taken to an interrogation centre outside the prison compound. He was first pinned to the ground by two guards, while a third, having knelt on his head, then took it in both hands and repeatedly banged his left temple against the ground for some ten minutes. He then described how he was subjected to the so-called 'hanging airplane' method of torture:

'I was picked up from the ground and two soldiers began to bind a rope around my arms. This long rope had a metal ring in the middle which was positioned behind my neck. Both ends were then passed in front of my shoulders and wound in a spiral tightly around my arms, finally trapping my fingers. One soldier then drew the two rope ends back through the metal ring, forcing my arms up between the shoulder blades. Holding on to the rope he kneed me hard in the small of the back, which caused a sharp pain in the chest. The rope was then passed over a hook in the ceiling and pulled downwards so that I was suspended with my toes just touching the ground. I quickly lost consciousness. I don't know how long I blacked out for, but I woke up back in my cell, naked except for handcuffs, and shackled around my ankles.'

Four days later he was again led naked from his cell, handcuffed but without leg shackles, outside the prison compound. He was not brought to the interrogation room, but was bound to a tree.

'One soldier took a thick piece of rope and tied me to a tree. The rope was wound around my body from the neck down to the knees. The soldier then stood behind the tree and put his foot against it, pulling the rope tight. Chinese soldiers were sitting around the tree having lunch. One stood up and threw the remains of his bowl of vegetables and chillies in my face. The chillies burned my eyes and I still suffer a little. I was then untied and taken back to my cell, but I stumbled often as I still found it difficult to walk and I was beaten every time I fell.'

Other ex-detainees have related how they were repeatedly given shocks from the electric cattle prods that police used while the demonstrations were actually taking place. A young man had one forced into his mouth, causing severe swelling, and a nun told investigators of how she had had this instrument of torture forced into both her anus and vagina.

While it is tempting to take this sort of information as definitive of the Chinese people as a whole, I know it would be wrong to do so. But equally, such depravity cannot be dismissed. So, although I have now spent the greater part of my life in exile and although I have naturally taken a keen interest in China's affairs throughout that time, as a result of which I have some experience as a 'China watcher', still I must admit that I do not fully understand the Chinese mind.

When I visited China in the early 1950s, I could see that a lot of people had given up everything in order to help bring about a transformation in society. Many bore physical scars from the struggle and most were men of the highest principle who genuinely sought to bring about real benefits for every person in their vast country. To do this, they constructed a party system which enabled them to know every last detail about one another, right down to the number of hours' sleep each one needed. They were so passionate about their ideals that they would stop at nothing to achieve them. And in their leader, Mao Tse-tung, they had a man of great vision and imagination, someone who realised the value of constructive criticism and frequently encouraged it.

Yet in no time at all, the new administration became paralysed by petty in-fighting and squabbling. I saw it happen in front of my own eyes. Soon, they began to exchange fact for fable, to tell falsehoods whenever it was necessary to show themselves in a good light. When I met Chou En-lai in India on that occasion in 1956 and told him of my fears, he replied by telling me not to worry. All would be well. In reality, things only changed for the worse.

When I returned to Tibet in 1957, I found the Chinese authorities openly persecuting my people, though simultaneously I was constantly assured there would be no interference. They lied without hesitation, just as they have ever since. Worse, it seemed that the vast majority of the outside world was prepared to believe this fiction. Then, during the 1970s, a number of prominent western politicians were taken to Tibet and came back saying that all was well there.

The truth remains that, since the Chinese invasion, over a million Tibetans have died as a direct result of Peking's policies. When adopting its resolution on Tibet in 1965, the United Nations stated plainly that China's occupation of my homeland has been characterised by 'acts of murder, rape and arbitrary imprisonment; torture and cruel, inhuman and degrading treatment of Tibetans on a large scale'.

I remain at a loss to explain how this happened, how the noble ideals of so many good men and women became transformed into senseless barbarity. Nor can I understand what motivated those people within the Chinese leadership who actively counselled the total destruction of the Tibetan race. It seems that China is a country which has lost its faith, as a result of which the Chinese people have themselves endured unspeakable misery over the past forty-one years – all in the name of Communism.

Yet the pursuit of Communism has been one of the greatest human experiments of all time, and I do not deny that I myself was very impressed with its ideology at first. The trouble was, as I soon discovered, that although Communism claims to serve 'the people' – for whom there are 'people's hotels', 'people's hospitals', and so on – 'the people' does not mean everyone, only those who hold views that are held by a minority to be 'the people's views'.

Some of the responsibility for the excesses of Communism rests squarely on the West. The hostility with which it greeted the first Marxist governments accounts in part for the often ludicrous precautions they took to protect themselves. They became suspicious of everything and everyone, and suspicion causes terrible unhappiness because it goes against a fundamental human trait – namely one person's desire to trust another person. In this connection, I remember, for example, the absurd situation of my visit to Lenin's room in the Kremlin during my visit to Moscow in 1982. I was watched over by an unsmiling plain-clothes security man who was clearly ready to shoot in an instant, whilst a woman guide mechanically explained the official history of the Russian Revolution.

However, in as much as I have any political allegiance, I suppose I am still half Marxist. I have no argument with Capitalism, so long as it is practised in a humanitarian fashion, but my religious beliefs dispose me far more towards Socialism and Internationalism, which are more in line with Buddhist principles. The other attractive thing about Marxism for me is its assertion that man is ultimately responsible for his own destiny. This reflects Buddhist thought exactly.

Against this, I set the fact that those countries which pursue Capitalist policies within a democratic framework are much freer than those which pursue the Communist ideal. So ultimately I am in favour of humanitarian government, one which aims to serve the whole community: the young, the old and the disabled, as much as those who can be directly productive members of society.

Having said that I remain half Marxist, if I were actually to vote in an election it would be for one of the Environmental parties. One of the most positive developments in the world recently has been the growing awareness of the importance of Nature. There is nothing sacred or holy about this. Taking care of our planet is like taking care of our houses. Since we human beings come from Nature, there is no point in our going against Nature, which is why I say the environment is not a matter of religion or ethics or morality. These are luxuries, since we can survive without them. But we will not survive if we continue to go against Nature.

We have to accept this. If we unbalance Nature, humankind will suffer. Furthermore, as people alive today, we must consider future generations: a clean environment is a human right like any other. It is therefore part of our responsibility towards others to ensure that the world we pass on is as healthy, if not healthier, than when we found it. This is not quite such a difficult proposition as it might sound. For although there is a limit to what we as individuals can do, there is no limit to what a universal response might achieve. It is up to us as individuals to do what we can, however little that may be. Just because switching off the light on leaving the room seems inconsequential, it does not mean that we should not do it.

This is where, as a Buddhist monk, I feel that belief in the concept of *karma* is very useful in the conduct of daily life. Once you believe in the connection between motivation and its effect, you will become more alert to the effects which your own actions have upon yourself and others.

Thus, despite the continuing tragedy of Tibet, I find much good in the world. I am especially encouraged that the belief in consumerism as an end in itself seems to be giving way to an appreciation that we humans must conserve the earth's resources. This is very necessary. Human beings are in a sense children of the earth. And, whereas up until now our common Mother tolerated her children's behaviour, she is presently showing us that she has reached the limit of her tolerance.

It is my prayer that one day I shall be able to carry this message of concern for the environment and for others to the people of China. Since Buddhism is by no means alien to the Chinese, I believe that I may be able to serve them in a practical way. The last Panchen Lama's predecessor once conducted a *Kalachakra* initiation ceremony in Peking. If I were to do the same, it would not be without precedent. For as a Buddhist monk, my concern extends to all members of the human family and, indeed, to all suffering sentient beings.

I believe that this suffering is caused by ignorance, and that people inflict pain on others in pursuit of their own happiness or satisfaction. Yet true happiness comes from a sense of inner peace and contentment, which in turn must be achieved through cultivation of altruism, of love, of compassion, and through the elimination of anger, selfishness and greed.

To some people this may sound naïve, but I would remind them that, no matter what part of the world we come from, fundamentally we are all the same human beings. We all seek happiness and try to avoid suffering. We have the same basic needs and concerns. Furthermore, all of us human beings want freedom and the right to determine our own destiny as individuals. That is human nature. The great changes taking place everywhere in the world, from Eastern Europe to Africa, are a clear indication of this.

At the same time, the problems we face today – violent conflicts, destruction of Nature, poverty, hunger, and so on – are mainly problems created by humans. They can be resolved – but only through human effort, understanding and the development of a sense of brotherhood and sisterhood. To do this, we need to cultivate a universal responsibility for one another and for the planet we share, based on a good heart and awareness. Now, although I have found my own Buddhist religion helpful in generating love and compassion, I am convinced that these qualities can be developed by anyone, with or without religion. I further believe that all religions pursue the same goals: those of cultivating goodness and bringing happiness to all human beings. Though the means might appear different, the ends are the same.

All this talk of universal responsibility may sound hopelessly naïve. Nevertheless, it is an idea that I have been expressing publicly ever since my first visit abroad from exile in India back in 1973. And whilst in those days, people were sceptical of the idea, just as they were not always easy to interest in the notion of world peace, I am encouraged to note that an increasing number are now beginning to respond favourably. As a result of the many extraordinary events humanity has experienced during the course of the twentieth century, we have, I feel, become more mature. For example, in the fifties and sixties, and even as late as in the seventies, many people felt that the ultimate decision must come through war.

Today, that thinking holds sway in the minds of only a small minority. And whereas in the early part of this century many people believed that progress and development within society should be pursued through strict regimentation, the collapse of fascism, followed by the disappearance of the Iron Curtain, has shown this to be a hopeless enterprise. Similarly we see that whilst for almost a century there has been a consensus that science and spirituality are incompatible, today, as the scientific understanding of the nature of reality deepens, especially in the field of quantum mechanics, this perception is changing. It is becoming clearer that we can no longer speak coherently of reality as a phenomenon which can be completely divorced from human experience. Because of this, people are beginning to show more interest in what I call our 'inner world', that is, the dynamics and functions of consciousness, or spirit, and its effects on the body. In addition, of course, there is the worldwide increase in environmental awareness.

To me, these are all extremely encouraging developments which are sure to have far-reaching consequences. So too is the growing awareness, in today's very clearly interdependent world, that neither individuals nor even whole nations can solve all their problems by themselves; that we need one another. And despite the fact that so much suffering continues to be inflicted on individuals and peoples in the name of ideology, or religion, or progress, or development, a new sense of hope is emerging for the downtrodden. People everywhere are displaying a willingness to sacrifice their own wellbeing, even at times their lives, for the rights and freedoms of their fellow human beings. Yet such sacrifices do not arise in isolation. The recent success of struggles for human rights and democracy in places like South Africa and the former Soviet Union could not have taken place without the sympathy, support and concern of individuals elsewhere who, despite not being involved directly, nonetheless felt a responsibility for others' rights and wellbeing. So although it is difficult to bring about positive change in society itself, it is undoubtedly worthwhile to try. It is possible. This is my firm belief. Whether or not we succeed is a different matter: what is important is that we do our best.

In my own life, therefore, I try always to be sincere, even towards those who may consider me their enemy. If I were instead to develop ill-will through anger or hatred, who would lose? No one but myself. My happiness, my ability to sleep well, even my appetite would suffer, but my ill-will alone could not hurt those towards whom it was directed. The agitation that came with it would instead do nothing but weaken my own constitution. As a result, those people I could help to be happy would not become happy. So whilst some might criticise me, I try to remain joyful. I know very well that if I want to work effectively for freedom and justice, it is best to do so without any sense of malice in my heart. If instead I remain calm and focused on my desire to serve others, I am sure to be able to make a contribution over time. I am quite certain that because of my commitment to non-violence, based on a genuine desire for universal brotherhood and sisterhood, there have been some positive results, however slight.

CHAPTER SIXTEEN

Return to a Free Tibet?

○

During the time since the first edition of this book, there have been so many changes in the world. At the dawn of the new millennium, although there are a few instances of new conflicts breaking out, I believe that we are witnessing the emergence of a new spirit of dialogue and reconciliation. The People's Republic of China has not been untouched by this. Indeed, in the past decade, China has developed in a remarkable and broadly commendable way. Its pragmatic and flexible handling of issues relating to Hong Kong since re-establishing sovereignty there has been most impressive. Sadly, however, the changes that have occurred within Tibet have mainly been for the worse. Certainly since around 1994, the situation in certain areas has deteriorated to a level not seen since the time of the Cultural Revolution. The basic human rights of Tibetans are violated systematically and on a daily basis. There continue to be mass arrests, beatings, torture and execution of those who call for the freedoms which are taken for granted in so many parts of the world today. One of the most disturbing developments is the way in which the Chinese authorities in Tibet have been trying, through the use of force, to suppress the slightest expression of dissent. After a brief period at the end of the last decade and the beginning of this, there was a considerable flow of information out of Tibet. However, whereas then, for example, foreign journalists were allowed relatively easy access to Tibet, today their presence is forbidden except under exceptional, carefully controlled circumstances. Moreover, the continuing influx of Chinese settlers, lured by economic bribes

– including the promise of higher wages than back home in China – is severely damaging Tibetan culture. Already Tibetans are reduced to a minority in their homeland. And in recent years the Chinese authorities have severely restricted the study of Tibetan subjects as well as the use of the Tibetan language as the medium of teaching. This economic *laissez-faire*, which has been so successful in attracting immigrants, though it has made a handful of Tibetans wealthy, is creating an underclass of ill-educated and thus unemployable Tibetans who are condemned to a pitiful existence.

In other respects too, the current situation in Tibet gives grounds for serious disquiet. One of the saddest events of the past ten years concerns the reincarnation of the late Panchen Lama who, as I mentioned earlier, died in 1989. To explain properly, it is necessary to give some of the background. First of all, I should point out that, as with the title of Dalai Lama, so it is with that of the Panchen Lama. It merely signifies an office, just in the same way as, for example, 'Archbishop of Canterbury' or even 'President of the Republic' does. The word 'Panchen' itself is a composite of two words, *pandita* – a Sanskrit word meaning 'scholar' – and *chenpo*, a Tibetan word meaning 'great'. Originally, this title was that by which successive abbots of Tashilunpo monastery were known. This particular monastery, situated adjacent to the city of Shigatse in south-western Tibet, was founded by Gendun Drup, the first Dalai Lama, in 1447 CE. However, it was only during the time of the fifth Dalai Lama (1617–1682 CE) that a particular lineage of incarnations came to be associated with 'Magnificent Auspiciousness', (the literal meaning of Tashilunpo). Subsequently, in part because it was one of the most important monasteries in all Tibet with perhaps 4,000 monks at its height, there developed a special relationship between the Dalai Lama and the Panchen Lama. As a result of this, it sometimes happened that, during the interregnum between the Dalai Lamas – the time between the death of one and the assumption of office of the next – the Panchen Lama took a special interest in the search for the reincarnation of the Dalai Lama.

The late Panchen Lama, whose full ordained name was Lobsang Trinley Lhundrup Choekyi Gyalsten, was the tenth to have been recognised. He had, as the reader will know, an extremely difficult life. Nevertheless, despite his terrible mistreatment at the hands of those who, when he was a young man, wooed him with promises of friendship, he was without doubt a great fighter for the cause of freedom in Tibet. This can be stated with confidence because, after his release, the Panchen Lama continued his brave and open criticism of various aspects of Chinese policies in Tibet. His brutal fifteen year imprisonment did nothing to lessen his commitment to justice and truth. Even though that other great freedom fighter, the Chinese political dissident Wei Jingshen – who was for a time in the same prison – has said that at one point the Panchen Lama considered suicide because the regime was so harsh, he survived with his courage intact. 'You can take my body to the Central Committee', he is reported to have said.

The real importance of the Panchen Lama lineage is spiritual rather than political, however. Amongst the Panchen Lamas there have been several great scholar-saints. And in the same way as the Dalai Lama is held to be the earthly manifestation of Chenrezig, Bodhisattva of Compassion, the Panchen Lama is considered by Tibetans to be that of Amithaba, or 'the Infinite Light'. I therefore assumed the traditional role of the Dalai Lama to determine and recognise the new incarnation of the late Panchen Lama with a strong sense of responsibility.

The most important aspect of this involved undertaking a number of religious practices which I performed with the greatest care. The first of these, comprising a divination called a *mo*, took place in early 1991. In all, thirteen rituals (not all of them divinations), were performed before I proclaimed Gendhun Choekyi Nyima, a six-year-old boy born to simple parents in Tibet's northern region of Nagchu, the true reincarnation. Originally there was a list of some thirty candidates. Having no desire to politicise the issue, I informed the Chinese government as early as March 1991 of my wish to assist in the search for the reincarnation – which was of course conducted primarily in Tibet from Tashilunpo monastery. Unfortunately, that and all later appeals went unheeded. Instead, the authorities in Peking pronounced my selection invalid. Gendhun Choekyi Nyima, 11th Panchen Lama, was subsequently taken by them to China. He thus became the world's youngest political prisoner.

Against this and many other deeply regrettable incidents, there are however many positive developments to be taken into consideration when assessing the prospects for freedom in Tibet. For example, more and more ordinary Chinese people are showing their sympathy and concern regarding the Tibetan issue. Indeed, it seems there is a growing sense of solidarity between politically aware Chinese and the oppressed people of Tibet. This is a development which encourages me greatly, especially as I have had personal experience of this sentiment on a number of occasions now. I recall, for example, attending a reception one time when I was travelling abroad – a welcome of some sort at a university campus. A young student came up to me and knelt down on the ground. As a Chinese, he told me, he wanted to express his sorrow for the negative actions of his fellow countrymen and women towards the Tibetans. Then on another recent occasion, I was introduced to a Chinese, a writer I was told – quite a distinguished looking man with a bald head, a person somewhere between fifty and sixty years of age – who also expressed to me his great sadness for what his people had done. He held my hand and cried as he said that no apology could be enough to wash away all the atrocities that the Chinese people had committed against the Tibetans. Then there was the time when, following a lecture I gave to some two hundred Chinese students whilst on a visit to Boston in America, I attended a lunch at which there were perhaps twenty people present. These included several professors, a number of students and a few political dissidents – all of them Chinese – who told me, almost unanimously, that if the Dalai Lama's middle-way approach to the Tibetan issue was known to the Chinese people, they were quite certain that the entire country would support it.

This personal experience of goodwill amongst ordinary Chinese towards Tibetans is corroborated by other reports I have received. For instance, I learned from one young Tibetan exile student undergoing higher education in a leading American university – studying, I think, law – that he too had received a very favourable impression from many of the Chinese he had met. There are presently considerable numbers of Chinese visiting scholars at this university. On many occasions, he told me, he had held conversations with these people, sometimes going on long walks together. During the course of them, they had spoken of their admiration for the Dalai Lama's approach and strongly criticised their own government's policies on Tibet. Now, the men and women to whom the Tibetan student has spoken are all important academics. It is reasonable to suppose that their opinions are respected back home. I therefore believe that, though their attitude towards freedom for Tibetans may be privately held, still this will have an important effect in the long run.

On top of all this is also the fact that increasing numbers of Chinese are taking an interest in Buddhism in general and in Tibetan Buddhism in particular. Indeed, there have been reports in the international press of mounting concern on the part of the Chinese authorities at this development. I recall reading an article which stated that in one Chinese province, Shanxi, which has traditionally been home to a strong Buddhist community, there had been such an increase in the number of temples and statues being built by the local community that the provincial government had become alarmed. A committee of enquiry was set up, chaired by the provincial leader himself. It was subsequently decreed that all those structures which had been erected without official permission must be demolished. This indicates that the spiritual faith of ordinary Chinese people is very strong, and increasing.

I myself have experienced directly this growing interest in spiritual matters amongst the Chinese people. Firstly, there has for some time now been a small but steadily increasing number of Chinese who come to Dharamsala in India from Taiwan,

Singapore and other places for Buddhist teachings. Indeed, we now have several Chinese who have joined the monastic order, a few of whom study at the Institute of Buddhist Dialectics here. Secondly, to my great joy, I have lately given several teachings in the West to predominantly Chinese audiences where the main language of translation has been into Chinese. The fact that these have been enthusiastically received has, of course, been a source of great satisfaction to me. However, I do not say it has come as a great surprise that some Chinese brothers and sisters wish to learn something about the Buddhist faith. In anticipation of this development there have been Tibetan monks studying the Chinese language for almost the last twenty years now, so that when the time came we would have translators ready prepared. Above all, it gives me hope that in the future I may be able to serve the Chinese people spiritually. Looked at from such a perspective, there are, after all, no differences between us as human beings. Indeed, there are none between any members of the human family, whether they be Chinese, Tibetan, Indian, European – whoever. We are all the same in wanting happiness and to avoid suffering.

One interesting discovery for me has been that I have felt no reservations, no hesitation in speaking about Buddhism to a Chinese audience. This I put down to the fact that traditionally many Chinese are Buddhists. By contrast, whenever lecturing on the subject to Westerners whose culture and background are essentially Judaeo-Christian, I always feel a slight reluctance. This is because I believe that, in general, it is much better for individuals to remain within their own traditions rather than change to one whose culture is basically foreign to them and not part of their daily experience. After all, I have always felt that the aims of all religions are essentially the same: namely to make us better, less selfish and ultimately happier human beings. That is the key, the point to the religious life. It is therefore better, in my opinion, for people to retain their traditional values, including their religion.

This attitude of mine has lately been reinforced by events in the

Republic of Mongolia. There, certain missionaries have been making efforts to convert people to Christianity by giving financial inducements on the one hand whilst, on the other, telling them that the reason Mongolia lost its freedom and remains backward is their superstitious adherence to Buddhism. Seeing the negative effects of this kind of proselytising, I feel even more reluctant to engage in any activity which could draw people away from their traditional culture and values. Where I feel that perhaps I can help in the spiritual life of those from different religious backgrounds, is in the field of inter-faith dialogue. Also, if, as I believe, there are certain aspects of Tibetan Buddhist insight or practise that could be useful to those of other faiths or traditions then I am, of course, very ready to share them. Indeed, I feel great satisfaction on those occasions when people tell me, as one Protestant woman did recently after a long lecture on Buddhism, that they have learned something from our approach that has been helpful to their own spiritual practice. I also feel happiness when people from other faiths show some acknowledgement, some appreciation, of my ecumenical approach to religion. To see some positive results from my efforts for harmony between the different religions strengthens my conviction that religious pluralism is a necessity.

Because of my devotion to non-denominationalism, I am of course deeply troubled whenever sectarianism occurs within the Tibetan community. Unfortunately, there has of late been one development in this sphere which has caused me tremendous sadness. Here I am referring to the controversy over the 'spirit' known as Dorje Shugden. As I mentioned in Chapter Twelve, there is acceptance, within Buddhism in the Tibetan tradition, of tutelary deities. These are held to be the earthly manifestations of certain spiritual energies associated with particular people, places or things. One such is known as Dorje Drakden, the personal spiritual protector of the Dalai Lamas, who manifests through the medium of Nechung Monastery. Those whose background is Judaeo-Christian or Islamic might think of these protectors, or tutelary deities, in approximately the same way as they do 'guardian angels'. However, it is essential to remember that in Buddhism the notion that any phenomenon exists independently, or intrinsically, is expressly refuted. In other words, according to Tibetan Buddhist understanding, these 'spirits' do not exist in and of themselves. They are not independent entities – though many people erroneously treat them as if they were.

Since the time of the Fifth Dalai Lama, more than three centuries ago, relations between the Dalai Lama and Dorje Shugden have not been good. An aspect of this is the troubled relationship between Shugden and the Tibetan government. This, then, is the first of three important reasons why I have for almost twenty years, at the time of writing, been cautioning people against associating with this particular 'spirit'. The second reason concerns the way in which Shugden is propitiated. There is a danger of it lapsing into mere 'spirit worship'. As such, the practices involved present a grave danger that the profound philosophical and psychological insights of Buddhism in the Tibetan tradition could be lost and that, as a result, it will degenerate into mere superstition. The third reason concerns my deep commitment to non-sectarianism, both within the context of Tibetan Buddhism and towards other faiths, other religions. Whereas my approach has always been to take spiritual instruction from teachers belonging to all four traditions, that of Shugden and Shugden's followers is avowedly hostile to such openness. For example, some of them hold that even to keep a book or text of scripture pertaining to the Nyingma tradition will incur Shugden's wrath. (As I mentioned earlier, there are four principle schools within the Tibetan Buddhist tradition: the Nyingma, the Sakya, the Kargyu, and the Gelugpa – that to which the Dalai Lama belongs. Shugden is held to be a protector of the Gelugpa tradition.)

Despite the fact that I have been cautioning people about the negative consequences of associating with this 'spirit', some Tibetans have continued their association as it were carelessly. Accordingly, I have of late put further emphasis on my concerns about propitiating Shugden. I have also reiterated that those who wish to receive teachings and initiations from me must not do so. In saying this, I have no intention of suppressing peoples' religious freedom, as some have alleged. On the contrary, the restrictions I have called for in relation to the propitiation of this 'spirit' are actually intended to protect religious freedom. One could thus speak in terms of a double negative. I have sought only to curtail a practise which is itself above all a restrictive practice, one which entails the idea that harm will come to those who follow any tradition other than that of the Gelugpa school, of which, let it be said, I am, as Dalai Lama, a supremely devoted adherent.

Turning now to the world at large, what else can be said of my life during the past ten years? Certainly I regard the continuing spread of democracy worldwide as a source of encouragement and hope. I am also very happy at the attempts being made in places like the Middle East and Northern Ireland to find peaceful solutions to long-running disputes. On a personal level, it was wonderful recently to visit the newly constituted Republic of South Africa where I had the privilege of meeting with President Nelson Mandela. I found him a very remarkable human being. His handling of power since election as president has been most impressive. Quite often it is the case that before individuals assume office they have plenty of nice words to say, but afterwards these are somehow forgotten. By contrast, it seems that here the only change has been for the better. It seems that President Mandela has become even more conciliatory, even more friendly. And though I had always received a good impression of him, I found that after my meeting with him, this increased. Sometimes the opposite happens and I come away feeling a little disappointed. In this case, however, I found myself really impressed. A very remarkable person. Also very moving to note in connection with South Africa has been the way in which the work of the Commission for Truth and Reconciliation has been carried out. Despite lack of remorse on the part of some members of the old regime, there has remained an attitude of forgiveness.

One of my most significant visits abroad was to the island of

Taiwan during March 1997. Certainly in respect of my efforts to reach out to our Chinese brothers and sisters, this trip was a milestone. For quite a number of years I had been receiving invitations to visit both from Buddhist and other organisations, so it was with pleasure that I was finally able to make the journey as a guest of the Buddhist Association of the Republic of China and of some non-Buddhist religious groups. Since Taiwan has a large population of Buddhists, I was naturally keen to meet them and serve them in any way I could. As Dalai Lama I was also particularly eager to learn about the Chinese Buddhist tradition of *bikshuni*, that is to say of full ordination of nuns. We in the Tibetan tradition do not at present follow this practice but I intend to introduce it.

On a personal level too, my visit was a most moving and memorable experience. The people of Taiwan responded to me with extraordinary warmth. Everywhere I went I was received with enthusiasm, sympathy and, I felt, respect. As an observer it was clear to me that Taiwan is very modern and successful and has achieved a high degree of material progress based on economic prosperity, as well as an impressive standard of education. Moreover, following the democratisation instituted by President Lee Teng-hui; the first direct presidential election of March 1996 saw the emergence of Taiwan as a fully fledged democracy. All this struck me as very positive. But what delighted me was to discover the manifestly strong interest the people have in spiritual matters in general and in Buddhism in particular. Indeed I was positively surprised by the strong faith of the Buddhists I met there. On one occasion, for example, I gave a teaching in an open stadium in Kaohsiung to an audience of about 50,000 people. Despite the fact that it was a miserable, rainy day, everyone remained for the full duration of two hours and was disciplined and attentive to the end. Similarly, the large number who attended my two-day teaching at the Tao Yuan Dome Stadium displayed a remarkable spirit of faith and devotion to the teachings of the Buddha. On a slightly different note, I greatly appreciated the simplicity and tidiness of the Buddhist temples and monasteries I visited whilst over there. I was pleased, too, to meet some of the young people of the island when I went to Fu Jen Catholic University and to Chungshan University where I was able to engage in an exchange of views with the students.

Meeting President Lee Teng-hui and Vice President and Premier Lien Chan was both a pleasure and an honour. I was greatly encouraged by the new attitude of the leadership in Taiwan and am hopeful of better relations between us Tibetans and the people of Taiwan. Premier Lien Chan stated during our meeting that there had been unnecessary misunderstandings in the past. 'This is a new beginning,' he said, and I am confident that this is the case. At my meeting with President Lee Teng-hui, there was a very warm atmosphere, full of human feeling. I had heard beforehand that he is a devout Presbyterian and indeed I was much inspired by his clearly genuine and strong interest in spiritual matters. And I was moved and greatly encouraged by his obviously sincere empathy for the plight of the Tibetan people.

Looking to the future, I believe that the likelihood of the Tibetan refugees returning to a free Tibet has increased considerably during the last ten years. Following the collapse of communist totalitarianism across Eastern Europe and Central Asia, I note that within the People's Republic of China, the criteria which would qualify its government to be called Marxist are no longer present. My reason for saying this is that if the government in Peking truly continued to follow Marxist ideology, it would take much more concern for the growing gap between rich and poor in China. It seems, however, that the present attitude is that, so long as the country as a whole continues to get richer, the government is not much bothered about this inequality. This, together with other developments, shows that the People's Republic of China is changing. And in the meantime, as I have already pointed out, more and more Chinese intellectuals – writers, academics and thinkers – are gaining deeper awareness about the reality of the Tibetan issue. Also, it is certain that, despite many problems, China itself is a better place to live than fifteen or twenty years ago. The reforms initiated by Deng Xiaoping have affected the country in such a way as to render the political system less ideological, less reliant on mass mobilisation, less coercive, and less stifling to the average citizen. It seems too that China has become more flexible in its international policy. One indication of this is China's greater participation in international fora and in China's co-operation with international agencies and organisations. These are welcome developments. Meanwhile, the morale of the Tibetan people within Tibet remains very strong. I therefore do not doubt that the day of our return is drawing ever closer, though of course we cannot say it is definite.

Nor can I, however, deny that inside Tibet there is growing impatience at the lack of tangible progress being made in respect of Tibetan rights. There have, as a result of this, regrettably been a few outbreaks of violence. At the same time, my own position in this regard remains unchanged. I remain convinced that decisions made out of desperation – and the situation in Tibet is desperate – often go wrong. Therefore, rather than make decisions based on emotion, we need to analyse carefully and make them according to reality. The fact is that the Tibetan people have already been wounded. They do not want further wounds so there is, therefore, no sense in resorting to violent methods to solve the Tibetan issue. My counsel to the Tibetan people is: 'Be patient'. The non-violent campaign for Tibetan rights can be seen as an experiment. As such, it may not work – but I firmly believe it will. Moreover, it seems reasonably certain that the growing support for our cause in China itself would not be there if Tibetans gave up and turned to violence.

A few people might think that the Dalai Lama is being unpatriotic in his attitude of willingness to talk to the Chinese without preconditions. I have lately suggested that Tibetans might be prepared to accept genuine autonomy for Tibet whereby China could maintain control over foreign policy and even maintain a limited presence within Tibet. The country would thus remain in association with the People's Republic of China. However, I cannot take this decision unilaterally on the part of the world's six million Tibetans and it would have to be put to them in a referendum. Just one person cannot take that decision. Likewise, there can be no question of accepting the Chinese demand that I acknowledge Tibet to be an inalienable part of China as a precondition to negotiations on the future of Tibet. To do so would be to tell an enormous historical lie which, as a Buddhist monk, I could not do. But if some people see me as unpatriotic nonetheless, this is perhaps a reflection of the fact that, because of my spiritual training, I do not really make a distinction between Tibetans and others. I believe that all human beings have an equal right to happiness and to freedom from suffering. My devotion is thus to the basic rights of the Tibetan people and I do not attach much importance to labels and political terminology.

I suppose that my attitude to the increase in personal popularity which I have noticed lately is also influenced by my spiritual training. The esteem in which the Dalai Lama is held somewhat surprises me. I have done little to merit it, despite what some people may say. On a few occasions I have been publicly commended for my efforts on behalf of world peace. But I have done nothing, really nothing for world peace. The only thing I do for peace is talk about it a great deal. Meanwhile there are, unquestionably, others who have done far more to advance the cause of peace in the world than this Dalai Lama. Also, the fact that already there have been two films made in Hollywood touching on my life story likewise does not mean much to me. I cannot say that I personally feel anything special in this regard. Of course, insofar as such media interest continues to bring the Tibetan issue before a much wider audience than ever before, I am very happy. However, perhaps even more important than these large scale demonstrations of support for the Tibetan people have been the smaller efforts of countless individuals around the world who have spoken up for the suffering millions of their fellow human beings in the Land of Snow.

I would therefore like to conclude this book with a personal note of thanks to all friends of Tibet. The concern and support which you have expressed for the plight of the Tibetans has touched us all greatly, and continues to give us courage to struggle for freedom and justice, not through the use of arms, but with the powerful weapons of truth and determination. I know that I speak on behalf of all of them when I thank you and ask you not to forget Tibet at this critical time in our country's history.

We, too, hope to contribute to the development of a more peaceful, more humane and more beautiful world. A future free Tibet will seek to help all those in need, to protect Nature and to promote peace. I believe that our Tibetan ability to combine spiritual qualities with a realistic and practical attitude will enable us to make a special contribution, in however modest a way.

Finally, I would like to share with my readers a short prayer which gives me great inspiration and determination:

> For as long as space endures,
> And for as long as living beings remain,
> Until then may I, too, abide
> To dispel the misery of the world.

Index

ANCIENT WISDOM, MODERN WORLD

CONTENTS

PART THREE — ETHICS AND SOCIETY

INTRODUCTION AND
ACKNOWLEDGEMENTS

Having lost my country at the age of sixteen and become a refugee at twenty-four, I have faced a great many difficulties during the course of my life. When I consider these, I see that a lot of them were insurmountable. Not only were they unavoidable, but they were incapable of favourable resolution. Nonetheless, in terms of my own peace of mind and physical health, I can claim to have coped reasonably well. As a result, I have been able to meet adversity with all my resources – mental, physical and spiritual. I could not have done so otherwise. Had I been overwhelmed by anxiety and despair, my health would have been harmed. I would also have been constrained in my actions.

Yet looking around, I see that it is not only we Tibetan refugees and members of other displaced communities who face difficulties. Everywhere and in every society, people endure suffering and adversity – even those who enjoy freedom and material prosperity. Indeed, it seems to me that much of the unhappiness we humans endure is actually of our own making. In principle, therefore, this at least is avoidable. I also see that, in general, those individuals whose conduct is ethically positive are happier and more satisfied than those who neglect ethics. This confirms my belief that if we can reorientate our thoughts and emotions, and reorder our behaviour, not only can we learn to cope with suffering more easily, but we can prevent a great deal of it from arising in the first place.

I shall try to show in this book what I mean by the term 'positive ethical conduct'. In doing so, I acknowledge that it is very difficult either to generalize successfully or to be absolutely precise about ethics and morality. Rarely, if ever, is any situation totally black and white. The same act will have different shades and degrees of moral value under different circumstances. At the same time, it is essential that we reach a consensus in respect of what constitutes positive conduct and what constitutes negative conduct, of what is right and what is wrong, of what is appropriate and what is inappropriate. In the past, the respect people had for religion meant that ethical practice was maintained through a majority following one religion or another. But this is no longer the case. We must therefore find some other way of establishing basic ethical principles.

Not that the reader should suppose that, as Dalai Lama, I have any special solution to offer. There is nothing in these pages which has not been said before. Indeed, I feel that the concerns and ideas expressed here are shared by many of those who think about and attempt to find solutions to the problems and suffering we humans face. In responding to the suggestion of some of my friends and offering this book to the public, my hope is to give voice to those millions who, not having an opportunity to articulate their views in public, remain members of what I take to be a silent majority.

The reader should, however, bear in mind that my formal learning has been of an entirely religious and spiritual character. Since my youth, my chief (and continuing) field of study has been Buddhist philosophy and psychology. In particular, I have studied the works of the religious philosophers of the Geluk tradition to which, historically, the Dalai Lamas have belonged. Being a firm believer in religious pluralism, I have also studied the principal works of other Buddhist traditions. But I have had comparatively little exposure to modern, secular, thought. Yet this is not a religious book. Still less is it a book about Buddhism. My aim has been to appeal for an approach to ethics based on universal rather than religious principles.

For this reason, producing a work for a general audience has not been without challenges, and it is the result of teamwork. One particular problem arose from the fact that it is difficult to render into modern language a number of the Tibetan terms it seemed essential to use. This book is by no means intended as a philosophical treatise. I have tried therefore to explain these terms in such a way that they could be understood readily by a non-specialist readership and also rendered clearly into other languages. But in doing so, and in trying to communicate unambiguously with readers whose language and culture may be quite different from my own, it is possible that some shades of meaning in the Tibetan are lost, and other, unintended ones are added. I trust that careful editing has minimized this. When any such distortions come to light, I would hope to correct them in a subsequent edition. In the meantime, for his assistance in this area, for his translation into English, and for innumerable suggestions, I wish to thank Dr Thupten Jinpa. I wish also to thank Mr A.R. Norman for his work of redaction. This has been invaluable. Finally, I would like to record my thanks to those others who have helped bring this work to fruition.

Dharamsala, February 1999

PART ONE

The Foundations of Ethics

CHAPTER ONE

MODERN SOCIETY AND THE QUEST FOR HUMAN HAPPINESS

I am a comparative newcomer to the modern world. Although I fled my homeland as long ago as 1959, and although my life since then as a refugee in India has brought me into much closer contact with contemporary society, my formative years were spent largely cut off from the realities of the twentieth century. This was partly due to my appointment as Dalai Lama: I became a monk at a very early age. It also reflects the fact that we Tibetans had chosen – mistakenly, in my view – to remain isolated behind the high mountain ranges which separate our country from the rest of the world.

Today, however, I travel a great deal, and both at home and abroad it is my good fortune continuously to be meeting new people. Moreover, individuals from all walks of life come to see me. Quite a lot – especially those who make the effort to travel to the Indian hill-station at Dharamsala where I live in exile – arrive seeking something. Among these are people who have suffered greatly: some have lost parents and children; some have friends or family who committed suicide; some are sick with cancer and with AIDS-related illnesses. Then, of course, there are fellow Tibetans with their own tales of hardship and suffering. Unfortunately, many have unrealistic expectations, supposing that I have healing powers or that I can give some sort of blessing. But I am only an ordinary human being. The best I can do is try to help them by sharing in their suffering.

For my part, meeting innumerable others from all over the world and from every walk of life reminds me of our basic sameness as human beings. Indeed, the more I see of the world, the clearer it becomes that no matter what our situation, whether we are rich or poor, educated or not, of one race, gender, religion or another, we all desire to be happy and to avoid suffering. Our every intended action, in a sense our whole life – how we choose to live it within the context of the limitations imposed by our circumstances – can be seen as our answer to the great question which confronts us all: 'How am I to be happy?'

We are sustained in this great quest for happiness, it seems to me, by hope. We know, even if we do not admit it, that there can be no guarantee of a better, happier life than the one we are leading today. As an old Tibetan proverb puts it, 'The next life or tomorrow – we can never be certain which will come first'. But we hope to go on living. We hope that through this or that action we can bring about happiness. Everything we do, not only as individuals but also at the level of society, can be seen in terms of this fundamental aspiration. Indeed, it is one shared by all sentient beings. The desire or inclination to be happy and to avoid suffering knows no boundaries. It is in our nature. As such, it needs no justification and is validated by the simple fact that we naturally and correctly want this.

And, in countries both rich and poor, this is precisely what we see. Everywhere, by all means imaginable, people are striving to improve their lives. Yet strangely, my impression is that those living in the materially developed countries, for all their industry, are in some ways less satisfied, are less happy, and to some extent suffer more than those living in the least developed countries. Indeed, if we compare the rich with the poor, it often seems that those with nothing are, in fact, the least anxious, though they may be plagued with physical pains and suffering. As for the rich, while a few know how to use their wealth intelligently – that is to say, not in luxurious living but sharing it with the needy – most do not.

They are so caught up with the idea of acquiring still more that they make no room for anything else in their lives. In their absorption they actually lose the dream of happiness which riches were to have provided. As a result, they are constantly tormented, torn between doubt about what might happen and the hope of gaining more, and plagued with mental and emotional suffering – even though outwardly they may appear to be leading entirely successful and comfortable lives. This is suggested both by the high degree and by the disturbing prevalence among the populations of the materially developed countries of anxiety, discontent, frustration, uncertainty, and depression. Moreover, this inner suffering is clearly connected with growing confusion as to what constitutes morality and what its foundations are.

I am often reminded of this paradox when I go abroad. It frequently happens that when I arrive in a new country, at first everything seems very pleasant, very beautiful. Everybody I meet is very friendly. There is nothing to complain about. But then, day by day as I listen, I hear people's problems, their concerns and worries. Below the surface, so many feel uneasy and dissatisfied with their lives. They experience feelings of isolation; then follows depression. The result is the troubled atmosphere which is such a feature of the developed world.

At first, this surprised me. Although I never imagined that material wealth alone could overcome suffering, looking at the developed world from Tibet, a country then, as now, materially very poor, I must admit that I thought wealth would have gone further toward reducing suffering than is actually the case. I expected that with physical hardship much reduced, as it is for the majority living in the industrially developed countries, happiness would be much easier to achieve than for those living under more severe conditions. Instead, the extraordinary advancements of science and technology seem to have achieved little more than numerical improvement. In many cases, progress has meant hardly anything more than greater numbers of opulent houses in more cities, with more cars driving between them. Certainly there has been a reduction in some types of suffering including especially certain illnesses. But it seems to me that there has been no overall reduction.

Saying this, I remember well an occasion on one of my early trips to the West. I was the guest of a very wealthy family which lived in a large, well-appointed house. Everyone was very charming and polite. There were servants to cater to one's every need, and I began to think that here, perhaps, was proof positive that wealth could be a source of happiness. My hosts definitely had an air of relaxed confidence. But when I saw in the bathroom, through a cupboard door which was slightly open, an array of tranquillizers and sleeping pills, I was reminded forcefully that there is often a big gap between outward appearances and inner reality.

This paradox whereby inner – or we could say

psychological and emotional – suffering is so often found amid material wealth is readily apparent throughout much of the West. Indeed, it is so pervasive that we might wonder whether there is something in Western culture which predisposes people living there to such kinds of suffering. This I doubt. So many factors are involved. Clearly, material development itself has a role to play. But we can also cite the increasing urbanization of modern society where high concentrations of people live in close proximity to one another. In this context, consider that in place of our dependence on one another for support, today, wherever possible, we tend to rely on machines and services. Whereas formerly farmers would call in all their family members to help with the harvest, today they simply telephone a contractor. We find modern living so organized so that it demands the least possible direct dependence on others. The more or less universal ambition seems to be for everyone to own their own house, their own car, their own computer, and so on in order to be as independent as possible. Of course this is natural and understandable. The increasing autonomy that people enjoy as a result of advances in science and technology has its good points. It is possible today to be far more independent of others than ever before. But with these developments, there has arisen a sense that my future is not dependent on my neighbour but rather on my job, or, at most, my employer. This in turn encourages us to suppose that because others are not important for my happiness their happiness is not important to me.

We have, in my view, created a society in which people find it harder and harder to show one another basic affection. In place of the sense of community and belonging, which we find such a reassuring feature of less wealthy (and generally rural) societies, we find a high degree of loneliness and alienation. Despite the fact that millions live in close proximity to one another, it seems that many people, especially among the old, have no one to talk to but their pets. Modern industrial society often strikes me as being like a huge self-propelled machine. Instead of human beings in charge, each individual is a tiny, insignificant component with no choice but to move when the machine moves.

All this is compounded by the contemporary rhetoric of growth and economic development which greatly reinforces people's tendency toward competitiveness and envy. And with this comes the perceived need to keep up appearances – itself a major source of problems, tension and unhappiness. Yet the psychological and emotional suffering we find so prevalent in the West is less likely to reflect a cultural shortcoming than an underlying human tendency. Indeed, I have noticed that similar forms of inner suffering are evident outside the West. In some parts of Southeast Asia, it is observable that, as prosperity has increased, traditional belief systems have begun to lose their influence over people. With this, we find a broadly similar manifestation of unease as that established in the West. This suggests that the potential exists in us all, and in the same way that physical disease reflects its environment, so it is with psychological and emotional suffering: it arises within the context of particular circumstances. Thus, in the southern, undeveloped or 'Third World' countries we find ailments broadly confined to that part of the world such as those arising from poor sanitation. By contrast, in urban industrial societies, we see illness manifest itself in ways that are consistent with that environment. So instead of water-borne diseases, we find stress-related disease. All this implies that there are strong reasons for supposing a link between our disproportionate emphasis on external progress and the unhappiness, the anxiety, and the lack of contentment of modern society.

This may sound a very gloomy assessment. But unless we acknowledge the extent and character of our problems, we will not be able even to begin to overcome them.

Clearly, a major reason for modern society's devotion to material progress is the very success of science and technology. Now the wonderful thing about these forms of human endeavour is that they bring immediate satisfaction. They're unlike prayer, the results of which are, for the most part, invisible – if indeed prayer works at all. And we are impressed by results. What could be more normal? Unfortunately, this devotion encourages us to suppose that the keys to happiness are material well-being on the one hand and the power conferred by knowledge on the other. And while it is obvious to anyone who gives this mature thought that the former cannot bring us happiness by itself, it is perhaps less apparent that the latter cannot. But the fact is, knowledge alone cannot provide the happiness that springs from inner development, the happiness that is not reliant on external factors. Indeed, though our very detailed and specific knowledge of external phenomena is an immense achievement, the urge to reduce, to narrow down in pursuit of it, far from bringing us happiness can actually be dangerous. It can cause us to lose touch with the wider reality of human experience and, in particular, to overlook our dependence on others.

We need also to recognize what happens when we rely too much on the external achievements of science. For example, as the influence of religion declines, there is mounting confusion with respect to the problem of how best we are to conduct ourselves in life. In the past, religion and ethics were closely interwined. Now, many people, believing that science has 'disproven' religion, make the further assumption that because there appears to be no final evidence for any spiritual authority, morality itself must be a matter of individual preference. And whereas in the past scientists and philosophers felt a pressing need to find solid foundations on which to establish immutable laws and absolute truths, nowadays this kind of research is held to be futile. As a result, we see a complete reversal, heading towards the opposite extreme, where ultimately nothing exists any longer, where reality itself is called into question. This can only lead to chaos.

In saying this, I do not mean to criticize scientific endeavour. I have learned a great deal from my encounters with scientists, and I see no obstacle to engaging in dialogue with them even when their perspective is one of radical materialism. Indeed, for as long as I can remember, I have been fascinated by the insights of science. As a boy, there was a time when I was rather more interested in learning about the mechanics of an old film projector I found in the storerooms of the summer residence of the Dalai Lama than in my religious and scholastic studies. My concern is rather that we are apt to overlook the limitations of science. In replacing religion as the final source of knowledge in popular estimation, science begins to look a bit like another religion itself. With this comes a similar danger on the part of some of its adherents to blind faith in its principles, and, correspondingly, to intolerance of alternate views. That this supplanting of religion has taken place is not surprising, however, given science's extraordinary achievements. Who could fail to be impressed at our ability to land people on the moon? Yet the fact remains that if, for example, we were to go to a nuclear physicist and say: 'I am facing a moral dilemma, what should I do?' he or she could only shake their head and suggest we look elsewhere for an answer.

Generally speaking, a scientist is in no better a position than a lawyer in this respect. For while both science and the law can help us forecast the likely consequence of our actions, neither can tell us how we ought to act in a moral sense. Moreover, we need to recognize the limits of scientific inquiry itself. For example, though we have been aware of human consciousness for millennia, and though it has been the subject of investigation throughout history, despite scientists' best efforts, they still do not understand what it actually is, nor why it exists, how it functions nor what is its essential nature. Neither can science tell us what the substantial cause of consciousness is, nor what its effects are. Of course, consciousness belongs to that category of phenomena without form, substance or colour. It is not susceptible to investigation by external means. But this does not mean such things do not exist, merely that science cannot find them.

Should we, therefore, abandon scientific inquiry on the grounds that it has failed us? Certainly not. Nor do I mean to suggest that the goal of prosperity for all is invalid. Because of our nature, bodily and physical experience plays a dominant role in our lives. The achievements of science and technology clearly reflect our desire to attain a better, more comfortable existence. This is very good. Who could fail to applaud many of the advances of modern medicine?

At the same time, I think it is genuinely true that members of certain traditional, rural communities do enjoy greater harmony and tranquillity than those settled in our modern cities. For example, in the Spiti area of northern India, it remains the custom for locals not to lock their houses when they go out. It is expected that a visitor who finds the house empty would go in and help themselves to a meal while waiting for the family to return. The same obtained in Tibet in former times. This is not to say that there is no crime in such places. As in the case of pre-occupation Tibet, such things did of course happen occasionally. But when they did, people would raise their eyebrows in surprise. It was a rare and unusual event. By contrast, in some modern cities, if a day goes by without a murder it is a remarkable event. With urbanization has come disharmony.

We must be careful not to idealize old ways of life, however. The high level of cooperation we find in undeveloped rural communities may be based more on necessity than on goodwill. People recognize it as an alternative to greater hardship. And the contentment we perceive may actually have more to do with ignorance. These people may not realize or imagine that any other way of life is possible. If they did, very likely they would embrace it eagerly. The challenge we face is therefore to find some means of enjoying the same degree of harmony and tranquillity as those more traditional communities while benefiting fully from the material developments of the world as we find it at the dawn of a new millennium. To say otherwise is to imply that these communities should not even try to improve their standard of living. Yet, I am quite certain that, for example, the majority of Tibet's nomads would be very glad to have the latest thermal clothing for winter, smokeless fuel to cook with, the benefits of modern medicine, and a portable television in their tents. And I, for one, would not wish to deny them these.

Modern society, with all its benefits and defects, has emerged within the context of innumerable causes and conditions. To suppose that merely by abandoning material progress we could overcome all our problems would be short-sighted. That would be to ignore their underlying causes. Besides, there is still much in the modern world to be optimistic about.

There are countless people even in the most developed countries who are active in their concern for others. Nearer home, I think of the enormous kindness we Tibetan refugees have been shown by those whose personal resources were also quite limited. For example, our children have benefited immeasurably from the selfless contribution of their Indian teachers, many of whom have been compelled to live under difficult conditions far away from their homes. On a wider scale, we might also consider the growing appreciation of fundamental human rights all over the world. This represents a very positive development in my view. The way in which the international community responds to natural disasters with immediate aid is also a wonderful feature of the modern world. Increasing recognition that we cannot forever continue to mistreat our natural environment without facing serious consequences is likewise a cause for hope. Moreover, I believe that, thanks largely to modern communications, people are probably more accepting of diversity now. And standards of literacy and education throughout the world are in general higher than ever before. Such positive developments I take to be an indication of what we humans are capable.

Recently, I had the opportunity to meet the Queen Mother in England. She has been a familiar figure to me throughout my life, so this gave me great pleasure. But what was particularly encouraging was to hear her opinion, as a woman as old as the twentieth century itself, that people have become much more aware of others than when she was young. In those days, she said, people were interested mainly in their own countries whereas today there is much more concern for the inhabitants of other countries. When I asked her whether she was optimistic about the future, she replied in the affirmative without hesitation.

It is, of course, true that we can point to an abundance of severely negative trends within modern society. There is no reason to doubt the escalation in murder, violence, and rape cases year by year. In addition, we hear constantly of abusive and exploitative relationships both in the home and within the wider community, of growing numbers of young people addicted to drugs and alcohol, and of how the high proportion of marriages ending in divorce is affecting children today. Not even our own small refugee community has escaped the impact of some of these developments. Whereas, for example, suicide was almost unheard of in Tibetan society, lately there have been one or two tragic incidents of this kind within our exile community. Likewise, whereas drug addiction among young Tibetans certainly did not exist a generation ago, we now have a few cases – mainly, it must be said, in those places where they are exposed to the modern urban lifestyle.

Yet, unlike the sufferings of sickness, old age and death, none of these problems are by nature inevitable. Nor are they due to any lack of knowledge. When we think carefully, we see that they are all ethical problems. They each reflect our understanding of what is right and wrong, of what is positive and what is negative, of what is appropriate and what is inappropriate. But beyond this we can point to something more fundamental: a neglect of what I call our inner dimension.

What do I mean by this? According to my understanding, our overemphasis on material gain reflects an underlying assumption that what it buys can, by itself alone, provide us with all the satisfaction we require. Yet by nature, the satisfaction material gain can provide us with will be limited to the level of the senses. If it were true that we human beings were no different from animals, this would be fine. However, given the complexity of our species – in particular the fact of our having thoughts and emotions as well as imaginative and critical faculties – it is obvious that our needs transcend the merely sensual. The prevalence of anxiety, stress, confusion, uncertainty and depression among those whose basic needs have been met is a clear indication of this. Our problems, both those we experience externally – such as wars, crime and violence – and those we experience internally – our emotional and psychological sufferings – cannot be solved until we address this underlying neglect. That is why the great movements of the last hundred years and more – democracy, liberalism, socialism – have all failed to deliver the universal benefits they were supposed to provide, despite many wonderful ideas. A revolution is called for, certainly. But not a political, an economic or even a technical revolution. We have had enough experience of these during the past century to know that a purely external approach will not suffice. What I propose is a spiritual revolution.

CHAPTER TWO

NO MAGIC, NO MYSTERY

In calling for a spiritual revolution, am I advocating a religious solution to our problems after all? No. As someone nearing seventy years of age at the time of writing, I have accumulated enough experience to be completely confident that the teachings of the Buddha are both relevant and useful to humanity. If a person puts them into practice, it is certain that not only they but others, too, will benefit. My meetings with many different sorts of people the world over have, however, helped me realize that there are other faiths, and other cultures, no less capable than mine of enabling individuals to lead constructive and satisfying lives. What is more,

I have come to the conclusion that whether or not a person is a religious believer does not matter much. Far more important is that they be a good human being.

I say this in acknowledgement of the fact that though a majority of the earth's nearly six billion human beings may claim allegiance to one faith tradition or another, the influence of religion on people's lives is generally marginal, especially in the developed world. It is doubtful whether globally even a billion are what I would call dedicated religious practitioners, that is to say, people who try, on a daily basis, faithfully to follow the principles and precepts of their faith. The rest remain, in this sense, non-practising. Those who are dedicated practitioners meanwhile follow a multiplicity of religious paths. From this it becomes clear that, given our diversity, no single religion satisfies all humanity. We may also conclude that we humans can live quite well without recourse to religious faith.

These may seem unusual statements, coming as they do from a religious figure. I am, however, Tibetan before I am Dalai Lama, and I am human before I am Tibetan. So while as Dalai Lama I have a special responsibility to Tibetans, and as a monk I have a special responsibility toward furthering interreligious harmony, as a human being I have a much larger responsibility toward the whole human family – which indeed we all have. And since the majority does not practise religion, I am concerned to try to find a way to serve all humanity without appealing to religious faith.

Actually, I believe that if we consider the world's major religions from the widest perspective, we find that they are all – Buddhism, Christianity, Hinduism, Islam, Judaism, Sikhism, Zoroastrianism, and the others – directed toward helping human beings achieve lasting happiness. And each of them is, in my opinion, capable of facilitating this. Under such circumstances, a variety of religions (each of which promotes the same basic values after all) is both desirable and useful.

Not that I always felt like this. When I was younger and living in Tibet, I believed in my heart that Buddhism was the best way. I told myself it would be marvellous if everyone converted. Yet this was due to ignorance. We Tibetans had, of course, heard of other religions. But what little we knew about them came from Tibetan translations of secondary, Buddhist, sources. Naturally, these focused on those aspects of other religions which are more open to debate from a Buddhist perspective. This was not because their authors wished deliberately to caricature their opponents. Rather, it reflected the fact that they had no need to address all those aspects with which they had no argument. In India, where they wrote, the works they were discussing were available in their entirety. Unfortunately, this was not the case in Tibet. There were no translations of these other scriptures available.

As I grew up, I was gradually able to learn more about the other world religions. Especially after going into exile, I began to meet people who, having dedicated their entire

lives to different faiths – some through prayer and meditation, others through actively serving others – had acquired
a profound experience of their particular tradition. Such
personal exchanges helped me recognize the enormous
value of each of the major faith traditions and led me to
respect them deeply. For me, Buddhism remains the most
precious path. It corresponds best to my personality. But
that does not mean I believe it to be the best religion for
everyone any more than I believe it necessary for everyone
to be a religious believer.

Of course, both as a Tibetan and as a monk, I have been
brought up according to, and educated in, the principles,
the precepts and the practice of Buddhism. I cannot,
therefore, deny that my whole thinking is shaped by my
understanding of what it means to be a follower of the
Buddha. However, my concern in this book is to try to
reach beyond the formal boundaries of my faith. I want to
show that there are indeed some universal ethical principles
which could help everyone to achieve the happiness we all
aspire to. Some people may feel that in this I am attempting
to propagate Buddhism by stealth. But while it is difficult for
me conclusively to refute the claim, that is not the case.

Actually, I believe there is an important distinction to
be made between religion and spirituality. Religion I take
to be concerned with faith in the claims to salvation of one
faith tradition or another, an aspect of which is acceptance
of some form of metaphysical or supernatural reality,
including perhaps an idea of heaven or *nirvana*. Connected

with this are religious teachings or dogma, rituals, prayer and so on. Spirituality I take to be concerned with those qualities of the human spirit – such as love and compassion, patience, tolerance, forgiveness, contentment, a sense of responsibility, a sense of harmony – which bring happiness to both self and others. While ritual and prayer, along with the questions of *nirvana* and salvation, are directly connected with religious faith, these inner qualities need not be, however. There is thus no reason why the individual should not develop them, even to a high degree, without recourse to any religious or metaphysical belief system. This is why I sometimes say that religion is something we can perhaps do without. What we cannot do without are these basic spiritual qualities.

Those who practise religion would, of course, be right to say that such qualities, or virtues, are fruits of genuine religious endeavour and that religion therefore has everything to do with developing them and with what may be called spiritual practice. But let us be clear on this point. Religious faith demands spiritual practice. Yet it seems there is much confusion, as often among religious believers as among non-believers, concerning what this actually consists in. The unifying characteristic of the qualities I have described as 'spiritual' may be said to be some level of concern for others' well-being. In Tibetan, we speak of *shen-pen kyi-sem*, meaning 'the thought to be of help to others'. And when we think about them, we see that each of the qualities noted is defined by an implicit concern for others' well-being.

Moreover, the one who is compassionate, loving, patient, tolerant, forgiving and so on to some extent recognizes the potential impact of their actions on others and orders their conduct accordingly. Thus spiritual practice according to this description involves, on the one hand, acting out of concern for others' well-being. On the other, it entails transforming ourselves so that we become more readily disposed to do so. To speak of spiritual practice in any terms other than these is meaningless.

My call for a spiritual revolution is thus not a call for a religious revolution. Nor is it a reference to a way of life that is somehow otherworldly, still less to something magical or mysterious. Rather, it is a call for a radical reorientation away from our habitual preoccupation with self. It is a call to turn toward the wider community of beings with whom we are connected, and for conduct which recognizes others' interests alongside our own.

Here the reader may object that while the transformation of character that such a reorientation implies is certainly desirable, and while it is good that people develop compassion and love, a revolution of spirit is hardly adequate to solve the variety and magnitude of problems we face in the modern world. Furthermore, it could be argued that problems arising from, for example, violence in the home, addiction to drugs and alcohol, family break-up and so on are better understood and tackled on their own terms. Nevertheless, given that they could each certainly be solved through people being more loving and compassionate toward one another – however improbable this may seem – they can also be characterized as spiritual problems susceptible to a spiritual solution. This is not to say that all we need do is cultivate spiritual values and these problems will automatically disappear. On the contrary, each of them needs a specific solution. But we find that when this spiritual dimension is neglected, we have no hope of achieving a lasting solution.

Why is this? Bad news is a fact of life. Each time we pick up a newspaper, or turn on the television or radio, we are confronted with sad tidings. Not a day goes by but, somewhere in the world, something happens that everyone agrees is unfortunate. No matter where we are from or what our philosophy of life, to a greater or lesser extent, we are all sorry to hear of others' suffering.

These events can be divided into two broad categories: those which have principally natural causes – earthquakes, drought, floods and the like – and those which are of human origin. Wars, crime, violence of every sort, corruption, poverty, deception, fraud, social, political and economic injustice are each the consequence of negative human behaviour.

And who is responsible for such behaviour? We are. From royalty, presidents, prime ministers and politicians through administrators, scientists, doctors, lawyers, academics, students, priests, nuns and monks such as myself, to industrialists, artists, shopkeepers, technicians, pieceworkers, manual labourers and those without work, there is not a single class or sector of society which does not contribute to our daily diet of unhappy news.

Fortunately, unlike natural disasters, about which we can do little or nothing, these human problems, because they are all essentially ethical problems, can be overcome. The fact that there are so many people, again from every sector and level of society, working to do so is a reflection of this intuition. There are those who join political parties to fight for a fairer constitution; those who become lawyers to fight for justice; those who join aid organizations to fight poverty; those who care, both on a professional and on a voluntary basis, for the victims of harm. Indeed, we are all, according to our own understanding and in our own way, trying to make the world – or at least our bit of it – a better place for us to live in.

Unfortunately, we find that no matter how sophisticated and well-administered our legal systems, and no matter how advanced our methods of external control, by themselves they cannot eradicate wrongdoing. Observe that nowadays our police forces have at their disposal technology that could barely have been imagined fifty years ago. They have methods of surveillance which enable them to see what formerly was hidden; they have DNA matching, forensic laboratories, sniffer dogs and, of course, highly trained personnel. Yet criminal methods are correspondingly advanced so that really we are no better off. Where ethical restraint is lacking, there can be no hope of overcoming problems like those of rising crime. In fact, without such inner discipline, we find that the very means we use to solve them becomes a source of difficulty itself. The increasing sophistication of criminal and police methods is a vicious and mutually reinforcing cycle.

What, then, is the relationship between spirituality and ethical practice? Since love and compassion and similar qualities all, by definition, presume some level of concern for others' well-being, they also presume ethical restraint. We cannot be loving and compassionate unless at the same time we curb our own harmful impulses and desires.

As to the foundations of ethical practice itself, it might be supposed that here at least I advocate a religious approach. Certainly each of the major religious traditions has a well-developed ethical system. However, the difficulty with tying our understanding of right and wrong to religion is that we must then ask, 'Which religion?' Which articulates the most complete, the most accessible, the most acceptable system? The arguments would never stop. Moreover, to do so would be to ignore the fact that many who reject religion do so out of convictions sincerely held, not merely because they are unconcerned with the deeper questions of human existence. We cannot suppose that such people are without a sense of right and wrong or of what is morally appropriate just because some who are anti-religion are immoral. Besides, religious belief is no guarantee of moral integrity. Looking at the history of our species, we see that among the major troublemakers – those who visited violence, brutality and destruction on their fellow human beings – there have been many who professed religious faith, often loudly. Religion can help us establish basic ethical principles. Yet we can still talk about ethics and morality without having recourse to religion.

Again, it could be objected that if we do not accept religion as the source of ethics, we must allow that people's understanding of what is good and right, of what is wrong and bad, of what is morally appropriate and what is not, of what constitutes a positive act and what a negative act must vary according to circumstances and even from person to person. But here let me say that no one should suppose it could ever be possible to devise a set of rules or laws to provide us with the answer to every ethical dilemma, even if we were to accept religion as the basis of morality. Such a formulaic approach could never hope to capture the richness and diversity of human experience. It would also give grounds for arguing that we are responsible only to the letter of those laws, rather than for our actions.

This is not to say that it is useless to attempt to construe principles which can be understood as morally binding. On the contrary, if we are to have any hope of solving our problems, it is essential we find a way to do so. We must have some means of adjudicating between, for example, terrorism as a means to political reform and Mahatma Gandhi's principles of peaceful resistance. We must be able to show that violence toward others is wrong. And yet we must find some way of doing so which avoids the extremes of crude absolutism on the one hand, and of trivial relativism on the other.

My own view, which does not rely solely on religious faith, nor even on an original idea, but rather on ordinary common sense, is that establishing binding ethical principles is possible when we take as our starting point the observation that we all desire happiness and wish to avoid suffering. We have no means of discriminating between right and wrong if we do not take into account others' feelings, others' suffering. For this reason, and also because – as we shall see – the notion of absolute truth is difficult to sustain outside the context of religion, ethical conduct is not something we engage in because it is somehow right in itself but because, like ourselves, all others desire happiness and to avoid suffering. Given that this is a natural disposition, shared by all, it follows that each individual has a right to pursue this goal. Accordingly, I suggest that one of the things which determines whether an act is ethical or not is its effect on others' experience or expectation of happiness. An act which harms or does violence to this is potentially an unethical act.

I say *potentially* because although the consequences of our actions are important, there are other factors to consider, including both the question of intent and the nature of the act itself. We can all think of things which we have done that have upset others, despite the fact that it was by no means our intention to do so. Similarly, it is also not hard to think of acts which, though they may appear somewhat forceful and aggressive and likely to cause hurt, could yet contribute to others' happiness in the long run. Disciplining children will often fall into this category. On the other hand, the fact that our actions may appear to be gentle does not mean that they are positive or ethical if our intentions are selfish. On the contrary, if, for example, our intention is to mislead, then to pretend kindness is a most unfortunate deed. Though force may not be involved, such an act is certainly violent. It does violence not only insofar as the end is harmful to the other but also in that it injures that person's trust and expectation of truth.

Again, it is not difficult to imagine a case where an individual may suppose their actions to be well intended and directed toward the greater good of others, but where they are in reality totally immoral. Here we might think of a soldier who carries out orders summarily to execute civilian prisoners. Believing the cause to be a just one, this soldier may suppose such actions to be directed toward the greater good of humanity. Yet according to the principle of non-violence I have described, such killing by definition would be an unethical act. Carrying out these orders would thus be gravely negative conduct. In other words, the content of our actions is also important in determining whether they are ethical or not, since certain acts are negative by definition.

The factor which is perhaps most important of all in determining the ethical nature of an act is neither its content, nor its consequence, however. In fact, since only rarely are the fruits of our actions directly attributable to us alone — whether the helmsman is able to bring his boat to safety in a storm depends not just on his actions — consequence could conceivably be the least important factor. In Tibetan, the term for what is considered to be of the greatest significance in determining the ethical value of a given action is the individual's *kun long*. Translated literally, the participle *kun* means 'thoroughly' or 'from the depths', and '*long (wa)*' denotes the act of causing something to stand up, to arise, or to awaken. But in the sense in which it is used here, *kun long* is understood as what drives or inspires our actions — both those we intend directly and those which are in a sense involuntary. It therefore denotes the individual's overall state of heart and mind. When this is wholesome, it follows that our actions themselves will be (ethically) wholesome.

From this description, it is clear that it is difficult to translate *kun long* succinctly. Generally, it is rendered simply as 'motivation', but this clearly does not capture the full range of its meaning. The word 'disposition', although it comes quite close, lacks the active sense of the Tibetan. On the other hand, to use the term 'overall state of heart and mind' seems unnecessarily long. Arguably, it could be abbreviated to 'mind-state', but this would ignore the wider meaning of mind as it is used in Tibetan. The word for mind, *lo*, includes the ideas of feeling and emotion (heart) alongside those of consciousness, or awareness. This reflects an understanding that emotions and thoughts cannot ultimately be separated. Even the perception of a quality, like colour, is held to carry within it an affective dimension. Nor is there an idea of pure sensation without any accompanying cognitive event. The inference is rather that we can identify different types of emotion. There are those which are primarily instinctual, such as revulsion at the sight of blood, and there are those which have a more developed rational component, such as fear of poverty. The reader is asked to remember this point whenever I speak of 'mind', of 'motivation', of 'disposition' or of 'states of mind'.

That this is so, that the individual's overall state of heart and mind, or motivation, in the moment of action is, generally speaking, the key to determining its ethical content, is easily understood when we consider how our actions are affected when we are gripped with powerful negative thoughts and emotions such as hatred and anger. In that moment, our mind and heart (lo) is in turmoil. Not only does this cause us to lose our sense of proportion and perspective, but we also lose sight of the likely impact of our actions on others. Indeed, we can become so distracted that we ignore the question of others, and of their right to happiness, altogether. Our actions under such circumstances – that is to say our deeds, words, thoughts, omissions and desires – will almost certainly be injurious of others' happiness. And this in spite of what our long-term intentions toward others may be or whether our actions are consciously intended or not. Consider a situation where we become embroiled in an argument with a family member.

How we deal with the charged atmosphere which develops will depend to a large extent on what underlies our actions at that moment – in other words, on our *kun long*. The less calm we are, the more likely we are to react negatively with harsh words, and the more certain we are to say or do things which later we regret bitterly, even though we feel deeply for that person.

Or imagine a situation where we inconvenience another in some small way, perhaps by bumping into them accidentally while walking along, and they shout at us for being careless. We are much more likely to shrug this off if our disposition (*kun long*) is wholesome, if our hearts are suffused with compassion, than if we are under the sway of negative emotions. When the driving force of our actions is wholesome, our actions will tend automatically to contribute to others' well-being. They will thus automatically be ethical. Further, the more this is our habitual state, the less likely we are to react badly when provoked. And even when we do lose our temper, any outburst will be free of any sense of malice or hatred. The aim of spiritual and, therefore, ethical practice is thus to transform and perfect the individual's *kun long*. This is how we become better human beings.

We find that the more we succeed in transforming our hearts and minds through cultivating spiritual qualities, the better able we will be to cope with adversity and the greater the likelihood that our actions will be ethically wholesome. So if I may be permitted to give my own case as an example, this understanding of ethics means that in striving continuously to cultivate a positive, or wholesome mind-state, I try to be of the greatest service to others that I can be. By making sure, in addition to this, that the content of my actions is, so far as I am able to make them, similarly positive, I reduce my chances of acting unethically. How effective this strategy is, that is to say, what the consequences are in terms of others' well-being, either in the short term or the long term, there is no way to tell. But provided my efforts are continual, and provided I pay attention, no matter what happens, I should never have cause for regret. At least I know I have done my best.

My description in this chapter of the relationship between ethics and spirituality does not address the question of how we are to resolve ethical dilemmas. We will come to that later. Rather, I have been concerned to outline an approach to ethics which, by relating ethical discourse to the basic human experience of happiness and suffering, avoids the problems which arise when we ground ethics in religion. The reality is that the majority of people today are unpersuaded of the need for religion. Moreover, there may be conduct which is acceptable to one religious tradition but not to another.

As to what I meant by the term 'spiritual revolution', I trust that I have made it clear that a spiritual revolution entails an ethical revolution.

CHAPTER THREE

DEPENDENT ORIGINATION AND THE NATURE OF REALITY

At a public talk I gave in Japan a few years ago, I saw some people coming toward me carrying a bunch of flowers. I stood up in anticipation of receiving their offering, but to my surprise, they walked straight past and laid the flowers on the altar behind me. I sat down feeling somewhat embarrassed! Yet again I was reminded that the way in which things and events unfold does not always coincide with our expectations. Indeed, this fact of life – that there is often a gap between the way in which we perceive phenomena and the reality of a given situation –

is the source of much unhappiness. This is especially true when, as in the example here, we make judgements on the basis of a partial understanding, which turns out not to be fully justified.

Before considering what a spiritual and ethical revolution might consist in, let us give some thought to the nature of reality itself. The close connection between how we perceive ourselves in relation to the world we inhabit and our behaviour in response to it means that our understanding of phenomena is crucially significant. Indeed, when we consider the matter, we start to see that we cannot finally separate out any phenomena from the context of other phenomena. We can only really speak in terms of relationships.

In the course of our daily lives, we engage in countless different activities and receive huge sensory input from all that we encounter. The problem of misperception, which, of course, varies in degree, usually arises because of our tendency to isolate particular aspects of an event or experience and see them as constituting its totality. This leads to a narrowing of perspective and from there to false expectations. But when we consider reality itself, we quickly become aware of its infinite complexity, and we realize that our habitual perception of it is often inadequate. If this were not so, the concept of deception would be meaningless. If things and events always unfolded as we expected, we would have no notion of illusion or of misconception.

As a means to understanding this complexity, I find the concept of dependent origination (in Tibetan, *ten del*), articulated by the Madhyamika (Middle Way) school of Buddhist philosophy, to be particularly helpful. According to this, we can understand how things and events come to be in three different ways. At the first level, the principle of cause and effect, whereby all things and events arise in dependence on a complex web of interrelated causes and conditions, is invoked. This suggests that no thing or event can be construed as capable of coming into, or remaining in, existence by itself. For example, if I take some clay and mould it, I can bring a pot into being. The pot exists as an effect of my actions. At the same time, it is also the effect of a myriad of other causes and conditions. These include the combination of clay and water to form its raw material. But beyond this, we can point to the coming together of the molecules, the atoms and other minute particles which form these constituents (which are themselves dependent on innumerable other factors). Then there are the circumstances leading up to my decision to make a pot. And there are the cooperative conditions of my actions as I give shape to the clay. All these different factors make it clear that my pot cannot exist independently of its causes and conditions. Rather it is dependently originated.

On another level, *ten del* can be understood in terms of the mutual dependence which exists between parts and whole. Without parts, there can be no whole; without a whole, the concept of parts makes no sense. The idea of 'whole' is predicated on parts, but these parts themselves must be considered to be wholes comprised of their own parts.

On the third level, all phenomena can be understood to be dependently originated because when we analyse them, we find that, ultimately, they lack independent identity. This can be understood from the way in which we refer to certain phenomena. For example, the words 'action' and 'agent' presuppose one another. So do 'parent' and 'child'. Someone is only a parent because he or she has children. Likewise, a daughter or son is so called only in relation to them having parents. The same relationship of mutual dependence is seen in the language we use to describe trades or professions. Individuals are called farmers on account of their work on the land. Doctors are so called because of their work in the field of medicine.

In a more subtle way, things and events can be understood in terms of dependent origination when, for example, we ask, What exactly is a clay pot? When we look for something we can describe as its final identity, we find that the pot's very existence – and by implication that of all other phenomena – is to some extent provisional and determined by convention. When we ask whether its identity is determined by its shape, its function, its specific parts (that is, its being compounded of clay, water and so on), we find that the term 'pot' is merely a verbal designation. There is no single characteristic which can be said to identify it. Nor indeed does the totality of its characteristics. We can imagine pots of different shapes that are no less pots. And because we can only really speak of its existing in relation to a complex nexus of causes and conditions, viewed from this perspective it has no one defining quality. In other words, it does not exist in and of itself, but rather it is dependently originated.

As far as mental phenomena are concerned, we see that again there is a dependence. Here it lies between perceiver and perceived. Take, for example, the perception of a flower. First, in order for a perception to arise, there must be a sense organ. Second, there must be a condition – in this case the flower itself. Third, in order for a perception to occur, there must be something which directs the focus of the perceiver to the object. Then, through the causal interaction of these conditions, a congnitive event occurs which we call the perception of a flower. Now let us examine what exactly constitutes this event. Is it only the operation of the sense faculty? Is it only the interaction between that faculty and the flower itself? Or is it something else? We find that in the end, we cannot understand the concept of perception except in the context of an indefinitely complex series of causes and conditions.

If we take consciousness itself as the object of our investigation, although we tend to think of it in terms of something intrinsic and unchangeable, we find that it, too, is better understood in terms of dependent origination.

This is because apart from individual perceptual, cognitive and emotional experiences, it is difficult to posit an independently existing entity called mind or consciousness. Understood this way, consciousness is more like a construct which arises out of a spectrum of complex events.

Another way to understand the concept of dependent origination is to consider the phenomenon of time. Ordinarily, we suppose that there is an independently existing entity which we call time. We speak of time past, present, and future. However, when we look more closely, we see that again this concept is merely a convention. We find that the term 'present moment' is just a label denoting the interface between the tenses 'past' and 'future'. We cannot actually pinpoint the present. Just a fraction of a second before the supposed present moment lies the past; just a fraction of a second after lies the future. Yet if we say that the present moment is 'now', no sooner have we spoken the word than it lies in the past. If we were to maintain that nevertheless there must be a single moment which is indivisible into either past or future, we would, in fact, have no grounds for any separation into past, present and future at all. If there is a single moment which is indivisible, then we would have only the present. But without a concept of the present, it becomes difficult to speak about the past and the future since clearly both depend on the present. Moreover, if we were to conclude from our analysis that the present does not then exist, we would have to deny not only worldly convention but also our own experience.

Indeed, when we begin to analyse our experience of time, we find that here the past disappears and the future is yet to come. We experience only the present.

Where do these observations leave us? Certainly, things become somewhat more complex when we think along these lines. The more satisfactory conclusion is surely to say that the present does indeed exist. But we cannot conceive of it doing so inherently or objectively. The present comes into being in dependence on the past and the future.

How does this help us? What is the value of these observations? They have a number of important implications. First, when we come to see that everything we perceive and experience arises as a result of an indefinite series of interrelated causes and conditions, our whole perspective changes. We begin to see that the universe we inhabit can be understood in terms of a living organism where each cell works in balanced cooperation with every other cell to sustain the whole. If, then, just one of these cells is harmed, as when disease strikes, that balance is harmed and there is danger to the whole. This, in turn, suggests that our individual well-being is intimately connected both with that of all others and with the environment within which we live. It also becomes apparent that our every action, our every deed, word and thought, no matter how slight or inconsequential it may seem, has an implication not only for ourselves but for all others too.

Furthermore, when we view reality in terms of dependent origination, it draws us away from our usual tendency to see things and events in terms of solid, independent, discrete entities. This is helpful because it is this tendency which causes us to exaggerate one or two aspects of our experience and make them representative of the whole reality of a given situation while ignoring its wider complexities.

Such an understanding of reality as suggested by this concept of dependent origination also presents us with a significant challenge. It challenges us to see things and events less in terms of black and white and more in terms of a complex interlinking of relationships, which are hard to pin down. And it makes it difficult to speak in terms of absolutes. Moreover, if all phenomena are dependent on other phenomena, and if no phenomena can exist independently, even our most cherished selves must be considered not to exist in the way we normally assume. Indeed, we find that if we search for the identity of the self analytically, its apparent solidity dissolves even more readily than that of the clay pot or that of the present moment. For whereas a pot is something concrete which we can actually point to, the self is more elusive: its identity as a construct quickly becomes evident. We come to see that the habitual sharp distinction we make between 'self' and 'others' is to some extent an exaggeration.

This is not to deny that every human being naturally and correctly has a strong sense of 'I'. Even though we might not be able to say why it is so, this sense of self is certainly there. But let us examine what constitutes the actual object we call self. Is it the mind? Sometimes it happens that an individual's mind becomes hyperactive, or it may become depressed. In either case, a doctor may prescribe medicine in order to improve that person's sense of well-being. This shows that generally we think of the mind as a possession of the self. Indeed when we think closely, statements such as 'my body', 'my speech', 'my mind' all have within them an implied notion of ownership. It is difficult, therefore, to see how mind can constitute self, although it is true that there have been Buddhist philosophers who tried to identify self with consciousness. But were self and consciousness the same thing, it would follow, absurdly, that the actor and the action, both the doer and what is done of knowing, are one and the same. We would have to say that the agent 'I' who knows and the process of knowing are identical. On this view it is also hard to see how the self could exist as an independent phenomenon outside the mind–body aggregate. This suggests that the word 'self' does not denote an independent object. Rather it is a label we apply to a complex web of interrelated phenomena.

Here let us step back and review how we normally relate to this idea of self. We say, 'I am tall; I am short; I did this; I did that', and nobody questions us. It is quite clear what we mean, and everybody is happy to accept the convention. On this level, we exist quite in accordance with these statements. Such convention is part of everyday discourse and is compatible with common experience. But this does not mean that something exists solely because it is said to or because there is a word that refers to it. No one has ever found a unicorn.

Conventions may be said to be valid when they do not contradict knowledge acquired either through empirical experience or through inference, and when they serve as the foundation for a common discourse within which we situate such notions as truth and falsity. This does not preclude us from accepting that although perfectly adequate as a convention, the self, as with all other phenomena, exists in dependence on the labels and concepts we apply to the term. Consider in this context an instance where, in the dark, we mistake a coiled rope for a snake. We stop still and feel afraid. Although what we see is in reality a length of rope that we may have forgotten about, because of the lack of light and due to our misconception, we think it is a snake. Actually, the coil of rope possesses not the slightest property of a snake other than in its appearance. The snake itself is not there. We have imputed its existence onto something else. So it is with the notion of an independently existing self.

We also find that the very concept of self is relative. Here consider the fact that we often find ourselves in situations in which we blame ourselves. We say 'Oh, on such and such a day I really let myself down' and we speak of feeling angry with ourselves. This would suggest that there are in fact two distinct selves, the one which did wrong and the one which criticizes. The former is a self understood in relation to a particular experience or event. The latter is understood from a perspective of the self as a generality. Yet even though it makes sense to have an internal dialogue like this, still there is only one continuum of consciousness at any given moment. Similarly, we can see that the personal identity of a single individual has many different aspects. In my own case, for example, there is a perception of a self that is a monk, of a self that is Tibetan, of a self that is from the Amdo region of Tibet, and so on. Some of these selves predate others. For instance, the 'self' which is Tibetan existed before the 'self' that is a monk. I did not become a novice monk until I was seven years old. The 'self' which is a refugee has only existed since 1959. In other words, on one single basis there are many designations. They are all Tibetan since that 'self' – or identity – existed at my birth. But they are all nominally different. To me, this is further reason to have doubts about the inherent existence of self. We cannot say that any one characteristic is what finally constitutes my 'self', nor, on the other hand, is the sum of them. For even if I were to relinquish one or more, the sense of 'I' would still continue.

There is thus no single thing that can be found under analysis to identify the self. Just as when we try to find the ultimate identity of a solid object, it eludes us. Indeed, we are forced to conclude that this precious thing which we take such care of, which we go to such lengths to protect and make comfortable, is, in the end, no more substantial than a rainbow in the summer sky.

If it is true that no object or phenomena, not even the self, exists inherently, should we then conclude that, ultimately, nothing exists at all? Or is the reality we perceive simply a projection of the mind, apart from which nothing exists? No. When we say that things and events can only be established in terms of their dependently originating nature, that they are without intrinsic reality, existence or identity, we are not denying the existence of phenomena altogether. The 'identitylessness' of phenomena points rather to the way in which things exist: not independently but in a sense interdependently. Far from undermining the notion of phenomenal reality, I believe the concept of dependent origination provides a robust framework within which to situate cause and effect, truth and falsity, identity and difference, harm and benefit. It is, therefore, quite wrong to infer from the idea any sort of nihilistic approach to reality. A simple nothingness, without any sense of an object being this and not that, is absolutely not my meaning. Indeed if we take lack of intrinsic identity as the object of further inquiry and search for its true nature, what we find is the identitylessness of identitylessness and so on, going into infinity – from which we must conclude that even the absence of intrinsic existence exists only conventionally. So while acknowledging that there is often a discrepancy between perception and reality, it is important not to go to the extreme of supposing that behind the phenomenal is a realm which is somehow more 'real'. The problem with this is that we may then dismiss everyday experience as nothing but an illusion. That would be quite wrong.

One of the most promising developments in modern science is the emergence of quantum and probability theory. To some degree at least, this appears to support the notion of the dependent origination of phenomena. Although I cannot claim to have a very clear understanding of this theory, the observation that at the subatomic level it becomes difficult to distinguish clearly between the observer of an object and the object itself seems to indicate a movement toward the conception of reality I have outlined. I would not wish to emphasize this too strongly, however. What science holds to be true today is liable to change. New discoveries mean that what is accepted today may be doubted tomorrow. Besides, on whatever premise we base our appreciation of the fact that things and events do not exist independently, the consequences are similar.

Such an understanding of reality allows us to see that the sharp distinction we make between self and others arises largely as a result of conditioning. Yet it is possible to imagine becoming habituated to an extended conception of self wherein the individual situates his or her interests within that of others' interests. For example, when an individual thinks in terms of his or her homeland, and says, 'We are Tibetan' or 'We are French', they understand their identity in terms of something that goes beyond that of the individual self.

If the self had intrinsic identity, it would be possible to speak in terms of self-interest in isolation from that of others'. But because this is not so, because self and others can only really be understood in terms of relationship, we see that self-interest and others' interests are closely interrelated. Indeed, within this picture of dependently originated reality, we see that there is no self-interest completely unrelated to others' interests. Due to the fundamental interconnectedness which lies at the heart of reality, your interest is also my interest. From this, it becomes clear that 'my' interest and 'your' interest are intimately connected. In a deep sense they converge.

Accepting a more complex understanding of reality where all things and events are seen to be closely interrelated does not mean we cannot infer that the ethical principles we identified earlier cannot be understood as binding, even if, on this view, it becomes difficult to speak in terms of absolutes, at least outside a religious context. On the contrary, the concept of dependent origination compels us to take the reality of cause and effect with utmost seriousness. By this I mean the fact that particular causes lead to particular effects, and that certain actions lead to suffering while others lead to happiness. Thus it is in everybody's interest to do what leads to happiness and avoid that which leads to suffering. And because, as we have seen, our interests are inextricably linked, we are compelled to accept ethics as the indispensable interface between my desire to be happy and yours.

CHAPTER FOUR

REDEFINING THE GOAL

I have observed that we all naturally desire happiness and not to suffer. I have suggested, furthermore, that these are rights from which in my opinion we can infer that an ethical act is one which does not harm others' experience or expectation of happiness. And I have described an understanding of reality which points to a commonality of interest in respect of self and others.

Let us now consider the nature of happiness. The first thing to note is that happiness is a relative quality. We experience it differently according to our circumstances. What makes one person glad may be a source of suffering to another. Most of us would be extremely sorry to be sent to prison for life. Yet a criminal under threat of the death penalty would likely be very happy to be reprieved with a sentence of life imprisonment. Second, it is important to recognize that we use the same word 'happiness' to describe very different states, although this is more obvious in Tibetan where the same word, *de-wa*, is also used for 'pleasure'. We speak of happiness in connection with bathing in cool water on a hot day. We speak of it in connection with certain ideal states, such as when we say, 'I would be so happy to win the lottery.' We also speak of happiness in relation to the simple joys of family life.

In this last case, happiness is more of a state that persists in spite of ups and downs and occasional intermissions. But in the case of bathing in cool water on a hot day, because it is the consequence of an activity which seeks to please the senses, it is necessarily transient. If we remain in the water too long, we start to feel cold. Indeed, the happiness we derive from such activities depends on their being short-lived. In the case of winning a large sum of money, the question of whether it would confer lasting happiness or merely the sort that is soon overwhelmed by problems and difficulties that cannot be solved by wealth alone depends upon the one who wins it. But generally speaking, even if money bring us happiness, it tends to be the kind which money can buy: material things and sensory experiences. And these, we discover, become a source of suffering themselves. So far as actual possessions are concerned, for example, we must admit that often they cause us more, not less, difficulties in life. The car breaks down, we lose our money, our most precious belongings are stolen, our house is damaged by fire. Either that or we suffer because we worry about these things happening.

If this were not the case – if in fact such actions and circumstances did not contain within them the seed of suffering – the more we indulged in them, the greater our happiness would be, just as pain increases the more we endure the causes of pain. But such is not the case. In fact, while occasionally we may feel we have found perfect happiness of this sort, this seeming perfection turns out to be as ephemeral as a drop of dew on a leaf, shining brilliantly one moment, gone the next.

This explains why placing too much hope in material development is a mistake. The problem is not materialism as such. Rather it is the underlying assumption that full satisfaction can arise from gratifying the senses alone. Unlike animals, whose quest for happiness is restricted to survival and to the immediate gratification of sensory desires, we human beings have the capacity to experience happiness at a deeper level, which, when achieved, has the capacity to overwhelm contrary experiences. Consider the case of a soldier who fights in a battle. He is wounded, but the battle is won. The satisfaction he experiences in victory means that his experience of suffering on account of his wounds will likely be far less than that of a soldier with the same wounds on the losing side.

This human capacity for experiencing deeper levels of

happiness also explains why such things as music and the arts offer a greater degree of happiness and satisfaction than merely acquiring material objects. However, even though aesthetic experiences are a source of happiness, they also have a strong sensory component. Music depends on the ears, art on the eyes, dance on the body. As with the satisfactions we derive from work or career, they are in general acquired through the senses. By themselves, they cannot offer the happiness we dream of.

Now, it could be argued that while it is all very well to distinguish happiness that is transient from that which is lasting, between ephemeral and genuine happiness, the only happiness it is meaningful to speak of when a person is dying from thirst is access to water. This is unarguable. When it comes to the question of survival, naturally our needs become so urgent that the majority of our efforts will go toward fulfilling them. Yet because the urge to survive comes out of physical need, it follows that bodily satisfaction is invariably limited to what the senses provide. So to conclude that we should seek immediate gratification of the senses in all circumstances would hardly be justified. Actually, when we think carefully, we see that the brief elation we experience when appeasing sensual impulses may not be very different from what the drug addict feels when indulging his or her habit. Temporary relief is soon followed by a craving for more. And in just the same way that taking drugs in the end only causes trouble, so, too, does much of what we undertake to fulfil our immediate sensory desires. This is not to say that the pleasure we take in certain activities is somehow mistaken. But we must acknowledge that there can be no hope of gratifying the senses permanently. At best, the happiness we derive from eating a good meal can only last until the next time we are hungry. As one ancient Indian writer remarked: *Indulging our senses and drinking salt water are alike: the more we partake, the more our desire and thirst grow.*

Indeed, we find that a great deal of what I have called internal suffering can be attributed to our impulsive approach to happiness. We do not stop to consider the complexity of a given situation. Our tendency is to rush in and do that which seems to promise the shortest route to satisfaction. Yet in doing so, all too frequently we deprive ourselves of the opportunity for a greater degree of fulfilment. This is actually quite strange. Usually we do not allow our children to do whatever they want. We realize that if given their freedom, they would probably spend their time playing rather than studying. So instead we make them sacrifice the immediate pleasure of play and compel them to study. Our strategy is more long term. And while this may be less fun for them, it confers a solid foundation for their future. But, as adults, we often neglect this principle. We overlook the fact that if, for example, one partner in a marriage devotes all their time to their own narrow interests, it is sure that the other partner will suffer. And when that happens, it is inevitable the marriage will become harder and harder to sustain.

Similarly, we fail to recognize that when the parents are interested only in each other and neglect their children, there are sure to be negative consequences.

When we act to fulfil our immediate desires without taking into account others' interests, we undermine the possibility of lasting happiness. Consider that if we live in a neighbourhood with ten other families and yet we never give a thought to their well-being, we rob ourselves of the opportunity to benefit from their society. On the other hand, if we make the effort to be friendly and have regard for their well-being, we provide for our own happiness as well as theirs. Or, again, imagine an instance where we meet somebody new. Perhaps we go for a meal together. Now this may cost us some money. But as a result, there is a good chance of founding a relationship, which brings many benefits over the years to come. Conversely, if on meeting someone we see a chance to defraud them, and we take it, though we have gained a sum of money instantly, the likelihood is that we completely destroy the possibility of a long-term benefit from interaction with them.

Let us now consider the nature of what I have characterized as genuine happiness. Here my own experience might serve to illustrate the state to which I refer. As a Buddhist monk, I have been trained in the practice, the philosophy and the principles of Buddhism. But as to any sort of education to cope with the demands of modern living, I have received almost none. During the course of my life, I have had to handle enormous responsibilities and difficulties. At sixteen, I lost my freedom when Tibet was occupied. At twenty-four, I lost my country itself when I came into exile. For forty years now I have lived as a refugee in a foreign country, albeit the one that is my spiritual home. Throughout this time, I have been trying to serve my fellow refugees and, to the extent possible, the Tibetans who remain in Tibet. Meanwhile, our homeland has known immeasurable destruction and suffering. And, of course, I have lost not only my mother and other close family members but also dear friends. Yet for all this, although I certainly feel sad when I think about these losses, still so far as my basic serenity is concerned, on most days I am calm and contented. Even when difficulties arise, as they must, I am usually not much bothered by them. I have no hesitation in saying that I am happy.

According to my experience, the principal character-istic of genuine happiness is peace: inner peace. By this I do not mean some kind of feeling of being 'spaced out'. Nor am I speaking of an absence of feeling. On the contrary, the peace I am describing is rooted in con-cern for others and involves a high degree of sensitivity and feeling, although I cannot claim personally to have succeeded very far in this. Rather, I attribute my sense of peace to the effort to develop concern for others.

This fact, that inner peace is the principal characteristic of happiness, explains the paradox that while we can all think of people who remain dissatisfied despite having every material advantage, there are others who remain happy, notwithstanding the most difficult circumstances. Consider the example of those eighty thousand Tibetans who, during the months following my escape into exile, left Tibet for the sanctuary offered them by the Indian government. The conditions they faced were hard in the extreme. There was little food available and even less medicine. The refugee camps could offer no better accommodation than canvas tents. Most people had few possessions beyond the clothes they had left home in. They wore heavy *chubas* (the traditional Tibetan dress) appropriate to our harsh winters, when what they really needed in India was the lightest cotton. And there was terrible sickness from diseases unknown in Tibet. Yet for all their hardship, today the survivors exhibit few signs of trauma. Even then, few entirely lost confidence. Fewer still gave in to their feelings of sorrow and despair. I would even say that once the initial shock had passed, the majority remained quite optimistic and, yes, happy.

The indication here is that if we can develop this quality of inner peace, no matter what difficulties we meet with in life, our basic sense of well-being will not be undermined. It also follows that though there is no denying the importance of external factors in bringing this about, we are mistaken if we suppose that they can ever make us completely happy.

Certainly our constitution, our upbringing and our circumstances all contribute to our experience of happiness. And we can all agree that the lack of certain things makes its attainment all the harder. So let us consider these in turn. Good health, friends, freedom and a degree of prosperity are all valuable and helpful. Good health speaks for itself. We all desire it. Similarly, we all need and want friends, no matter what our situation or how successful we become. I have always been fascinated by watches, but though I am particularly fond of the one I generally wear, it never shows me any affection. In order to attain the satisfaction of love, we need friends who can return our affection. Of course, there are different kinds of friends. There are those who are really the friends of status, money and fame, and not friends of the person who possesses these things. But I refer to those who are there to help us when we encounter a difficult stage in life and not those who base their relationship with us on superficial attributes.

Freedom, in the sense of liberty to pursue happiness and to hold and express personal views, likewise contributes to our sense of inner peace. In societies where this is not permitted, we find spies who pry into the lives of every community, even the family itself. The inevitable result is that people start to lose confidence in one another. They become suspicious and doubt others' motives. Once a person's basic sense of trust is destroyed, how can we expect them to be happy?

Prosperity too – not so much in the sense of having an abundance of material wealth but more in the sense of flourishing mentally and emotionally – makes a significant contribution to our sense of inner peace. Here again we might think of the example of the Tibetan refugees who prospered in spite of their lack of resources.

Indeed, each of these factors plays an important part in establishing a sense of individual well-being. Yet without a basic feeling of inner peace and security, they are of no avail. Why? Because, as we saw, our possessions themselves are often a source of anxiety. So are our jobs insofar as we worry about losing them. Even our friends and relatives can become a source of trouble. They may get sick and need our attention when we are busy with important business. They may even turn against us and cheat us. Similarly, our bodies, however fit and beautiful they may be at present, must eventually give in to old age. Nor are we ever invulnerable to sickness and pain. Thus there is no hope of attaining lasting happiness if we lack inner peace.

Where, then, are we to find inner peace? There is no single answer. But one thing is for sure. No external factor can create it. Nor would it be any use asking for inner peace from a doctor. The best he or she can do is offer us an antidepressant, or a sleeping pill. Similarly, no machine or computer, however sophisticated and powerful, could give us this vital quality. In my view, developing inner peace, on which lasting – and therefore – meaningful happiness is dependent, is like any other task in life: we have to identify its causes and conditions and then diligently set about cultivating them. This, we find, entails a two-pronged approach. On the one hand, we need to guard against those factors which obstruct it. On the other, we need to cultivate those which are conducive to it.

So far as the conditions of inner peace are concerned, one of the most important is our basic attitude. Let me explain this by giving another personal example. Despite my habitual serenity today, I used to be somewhat hot-tempered and prone to fits of impatience and sometimes anger. Even today, there are, of course, times when I lose my composure. When this happens, the least annoyance can take on undue proportions and upset me considerably. I may, for example, wake up in the morning and feel agitated for no particular reason. In this state, I find that even what ordinarily pleases me may irritate me. Just looking at my watch can give rise to feelings of annoyance. I see it as nothing but a source of attachment and, through this, of further suffering. But then on other days I will wake up and see it as something beautiful, so intricate and delicate. Yet, of course, it is the same watch. What has changed? Are my feelings of revulsion one day and satisfaction the next purely the result of chance? Or is some neurological mechanism over which I have no control at work here? Although of course our constitution must have something to do with it, the governing factor is surely my mental attitude. Our basic attitude – how we relate to external circumstances – is thus the first consideration in any discussion on developing inner peace. In this context, the great Indian scholar-saint Shantideva once observed that while we have no hope of finding enough leather to cover the earth so that we never prick our feet on a thorn, actually we do not need to. As he went on to say, enough to cover the soles of our feet will suffice. In other words, while we cannot always change our external situation to suit us, we can change our attitude.

The other major source of inner peace, and thus of genuine happiness, is, of course, the actions we undertake in our pursuit of happiness. We can classify these in terms of those which make a positive contribution towards it, those whose effect is neutral, and those which have a negative effect on it. By considering what differentiates those acts which make for lasting happiness from those which offer only a transient sense of well-being, we see that in the latter case the activities themselves have no positive value. We have a desire for something sweet, perhaps, or for some fashionable item of clothing, or to experience something new. We have no real need of it. We simply want that thing or to enjoy that experience or sensation, and we set about satisfying our craving without much thought. Now I am not suggesting there is necess-arily anything wrong in this. An appetite for the concrete is part of human nature: we want to see, we want to touch, we want to possess. But, as I suggested earlier, it is essential we recognize that when we desire things for no real reason beyond the sensual pleasure they give us, ultimately they tend to bring us more problems. Moreover, we find that like the happiness which gratifying such needs brings, they are themselves in fact transient.

We must also acknowledge that it is this very lack of concern for consequences that underlies extreme actions, like inflicting pain on others, and even killing itself – either of which can certainly satisfy a person's desires for a short time – though those desires are severely negative ones. Or again, in the field of economic activity, the pursuit of profit without consideration of potentially negative consequences can undoubtedly give rise to feelings of great joy when success comes. But in the end there is suffering: the environment is polluted, our unscrupulous methods drive others out of business, the bombs we manufacture cause death and injury.

As to those activities which can lead to a sense of peace and lasting happiness, consider what happens when we do something we consider to be worthwhile. Perhaps we conceive of a plan to help our community and, eventually, after much effort, bring it to fruition. When we analyse activities of this sort, we find they involve discernment. They entail weighing up different factors, including both the likely and the possible consequences for ourselves and for others. In this process of evaluation, the question of morality, of whether our intended actions are ethical, arises automatically. So while the initial impulse might be to be deceitful in order to attain some end, we reason that although we may gain temporary happiness this way, actually the long-term consequences of behaving thus are likely to bring trouble. We therefore deliberately renounce one course of action in favour of another. And it is through achieving our aim by means of effort and self-sacrifice, through considering both the short-term benefit to us and the long-term effects on others' happiness, and sacrificing the former for the latter, that we attain the happiness which is characterized by peace, and by genuine satisfaction. Our differing responses to hardship confirm this. When we go on holiday, our basic motive is leisure. If, then, due to bad weather, due to clouds and rain, we are frustrated in our desire to spend time relaxing outside, our happiness is easily destroyed. On the other hand, when we seek not merely temporary satisfaction, when striving to achieve a goal, the hunger, fatigue or discomfort we may experience hardly bother us. In other words, altruism is an essential component of those actions which lead to genuine happiness.

There is thus an important distinction to be made between what we might call ethical and spiritual acts. An ethical act is one where we refrain from causing harm to others' experience or expectation of happiness. Spiritual acts we can describe in terms of those qualities mentioned earlier of love, compassion, patience, forgiveness, humility, tolerance and so on which presume some level of concern for others' well-being. We find that the (spiritual) actions we undertake which are motivated not by narrow self-interest but out of our concern for others actually benefit ourselves. And not only that, but they make our lives meaningful. At least this is my experience. Looking back over my life, I can say with full confidence that such things as the office of Dalai Lama, the political power it confers, even the comparative wealth it puts at my disposal, contribute not even a fraction to my feelings of happiness compared with the happiness I have felt on those occasions when I have been able to benefit others.

Does this proposition stand up to analysis? Is conduct inspired by the wish to benefit others the most effective way to bring about genuine happiness? Consider the following. We humans are social beings. We come into the world as the result of others' actions. We survive here in dependence on others. Whether we like it or not, there is hardly a moment of our lives when we do not benefit from others' activities. For this reason, it is hardly surprising that most of our happiness arises in the context of our relationships with others. Nor is it so remarkable that our greatest joy should come when we are motivated by concern for others. But that is not all. We find that not only do altruistic actions bring about happiness, but they also lessen our experience of suffering. Here I am not suggesting that the individual whose actions are motivated by the wish to bring others happiness necessarily meets with less misfortune than the one who does not. Sickness, old age and mishaps of one sort or another are the same for us all. But the sufferings which undermine our internal peace – anxiety, frustration, disappointment – are definitely less. In our concern for others, we worry less about ourselves. When we worry less about ourselves, the experience of our own suffering is less intense.

What does this tell us? Firstly, because our every action has a universal dimension, a potential impact on others' happiness, ethics are necessary as a means to ensure that we do not harm others. Secondly, it tells us that genuine happiness consists in those spiritual qualities of love and compassion, patience, tolerance, forgiveness, humility and so on. It is these which provide happiness both for ourselves and for others.

CHAPTER FIVE

THE SUPREME EMOTION

On a recent trip to Europe, I took the opportunity to visit the site of the Nazi death camp at Auschwitz. Even though I had heard and read a great deal about the place, I found myself completely unprepared for the experience. My initial reaction to the sight of the ovens in which hundreds of thousands of my fellow human beings were burned was one of total revulsion. I was dumbfounded at the sheer calculation and detachment from feeling to which they bore horrifying testimony. Then, in the museum which forms part of the visitor centre, I saw a collection of shoes. A lot of them were patched or small, having obviously belonged to children and poor people. This saddened me particularly. What wrong could *they* possibly have done, what harm? I stopped and prayed – moved profoundly both for the victims and for the perpetrators of this iniquity – that such a thing would never happen again. And, in the knowledge that, just as we all have the capacity to act selflessly out of concern for others' well-being, so do we all have the potential to be murderers and torturers, I vowed to do all I could to ensure that nothing like this happened again.

Events such as those which occurred at Auschwitz are violent reminders of what can happen when individuals – and by extension, whole societies – lose touch with basic human feeling. This explains why, although it is necessary to have legislation and international conventions in place as safeguards against future disasters of this kind, much more effective and important than such legislation is our regard for one another's feelings at a simple human level.

When I speak of basic human feeling, I am not only thinking of something fleeting and vague, however. I refer to the capacity we all have to empathize with one another, which, in Tibetan we call *shen dug ngal wa la mi sö pa*. Translated literally, this means 'the inability to bear the sight of another's suffering'. Given that this is what enables us to enter into, and to some extent participate, in others' pain, it is one of our most significant characteristics. It is what causes us to start at the sound of a cry for help, to recoil at the sight of harm done to another, to suffer when confronted with others' suffering. And it is what compels us to shut our eyes when we want to ignore others' distress.

Here, imagine walking along a road, deserted save for an elderly person just ahead of you. Suddenly, that person trips and falls. What do you do? I have no doubt that the majority of readers would go over to see whether they might help. Not all, perhaps. But in admitting that not everyone would go to the assistance of another in distress, I do not mean to suggest that in those few exceptions this capacity for empathy, which I have suggested to be universal, is entirely absent. Even in the case of those who did not, surely there will at least be the same feeling, however faint, of concern, which would motivate the majority to offer their assistance. It is certainly possible to imagine people who, after enduring years of warfare, are no longer moved at the sight of others' suffering. The same could be true of those who live in places where there is an atmosphere of violence and indifference to others. It is even possible to imagine a few who would exult at the sight of another's suffering. Yet this does not prove that the capacity for empathy is not present in such people. That we all, excepting perhaps only the most disturbed, appreciate being shown kindness, suggests that however hardened we may become, the capacity for empathy remains.

This characteristic of appreciating others' concern is, I believe, a reflection of our 'inability to bear the sight of another's suffering'. I say this because alongside our natural ability to empathize with others, we also have a need for others' kindness which runs like a thread throughout our whole life. It is most apparent when we are young and when we are old. But we have only to fall ill to be reminded of how important it is to be loved and cared about even during our prime years. Though it may seem a virtue to be able to do without affection, in reality a life lacking this precious ingredient must be a miserable one. It is surely not a coincidence that the lives of most criminals turn out to have been lonely and lacking in love.

We see this appreciation of kindness reflected in our response to the human smile. For me, human beings' ability to smile is one of our most beautiful characteristics. It is something no animal can do. Not dogs, nor even whales or dolphins, each of them very intelligent beings with a clear affinity for humans, can smile as we do. Personally, I always feel a bit curious when I smile at someone and they remain serious and unresponding. On the other hand, my heart is gladdened when they reciprocate. Even in the case of someone I have nothing to do with, when that person smiles at me, I am touched. But why? The answer surely is that a genuine smile touches something fundamental in us: our natural appreciation of kindness.

Despite the body of opinion suggesting that human nature is basically aggressive and competitive, my own view is that our appreciation for affection and love is so profound that it begins even before our birth. Indeed, according to some scientist friends of mine, there is strong evidence to suggest that a mother's mental and emotional state greatly affects the well-being of her unborn child, that it benefits her baby if she maintains a warm and gentle state of mind. A happy mother bears a happy child. On the other hand, frustration and anger are harmful to the healthy development of the baby. Similarly, during the first weeks after birth, warmth and affection continue to play a supreme role in the infant's physical development. At this stage the brain is growing very rapidly, a function which doctors believe is somehow assisted by the constant touch of the mother or surrogate. This shows that though the baby may not know or care who is who, it has a clear physical need of affection. Perhaps, too, it explains why even the most fractious, agitated and paranoid individuals respond positively to the affection and care of others. As infants they must have been nurtured by someone. Should a baby be neglected during this critical period, clearly it could not survive.

Fortunately, this is very rarely the case. Almost without exception, the mother's first act is to offer her baby her nourishing milk – an act which to me symbolizes unconditional love. Her affection here is totally genuine and uncalculating: she expects nothing in return. As for the baby, it is drawn naturally to its mother's breast. Why? Of course we can speak of the survival instinct. But in addition I think it reasonable to conjecture a degree of affection on the part of the infant towards its mother. If it felt aversion, surely it would not suckle? And if the mother felt aversion, it is doubtful her milk would flow freely. What we see instead is a relationship based on love and mutual tenderness, which is totally spontaneous. It is not learned from others, no religion requires it, no laws impose it, no schools have taught it. It arises quite naturally.

This instinctual care of mother for child – shared it seems with many animals – is crucial because it suggests that alongside the baby's fundamental need of love in order to survive, there exists an innate capacity on the part of the mother to give love. So powerful is it that we might almost suppose a biological component to be at work. Of course it could be argued that this reciprocal love is nothing more than a survival mechanism. That could well be so. But that is not to deny its existence. Nor indeed does it undermine my conviction that this need and capacity for love suggests that we are, in fact, loving by nature.

If this seems improbable, consider our differing response to acts of kindness and to acts of violence. Most of us find violence intimidating. Conversely, when we are shown kindness, we respond with greater trust. Similarly, consider the relationship between peace – which as we have seen is the fruit of love – and good health. According to my understanding, our constitution is more suited to peace and tranquillity than to violence and aggression.

We all know that stress and anxiety can lead to high blood pressure and other negative symptoms. In the Tibetan medical system, mental and emotional disturbances are held to be a cause of many constitutional diseases, including cancer. Moreover, peace, tranquillity and others' care are essential to recovery from illness. We can also identify a basic longing for peace. Why? Because peace suggests life and growth whereas violence suggests only misery and death. This is why the idea of a Pure Land, or of Heaven, attracts us. If such a place were described in terms of unending warfare and strife, we would much rather remain in this world.

Notice, too, how we respond to the phenomenon of life itself. When spring follows winter, the days become longer, there is more sunshine, the grass grows afresh: automatically our spirits lift. On the other hand, at the approach of winter, the leaves begin to fall one by one and much of the vegetation around us becomes as though dead. Small wonder if we tend to feel a bit downcast at that time of year. The indication here is surely that our nature prefers life over death, growth over decay, construction over destruction.

Consider also the behaviour of children. In them we see what is natural to the human character before it has been overlaid with learned ideas. We find that very young babies do not really differentiate between one individual and another. They attach much more importance to the smile of the person in front of them than to anything else.

Even when they start to grow up they are not much interested in differences of race, nationality, religion or family background. When they meet with other children they do not stop to discuss these things. They immediately begin the much more important business of play. Nor is this just sentimentalism. I see the reality whenever I visit one of the children's villages in Europe, where numbers of Tibetan refugee children have been educated since the early 1960s. These villages were founded to care for orphaned children from countries at war with one another. To no one's great surprise, it was found that despite their different backgrounds, when these children are put together they live in complete harmony with one another.

Now it could be objected that while we may all share a capacity for loving-kindness, human nature is such that inevitably we tend to reserve it for those closest to us. We are biased toward our families and friends. Our feelings of concern for those outside this circle will depend very much on individual circumstances: those who feel threatened are not likely to have very much goodwill for those who threaten them. All this is true enough. Nor do I deny that whatever our capacity to feel concern for our fellow human beings, when our very survival is threatened, it may but rarely prevail over the instinct for self-preservation. Still, this does not mean that the capacity is no longer there, that the potential does not remain. Even soldiers after a battle will often help their enemies retrieve the dead and wounded.

In all of what I have said about our basic nature, I do not mean to suggest that I believe it has no negative aspects. Where there is consciousness, hatred, ignorance and violence do indeed arise naturally. This is why, although our nature is basically disposed towards kindness and compassion, we are all capable of cruelty and hatred. It is why we have to struggle to better our conduct. It also explains how individuals raised in a strictly non-violent environment have turned into the most horrible butchers. In connection with this, I recall my visit some years ago to the Washington Memorial, which pays tribute to the martyrs and heroes of the Jewish Holocaust at the hands of the Nazis. What struck me most forcefully about the monument was its simultaneous cataloguing of different forms of human behaviour. On one side it lists the victims of acts of unspeakable atrocity. On the other, it remembers the heroic acts of kindness on the part of Christian families and others who willingly took terrible risks in order to harbour their Jewish brothers and sisters. I felt that this was entirely appropriate, and very necessary: to show the two sides of human potential.

The existence of this negative potential does not give us grounds to suppose that human nature is inherently violent, or even necessarily disposed towards violence, however. Perhaps one of the reasons for the popularity of the belief that human nature is aggressive lies in our continual exposure to bad news through the media. Yet the very cause of this is surely that good news is not news.

To say that human nature is not only non-violent but actually disposed toward love and compassion, kindness, gentleness, affection, creation and so on does, of course, imply a general principle which must, by definition, be applicable to each individual human being. What, then, are we to say about those individuals whose lives seem to be given over wholly to violence and aggression? During the past century alone there are several obvious examples to consider. What of Hitler and his plan to exterminate the entire Jewish race? What of Stalin and his pogroms? What of Chairman Mao, the man I once knew and admired, and the barbarous insanity of the Cultural Revolution? What of Pol Pot, architect of the Killing Fields? And what about those who torture and kill for pleasure?

Here I must admit that I can think of no single explanation to account for the monstrous acts of these people. However, we must recognize two things. Firstly, such people do not come from nowhere but from within a particular society at a particular time and in a particular place. Their actions need to be considered in relation to these circumstances. Secondly, we need to recognize the role of the imaginative faculty in their actions. Their schemes were and are carried out in accordance with a vision, albeit a perverted one. Notwithstanding the

fact that nothing could justify the suffering they insti-
gated, whatever their explanation might be and whatever
positive intentions they might point to, Hitler, Stalin,
Mao and Pol Pot each had goals toward which they
were working. If we examine those actions which are
uniquely human, which animals cannot perform, we find
this imaginative faculty plays a vital role. The faculty
itself is a unique asset. But the use to which it is put
determines whether the actions it conceives are positive or
negative, ethical or unethical. The individual's motivation
(*kun long*) is thus the governing factor. And whereas a
vision properly motivated – which recognizes others'
desire for and equal right to happiness and to be free
of suffering – can lead to wonders, when divorced from
basic human feeling the potential for destruction cannot
be overestimated.

As for those who kill for pleasure or, worse, for no
reason at all, we can only conjecture a deep submergence
of the basic impulse toward care and affection for others.
Still this need not mean that it is entirely extinguished. As
I pointed out earlier, except perhaps in the most extreme
cases, it is possible to imagine even these people appreciating being shown affection. The disposition remains.

Actually, the reader does not need to accept my proposition that human nature is basically disposed toward
love and compassion to see that the capacity for empathy which underlies it is of crucial importance when it
comes to ethics. We saw earlier how an ethical act is a

non-harming act. But how are we to determine whether an act is genuinely non-harming? We find that in practice, if we are not able to connect with others to some extent, if we cannot at least imagine the potential impact of our actions on others, then we have no means to discriminate between right and wrong, between what is appropriate and what is not, between harming and non-harming. It follows that if we could enhance this capacity – that is to say, our sensitivity towards others' suffering – the more we did so, the less we could tolerate seeing others' pain and the more we would be concerned to ensure that no action of ours caused harm to others.

The fact that we can indeed enhance our capacity for empathy becomes obvious when we consider its nature. We experience it mainly as a feeling. And, as we all know, to a greater or lesser extent we can not only restrain our feelings through reasoning, but we can enhance them in the same way. Our desire for objects – perhaps a new car – is enhanced by our turning it over and over in our imagination. Similarly, when, as it were, we direct our mental faculties onto our feelings of empathy, we find that not only can we enhance them, but we can transform them into love and compassion itself.

As such, our innate capacity for empathy is the source of that most precious of all qualities, which in Tibetan we call *nying je*. Now while generally translated simply as 'compassion', the term *nying je* has a wealth of meaning that is difficult to convey succinctly, though the ideas it contains are universally understood. It connotes love, affection, kindness, gentleness, generosity of spirit and warm-heartedness. It is also used as a term of both sympathy and of endearment. On the other hand, it does not imply 'pity' as the word 'compassion' may. There is no sense of condescension. On the contrary, *nying je* denotes a feeling of connection with others, reflecting its origins in empathy. Thus while we might say, 'I love my house' or 'I have strong feelings of affection for this place', we cannot say, 'I have compassion' for these things. Having no feelings themselves, we cannot empathize with objects. We cannot, therefore, speak of having compassion for them.

Although it is clear from this description that *nying je*, or love and compassion, is understood as an emotion, it belongs to that category of emotions which have a more developed cognitive component. As already mentioned, some emotions, such as the revulsion we tend to feel at the sight of blood, are basically instinctual. Others, such as fear of poverty, have this more developed cognitive component. We can thus understand *nying je* in terms of a combination of empathy and reason. We can think of empathy as the characteristic of a very honest person, reason as that of someone who is very practical. When the two are put together, the combination is highly effective. As such, *nying je* is quite different from those random feelings, like anger and lust, which, far from bringing us happiness, only trouble us and destroy our peace of mind.

To me, this suggests that by means of sustained reflection on, and familiarization with compassion, through rehearsal and practice, we can develop our innate ability to connect with others, a fact which is of supreme importance given the approach to ethics I have described. The more we develop compassion, the more genuinely ethical our conduct will be.

As we have seen, when we act out of concern for others, our behaviour towards them is automatically positive. This is because we have no room for suspicion when our hearts are filled with love. It is as if an inner door is opened, allowing us to reach out. Having concern for others breaks down the very barriers which inhibit healthy interaction with others. And not only that. When our intentions toward others are good, we find that any feelings of shyness or insecurity we may have are greatly reduced. To the extent that we are able to open this inner door, we experience a sense of liberation from our habitual preoccupation with self. Paradoxically, we find this gives rise to strong feelings of confidence. Thus, if I may give an example from my own experience, I find that whenever I meet new people and have this positive disposition, there is no barrier between us. No matter who or what they are, whether they have blonde hair or black hair, or hair dyed green, I feel that I am simply encountering a fellow human being with the same desire to be happy and to avoid suffering as myself. And I find I can speak to them as if they were old friends, even at our first meeting. By keeping in mind that ultimately we are all brothers and sisters, that there is no substantial difference between us, that just as I do, all others share my desire to be happy and to avoid suffering, I can express my feelings as readily as to someone I have known intimately for years. And not just with a few nice words or gestures but really heart to heart, no matter what the language barrier.

We also find that when we act out of concern for others, the peace this creates in our own hearts brings peace to everyone we associate with. We bring peace to the family, peace to our friends, to the workplace, to the community and so to the world. Why, then, would anyone not wish to develop this quality? Could anything be more sublime than that which brings peace and happiness to all? For my own part, the mere ability we human beings have to sing the praises of love and compassion is a most precious gift.

Conversely, not even the most sceptical reader could suppose that peace comes about as the result of aggressive and inconsiderate, that is to say unethical, behaviour. Of course it cannot. I well remember how I learned this particular lesson when I was a small boy in Tibet. One of my attendants, Kenrab Tenzin, had made a pet of a small parrot, which he used to feed with nuts. Although he was a rather stern man with bulging eyes and a somewhat forbidding aspect, merely at the sound of his footsteps, or of his coughing, this parrot would show signs of excitement. As the bird nibbled from his fingers, Kenrab Tenzin would stroke its head, which appeared to put it into a state of ecstasy. I was very envious of this relationship and desired the bird to show me the same friendliness. But when I tried on a few occasions to feed it myself, I failed to get a good response. So I tried poking at it with a stick in the hope of provoking a better reaction. Needless to say, the result was totally negative. Far from forcing it to behave better toward me, the bird took fright. What little prospect of establishing friendly relations there may have been were totally destroyed. I learned thereby that friendships come about not as the result of bullying but as a result of kindness and compassion.

The world's major religious traditions each give the development of love and compassion a key role. Because they are both the source and the result of patience, tolerance, forgiveness and all good qualities, their importance is considered to extend from the beginning to the end of spiritual practice. But even without a religious perspective, love and compassion are clearly of fundamental importance to us all. Given our basic premise that an ethical conduct consists in not harming others, it follows that we need to take others' feelings into consideration, the basis for which is our innate capacity for empathy. And as we transform this capacity into love and compassion, through the guarding against those factors which obstruct it and cultivating those conducive to it, so our practice of ethics improves. This, we find, leads to happiness both for ourselves and others.

PART TWO

Ethics and the Individual

CHAPTER SIX

THE ETHIC OF RESTRAINT

I have suggested that developing the compassion on which happiness depends demands a two-pronged approach. On the one hand, we need to restrain those factors which inhibit compassion. On the other, we need to cultivate those which are conducive to it. As we have seen, what is conducive to compassion is love, patience, tolerance, forgiveness, humility and so on. What inhibits compassion is that lack of inner restraint which we have identified as the source of all unethical conduct. We find that by transforming our habits and dispositions we can begin to perfect our overall state of heart and mind (*kun*

long) – that from which all our actions spring. The first thing, then – because the spiritual qualities conductive to compassion entail positive ethical conduct – is to cultivate a habit of inner discipline. Now I cannot deny that this is a major undertaking, but at least we are familiar with the principle. For example, knowing its destructive potential, we restrain both ourselves and our children from indulging in drug abuse. However, it is important to recognize that restraining our response to negative thoughts and emotions is not a matter of just suppressing them: insight into their destructive nature is crucial. Merely being told that envy, potentially a very powerful and destructive emotion, is negative cannot provide a strong defence against it. If we order our lives externally but ignore the inner dimension, inevitably we will find that doubt, anxiety and other afflictions develop, and happiness eludes us. This is because, unlike physical discipline, true inner – or spiritual – discipline cannot be achieved by force but only through voluntary and deliberate effort based on understanding. In other words, conducting ourselves ethically consists in more than merely obeying laws and precepts.

The undisciplined mind is like an elephant. If left to blunder around out of control, it will wreak havoc. But the harm and suffering we encounter as a result of failing to restrain the negative impulses of mind far exceed the damage a rampaging elephant can cause. Not only are these impulses capable of bringing about the destruction of things, they can also be the cause of lasting pain to others and to ourselves. By this I do not mean to suggest that the mind (*lo*) is inherently destructive. Under the influence of a strongly negative thought or emotion, the mind may seem to be characterized by a single quality. But if, for instance, hatefulness were an unchangeable characteristic of consciousness, then consciousness must always be hateful. Clearly this is not the case. There is an important distinction to be made between consciousness as such and the thoughts and emotions it experiences.

Similarly, while at the time a powerful experience may overwhelm us, when we consider it later, we are unmoved. When very young, I used to become highly excited, as the old year drew to a close, at the thought of *Monlam Chenmo*. This was the Great Prayer Festival which marked the start of the Tibetan New Year. In my capacity as Dalai Lama, I had an important role in this, which meant moving from the Potala to a set of rooms in the Jokhang temple, one of Tibet's holiest shrines. As the day drew closer, I would spend more and more time daydreaming at the prospect, half-terrified and half-elated, and less and less time studying. My feelings of terror were caused by the thought of the long recital I had to give from memory during the main ceremony, my excitement by the thought of passing among the huge crowd of pilgrims and traders thronging the market place in front of the temple complex. Even though both the overexcitement and the aversion I felt were real enough then, today, of course, I can laugh at these memories. I am now quite used to crowds. And, after so many years of practice, the recitation no longer troubles me.

We can conceive of the nature of mind in terms of the water in a lake. When the water is stirred up by a storm, the mud from the lake's bottom clouds it, making it appear opaque. But the nature of the water is not dirty. When the storm passes, the mud settles and the water is left clear once again. So although generally we may suppose mind, or consciousness, to be an inherent and unchangeable entity, when we consider it more deeply, we see that it consists in a whole spectrum of events and experiences. These include our sensory perception, which engages with objects directly, as well as our thoughts and feelings, which are mediated by language and concepts. It is also dynamic: through deliberate engagement we can effect changes in our mental and emotional states. We know, for example, how comfort and reassurance can help dispel fear. Similarly, those forms of counselling which lead to greater awareness, and affection, can help alleviate depression.

This observation, that emotion and consciousness are not the same thing, tells us that we do not have to be controlled by our thoughts and emotions. Prior to our every action, there must be a mental and emotional event to which we are more or less free to respond, albeit that, until we have learned to discipline our mind to some degree, we will have difficulty in exercising this freedom. How we respond to these events and experiences is, moreover, that which – generally speaking – determines the moral content of our acts. In simple terms, this means that if we do so positively, keeping others' interests before us, our acts will be positive. If we respond negatively, neglecting others, our acts will be negative and unethical.

According to this understanding, we might think of mind, or consciousness, in terms of a president or monarch who is very honest, very pure. On this view, our thoughts and emotions are like cabinet ministers. Some of them give good advice, some bad. Some have the well-being of others as their principal concern, others only their own narrow interests. The responsibility of the main consciousness – the leader – is to determine which of these subordinates give good advice and which bad, which of them are reliable and which are not, and to act on the advice of the one sort, and not the other.

Mental and emotional events which, in this sense, give bad advice can themselves be described as a form of suffering. Indeed, we find that when they are allowed to develop to any significant degree, the mind becomes swamped with emotion, and we experience a kind of inner turbulence. This also has a physical dimension. In a moment of anger, for example, we experience a powerful disturbance of our habitual equilibrium, which can often be sensed by others. We are all familiar with the way in which the whole atmosphere is spoiled when just one member of the household is in a bad mood.

When we become enraged, both people and animals tend to avoid us. Sometimes this turbulence is so strong that we find great difficulty containing it. This may cause us to lash out at others. In doing so, we externalize our inner turbulence.

This is not to say that all thoughts and emotions which cause us discomfort are necessarily negative. The primary attribute distinguishing ordinary emotions from those which undermine peace, is its negative cognitive component. A moment of sorrow does not become disabling grief unless we hold onto it and add negative thoughts and imaginings. In the case of the overexcitement I felt about those crowds of pilgrims and traders, and the fear I had of the long recitation, there was an added cognitive component on top of the basic feeling. Through my somewhat obsessive daydreaming, my imagination superimposed something beyond the reality of the situation. And it was the stories I told myself about the forthcoming event that undermined my basic serenity.

Nor is all fear like the childish one I have just described. There are occasions when we experience a more rational kind of fear. Far from being negative, this may actually be helpful. It can heighten our awareness and give us the energy we need to protect ourselves. On the first night of my escape from Lhasa in 1959, when I left home dressed as a soldier, I certainly felt this kind of fear. But because I had neither the time nor the inclination to think about it, it did not unsettle me very much. Its main effect was to make me very alert. One could say that this was an instance of fear which was both justified and useful.

The fear we feel in relation to a situation which is quite delicate or critical may also be justified. Here I am thinking of what we feel when we have to make a decision we know will have a significant effect on others' lives. Such fear may disconcert us somewhat. But the most dangerous and negative is that fear which is completely unreasonable and which can totally overwhelm and paralyse us.

In Tibetan, we call such negative and emotional events *nyong mong*, literally, 'that which afflicts from within' or, as the term is usually translated, 'afflictive emotion'. On this view, generally speaking, all those thoughts, emotions and mental events which reflect a negative or uncompassionate state of mind (*kun long*) inevitably undermine our experience of inner peace. All negative thoughts and emotions such as hatred, anger, pride, lust, greed, envy and so on – are considered to be afflictions in this sense. We find that these afflictive emotions are so strong that, if we do nothing to counter them, though there is no one who does not value their life, they can lead us to the point of madness and even suicide itself. But because such extremes are unusual, we tend to see negative emotions as an integral part of our mind about which we can do very little. And, in failing to recognize their destructive potential we do not see the need to challenge them. Indeed, far from doing so, we have a tendency to nurture and reinforce them. This provides them with the ground in which to grow. Yet, as we shall see, their nature is wholly destructive.

Negative thoughts and emotions are what obstruct our most basic aspiration – to be happy and to avoid suffering. When we act under their influence, we become oblivious to the impact our actions have on others: they are thus the cause of our destructive behaviour both toward others and to ourselves. They are the very source of unethical conduct. Murder, scandal and deceit all have their origin in afflictive emotion. They are also the basis of the anxiety, depression, confusion and stress, which are such a feature of our lives today. This is why I say that the undisciplined mind – that is, the mind under the influence of anger, hatred, greed, pride, selfishness and so on – is the source of all of our troubles which do not fall into the category of unavoidable suffering (which includes sickness, old age, and death). Our failure to check our response to afflictive emotions opens the door to suffering for both self and others.

To say that when we cause others to suffer we ourselves suffer does not mean, of course, we can logically infer that in every instance when, for example, I hit someone, I will be hit myself. The proposition I am making is much more general than this. Rather, I mean to suggest that the impact of our actions – both positive and negative – registers deep within us. If it is correct that, on some level, we all have the capacity for empathy, it follows that for one individual to harm another, this potential must be overwhelmed, or submerged in some way. Take the case of a person who cruelly tortures another, their mind (lo) must be strongly gripped at the gross, or conscious level, by some kind of harmful thinking or ideology which causes them to believe their victim is deserving of such treatment. Such a belief – which to some degree must have been deliberately chosen – is what enables the cruel person to suppress their feelings. Nevertheless, deep down, there is bound to be some kind of effect. In the long run, there is a high degree of probability that discomfort will be felt by the torturer. Consider in this context the example we looked at earlier – of merciless dictators like Hitler and Stalin. It seems that as they neared the end of their lives, they became lonely, anxious, full of dread and suspicion, like crows afraid of their own shadows.

Of course, the number of people who go to such extremes is very small. The impact of minor negative actions is also much more subtle than major ones. So, as a less extreme example of the way in which negative actions cause suffering both to ourselves as well as others, consider a child going out to play who gets into a fight with another child. Immediately after, the victorious child may experience a sense of satisfaction. But on returning home, that emotion will subside and a more subtle state of mind will manifest. At that point, a sense of unease sets in. We could almost describe this sort of feeling as a sense of alienation from self: the individual doesn't feel quite 'right'. In the contrary case of a child who goes out to play with a friend and shares an enjoyable afternoon with that playmate, afterwards not only will there be an immediate sense of satisfaction, but when the mind has settled down and the excitement worn off, there will be a sense of calm and comfort.

Another example of the way in which negative actions harm the one who indulges them can be seen in the context of an individual's reputation. Generally, it seems, we humans – even for that matter animals – abhor meanness, aggressiveness, deceit and so on. For this reason, if we engage in activities which harm others, despite the temporary satisfaction we might gain thereby, people will at some point begin to look at us askance. They will become apprehensive of us, nervous and suspicious on account of our bad reputation. In time, we will start to lose friends. In this way, because a good reputation is a source of happiness, we bring suffering on ourselves if we spoil it.

Indeed, though there may be a few exceptions, we find that if a person lives a very selfish life, without concern for others' welfare, they tend to become quite lonely and miserable. Though they may be surrounded by people who are friends of their wealth or status, when the selfish or aggressive individual faces tragedy, not only do these so-called friends vanish, they may even secretly rejoice. And if, moreover, he or she is actively malicious too, it is likely that when they die they will not be much missed.

People may actually be glad – as many of the inmates of the Nazi death camps must have been at the subsequent execution of their captors. Conversely, we find that when people are actively concerned for others, they are much respected, even venerated. When such people die, many mourn and regret their passing. Consider the case of Mahatma Gandhi. Despite a Western education, and the opportunities this gave him to lead a comfortable life, he chose out of consideration for others to live in India almost as a beggar in order to devote himself to his life's work. Yet though his name is now just a memory, millions still draw comfort and inspiration from his noble deeds.

As far as the actual cause of afflictive emotion is concerned, we can point to a number of different factors. These include the habit we all have of thinking of ourselves before others. We can also cite our tendency to project characteristics onto things and events above and beyond what actually is there – as in the example of mistaking the coiled rope for a snake. But beyond these, because our negative thoughts and emotions do not exist independently of other phenomena, the very objects and events we come into contact with themselves play a role in shaping our responses. There is thus nothing which does not have the potential to trigger them. Anything can be a source of afflictive emotion – not just our adversaries but our friends and our most valued possessions too – even our own selves.

This suggests that the first step in the process of actually countering our negative thoughts and emotions is to avoid those situations and activities which would normally give rise to them. If, for example, we find we become angry whenever we meet with a particular person, it may be best to keep away from them until we develop our internal resources more. The second step is to avoid the actual conditions which lead to these strong thoughts and emotions. This, however, presupposes that we have learned to recognize afflictive emotions as they arise in us. This is not always easy. While hatred is a very strong emotion when fully developed, in its beginning stages the aversion we feel toward a particular object or event may be quite subtle. And even at their most advanced stages of development, afflictive emotions do not always manifest dramatically. The assassin may be relatively calm in the moment that he pulls the trigger.

To this end, we need to pay close attention and be aware of our body and its actions, of our speech and what we say, and of our hearts and minds and what we think and feel. We must be on the lookout for the slightest negativity and keep asking ourselves such questions as, 'Am I happier when my thoughts and emotions are negative and destructive or when they are wholesome?', 'What is the nature of consciousness? Does it exist in and of itself, or does it exist in dependence on other factors?', We need to think, think, think. We should be like a scientist who collects data, analyses it, and draws the appropriate conclusion. Gaining insight into our own negativity is a lifelong task, and one which is capable of almost infinite refinement. But unless we undertake it, we will be unable to see where to make the necessary changes in our lives.

Were we to expend even a fraction of the time and effort we waste in trivial activities – pointless gossip and the like – on gaining insight into the actual nature of afflictive emotion, I believe it would have a huge impact on our quality of life. Both individuals and society would benefit. One of the first things we would discover is how destructive afflictive emotions are. And the more we developed an appreciation of their destructive nature, the more disinclined we would become to follow them. This alone would have a significant impact on our lives.

Consider that not only do negative thoughts and emotions destroy our experience of peace, they also undermine our health. In the Tibetan medical system, anger is understood as a primary source of many illnesses, including those associated with high blood pressure, sleeplessness and degenerative disorders – a view which seems to be increasingly accepted in allopathic medicine.

Another childhood memory illustrates the way in which afflictive emotions harm us. When I was a teenager, one of my favourite pastimes was tinkering with the old cars that my predecessor, the Thirteenth Dalai Lama, had acquired not long before he died in 1933. There were four of them, two baby Austins of British manufacture, a Dodge and a beaten-up jeep, both of American origin. Together they comprised almost the only powered vehicles in Tibet. For the young Dalai Lama, these dusty relics held an irresistible attraction, and I longed to have them running again. My secret dream was actually to learn to drive. But it was only after a lot of pestering of various government officials that finally I found someone who knew anything about cars. This was Lhakpa Tsering, who came from Kalimpong, a town just over the Indian border. One day, I recall, he was working on the engine of one of the cars when, dropping his spanner, he shouted an oath and stood up abruptly. Unfortunately, he had forgotten that the bonnet was open above him and he hit his head with a terrible crack. But then to my great surprise, instead of extracting himself carefully, he became further enraged and, straightening up again, hit his head even harder a second time. For a moment, I stood astonished at these antics. Then I found I could not stop laughing.

Lhakpa Tsering's outburst resulted in nothing more than two generous bruises. That was merely unfortunate for him. But from this we see how the afflictive emotions destroy one of our most precious qualities, namely, our capacity for discriminative awareness. Robbed of what enables us to judge between right and wrong, to evaluate what is likely to be of lasting benefit and what of merely temporary benefit to self and others, and to discern the likely outcome of our actions, we are no better off than animals. Small wonder that under their influence we do what ordinarily we would never consider doing.

This obliteration of our critical faculties points to another negative characteristic of this type of mental and emotional event. Afflictive emotions deceive us. They seem to offer satisfaction. But they do not provide it. In fact, although such emotion comes to us in the guise of a protector giving us, as it were, boldness and strength, we find that this energy is essentially blind. Decisions taken under its influence are often a source of regret. More often than not, such anger is actually an indication of weakness rather than of strength. Most people have experienced an argument deteriorating to the point where one person becomes verbally abusive, a clear sign of the fragility of their position. Moreover, we do not need anger to develop courage and confidence. As we shall see, it can be done through other means.

The afflictive emotions also have an irrational dimension. They encourage us to suppose that appearances are invariably commensurate with reality. When we become angry or feel hatred, we tend to relate to others as if their characteristics were immutable. A person can appear to be objectionable from the crown of their head to the soles of their feet. We forget that they, like us, are merely suffering human beings with the same wish to be happy and to avoid suffering as we ourselves. Yet common sense alone tells us that when the force of our anger diminishes, they are sure to seem a little better at least. The same is true in reverse if individuals become infatuated. The other appears to be wholly desirable – until such time as the grip of afflictive emotion subsides and they come to seem a little less than perfect. Indeed, when our passions become so strongly aroused, there is considerable danger of going to the opposite extreme. The individual once idolized now seems despicable and hateful, though of course it is the same person throughout.

The afflictive emotions are also useless. The more we give in to them, the less room we have for our good qualities – such as kindness and compassion – and the less able we are to solve our problems. Indeed, there is no occasion on which these disturbing thoughts and emotions are helpful, either to ourselves or to others. The more angry we are, the more people shun us. The more suspicious we are, the more cut off from people we become and thus the more lonely. The more lustful we are, the less we are able to develop proper relationships with others and, again, the more lonely we become. Consider the individual whose activities are directed principally by afflictive emotion or, to put it another way, by gross attachments and aversions: by greed, arrogant ambition and so forth. Such a person may become very powerful and very famous. Their name may even go down in history. But after they die, their power is gone and their fame is no more than an empty word. So what have they really achieved?

Nowhere is the uselessness of afflictive emotion more obvious than in the case of anger. When we become angry, we stop being compassionate, loving, generous, forgiving, tolerant and patient altogether. We thus deprive ourselves of the very things that happiness consists in. And not only does anger immediately destroy our critical faculties, it tends towards rage, spite, hatred and malice – each of which are always negative because they are a direct cause of harm to others. Anger causes suffering. At the very least, it causes the pain of embarrassment. For example, I have always enjoyed repairing watches. But I can recall a number of occasions as a boy when, completely losing my patience with those tiny, intricate parts, I picked the mechanism up and smashed it down on the table. Of course, I later felt very sorry and ashamed at my behaviour – especially when, as on one occasion, I had to return the watch to its owner in a condition worse than it was in before!

This story, trivial in itself, also makes the point that though we may have an abundance of material wealth – good food, fine furnishings, a nice television set – when we become angry, we lose all inner peace. We no longer enjoy even our breakfast. And when it becomes habitual, we may be ever so learned, rich or powerful, but others will simply avoid us. They will say, 'Oh yes, he is very clever, but he has such bad moods you know', and people will keep away. Or they will say, 'Yes she is extraordinarily talented, but she gets upset so easily. You had better watch out.' Just as when a dog is always growling and showing its teeth, we are cautious of those whose hearts are disturbed by anger. We would rather forgo their company than risk an outburst.

I do not deny that, as in the case of fear, there is a kind of 'raw' anger that we experience more as a rush of energy than as a cognitively enhanced emotion. Conceivably, this form of anger could have positive consequences. It is not impossible to imagine anger at the sight of injustice causing someone to act altruistically. The anger that causes us to go to the assistance of someone who is being attacked in the street could be characterized as positive. But if this goes beyond meeting the injustice, if it becomes personal and turns into vengefulness or maliciousness, then danger arises. When we do something negative, we are capable of recognizing the difference between ourselves and the negative act. But we often fail to separate action and agent when it comes to others. This shows us how unreliable is even apparently justified anger.

Should it still seem too much to say that anger is an entirely useless emotion, we can ask ourselves if anyone ever says anger can bring happiness. Nobody. What doctor prescribes anger as treatment for any disease? There isn't one. Anger can only hurt us. It has nothing to recommend it. Let the reader ask himself or herself: when we become angry, do we feel happy? Does our mind become calmer and our body relax? Or rather is it not that we feel tense in body and unsettled of mind?

If we are to retain our peace of mind and thereby our happiness, it follows that alongside a more rational and disinterested approach to our negative thoughts and emotions, we must cultivate a strong habit of restraint in response to them. Negative thoughts and emotions are what cause us to act unethically. Furthermore, because afflictive emotion is also the source of our own internal suffering – in that it is the basis of frustration, confusion, insecurity, anxiety and the very loss of self-respect which undermines our sense of confidence – failure to do so means that we will remain in a state of perpetual mental and emotional discomfort. Inner peace will be impossible. In place of happiness there will be insecurity. Anxiety and depression will never be far away.

Some people may feel that although it is right to curb the feelings of intense hatred which can cause us to be violent and even to kill, we are in danger of losing our independence when we restrain our emotions and discipline the mind. Actually, the opposite is true. Like their counterparts of love and compassion, anger and the afflictive emotions can never be used up. They have, rather, a propensity to increase, like a river flooding in summer when the snow melts, so that far from being free, our minds are enslaved and rendered helpless by them. When we indulge our negative thoughts and feelings, inevitably we become accustomed to them. As a result, gradually we become more prone to them and more controlled by them. And we become habituated to exploding in the face of displeasing circumstance.

Inner peace, which is the principal characteristic of

happiness, and anger cannot coexist without undermining one another. Indeed, negative thoughts and emotions undermine the very causes of peace and happiness. In fact, when we think properly, it is totally illogical to seek happiness if we do nothing to restrain angry, spiteful and malicious thoughts and emotions. Consider that when we become angry, we often use harsh words. Harsh words can destroy friendship. Since happiness arises in the context of our relationships with others, if we destroy friendships, we undermine one of the very conditions of happiness itself.

To say that we need to curb anger and our negative thoughts and emotions does not mean that we should deny our feelings. There is an important distinction to be made between denial and restraint. The latter constitutes a deliberate and voluntarily adopted discipline based on an appreciation of the benefits of doing so. This is very different from the case of someone who suppresses emotions such as anger out of a feeling that they need to present a façade of self-control, or out of fear of what others may think. Such behaviour is like closing a wound which is still infected. We are not talking about rule-following. Where denial and suppression occur, there comes the danger that in doing so the individual stores up anger and resentment. The trouble here is that at some future point they may find they cannot contain these feelings any longer.

In other words, there are, of course, thoughts and emotions which it is appropriate, even important, to express openly – including negative ones – albeit there are more or less appropriate ways to do so. It is far better to confront a person or situation than to hide our anger away, brood on it and nurture resentment in our hearts. Yet if we indiscriminately express negative thoughts and emotions simply on the grounds that they must be articulated, there is a strong possibility, for all the reasons I have given, that we will lose control and overreact. Thus the important thing is to be discriminating, both in terms of the feelings we express and in how we express them.

As I understand it, genuine happiness is characterized by inner peace and arises in the context of our relationships with others. It therefore depends on ethical conduct. This in turn consists in acts which take others' well-being into account. What obstructs us from engaging in such compassionate conduct is afflictive emotion. If, then, we wish to be happy, we need to curb our response to negative thoughts and emotions. This is what I mean when I say that we must tame the wild elephant that is the undisciplined mind. When I fail to restrain my response to afflictive emotion, my actions become unethical and obstruct the conditions of my happiness. We are not talking about attaining Buddhahood here, we are not talking about achieving union with God. We are merely recognizing that my interests and future happiness are closely connected to others' and learning to act accordingly.

CHAPTER SEVEN

THE ETHIC OF VIRTUE

I have suggested that if we are to be genuinely happy, inner restraint is indispensable. We cannot stop at restraint, however. Though it may prevent us from performing any grossly negative misdeeds, mere restraint is insufficient if we are to attain that happiness which is characterized by inner peace. In order to transform ourselves – our habits and dispositions – so that our actions are compassionate, it is necessary to develop what we might call an *ethic of virtue*. As well as refraining from negative thoughts and emotions, we need to cultivate and reinforce our positive qualities. What are these positive qualities? The basic human, or spiritual, qualities of love and compassion, patience, tolerance, humility, forgiveness and so on.

After compassion (*nying je*) itself, the chief of these is the one which in Tibetan is called *sö pa*. Here again, we have a term which appears to have no ready equivalent in other languages, though the ideas it conveys are universal. Often, *sö pa* is translated simply as 'patience', though its literal meaning is 'able to bear' or 'able to withstand'. But the word also carries a notion of resolution. It thus denotes a deliberate response (as opposed to an unreasoned reaction) to the strong negative thoughts and emotions that tend to arise when we encounter harm. As such, *sö pa* is what provides us with the strength to resist suffering and protects us from losing our compassion even for those who would harm us.

In this context, I am reminded of the example of Lopon-la, a monk from Namgyal monastery. Following my escape from Tibet, Lopon-la was one of many thousands of monks and officials imprisoned by the occupying forces. When he was finally released, he was allowed to come to India, where he rejoined his old monastery now refounded in exile. More than twenty years after last seeing him, I found Lopon-la much as I remembered him. He looked older, of course, but physically he was unscathed. And mentally his ordeal had not affected him adversely at all. His gentleness and serenity remained. From our conversation, I learned that he had, nevertheless, endured grievous treatment during those long years of imprisonment. In common with all others, he had been subjected to 're-education', during which he had been forced to denounce his religion and, on many occasions, he was tortured as well. When I asked him whether he had ever been afraid, he admitted that there was one thing that had scared him: the possibility that he might lose compassion and concern for his jailers.

I was very moved at this, and also very inspired. Hearing Lopon-la's story confirmed what I had always believed. It is not just a person's physical constitution, nor their intelligence, nor their education, nor even their social conditioning which enables them to withstand hardship. Much more significant is their spiritual state. And while some may be able to survive through sheer willpower, the ones who suffer the least are those who attain a high level of *sö pa*.

Forbearance, and also fortitude (courage in the face of adversity) are two words which come quite close to describing *sö pa* at a basic level. But when a person develops it more, there comes composure in adversity, a sense of being unperturbed, reflecting a voluntary acceptance of hardship in pursuit of a higher, spiritual, aim. This involves accepting the reality of a given situation through recognizing that underlying its particularity, there is a vastly complex web of interrelated causes and conditions.

Sö pa is thus the means by which we practise true non-violence. It is what enables us not only to refrain from physical reactions when we are provoked, but it enables us to let go of our negative thoughts and emotions too. We cannot speak of *sö pa* if we give in to someone yet we do so grudgingly or resentfully. If, for example, a superior in the workplace upsets us yet we are obliged to defer to them despite our feelings that is not *sö pa*. The essence of *sö pa* is resolute forbearance in the face of adversity. In other words, the one who practises patient forbearance is determined not to give in to negative impulses (which are experienced as afflictive emotion in the form of anger, hatred, desire for revenge and so on) but rather counters their sense of injury and does not return harm for harm.

None of the foregoing should be taken to imply that there are not times when it is appropriate to respond to others with strong measures. Nor does practising patience in the sense I have described it mean that we must accept whatever people would do to us and simply give in. Nor does it mean that we should never act at all when we meet with harm. *Sö pa* should not be confused with mere passivity. On the contrary, adopting vigorous counter-measures may be compatible with the practice of *sö pa*. There are times in everyone's life when harsh words – or even physical intervention – may be called for. But since it safeguards our inner composure, *sö pa* means we are in a stronger position to judge an appropriately non-violent response than if we are overwhelmed by negative thoughts and emotions. From this, we see that it is the very opposite of cowardice. Cowardice arises when we lose all confidence as a result of fear. Patient forbearance means that we remain firm even if we are afraid.

Nor, when I speak of acceptance, do I mean that we

should not do everything in our power to solve our problems whenever they can be solved. But in the case of present suffering – that which we are already undergoing – acceptance can help ensure that the experience is not compounded by the additional burden of mental and emotional suffering. For example, there is nothing much we can do about old age. Far better to accept our condition than to fret about it. Indeed, it always strikes me as a bit foolish when very elderly people proudly turn help away, when obviously they need it.

Patient forbearance, then, is the quality which enables us to prevent negative thoughts and emotions from taking hold of us. It safeguards our peace of mind in the face of adversity. Through practising patience in this way, our conduct is rendered ethically wholesome. As we have seen, the first step in ethical practice is to check our response to negative thoughts and emotions as they arise. The next step – what we do after applying the brakes – is to counter that provocation with patience.

Here the reader may object that surely there will be occasions when this is impossible. What about the times when someone we are close to, who knows all our weaknesses, behaves toward us in such a way that we find ourselves unable to prevent anger from completely overwhelming our defences? Under such circumstances, we may indeed find it impossible to preserve our compassion for the other, but at least we should take care not to react violently, or aggressively. Leaving the room and going for a walk, or even counting twenty breaths, may be the best thing: we need to find some means of calming down a bit. This is why we need to put the practice of patience at the heart of our daily lives. It is a question of familiarizing ourselves with it, at the deepest level, so that when we do find ourselves in a difficult situation, although we may have to make an extra effort, we know what is involved. If on the other hand, we ignore the practice of patience until we are actually experiencing trouble, it is quite likely we will not succeed in resisting provocation.

One of the best ways to begin familiarizing ourselves the virtue of patience, or *sö pa*, is by taking time to reflect systematically on its benefits. It is the source of forgiveness. When *sö pa* is combined with our ability to discriminate between action and agent, forgiveness arises naturally. Moreover, *sö pa* has no equal in protecting our concern for others, whatever their behaviour toward us. It enables us to reserve our judgement towards the act, and it enables us to have compassion for the individual. Similarly, when we develop the ability patiently to forbear, we find that we develop a proportionate reserve of calmness and tranquillity. We tend to be less antagonistic and more pleasant to associate with. This, in turn, creates a positive atmosphere around us so that it is easy for others to relate to us. And being better grounded emotionally through the practice of patience, we find that not only do we become much stronger mentally and spiritually, but we tend also to be healthier physically. Certainly I attribute the good health I enjoy to a generally calm and peaceful mind.

But the most important benefit of *sö pa*, or patience, consists in the way it acts as a powerful antidote to the affliction of anger – the greatest threat to our inner peace and therefore our happiness. Indeed, we find that patience is the best means we have of defending ourselves internally from its destructive effects. Consider: riches are no defence against anger. Nor is a person's education, no matter how accomplished and intelligent they may be. Nor, for that matter, can the law be of any help. And fame is useless. Only the inner protection of patient forbearance can keep us from experiencing the turmoil of negative thoughts and emotions. The mind, or spirit (*lo*), is not physical. It cannot be touched or harmed directly. Only negative thoughts and emotions can harm it. Therefore, only the corresponding positive quality can protect it.

As a second step to familiarizing ourselves with the virtue of patience, it is also very helpful to think of adversity not so much as a threat to our peace of mind but rather as the very means by which patience is attained. From this perspective, we see that those who would harm us are, in a sense, teachers of patience. Such people teach us what we could never learn merely from hearing someone speak, be they ever so wise or holy. No more can the reader hope to learn virtue merely by reading this book – unless, of course, it is so boring as to demand perseverance! From adversity we can, however, learn the value of patient forbearance. And, in particular, those who would harm us give us unparalleled opportunities to practise disciplined behaviour.

This is not to say that people are not responsible for their actions. But let us remember that they may be acting largely out of ignorance. A child brought up in a violent environment may not know any other way to behave. As a result, the question of blame is rendered largely redundant. The appropriate response to someone who causes us to suffer – and here, of course, I am not referring to those instances when others oppose us legitimately, as when they refuse to give in to our unreasonable demands – is to recognize that in harming us, ultimately they lose their peace of mind, their inner balance and thereby their happiness. And we do best if we have compassion for them, especially since a simple wish to see them hurt cannot actually harm them. It will certainly harm us, though.

Imagine two neighbours in dispute. One of them is able to take this dispute lightly. The other is obsessed with it and constantly schemes to find a way to hurt his or her opponent. But what happens? Nurturing malice, it will not be long before the one who broods begins to suffer. First, he or she will lose their appetite, then their sleep. Eventually, their health begins to go. They pass their days and nights in misery – with the result that, ironically, they end up fulfilling the wishes of their adversary.

In fact, when we really think about it, there is something not fully rational about singling out individual persons as the objects of our anger. Let us conduct a simple exercise in our imagination. Consider the case of someone who abuses us verbally. If we feel inclined to anger on account of the pain this causes us, should not the focus of our feelings really be on the words themselves, since these are what is actually causing us pain? Yet we become angry with the individual shouting at us. It could, of course, be objected that since it is the person who is doing the shouting, we are justified in becoming angry with them on the grounds that we are right to assign moral responsibility to the individual and not to his or her words. This may be true. At the same time, if we are to be angry at what actually caused the pain, their words are actually the more immediate cause. Better still, should we not direct our anger toward what drove that person to abuse us: their afflictive emotions? For if the person were calm and at peace, they would not act in this way. Yet of these three factors – the words which hurt, the person uttering them, and the negative impulses which drive them – it is toward the person that we direct our anger. There is something inconsistent in this.

If it be objected that it is the evil nature of the one who is abusing us which is truly the cause of our pain, still we would have no reasonable grounds for anger with that individual. For if it were that person's ultimate nature to be hostile toward us, they would be incapable of behaving differently. In that case, anger toward them would be pointless. If we are burned, there is no sense being angry with fire. It is in the nature of fire to burn. But to remind ourselves that the notion of inherent hostility or inherent evil is false, let us observe that under different circumstances, the same person who is causing us pain could become a good friend. It is not unusual to hear of soldiers on opposing sides during conflict becoming close in peacetime. And most of us have had the experience of meeting someone who despite a bad reputation in the past turns out to be quite pleasant.

Of course, I am not suggesting that we should engage in such reflections in every situation. When we are physically threatened, we might do better to concentrate our energies not on reasoning like this but in running away! But it is helpful to spend time familiarizing ourselves with the various aspects and benefits of patience. This will enable us to meet the challenges posed by adversity in a constructive manner.

I mentioned earlier the way that *sö pa*, or patience, acts as a counterforce to anger. In fact, for every negative state, we find that we can identify one which opposes it. For example, humility opposes pride; contentment opposes greed; perseverance opposes indolence. If, therefore, we wish to overcome the unwholesome states which arise when negative thoughts and emotions are allowed to develop, cultivating virtue should not be seen as separate from restraining our response to afflictive emotion. They go hand in hand. This is why ethical discipline cannot be confined either to mere restraint or to mere affirmation of positive qualities.

To see how this process of restraint coupled with counteraction works, let us consider anxiety. We can describe this as a form of fear, but one with a well-developed mental component. Now we are bound to encounter experiences and events we feel concerned about. But what turns concern into anxiety is when we start to brood and let the imagination add negative reflections. Then we begin to feel anxious and start to worry. And the more we indulge in worry, the more reasons we find for it. Eventually we find ourselves in a state of permanent distress. The more developed this state, the less we are able to take action against it, and the stronger it becomes. But when we think carefully, we see that underlying this process is principally narrowness of vision and a lack of proper perspective. This causes us to ignore the fact that things and events come into being as the result of innumerable different causes and conditions. We tend to concentrate on just one or two aspects of our situation. We attribute our suffering solely to negative childhood experiences, to our social or economic circumstances, or to some perceived failure or failing. Yet in so doing, inevitably we restrict ourselves to finding means to overcoming only these aspects. The trouble with this is that if we are unable to do so, there is a danger of becoming totally demoralized. The first step in overcoming anxiety is thus to develop a proper perspective of our situation.

This we can do in a number of different ways. One of the most effective is to try to shift the focus of attention away from self and toward others. When we succeed in this, we find that the scale of our own problems diminishes. This is not to say we should ignore our own needs altogether, but rather that we should try to remember others' needs alongside our own, no matter how pressing ours may be. This is helpful, because when our concern for others is translated into action, we find that confidence arises automatically and worry and anxiety diminish. Indeed, we find that almost all the mental and emotional suffering which is such a feature of modern living – including the sense of hopelessness, of loneliness and so on – lessen the moment we begin to engage in actions motivated by concern for others. In my opinion, this explains why merely performing outwardly positive actions will not suffice to reduce anxiety. Where the underlying motive is to further one's short-term aims, we only add to our problems.

What, though, of those occasions when we find our whole lives unsatisfactory, or when we feel on the point of being overwhelmed by our suffering – as happens to us all in varying degrees from time to time? When this occurs, it is vital that we make every effort to find a way of lifting our spirits. We can do this by recollecting our good fortune. We may, for example, be loved by someone; we may have certain talents; we may have received a good education; we may have our basic needs provided for – food to eat, clothes to wear, somewhere to live – we may have performed certain altruistic deeds in the past. Not unlike a banker who collects interest even on the smallest amounts of money he has out on loan, we must take into consideration even the slightest positive aspect of our lives. For if we fail to find some way of uplifting ourselves, there is every danger of sinking further into our sense of powerlessness. This can lead us to believe that we have no capacity for doing good whatsoever. Thus we create the conditions of despair itself. At that point, suicide may seem the only option.

In most cases of hopelessness and despair, we find that it is the individual's perception of their situation rather than its reality which is the issue. Certainly, it may not be resolvable without others' cooperation. In that case, it becomes a matter of asking for help. However, there may indeed be some circumstances which are hopeless. This is where religious belief can be a source of comfort, but that is a separate matter.

What else might an ethic of virtue consist in? As a general principle, it is essential to avoid extremes. Just as overeating is as dangerous as undereating, so it is with the pursuit and practice of virtue. We find that even noble causes when carried to extremes can become a source of harm. For example, courage taken to excess and without due regard for circumstances quickly becomes foolhardiness. Indeed, excess undermines one of the principal purposes of practising virtue, which is to offset our tendency to drastic mental and emotional reactions to others and to those events which cause us unavoidable suffering.

It is also important to realize that transforming the mind and heart (lo) so that our actions become spontaneously ethical requires that we put the pursuit of virtue at the heart of our daily lives. This is because love and compassion, patience, generosity, humility and so on are all complementary. And because it is so difficult to eradicate afflictive emotion, it is necessary that we habituate ourselves to their opposites even before negative thoughts and emotions arise. For example, the cultivation of generosity is essential to counteract our tendency to guard our possessions and even our energy too closely. The practice of giving helps us to overcome our habit of miserliness, which we tend to justify by asking, 'What will I have for myself if I start giving things away?'

Giving is recognized as a virtue in every major religion and in every civilized society, and it clearly benefits both the giver and the receiver. The one who receives is relieved from the pangs of want. The one who gives can take comfort from the joy his or her gift brings to others. At the same time, we must recognize that there are different types and degrees of giving. When we give with the underlying motive of inflating the image others have of us – to gain renown and have them think of us as virtuous or holy – we defile the act. In that case, what we are practising is not generosity but self-aggrandizement. Similarly, the one who gives much may not be so generous as the one who gives little. It all depends on the giver's means and motivation.

Though not a substitute, giving of our time and energy may represent a somewhat higher order of giving than making gifts. Here I am thinking especially of the gift of service to those with mental or physical disabilities, to the homeless, to those who are lonely, to those in prison and those who have been in prison. But this type of giving also includes, for example, teachers who impart their knowledge to students. Then, as I understand it, the most valuable form of giving is when there is no thought or expectation of reward, and when it is grounded in genuine concern for others. This is because the more we can expand our focus to include others' interests alongside our own, the more securely we build the foundations of our own happiness.

To say that humility is an essential ingredient in our pursuit of transformation may seem to be at odds with what I have said about the need for confidence. But just as there is clearly a distinction between valid confidence, in the sense of self-esteem, and conceit – which we can describe as an inflated sense of importance grounded in a false image of self – so it is important to distinguish between genuine humility, which is a species of modesty, and a lack of confidence. They are not the same thing at all, though many confuse them. That may, in part, explain why today humility is often thought of as a weakness rather than as an indication of inner strength – especially in the context of business and professional life. Certainly, modern society does not accord humility the place it had in Tibet when I was young. Then, both our culture and people's basic admiration of humility provided a climate in which it flourished, while ambition (to be differentiated from the entirely appropriate aspiration to succeed in wholesome tasks) was seen as a quality which leads all too easily to self-centred thinking. Yet in contemporary life, humility is more important than ever. The more successful we humans become, both as individuals and as a family through our development of science and technology, the more essential it becomes to preserve humility. For the greater our temporal achievements, the more vulnerable we become to pride and arrogance.

One technique helpful in developing real confidence and humility is to reflect on the example of those whose self-importance makes them an object of ridicule to others. They may not be aware of how foolish they look, but it is plain to everyone else. This is not a matter of sitting in judgement on others, however. Rather it is a question of bringing home to ourselves the negative consequences of such states of heart and mind. By seeing, through the example of others, where they lead, we will be all the more determined to avoid them. In a sense, we are reversing the principle of not harming others on the basis that we ourselves do not wish to be harmed and making use of the fact that it is much easier to identify others' failings than it is to acknowledge their virtues. It is also much easier to find fault in others than in ourselves.

Here I should perhaps add that if humility is not to be confused with lack of confidence, still less has it anything to do with a sense of worthlessness. Lack of a proper recognition of one's own value is always harmful and can lead to a state of mental, emotional and spiritual paralysis. Under such circumstances, the individual may even come to hate themselves, although I must admit that the concept of self-hatred seemed incoherent when it was first explained to me by some Western psychologists. It seemed to contradict the principle that our fundamental desire is to be happy and to avoid suffering. But I do now accept that when a person loses all sense of perspective, there is a danger of self-hatred. Yet we all have the capacity for empathy. We all, therefore, have the potential to engage in wholesome conduct even if this only takes the form of positive thoughts. To suppose ourselves worthless is simply incorrect.

Another way to avoid the narrowing of vision that can lead to such extreme states as self-hatred and despair is to rejoice in others' good fortune, where we find it. As part of this practice, it is helpful to take every opportunity to show our respect for others, even to encourage them with praise when that seems appropriate. If such praise seems likely to come across as flattery or to make them feel conceited, it may, of course, be better to keep our goodwill private. And when it is we ourselves who are being praised, it is vital not to let this make us feel puffed up and important. Instead, let us merely recognize the other's generosity in appreciating our good qualities.

As a means of overcoming negative feelings toward ourselves, which arise in connection with those occasions in the past when we have neglected others' feelings and indulged our own selfish desires and interests at their expense, it is very helpful to develop an attitude of regret and repentance. Here though, the reader should not suppose that I am advocating that sense of guilt which so many of my Western friends speak of. We do not seem to have a word in Tibetan which could translate the word 'guilt' exactly. And because of its strong cultural associations, I am not certain that I have understood the concept to its fullest extent. But it seems to me that while it is natural and to be expected that we should have feelings of discomfort in relation to our past misdeeds, there is sometimes an element of self-indulgence when this is extended to feelings of guilt. It makes no sense to brood anxiously on the harmful actions we have committed in the past to the point where we become paralysed. If the person is a believer in God, the appropriate action is to find some means of reconciliation with Him. So far as Buddhist practice is concerned, there are various rites and practices for purification. When the individual has no religious beliefs, however, it is surely a matter of acknowledging and accepting any negative feelings we may have in relation to our misdeeds and developing a sense of sorrow and regret for them. But then, rather than stopping at mere sorrow and regret, it is important to use this as the basis for resolve, for a deep-seated commitment never again to harm others and to direct our actions all the more determinedly to the benefit of others. The act of disclosure, or confession, of our negative actions to another – especially to someone we really respect and trust – will be found to be very helpful in this. Above all, we should remember that as long as we retain the capacity of concern for others, the potential for transformation remains. We are quite wrong if we merely acknowledge the gravity of our actions inwardly and then, instead of confronting our feelings, give up all hope and do nothing. This only compounds the error.

We have a saying in Tibet that engaging in the practice of virtue is as hard as driving donkey uphill, whereas engaging in destructive activities is as easy as rolling boulders downhill. It is also said that negative impulses arise as spontaneously as rain and gather momentum just like water following the course of gravity. What makes matters worse is our tendency to indulge negative thoughts and emotions even while agreeing that we should not. It is essential, therefore, to address directly our tendency to put things off and while away our time in meaningless activities and to shrink from the challenge of transforming our habits on the grounds that it is too great a task. In particular, it is important not to allow ourselves to be put off by the magnitude of others' suffering. The misery of millions is not a cause for pity. Rather it is a cause for compassion.

We must also recognize that the failure to act when it is clear that action is required may itself be a negative action. Where inaction is due to anger or malice or envy, afflictive emotion can be clearly cited as the motivating factor. This is as true of simple things as it is of more complex situations. If a husband does not warn his wife that a plate she is about to pick up is hot because he desires her to be burned, clearly afflictive emotion is likely to be present. On the other hand, where inaction is simply the result of indolence, the mental and emotional state of the individual may not be so gravely negative. But the consequence may still be very serious, although such inaction is attributable less to negative thoughts and emotions as to a lack of compassion. It is thus important that we are no less determined to overcome our habitual tendency to laziness than we are to exercise restraint in response to afflictive emotion.

This is no easy task and those who are religiously minded must understand that there is no blessing or initiation – which, if only we could receive it, – nor any mysterious or magical formula or mantra or ritual – if only we could discover it – that can enable us to achieve transformation instantly. It comes little by little, just as a building is constructed brick by brick or, as the Tibetan expression has it, an ocean is formed drop by drop. And, because, unlike our bodies which soon get sick, old and worn out, the afflictive emotions never age, it is important to realize that dealing with them is a life-long struggle. Nor should the reader suppose that what we are talking about here is the mere acquisition of knowledge. It is not even a question of developing the conviction that may come from such knowledge. What we are talking about is gaining an experience of virtue through constant practice and familiarization so that it becomes spontaneous. What we find is that the more we develop concern for others' well-being, the easier it becomes to act in others' interests. As we become habituated to the effort required, so the struggle to sustain it lessens. Eventually, it will become second nature. But there are no shortcuts.

Engaging in virtuous activities is a bit like bringing up a young child. A great many factors are involved. And, especially at the beginning, we need to be prudent and skilful in our endeavours to transform our habits and dispositions. We also need to be realistic about what we can expect to achieve. It took us a long time to become the way we are, and habits are not changed overnight. So while it is good to raise our sights as we progress, it is a mistake to judge our behaviour by using the ideal as a standard, just as it would be foolish to judge our child's performance as a first-year student from the perspective of a graduate. For this reason, far more effective than short bursts of heroic effort followed by periods of laxity is to work steadily like a stream flowing toward our goal of transformation.

One method that is very helpful in sustaining us in this life-long task of transformation is to adopt a daily routine which can be adjusted according to our progress. Of course, as with the practice of virtue in general, this is something religious practice encourages. But that is no reason why non-believers should not use some of the ideas and techniques which have served humanity so well over the course of millennia. Making a habit of concern for others' well-being, and spending a few minutes on waking in the morning reflecting on the value of conducting our lives in an ethically disciplined manner, is a good way to start the day no matter what our beliefs or lack of them.

The same is true of taking some time at the end of each day to review how successful in this we have been. Such a discipline is very helpful in developing our determination not to behave self-indulgently.

If these suggestions sound somewhat onerous to the reader searching not for *nirvana* or salvation, but simply for human happiness, it is worth reminding ourselves that what brings us greatest joy and satisfaction in life are those actions we undertake out of concern for others. Indeed, we can go further. For whereas the fundamental questions of human existence, such as why we are here, where we are going and whether the universe had a beginning, have each elicited different responses in different philosophical traditions, it is self-evident that a generous heart and wholesome actions lead to greater peace. And it is equally clear that their negative counterparts bring undesirable consequences. Happiness arises from virtuous causes. If we truly desire to be happy, there is no other way to proceed but by way of virtue: it is the method by which happiness is achieved. And, we might add, the basis of virtue, its ground, is ethical discipline.

CHAPTER EIGHT

THE ETHIC OF
COMPASSION

We noted earlier that all the world's major
religions stress the importance of cultivating love and
compassion. In the Buddhist philosophical tradition, different levels of attainment are described. At a basic level,
compassion (*nying je*) is understood mainly in terms of
empathy – our ability to enter into and, to some extent,
share others' suffering. But Buddhists – and perhaps others
– believe that this can be developed to such a degree that
not only does our compassion arise without any effort,
but it is unconditional, undifferentiated and universal in
scope. A feeling of intimacy toward all other sentient

beings, including, of course, those who would harm us, is generated. This is likened in the literature to the love a mother has for her only child.

But this sense of equanimity toward all others is not seen as an end in itself. Rather it is seen as the springboard to a love still greater. Because our capacity for empathy is innate, and because the ability to reason is also an innate faculty, compassion shares the characteristics of consciousness itself. The potential we have to develop it is therefore stable and continuous. It is not a resource which can be used up – as water is used up when we boil it. And though it can be described in terms of activity, it is not a physical activity which we train for, like jumping, where once we reach a certain height we can go no further. On the contrary, when we enhance our sensitivity toward others' suffering through deliberately opening ourselves up to it, it is believed that we can gradually extend our compassion to the point where the individual feels so moved by even the subtlest suffering of others that they come to have an overwhelming sense of responsibility toward those others. This causes the one who is compassionate to dedicate themselves entirely to helping others overcome both their suffering and the causes of their suffering. In Tibetan, this ultimate level of attainment is called *nying je chenmo*, literally 'great compassion'.

Now I am not suggesting that each individual must attain these advanced states of spiritual development in order to lead an ethically wholesome life. I have described *nying je chenmo* not because it is a precondition of ethical conduct but rather because I believe that pushing the logic of compassion to the highest level can act as a powerful inspiration. If we can just keep the aspiration to develop *nying je chenmo*, or great compassion, as an ideal, it will naturally have a significant impact on our outlook. Based on the simple recognition that, just as I do, so do all others desire to be happy and not to suffer, it will serve as a constant reminder against selfishness and partiality. It will remind us that if we reserve ethical conduct for those whom we feel close to, the danger is that we will neglect our responsibilities towards those outside this circle. It will remind us that there is little to be gained from being kind and generous because we hope to win something in return. It will remind us that actions motivated by the desire to create a good name for ourselves are still selfish, however much they may appear to be acts of kindness. It will also remind us that there is nothing exceptional about acts of charity toward those we already feel close to. And it will help us recognize that the bias we naturally feel toward our families and friends is actually a highly unreliable thing on which to base ethical conduct.

Why is this? So long as the individuals in question continue to meet our expectations, all is well. But should they fail to do so, someone we consider a dear friend one day can become our sworn enemy the next. As we saw earlier, we have a tendency to react badly to all who threaten fulfilment of our cherished desires, though they may be our closest relations. For this reason, compassion and mutual respect offer a much more solid basis for our relations with others. Likewise if our love for someone is based largely on attraction, whether it be their looks or some other superficial characteristic, our feelings for that person are liable, over time, to evaporate. When they lose the quality we found alluring, or we find ourselves no longer satisfied by it, the situation can change completely, this despite their being the same person. This is why intimate relationships based purely on attraction are almost always unstable. On the other hand, when we begin to perfect our compassion, neither the other's appearance nor their behaviour affect our underlying attitude.

Consider, too, that habitually our feelings toward others depend very much on their circumstances. Most people, when they see someone who is handicapped, feel sympathetic toward that person. But when they see others who compared with themselves are wealthier, or better educated, or better placed socially, they immediately feel envious and competitive toward them. Our negative feelings prevent us from seeing the sameness of ourselves and all others. We forget that just like us, whether fortunate or unfortunate, distant or near, they desire to be happy and not to suffer.

The struggle is thus to overcome these feelings of partiality. Certainly, developing genuine compassion for our loved ones is the obvious and appropriate place to start. The impact our actions have on our close ones will generally be much greater than on others, and therefore our responsibilities towards them are greater. Yet we need to recognize that ultimately there are no grounds for discriminating in their favour. In this sense, we are all in the same position as a doctor confronted by ten patients suffering the same serious illness. They are each equally deserving of treatment. The reader should not suppose that what is being advocated here is a state of detached indifference, however. The further essential challenge, as we begin to extend our compassion toward all others, is to maintain the same level of intimacy as we feel towards those closest to us. In other words, what is being suggested is that we need to strive for even-handedness in our approach toward all others, a level ground into which we can plant the seed of *nying je chenmo*, of great love and compassion.

If we can begin to relate to others on the basis of such equanimity, our compassion will not depend on the fact that so and so is my husband, my wife, my relative, my friend. Rather, a feeling of closeness toward all others can be developed based on the simple recognition that, just like myself, all wish to be happy and to avoid suffering. In other words, we will start to relate to others on the basis of their sentient nature. Again, we can think of this in terms of an ideal, one which it is immensely difficult to attain. But for myself, I find it one which is profoundly inspiring and helpful.

Let us now consider the role of compassionate love and kind-heartedness in our daily lives. Does the ideal of developing it to the point where it is unconditional mean that we must abandon our own interests entirely? Not at all. In fact, it is the best way of serving them – indeed, it could even be said to constitute the wisest course for fulfilling self-interest. For if it is correct that those qualities such as love, patience, tolerance and forgiveness are what happiness consists in, and if it is also correct that *nying je*, compassion, as I have defined it, is both the source and the fruit of these qualities, then the more we are compassionate, the more we provide for our own happiness. Thus, any idea that concern for others, though a noble quality, is a matter for our private lives only, is simply short-sighted. Compassion belongs to every sphere of activity, including, of course, the workplace.

Here, though, I must acknowledge the existence of a perception – shared by many, it seems – that compassion is, if not actually an impediment, at least irrelevant to professional life. Personally, I would argue that not only is it relevant, but that when compassion is lacking, our activities are in danger of becoming destructive. This is because when we ignore the question of others' well-being, inevitably we end up hurting them. The ethic of compassion helps provide the necessary foundation and motivation for both restraint and the cultivation of virtue. When we begin to develop a genuine appreciation of the value of compassion, our outlook on others begins automatically to change. This alone can serve as a powerful influence on the conduct of our lives. When, for example, the temptation to deceive others arises, our compassion for them would prevent us from entertaining the idea. And when we realize that our work itself is in danger of being exploited to the detriment of others, compassion will cause us to disengage from it. So to take an imaginary case of a scientist whose research seems likely to be a source of suffering, they will recognize this and act accordingly, even if this means abandoning the project.

I do not deny that genuine problems can arise when we dedicate ourselves to the ideal of compassion. In the case of a scientist who felt unable to continue in the direction their work was taking them, this could have profound consequences both for themselves and for their families. Likewise, those engaged in the caring professions – in medicine, counselling, social work and so on – or even those looking after someone at home may sometimes become so exhausted by their duties that they feel overwhelmed. Constant exposure to suffering, coupled occasionally with a feeling of being taken for granted, can induce feelings of helplessness and even despair. Or it can happen that individuals may find themselves performing outwardly generous actions merely for the sake of it – simply going through the motions, as it were. Of course this is better than nothing. But when left unchecked, this can lead to insensitivity towards others' suffering. If this starts to happen, it may be best to disengage for a short while and make a deliberate effort to reawaken our sensitivity. In this it can be helpful to remember that despair is never a solution. It is, rather, the ultimate failure. Therefore, as the Tibetan expression has it, even if the rope breaks nine times, we must splice it back together a tenth time. In this way, even if ultimately we do fail, at least there will be no feelings of regret. And when we combine this insight with a clear appreciation of our potential to benefit others, we find that we can begin to restore our hope and confidence.

Some people may object to this ideal of compassion on the grounds that by entering into others' suffering we bring suffering on ourselves. To an extent, this is true. But I suggest that there is an important qualitative distinction to be made between experiencing one's own suffering and experiencing suffering in the course of sharing in others'. In the case of one's own suffering, given that it is involuntary, there is a sense of oppression: it seems to come from outside us. By contrast, sharing in someone else's suffering must at some level involve a degree of voluntariness, which itself is indicative of a certain inner strength. For this reason, the disturbance it may cause is considerably less likely to paralyse us than our own suffering.

Of course, even as an ideal, the notion of developing unconditional compassion is daunting. Most people, including myself, must struggle to reach the point where putting others' interests on a par with our own becomes easy. We should not allow this to put us off, however. And while undoubtedly there will be obstacles on the way to developing a genuinely warm heart, there is the deep consolation of knowing that in doing so we are creating the conditions for our own happiness. As I mentioned earlier, the more we truly desire to benefit others, the greater the strength and confidence we develop and the greater the peace and happiness we experience. If this still seems unlikely, it is worth asking ourselves how else we are to do so. With violence and aggression? Of course not. With money? Perhaps up to a point, but no further. But with love, by sharing in others' suffering, by recognizing ourselves clearly in all others – especially those who are disadvantaged and those whose rights are not respected – by helping them to be happy: yes. Through love, through kindness, through compassion we establish understanding between ourselves and others. This is how we forge unity and harmony.

Compassion and love are not mere luxuries. As the source both of inner and external peace, they are fundamental to the continued survival of our species. On the one hand, they constitute non-violence in action. On the other, they are the source of all spiritual qualities: of forgiveness, tolerance and all the virtues. Moreover, they are the very things that give meaning to our activities. They are what makes them constructive. There is nothing amazing about being highly educated; there is nothing amazing about being rich. Only when the individual has a warm heart do these attributes become worthwhile.

So to those who say that the Dalai Lama is being unrealistic in advocating this ideal of unconditional love, I urge them to experiment with it nonetheless. They will discover that when we reach beyond the confines of narrow self-interest, our hearts become filled with strength. Peace and joy become our constant companion. It breaks down barriers of every kind and in the end destroys the notion of my interest as independent from others' interest. But most important, so far as ethics is concerned, where love of one's neighbour, affection, kindness and compassion live, we find that ethical conduct is automatic. Ethically wholesome actions arise naturally in the context of compassion.

CHAPTER NINE

ETHICS AND SUFFERING

I have suggested that we all desire happiness, that genuine happiness is characterized by peace, that peace is most surely attained when our actions are motivated by concern for others, and that this, in turn, entails ethical discipline and dealing positively with afflictive emotion. I have also suggested that in our quest for happiness we naturally and properly seek to avoid suffering. Let us now examine this quality, or state, that we wish so strongly to be free from but which lies at the very heart of our existence.

Suffering and pain are inalienable facts of life. A sentient being, according to my usual definition, is one which has the capacity to experience pain and suffering. One could also say that it is our experience of suffering which connects us to others. It is thus the basis of our capacity for empathy. But beyond this, we can observe that suffering falls into two (interrelated) categories. There are the avoidable forms which arise as a consequence of such phenomena as war, poverty, violence, crime – and even things like illiteracy and certain diseases. Then there are the unavoidable forms which include such phenomena as the problems of sickness, old age and death. So far, we have mainly been speaking about dealing with avoidable, human-created suffering. Now I want to look more closely at that which is unavoidable.

The problems and difficulties we face in life are not all like natural disasters. We cannot protect ourselves from them merely by taking suitable precautions, such as by storing food. In the case of sickness, for example, no matter how fit we keep ourselves, or how carefully we regulate our diet, eventually our bodies give in to physical problems. And when they do, the impact on our lives can be serious: we may be prevented from doing the things we want to do and from going to the places we want to go. Often we are prevented from eating the foods we like. Instead, we have to take medicines which taste awful. When things get really bad, we can find ourselves enduring days and nights wracked with pain – to the extent that we may long to die.

So far as ageing is concerned, from the day we are

born, we are faced with the prospect of growing old and losing the suppleness of youth. In time, our hair falls out, our teeth fall out, we lose our eyesight and our hearing. We can no longer digest the foods we once enjoyed. Eventually, we find that we cannot recall events which once were so vivid, or even remember the names of those closest to us. Should we live long enough, we will reach such a state of decrepitude that others may find the mere sight of us repulsive, though that is precisely the time we will have most need of them.

Then death comes – almost a taboo subject in modern society, it seems. Though eventually we may look forward to it as a relief and regardless of what may come afterwards, death means that we are parted from our loved ones, from our precious belongings, indeed from all that we hold dear.

To this brief description of unavoidable suffering we must, however, add another category. There is the suffering entailed in meeting with the unwanted – of mishaps and accident. This is the suffering of having what we want taken away from us – as we refugees have lost our countries, many forcibly parted from their loved ones. This is the suffering caused by not obtaining what we desire, though we may put great effort into doing so. Despite breaking our back working in the fields, the harvest fails; despite working night and day at a business venture, it is not successful, though through no fault of our own. It includes also the suffering of uncertainty, of never knowing when and where we will meet with adversity. From our own experience, we all know how this can lead to feelings of insecurity and anxiety. And undermining everything we do, there is the suffering of lack of contentment, which arises even when we achieve all that we have striven for. Such events are part of our everyday experience as human beings who desire happiness and not to suffer.

As if this were not enough, there is furthermore the fact that the very experiences which ordinarily we suppose to be pleasurable turn out themselves to be a source of suffering. They seem to offer fulfilment, but they do not actually provide it, a phenomenon we looked at earlier in the discussion on happiness. In fact, if we think carefully, we will find that we perceive such experiences as pleasurable only insofar as they offset more explicit suffering, as when, for example, we eat to assuage hunger. We take one mouthful, then two, three, four, five and enjoy the experience – but quite soon, although it is the same person and the same food, we begin to find eating objectionable. If we do not stop, eventually it will harm us – just as nearly every worldly pleasure comes to harm us when carried to an extreme. This is why contentment is indispensable if we are to be genuinely happy.

All these manifestations of suffering are essentially unavoidable and are indeed natural facts of existence. This does not mean that, finally, there is nothing we can do about them. Nor do I mean to suggest that it is unrelated to the question of ethical discipline. It is true that, according to Buddhist and other ancient Indian religious philosophies, suffering is seen as a consequence of *karma*. To suppose, as do quite a lot of people, Easterners and Westerners alike it seems, that this means that everything we experience is predetermined is totally wrong, however. Still less is it an excuse not to take responsibility in whatever situation we find ourselves.

Since the term *karma* appears to have entered everyday vocabulary, it might be worthwhile to clarify the concept somewhat. *Karma* is a Sanskrit word meaning 'action'. It denotes an active force, the inference being that the outcome of future events can be influenced by our actions. To suppose that *karma* is some sort of independent energy which predestines the course of our whole life is simply incorrect. Who creates *karma*? We ourselves. What we think, say, do, desire and omit creates *karma*. As I write, for example, the very action creates new circumstances and causes some other event. My words cause a response in the reader's mind. In everything we do, there is cause and effect, cause and effect. In our daily lives the food we eat, the work we undertake, our relaxation are all a function of action: our action. This is *karma*. We cannot, therefore, throw up our hands whenever we find ourselves confronted by unavoidable suffering. To say that every misfortune is simply the result of *karma* is tantamount to saying that we are totally powerless in life. If this were correct, there would be no cause for hope. We might as well pray for the end of the world.

A proper appreciation of cause and effect suggests that far from being powerless, there is much we can do to influence our experience of suffering. Old age, sickness and death are inevitable. But, as with the torments of negative thoughts and emotions, we certainly have a choice in how we respond to the occurrence of suffering. If we wish, we can adopt a more dispassionate and rational approach, and on that basis we can discipline our response to it. On the other hand, we can simply fret about our misfortunes. But when we do, we become frustrated. As a result, afflictive emotions arise and our peace of mind is destroyed. When we do not restrain our tendency to respond negatively to suffering, it becomes a source of negative thoughts and emotions. There is thus a clear relationship between the impact suffering has on our heart and mind and our practice of inner discipline.

Our basic attitude toward suffering makes a great difference to the way in which we experience it. Imagine, for example, two people suffering an identical form of terminal cancer. The only difference between these two patients is their outlook on it. One sees it as something to be accepted and, if possible, transformed into an opportunity for developing inner strength. The other responds to his or her circumstances with fear, bitterness and anxiety about the future. Now although on the physical level, there may be no difference between the two of them in terms of what they are suffering, in actual fact there is a profound difference in their experience of this illness. In the case of the latter, in addition to the physical suffering itself, there is the added pain of inner suffering.

This suggests that the degree to which suffering affects us is largely up to us. It is, therefore, essential to keep a proper perspective on our experience of suffering. When we look at a particular problem from close up, it tends to fill our whole field of vision and look enormous. If, however, we look at the same problem from a distance, automatically we will start to see it in relation to other things. This simple act makes a tremendous difference. It enables us to see that though a given situation may truly be tragic, even the most unfortunate event has innumerable aspects and can be approached from many different angles. Indeed, it is very rare, if not impossible, to find a situation which is negative no matter how we look at it.

When tragedy or misfortune come our way, as surely they must, it can be very helpful to make a comparison with another event, or to call to mind a similar or worse situation that has befallen, if not ourselves, then others before us. If we can shift our focus away from self and toward others, we experience a freeing effect. There is something about the dynamics of self-absorption, or worrying about ourselves too much, which tends to magnify our suffering. Conversely, when we come to see it in relation to others' suffering, we begin to recognize that, relatively speaking, it is not all that unbearable. This enables us to maintain our peace of mind much more easily than if we concentrate on our problems to the exclusion of all else.

As far as my own experience is concerned, I find that when, for example, I hear bad news from Tibet – and sadly this is quite often – naturally my immediate response is one of great sadness. However, by placing it in context and by reminding myself that the basic human disposition towards affection, freedom, truth and justice must eventually prevail, I find I can cope reasonably well. Feelings of helpless anger, which do nothing but poison the mind, embitter the heart and enfeeble the will seldom arise, even following the worst news.

It is also worth remembering that the time of greatest gain in terms of wisdom and inner strength is often that of greatest difficulty. With the right approach – and here we see once more the supreme importance of developing a positive attitude – the experience of suffering can open our eyes to reality. For example, my own experience of life as a refugee has helped me realize that the endless protocol, which was such an important part of my life in Tibet, was quite unnecessary.

We also find that our confidence and self-reliance can grow and our courage become strengthened as a result of suffering. This can be inferred from what we see in the world around us. Within our own refugee community, for example, among the survivors of our early years in exile are a number who, though they suffered terribly, are among the strongest spiritually – and the most cheerfully carefree – individuals I have the privilege to know. Conversely, we find that in the face of even relatively slight adversity, some people who have everything are inclined to lose hope and become despondent. There is a natural tendency for wealth to spoil us. The result is that we find it progressively more difficult to bear easily the problems everyone must encounter from time to time.

Let us now consider what options are open to us when we actually encounter a particular problem. At one extreme, we can allow ourselves to be overwhelmed. At the other, we can simply go on a picnic or take a holiday and ignore it. The third possibility is to face up to the situation directly. This involves examining it, analysing it, determining its causes and finding out how to deal with them.

Though this third course may occasion us additional pain in the short term, it is clearly preferable to the other two courses of action. If we try to avoid or deny a given problem by simply ignoring it or taking to drink or drugs, or even some forms of meditation or prayer, as a means of escape, while there is a chance of short-term relief, the problem itself remains. Such an approach is simply avoiding the issue, not resolving it. Once again, the danger is that, in addition to the initial problem, there will follow mental and emotional unrest. The afflictions of anxiety, fear and doubt build up. Eventually this can lead to anger and despair, with all the further potential for suffering (both for self and others) which that entails.

Imagine being shot in the stomach. The pain is excruciating. What are we to do? Of course, we need to have the bullet removed and we undergo surgery. This adds to the trauma. Yet we gladly accept this in order to overcome the original problem. Similarly, due to infection, or to catastrophic damage, it may be necessary to lose a limb in order to save our life. But again, naturally, we are prepared to accept this lesser form of suffering if it will spare us the greater suffering of death. It is only common sense voluntarily to undergo hardship when we see that by doing so we are able to avoid worse. Saying this, I admit that this is not always an easy judgement to make. When I was around six or seven years of age, I was inoculated against smallpox. Had I realized how much it would hurt, I doubt whether I could have been persuaded that vaccination constituted a lesser suffering than the disease itself. The pain lasted fully ten days and I still have four large scars as a result!

If the prospect of confronting our suffering head-on can sometimes seem a bit daunting, it is very helpful to remember that nothing within the realm of what we commonly experience is permanent. All phenomena are subject to change and decay. Also, as the description of reality I gave earlier suggests, we are mistaken if we ever suppose that our experience of suffering – or happiness, for that matter – can be attributed to a single source. Everything that arises does so within the context of innumerable causes and conditions. If this was not so, as soon as we came into contact with something that we considered good, automatically we would become happy; whenever we came into contact with something that we considered bad, automatically we would become sad. The causes of joy and sorrow would be easy to identify and life would be very simple. We would have good reason to become attached to one sort of person or thing or event and to be angry with and want to avoid others. But that is not reality.

Personally, I find enormously helpful the advice given in respect of suffering by the great Indian scholar-saint, Shantideva. It is essential, he said, that when we face difficulties of whatever sort we do not let them paralyse us. If we do, we are in danger of being totally overwhelmed by them. Instead, using our critical faculties, we should exam-ine the nature of the problem itself. If we find that there exists the possibility we could solve it by some means or other, there is no need for anxiety. The rational thing would then be to devote all one's energy to finding that means and acting on it. If, on the other hand, we find that the nature of the problem admits simply to no solution, there is no point worrying about it. If nothing can change the situation, worrying only makes it worse. Taken out of context of the philosophical text in which it appears as the culmination of a complex series of reflections,

Shantideva's approach may sound somewhat simplistic. But its very beauty lies in this quality of simplicity. And no one could argue with its sheer common sense.

As to the possibility that suffering has some actual purpose, we will not go into that here. But to the extent that our experience of suffering reminds us of what all others also endure, it serves as a powerful injunction to practise compassion and refrain from causing others pain. And to the extent that suffering awakens our empathy and causes us to connect with others, it can serve as the basis of compassion and love. Here I am reminded of the example of a great Tibetan scholar and religious practitioner who spent more than twenty years in prison enduring the most terrible treatment including torture, following the occupation of our country. During that time, those students of his who had escaped into exile would often tell me that the letters he wrote and had smuggled out of jail contained the most profound teachings on love and compassion they had ever encountered. Unfortunate events, though potentially a source of anger and despair, have equal potential to be a source of spiritual growth. Whether or not this is the outcome depends on our response.

CHAPTER TEN

THE NEED FOR DISCERNMENT

In our survey of ethics and spiritual development, we have spoken a great deal about the need for discipline. This may seem somewhat old-fashioned, even implausible in an age and culture where so much emphasis is placed on the goal of self-fulfilment. But the reason for people's negative view of discipline is, I suggest, mainly due to what is generally understood by the term. People tend to associate it with something imposed against their will. It is worth repeating, therefore, that what we are talking about when we speak of ethical discipline is something that we adopt voluntarily on the basis of full recognition of its benefits. This is not an alien concept. We do not hesitate to accept discipline when it comes to our physical health. On doctors' advice, we avoid foods that are harmful even when we crave them. Instead we eat those that benefit us. And while it is true that, at the initial stage, self-discipline, even when voluntarily adopted, may involve hardship and even a degree of struggle, through habituation and diligent application, this lessens over time. It is a bit like diverting the course of a stream. First we have to dig the channel and build up its banks. Then, when the water is released into it, we may have to make adjustments here and there. But when the course is fully established, water flows in the direction we desire.

Ethical discipline is indispensable because it is the means by which we mediate between the competing claims of my right to happiness and all others' equal right. Naturally, there will always be those who suppose their own happiness to be of such importance that others' pain is of no consequence. But this is short-sighted. No one truly benefits from causing harm to others. Whatever immediate advantage is gained at the expense of someone else is necessarily only temporary. In the long run, causing others hurt and disturbing their peace and happiness causes us anxiety. Because our actions have an impact both on ourselves and others, when we lack discipline, eventually anxiety arises in our mind and deep in our heart we come to feel a sense of disquiet. Conversely, whatever hardship it entails, disciplining our response to negative thoughts and emotions will be found to cause us fewer problems in the long run than indulging in acts of selfishness.

Nevertheless, it is worth saying again that ethical discipline entails more than just restraint. It also entails the cultivation of virtue. Love and compassion, patience, tolerance and forgiveness are essential qualities. When they are present in our lives, everything we do becomes an instrument to benefit the whole human family. Even in terms of our daily occupation – whether this is looking after children in the home, working in a factory, or serving the community as a doctor, lawyer, business person or teacher – our actions contribute towards the well-being of all. And because ethical discipline is what facilitates these, the very qualities which give meaning and value to our existence, it is clearly something to be embraced with enthusiasm and conscious effort.

Before looking at how we apply this inner discipline in our interactions with others, it may be worth reviewing the grounds for defining ethical conduct in terms of non-harming. As we have seen, given the complex nature of reality, it is very difficult to say that a particular act or type of act is right or wrong in itself. Ethical conduct is thus not something we engage in because it is somehow right in itself. We do so because we recognize that, just as I desire to be happy and to avoid suffering, so do all others. For this reason, a meaningful ethical system divorced from the question of an individual's experience of suffering and happiness is hard to envisage.

Of course, if we want to ask all sorts of difficult questions based on metaphysics, ethical discourse can become exceedingly complicated. Yet while it is true that ethical practice cannot be reduced to a mere exercise in logic, whichever way we look at it, in the end we are brought back to the fundamental questions of happiness and suffering. Why is happiness good and suffering bad for us? Perhaps there is no conclusive answer. But we can observe that it is in our nature to prefer the one to the other, just as it is to prefer the better over that which is merely good. We simply aspire to happiness and not to suffering. If we were to go further and ask why this is so, surely the answer would have to be something like, 'That's the way it is', or, for theists, 'God made us this way'.

So far as the ethical character of a given action is concerned, we have seen how this is dependent on a great many factors. Time and circumstance have an important bearing on the matter. But so, too, does an individual's freedom or lack of it. A negative act can be considered more serious when the perpetrator commits the deed with full freedom as opposed to someone who is acting against his or her will. Similarly, given the lack of remorse this reflects, negative acts repeatedly indulged can be considered graver than an isolated act. But we must also consider the intention behind the action, as well as its content. The overriding question, however, concerns the individual's spiritual state, their overall state of heart and mind (*kun long*) in the moment of action. Because, generally speaking, this is the area over which we have the most control, it is the most significant element in determining the ethical character of our acts. As we have seen, when our intentions are polluted by selfishness, by hatred, or by desire to deceive, however much our acts may have the appearance of being constructive, inevitably their impact will be negative, both for self and others.

How, though, are we to apply this principle of nonharming when confronted with an ethical dilemma? This is where our critical and imaginative powers come in. I have described these as two of our most precious resources, and suggested that possessing them is one of the things that distinguish us from animals. We have seen how afflictive emotions destroy them. And we have seen how important they are in learning to deal with suffering. As far as ethical practice is concerned, these qualities are what enable us to discriminate between temporary and long-term benefit, to determine the degree of ethical fitness of the different courses of action open to us, and to assess the likely outcome of our actions and thereby to set aside lesser goals in order to achieve greater ones. In the case of a dilemma, we need in the first instance to consider the particularity of the situation in the light of what, in the Buddhist tradition, is called the 'union of skilful means and insight'. 'Skilful means' can be understood in terms of the efforts we make to ensure that our deeds are motivated by compassion. 'Insight' refers to our critical faculties and how, in response to the different factors involved, we adjust the ideal of non-harming to the context of the situation. We could call it the faculty of wise discernment.

Employing this faculty – which is especially important when there is no appeal to religious belief – involves constantly checking our outlook and asking ourselves whether we are being broad-minded or narrow-minded. Have we taken into account the overall situation or are we considering only specifics? Is our view short-term or long-term? Are we being short-sighted or clear-eyed? Is our motive genuinely compassionate when considered in relation to the totality of all beings? Or is our compassion limited just to our families, our friends and those we identify with closely? Just as in the practice of discovering the true nature of our thoughts and emotions, we need to think, think, think.

Of course, it will not always be possible to devote time to careful discernment. Sometimes we have to act at once. This is why our spiritual development is of such critical importance in ensuring that our actions are ethically sound. The more spontaneous our actions, the more they will tend to reflect our habits and dispositions in that moment. If these are unwholesome, our acts are bound to be destructive. At the same time, I believe it is very useful to have a set of basic ethical precepts to guide us in our daily lives. These can help us to form good habits, although I should add my opinion that in adopting such precepts, it is perhaps best to think of them less in terms of moral legislation than as reminders always to keep others' interests at heart and in the forefront of our minds.

So far as the content of such precepts is concerned, it is doubtful whether we could do better than turn to the basic ethical directives articulated not only by each of the world's great religions but also by the greater part of the humanist philosophical tradition. The consensus among them, despite differences of opinion concerning metaphysical grounding, is to my mind compelling. All agree on the negativity of killing, stealing, telling lies and sexual misconduct. In addition, from the point of view of motivational factors, all agree on the need to avoid hatred, pride, covetousness, envy, greed, lust, harmful ideologies (such as racism) and so on.

Some people may wonder whether the injunctions against sexual misconduct are really necessary in these times of simple and effective contraception. However, as human beings, we are naturally attracted to external objects, whether it be through the eyes, when we are attracted by form, through the ears, when the attraction arises in relation to sound, or through any of the other senses. Each of them has the potential to be a source of difficulty for us. Yet sexual attraction involves all five senses. As a result, when extreme desire accompanies sexual attraction, it has the ability to cause us enormous problems. It is, I believe, this fact that is recognized in the ethical directives against sexual misconduct articulated by every major religion. And, at least in the Buddhist tradition, they remind us of the tendency for sexual desire to become obsessive. It can quickly reach the point where a person has almost no room left for constructive activity. In this connection, consider, for example, a case of infidelity. Given that wholesome ethical conduct entails considering the impact of our actions not only on ourselves but on others, too, there are the feelings of third parties to consider. In addition to our actions being violent toward our partner, given the trust that the relationship implies, there is the question of the lasting impact this kind of upset in the family can have on our children. It is now more or less universally accepted that they are the principal victims both of family break-up and of unhealthy relationships in the home. From our own perspective as the person who has commited the act, we must also acknowledge that it is likely to have the negative effect of gradually corroding our self-respect. Finally, there is the fact that in being unfaithful, other gravely negative acts may result as a direct consequence – lying and deception being perhaps the least of them. An unwanted pregnancy could easily cause a desperate prospective parent to seek an abortion.

When we think in this way, it becomes obvious that the momentary pleasures afforded by an adulterous liaison are far outweighed by the risk of the likely negative impact of our actions on both ourselves and others. So rather than seeing strictures against sexual misconduct as limiting freedom, we do better to see them as common-sense reminders that such actions directly affect the well-being of both oneself and others.

Does this mean that merely following precepts takes precedence over wise discernment? No. Ethically wholesome conduct depends on us applying the principle of non-harming. However, there are bound to be situations where any course of action would appear to involve breaking a precept. Under such circumstances, we must use our intelligence to judge which course of action will be least harmful in the long run. Imagine, for example, a situation where we witness someone running away from a group of people armed with knives and clearly intent on doing harm. We see the fugitive disappear into a doorway. Moments later, one of the pursuers comes up to us and asks which way he went. Now, on the one hand, we do not want to lie or to injure the other's trust. On the other, if we tell the truth, we realize that we may contribute to the injury or death of a fellow human being. Whatever we decide, the appropriate course of action would appear to involve a negative deed. Under such circumstances, because we are certain that in so doing we are serving a higher purpose – preserving someone from harm – it might well be appropriate to say, 'Oh, I didn't see him' or vaguely, 'I think he went the other way.' We have to take into account the overall situation and weigh the benefits of telling a lie and telling the truth and do what we judge to be least harmful overall. In other words, the moral value of a given act is to be judged in relation both to time, place and circumstance and to the interests of the totality of all others in the future as well as now. But while it is conceivable that a given act is ethically sound under one set of circumstances, the same act at another time and place and under a different set of circumstances may not be.

What, though, are we to do when it comes to others? What are we to do when they seem clearly to be engaging in actions we consider wrong? The first thing is to remember that unless we know down to the last detail the full range of circumstances, both internal and external, we can never be sufficiently clear about individual situations to be able to pronounce with complete certainty on the moral content of others' actions. Of course, there will be extreme situations when the negative character of others' acts will be self-evident. But mostly this is not the case. This is why it is far more useful to be aware of a single shortcoming in ourselves than it is to be aware of a thousand in somebody else. For when the fault is our own, we are in a position to correct it.

Nevertheless, recognizing that there is an essential distinction to be made between a person and their particular act, we may come across circumstances when it is appropriate to take action. In everyday life, it is normal and fitting to adapt in some degree to one's friends and acquaintances and to respect their wishes. The ability to do so is considered a good quality. But when we mix with those who clearly indulge in negative behaviour, seeking only their own benefit and ignoring others', we risk losing our own sense of direction. As a result, our ability to help others becomes endangered. There is a Tibetan proverb which says that when we lie on a mountain of gold, some of it rubs off on us; the same happens if we lie on a mountain of dirt. We are right to avoid such people, though we must be careful not to cut them off completely. Indeed, there are sure to be times when it is appropriate to try to stop them from acting in this way – provided, of course, that our motives in doing so are pure and our methods are non-harming. Again, the key principles are compassion and insight.

The same is true in respect of those ethical dilemmas we face at the level of society, especially the difficult and challenging questions posed by modern science and technology. For example, in the field of medicine, it has become possible to prolong life in cases which just a few years ago would have been hopeless. This can, of course, be a source of great joy. But quite often, there arise complicated and very delicate questions concerning the limits of care. I think that there can be no general rule in respect to this. Rather, there is likely to be a multiplicity of competing considerations, which we must assess in the light of reason and compassion. When it becomes necessary to take a difficult decision on behalf of a patient, we must take into account all the various elements. These will, of course, be different in each case. For example, if we prolong the life of a person who is critically ill but whose mind remains lucid, we give that person the opportunity to think and feel in a way that only a human being can. On the other hand, we must consider whether in doing so they will experience great physical and mental suffering as a result of extreme measures taken to keep them alive. This in itself is not an overriding factor, however. As someone who believes in the continuation of consciousness after the death of the body, I would argue that it is much better to have pain with this human body. At least we can benefit from the care of others' whereas, if we choose to die, we may find that we have to endure suffering in some other form.

If the patient is not conscious and is therefore unable to participate in the decision-making process, that is yet another problem. And on top of everything, there may be the wishes of the family to take into account, along with the immense problems that prolonged care can cause them and others. For example, it may be that in order to continue to support one life, valuable funds are kept from projects which would benefit many others. But if there is a general principle, I think it is simply that we recognize the supreme preciousness of life and try to ensure that when the time comes, the dying person departs as serenely and peacefully as possible.

In the case of work in such fields as those of genetics

and biotechnology, the principle of non-harming takes on special importance because lives may be at stake. When the motivation behind such research is merely profit, or fame, or even if research is carried out just for its own sake, it is very much open to question where it will lead. I am thinking particularly of the development of techniques to manipulate physical attributes, such as gender or even hair and eye colour, which can be used commercially to exploit the prejudices of parents. Indeed, let me say here that while it is difficult to be categorically against all forms of genetic experimentation, this is such a delicate area that it is essential that all those involved proceed with caution and deep humility. They must be especially aware of the potential for abuse. It is vital that they keep in mind the wider implications of what they are doing and, most importantly, ensure that their motives are genuinely compassionate. For if the general principle behind such work is simply utility, whereby those that are deemed useless can legitimately be used to benefit those judged to be useful, then there is nothing to stop us from subordinating the rights of those who fall into the former category to those who fall into the latter. Yet the attribute of utility can surely never justify the deprivation of an individual's rights. This is a highly dangerous and very slippery slope.

Recently I saw a BBC television documentary about cloning. Using computer-generated imagery, this film showed a creature some scientists were working on, a sort of semi-human being with large eyes and several other recognizably human features lying down in a cage. Of course, at present this is just fantasy but, they explained, it is possible to foresee a time when it will be possible to create beings like this. They could then be bred and their organs and other parts of their anatomy used in 'spare parts' surgery for the benefit of human beings. I was utterly appalled at this. Oh, terrible. Surely this is taking scientific endeavour to an extreme? The idea that one day we might actually create sentient beings specifically for that purpose revolts me. I felt the same at this prospect as I do at the idea of experiments involving human foetuses.

At the same time, it is difficult to see how this kind of thing can be prevented in the absence of individuals' disciplining their own actions. Yes, we can promulgate laws. Yes, we can have international codes of conduct – as indeed we should have both. Yet if the individual scientists do not have any sense that what they are doing is grotesque, destructive and negative in the extreme, then there is no real prospect of putting an end to such disturbing endeavours.

What about issues like vivisection, where animals are routinely caused terrible suffering before being killed as a means to furthering scientific knowledge? Here I only want to say that to a Buddhist, such practices are equally shocking. I can only hope that the rapid advances being made in computer technology will mean there is less and less call for animal experimentation in scientific research.

One positive development within modern society is the way in which, together with a growing appreciation of the importance of human rights, people are coming to have greater concern for animals. For example, there is growing recognition of the inhumanity of factory farming. It seems, too, that more and more people are taking an interest in vegetarianism and cutting down on their consumption of meat. I welcome this. My hope is that in future, this concern will be extended to consideration for even the smallest creatures of the sea.

Here, though, I should perhaps sound a word of warning. The campaigns to protect human and animal life are noble causes. But it is essential that we do not allow ourselves to be so carried away by our sense of injustice that we ignore others' rights. We need to ensure that we are wisely discerning in pursuit of our ideals.

Exercising our critical faculties in the ethical realm entails taking responsibility both for our acts and for their underlying motives. If we do not take responsibility for our motives, whether positive or negative, the potential for harm is much greater. As we have seen, negative emotions are the source of unethical behaviour. Each act affects not only the people closest to us but our friends, colleagues, community and ultimately the world.

PART THREE

Ethics and Society

CHAPTER ELEVEN

UNIVERSAL
RESPONSIBILITY

I believe that our every act has a universal dimension. Because of this, ethical discipline, wholesome conduct and careful discernment are crucial ingredients for
a meaningful, happy life. But let us now consider this
proposition in relation to the wider community.

In the past, families and small communities could exist
more or less independently of one another. If they took
into account their neighbours' well-being, so much the
better. Yet they could survive quite well without this kind
of perspective. Such is no longer the case. Today's reality
is so complex and, on the material level at least, so clearly

interconnected that a different outlook is needed. Modern economics is a case in point. A stock-market crash on one side of the globe can have a direct effect on the economies of countries on the other. Similarly, our technological achievements are now such that our activities have an unambiguous effect on the natural environment. And the very size of our population means that we cannot afford to ignore others' interests any longer. Indeed, we find that these are often so intertwined that serving our own interests benefits others, even though this may not be our explicit intention. For example, when two families share a single water source, ensuring that it is not polluted benefits both.

In view of this, I am convinced that it is essential to cultivate a sense of what I call universal responsibility. This may not be an exact translation of the Tibetan term I have in mind, *chi sem*, which means, literally, universal (*chi*) consciousness (*sem*). Although the notion of responsibility is implied rather than explicit in the Tibetan, it is definitely there. When I say that on the basis of concern for others' well-being we can, and should, develop a sense of universal responsibility, I do not, however, mean to suggest that each individual has a direct responsibility for the existence of, for example, wars and famines in different parts of the world. It is true that in Buddhist practice we constantly remind ourselves of our duty to serve all sentient beings in every universe. Similarly, the theist recognizes that devotion to God includes consideration for all His creatures. But clearly certain things, such as the poverty of a single village ten thousand miles away, are completely beyond the scope of the individual. What is entailed, therefore, is not an admission of fault but, again, a reorientation of our heart and mind away from self and toward others. To develop a sense of universal responsibility – of the universal dimension of our every act and of the equal right of all others to happiness and not to suffer – is to develop an attitude of mind whereby, if we see an opportunity to benefit others, we will take it in preference to merely looking after our own narrow interests. But though, of course, we care about what is beyond our scope, we accept it as part of nature and concern ourselves with doing what we can.

An important benefit of developing such a sense of universal responsibility is that it helps us become sensitive to all others – not just those closest to us. We come to see the need to care especially for those members of the human family who suffer most. We recognize the need to avoid causing divisiveness among our fellow human beings. And we become aware of the overwhelming importance of contentment.

When we neglect others' well-being and ignore the universal dimension of our actions, it is inevitable that we will come to see our interests as separate from theirs. We will overlook the fundamental oneness of the human family. Of course, it is easy to point to numerous factors which work against this notion of unity. These include differences of religious faith, of language, customs, culture and so on. But when we put too much emphasis on superficial differences, and on account of them make small rigid discriminations, we cannot avoid bringing about additional suffering both for ourselves and others. This makes no sense. We humans already have enough problems. We all face death, old age and sickness – not to mention the inevitability of meeting with disappointment. These we simply cannot avoid. Is this not enough? What is the point of creating still more unnecessary problems simply on the basis of different ways of thinking or different skin colour?

Judging these realities, we see that both ethics and necessity call for the same response. In order to overcome our tendency to ignore others' needs and rights, we must continually remind ourselves of what is obvious: that basically we are all the same. I come from Tibet; most of the readers of this book will not be Tibetans. If I were to meet each reader individually and look them over, I would see that the majority do indeed have characteristics superficially different from mine. If I were then to concentrate on these differences, I could certainly amplify them and make them into something important. The result would be that we grow more distant rather than closer. If, on the other hand, I were to look on each as one of my own kind – as a human being like myself with one nose, two eyes and so forth, ignoring differences of shape and colour – then automatically that sense of distance would fade. I would see that we have the same human flesh and that, moreover, just as I want to be happy and to avoid suffering, so do they. On the basis of this recognition, I would quite naturally feel well disposed toward them. And concern for their well-being would arise almost by itself.

Yet it seems to me that while most people are willing to accept the need for unity within their own group and, within this, the need to consider others' welfare, the tendency is to neglect the rest of humanity. In doing so, we ignore not only the interdependent nature of reality but the reality of our situation. If it were possible for one group, or one race, or one nation to gain complete satisfaction and fulfilment by remaining totally independent and self-sufficient within the confines of their own society, then perhaps it could be argued that discrimination against outsiders is justifiable. But this is not the case. In fact, the modern world is such that the interests of a particular community can no longer be considered to lie within the confines of its own boundaries.

Cultivating contentment is therefore crucial to maintaining peaceful coexistence. Discontent breeds acquisitiveness, which can never be satisfied. It is true that, if what the individual seeks is by nature infinite, such as the quality of tolerance, the question of contentment does not arise. The more we enhance our ability to be tolerant, the more tolerant we will become. In respect of spiritual qualities, contentment is neither necessary nor in fact is it desirable. But if what we seek is finite and we lack contentment, the danger is that having acquired it, we will still not be satisfied. In the case of the desire for wealth, even if a person were somehow able to take over the economy of an entire country, there is every chance they would begin to think in terms of acquiring that of other countries too. Desire for what is finite can never really be sated. On the other hand, when we develop contentment, we can never be disappointed or disillusioned.

Lack of contentment – which really comes down to greed – sows the seed of envy and aggressive competitiveness, and leads to a culture of excessive materialism. The negative atmosphere this creates becomes the context for all kinds of social ills which bring suffering to all members of that community. If it were the case that greed and envy had no side effects, arguably this would be a matter for that community alone. But, again, such is not the case. In particular, lack of contentment is the source of damage to our natural environment and, thereby, of harm to others. Which others? In particular, the poor and the weak. Within their own community, though the rich may be able to move house to avoid, for example, high levels of pollution, the poor have no choice.

Similarly, the people of the poorer nations, which do not have the resources to cope, also suffer both from the richer nations' excesses and from the pollution of their own cruder technology. The coming generations, too, will suffer. And eventually we ourselves will suffer. How? We have to live in the world we are helping to create. If we choose not to modify our behaviour out of respect for others' equal right to happiness and not to suffer, it will not be long before we begin to notice the negative consequences. Imagine the pollution of an extra two billion cars, for example. It would affect us all. So contentment is not merely an ethical matter. If we do not wish to add to our own experience of suffering, it is a matter of necessity.

This is one of the reasons why I believe that the culture of perpetual economic growth needs to be questioned. In my view it fosters discontent, and with this comes a great number of problems, both social and environmental. There is also the fact that in devoting ourselves so wholeheartedly to material development we neglect the implications this has for the wider community. Again, this is less a matter of the gap between First and Third World, North and South, between developed and underdeveloped, between rich and poor, being immoral and wrong. It is both of these. But in some ways more significant is the fact that such inequality is itself the source of trouble for everyone. If it were the case that, for example, Europe was the whole world, rather than home to less than ten per cent of the world's population, the prevailing ideology of endless growth might be justifiable. Yet the world is more than just Europe. The fact is that elsewhere people are starving. And where there are imbalances as profound as these, there are bound to be negative consequences for all, even if they are not equally direct: the rich also feel the symptoms of poverty in their daily lives. Consider, in this context, how the sight of surveillance cameras, and of iron security bars over our windows, actually detracts a little from our sense of security.

Universal responsibility also leads us to commitment to the principle of honesty. What do I mean by this? We can think of honesty and dishonesty in terms of the relationship between appearance and reality. Sometimes these synchronize, often they do not. But when they do, that is honesty, as I understand it. So we are honest when our actions are what they seem to be. When we pretend to be one thing but in reality we are something else, suspicion develops in others, causing fear. And fear is something we all wish to avoid. Conversely, when in our interactions with our neighbours we are open and sincere in everything we say and think and do, people have no need to fear us. This holds true both for the individual and for communities. Moreover, when we understand the value of honesty in all our undertakings, we recognize that there is no ultimate difference between the needs of the individual and the need of whole communities. Their numbers vary, but their desire, and right, not to be deceived remains the same. Thus when we commit ourselves to honesty, we help reduce the level of misunderstanding, doubt and fear throughout society. In a small but significant way, we create the conditions for a happy world.

The question of justice is also closely connected both with universal responsibility and the question of honesty. Justice entails a requirement to act when we become aware of injustice. Indeed, failure to do so may be wrong, although not wrong in the sense that it makes us somehow intrinsically bad. But if our hesitance to speak out comes from a sense of self-centredness then there may be a problem. If our response to injustice is to ask, 'What will happen to me if I speak out? Maybe people won't like me', this could well be unethical if in doing so we are ignoring the wider implications of our silence. It could also be inappropriate and unhelpful when set in the context of all others' equal right to happiness and to avoid suffering. This remains true even – perhaps especially – when people say, 'This is our business' or 'This is an internal affair.' Not only can our speaking out under such circumstances be a duty, more importantly it can be a service to others.

It may, of course, be objected that such honesty is not always possible, that we need to be 'realistic'. Our circumstances may prevent us from always acting in accordance with our responsibilities. Our own families may be harmed if, for example, we speak out when we witness injustice. But while we do have to deal with the day-to-day reality of our lives, it is essential to keep a broad perspective. We must evaluate our own needs in relation to the needs of others and consider how our actions and inactions are likely to affect them in the longer term. It is hard to criticize those who fear for their loved ones. But occasionally it will be necessary to take risks in order to benefit the wider community.

A sense of responsibility towards all others also means that both as individuals and as a society of individuals, we have a duty to care for each member of our society. This is true irrespective of their physical capacity or of their capacity for mental reflection. Just like ourselves, such people have a right to happiness and to avoid suffering. We must therefore avoid, at all cost, the urge to shut away those who are grievously afflicted as if they were a burden. The same goes for those who are diseased or marginalized. To push them away would be to heap suffering on suffering. If we ourselves were in the same condition, we would look to others for help. We need, therefore, to ensure that the sick and afflicted person never feels helpless, rejected or unprotected. Indeed, the affection we show to such people is, in my opinion, the measure of our spiritual health, both at the level of the individual and at that of society.

I may sound hopelessly idealistic in all this talk of universal responsibility. Nevertheless, it is an idea I have been expressing publicly ever since my first trip to the West, back in 1973. In those days, many people were sceptical of such notions. Similarly, it was not always easy to interest people in the concept of world peace. I am encouraged to note that today, however, an increasing number are beginning to respond favourably to these ideas.

Indeed, as a result of the many extraordinary events humanity has experienced during the course of the twentieth century, we have, I feel, become more mature. In the 1950s and 1960s, and in some places even more recently, many people felt that ultimately conflicts should be resolved through war. Today, that thinking holds sway only in the minds of a small minority. And whereas in the early part of this century many people believed that progress and development within society should be pursued through strict regimentation, the collapse of fascism, followed later by the disappearance of the so-called Iron Curtain, has shown this to be a hopeless enterprise. It is also worth noting the lesson from history which shows that order imposed by force is only ever short-lived. Moreover, the consensus (among some Buddhists too) that science and spirituality are incompatible no longer holds so firmly. Today, as the scientific understanding of the nature of reality deepens, this perception is changing. Because of this, people are beginning to show more interest in what I have called our inner world. By this, I mean the dynamics and functions of consciousness, or spirit: our hearts and minds. There has also been a worldwide increase in environmental awareness, and a growing recognition that neither individuals nor even whole nations can solve all their problems by themselves, that we need one another. To me, these are all very encouraging developments, which are sure to have far-reaching consequences. I am also encouraged by the fact that regardless of its implementation, there is at least clearer acknowledgement of the need to seek non-violent resolutions of conflict in a spirit of reconciliation. There is also, as we have noted, growing acceptance of the universality of human rights and indeed of the need to accept diversity in areas of common importance, such as, for example, in religious affairs. This I believe to reflect a recognition of the need for a wider perspective in response to the diversity of the human family itself. As a result, despite so much suffering continuing to be inflicted on individuals and peoples in the name of ideology, or religion, or progress, or development, or economics, a new sense of hope is emerging for the downtrodden. Although it will undoubtedly be difficult to bring about genuine peace and harmony, clearly it can be done. The potential is there. And its foundation is a sense of responsibility on the part of each of us as individuals towards all others.

CHAPTER TWELVE

LEVELS OF COMMITMENT

Through developing an attitude of responsibility toward others, we can begin to create the kinder, more compassionate world we all dream of. The reader may or may not agree with my advocacy of universal responsibility. But if it is correct that, given the broadly interdependent nature of reality, our habitual distinction between self and other is in some sense an exaggeration, and if on the basis of this I am right in suggesting that our aim should be to extend our compassion towards all others, we cannot avoid the conclusion that compassion – which entails ethical conduct – belongs at the heart of all our actions, both individual and social. Saying this, I trust it is clear that I am not calling on everyone to renounce their present way of life and adopt a new rule or way of thinking. Rather, my intention is to suggest that the individual, keeping his or her daily life, can change, can become a better, more compassionate and happier human being. And through being better, more compassionate individuals, we can make a significant contribution to society itself.

The work of a person labouring in some humble occupation is no less relevant to the well-being of society than that of, for example, a doctor, a teacher, a monk or a nun. All human endeavour is potentially great and noble. So long as we carry out our work with good motivation, reminding ourselves that 'My work is for others', it will be of benefit to the wider community. But when concern for others' feelings and welfare are missing, our activities tend to become spoiled. Through lack of basic human feeling, religion, politics, economics and so on can be rendered dirty. Instead of serving humanity, they become agents of its destruction.

Therefore, in addition to developing a sense of universal responsibility, we need actually to be responsible people. Until we put our principles into practice, they remain just that. So, for example, it is appropriate for a politician who is genuinely responsible to conduct himself or herself with honesty and integrity. It is appropriate for a businessman or woman to consider the needs of others in every enterprise they undertake. It is appropriate for a lawyer to use his or her expertise to fight for justice.

Of course, it is difficult to articulate precisely how our behaviour would be shaped by a commitment to the principle of universal responsibility. For this reason, I do not have any particular standard in mind. All that I hope is that, if what is written here makes sense to you, the reader, you will strive to be compassionate in your daily life, and that out of a sense of responsibility toward all others you will do what you can to help them. When you walk past a dripping tap, you will turn it off. If you see a light burning unnecessarily, you will do the same. If you are a religious practitioner and tomorrow you meet someone of another religious tradition, you will show them the same respect as you would hope them to show you. Or if you are a scientist and you see that the research you are engaged in may cause harm to others, out of a sense of responsibility, you will desist from it. According to your own resources, and recognizing the limitations of your circumstances, you will do what you can. Apart from this, I am not calling for any commitment as such. And if some days your actions are more compassionate than on others – well, that is normal. Likewise, if what I say does not seem helpful, then no matter. The important thing is that whatever we do for others, whatever sacrifices we make, it should be voluntary and arise from understanding the benefit of such actions.

But let us be clear on this. Recently I was told that the number of billionaires in America had increased from seventeen just a few years ago to several hundred today. Yet at the same time, the poor remain poor and in some cases are becoming poorer. This I consider to be completely immoral. It is also a potential source of problems. While millions do not even have the basic necessities of life – adequate food, shelter, education and medical facilities – the inequity of wealth distribution is a scandal. If it were the case that everyone had a sufficiency for their needs and more, then perhaps a luxurious lifestyle would be tenable. If that was what the individual really wanted, it would be difficult to argue that they need refrain from exercising their right to live as they see fit. Yet things are not like that. In this one world of ours, there are areas where people throw surplus food away while others close by – our fellow humans, innocent children among them – are reduced to scavenging among rubbish, and many starve. Thus although I cannot say that the life of luxury led by the rich is wrong of itself, assuming they are using their own money and have not acquired it dishonestly, I do say that it is unworthy, that it is spoiling.

Moreover, it strikes me that the lifestyles of the rich are often absurdly and pointlessly complicated. One friend of mine, who stayed with an extremely wealthy family, told me that every time they went swimming, they were handed a bathing robe to wear. This would then be changed for a fresh one each time they used the pool, even if they did so several times in one day. Extraordinary! Ridiculous, even. I do not see how living like this adds anything to one's comfort. As human beings we have only one stomach. There is a limit to the amount we can eat. Similarly, we have only eight fingers and two thumbs, so we cannot wear a hundred rings. Whatever argument there may be concerning choice, the extra we have is of no purpose in the moment when we are actually wearing a ring. The rest lie useless in their boxes. In my opinion, the appropriate use of wealth, as I said recently to the members of one very prosperous Indian family, is found in philanthropic giving. In this particular case, I suggested – since they asked – that spending their money on education would be the best thing they could do. The future of the world is in our children's hands. Therefore, if we wish to bring about a more compassionate – and therefore fairer – society, it is essential that we educate our children to be responsible, caring human beings. When a person is born rich, or acquires wealth by some other means, they have a tremendous opportunity to benefit others. What a waste when that opportunity is squandered on self-indulgence.

I feel strongly that luxurious living is inappropriate, so much so that I must admit that whenever I stay in a comfortable hotel and see others eating and drinking expensively while outside there are people who do not even have anywhere to spend the night, I feel greatly disturbed. It reinforces my feeling that I am no different from either the rich or the poor. We are the same in wanting happiness and not to suffer. And we have an equal right to that happiness. As a result, I feel that if I were to see a workers' demonstration going by, I would certainly join in. And yet, of course, the person who is saying these things is one of those enjoying the comforts of the hotel. Indeed, I must go further. It is also true that I possess several valuable wrist watches. And while I sometimes feel that if I were to sell them I could perhaps build some huts for the poor, so far I have not. In the same way, I do feel that if I were to observe a strictly vegetarian diet not only would I be setting a better example, but I would also be helping to save innocent animals' lives. Again, so far I have not and therefore must admit a discrepancy between my principles and my practice in certain areas. At the same time, I do not believe everyone can or should be like Mahatma Gandhi and live the life of a poor peasant. Such dedication is wonderful and greatly to be admired. But the watchword is 'As much as we can' – without going to extremes.

CHAPTER THIRTEEN

FURTHER
RESPONSIBILITIES

When we are committed to the ideal of concern for all others, it follows that this should inform our social and political policies. I say this not because I suppose that thereby we will be able to solve all society's problems overnight. Rather, it is my conviction that unless this wider sense of compassion which I have been urging on the reader inspires our politics, our policies are likely to harm instead of serve humanity as a whole. We must, I believe, take practical steps to acknowledge our responsibility to all others both now and in the future. This is true even where there may be little practical difference between those policies that are motivated by this compassion and those that are motivated by, for example, national interest.

Now although it is certainly the case that if all my suggestions concerning compassion, inner discipline, wise discernment, and the cultivation of virtue were to be implemented widely, the world would automatically become a kinder, more peaceful place, I believe that reality compels us to tackle our problems at the level of society at the same time as that of the individual. The world will change when each individual makes the attempt to counter their negative thoughts and emotions and when we practice compassion for its inhabitants irrespective of whether or not we have direct relationships with them.

In view of this, there are, I believe, a number of areas to which we need to give special consideration in the light of universal responsibility. These include education, the media, our natural environment, politics and economics, peace and disarmament, and interreligious harmony. Each has a vital role to play in shaping the world we live in, and I propose to examine them briefly in turn.

Before doing so, I must stress that the views I express are personal. They are also the views of someone who claims no expertise with respect to the technicalities of these matters. But if what I say seems objectionable, my hope is that it will at least give the reader pause for thought. For although it would not be surprising to see a divergence of opinion concerning how they are to be translated into actual policies, the need for compassion, for basic spiritual values, for inner discipline and for wholesome ethical conduct generally are in my view incontrovertible.

EDUCATION AND THE MEDIA

Whether visiting one of our schools for Tibetan refugees in India or speaking to student audiences abroad, I am always very happy to meet young people. They have a natural enthusiasm for justice and peace, and they tend to be much more open and flexible of mind than adults. No matter how well disposed towards change we are, we adults undoubtedly find it more difficult. Meeting the young also reminds me that children constitute humanity's most precious resource. Given that their moral outlook is largely shaped by their upbringing, it is essential we educate them responsibly.

The human mind (lo) is both the source and, properly directed, the solution to all our problems. Those who attain great learning but lack a good heart are in danger of falling prey to the anxieties and restlessness which result from desires incapable of fulfilment. This is because what I call material knowledge can easily be a source of negative thoughts and feelings. Conversely, a genuine understanding of spiritual values brings peace. If we bring up our children to have knowledge without compassion, their attitude towards others is likely to be a mixture of envy of those in positions above them, aggressive competitiveness toward their peers and scorn for those less fortunate. This leads to a propensity towards greed, presumption, excess and, very quickly, to loss of happiness. Knowledge is important, but much more important is the use towards which it is put. This depends on the heart and mind of the one who uses it.

Education is much more than a matter of imparting the knowledge and skills by which narrow goals are achieved. It is also about opening the child's eyes to the needs and rights of others. We must show children that their actions have a universal dimension. And we must somehow find a way to build on their natural feelings of empathy so that they come to have a sense of responsibility toward others. For it is this which stirs us into action. Indeed, if we had to choose between learning and virtue, the latter is definitely more valuable. The good heart which is the fruit of virtue is by itself a great benefit to humanity. Mere knowledge is not.

How, though, are we to teach morality to our children? I have a sense that, in general, modern educational systems neglect discussion of ethical matters. This is probably not intentional as much as a by-product of historical reality. Secular educational systems were developed at a time when religious institutions were still highly influential throughout society. Because ethical and human values were and still are generally held to fall within the purview of religion, it was assumed that this aspect of a child's education would be looked after through his or her religious upbringing. This worked well enough until the influence of religion began to decline. But now, although the need is still there, it is not being met. Therefore, we must find another way of showing children that basic human values are important. And we must also help them to develop them.

Ultimately, of course, the importance of concern for others is learned not from words but from actions: the example we set. This is why the family environment itself is such a vital component in a child's upbringing. When a caring and compassionate atmosphere is absent from the home, when children are neglected by their parents, it is easy to recognize the damaging effects. The children tend to feel helpless and insecure, and their minds are often agitated. Conversely, when children receive consistent affection and protection, they tend to be much happier and more confident in their abilities. Their physical health tends to be better too. And we find that they are concerned not just for themselves but for others as well. The home environment is also important because children learn negative behaviour from their parents. If, for example, the father is always getting into fights with his associates, or if the father and mother are always arguing destructively, although at first the child may find this objectionable, eventually they will come to understand it as quite normal. This learning is then taken out of the home and into the world.

It also goes without saying that what children learn about ethical conduct has to be practised first. In this, teachers have a special responsibility. By their own behaviour, they can make children remember them for their whole lives. If this behaviour is principled, disciplined and compassionate, their values will be readily impressed on the child's mind. This is because the lessons taught by a teacher with a positive motivation (*kun long*) penetrate deepest into their students' minds. I know this from my own experience. As a boy, I was very lazy. But when I was aware of the affection and concern of my tutors, their lessons would generally sink in much more successfully than if one of them was harsh or unfeeling that day.

So far as the specifics of education are concerned, that is for the experts. I will, therefore, confine myself to a few suggestions. The first is that in order to awaken young people's consciousness to the importance of basic human values, it is better not to present society's problems purely as an ethical matter or as a religious matter. It is important to emphasize that what is at stake is our continued survival. This way, they will come to see that the future lies in their hands. Secondly, I do believe that dialogue can and should be taught in class. Presenting students with a controversial issue and having them debate it is a wonderful way to introduce them to the concept of resolving conflict non-violently. Indeed, one would hope that if schools were to make this a priority, it could have a beneficial effect on family life itself. On seeing his or her parents wrangling, a child that had understood the value of dialogue would instinctively say, 'Oh no. That's not the way. You have to talk, to discuss things properly.'

Finally, it is essential that we eliminate from our schools' curricula any tendency toward presenting others in a negative light. There are undoubtedly some parts of the world where the teaching of history, for example, fosters bigotry and racism toward other communities. Of course this is wrong. It contributes nothing to the happiness of humanity. Now more than ever we need to show our children that distinctions between 'my country' and 'your country', 'my religion' and 'your religion' are secondary considerations. Rather, we must insist on the observation that my right to happiness carries no more weight than others' right. This is not to say that I believe we should educate children to abandon or ignore the culture and historical tradition they are born into. On the contrary, it is very important they be grounded in these. It is good for children to learn to love their country, their religion, their culture and so on. But the danger comes when this develops into narrow-minded nationalism, ethnocentricity and religious bigotry. The example of Mahatma Gandhi is pertinent here. Even though he had a very high level of Western education, he never forgot or became estranged from the rich heritage of his Indian culture.

If education constitutes one of our most powerful weapons in our quest to bring about a better, more peaceful world, the mass media is another. As every political figure knows, they are no longer the only ones with authority in society. In addition to that of newspapers and books, radio, film and television together have an influence over individuals unimagined a hundred years ago. This power confers great responsibility on all who work in the media. But it also confers great responsibility on each of us who, as individuals, listen and read and watch. We, too, have a role to play. We are not powerless before the media. The control switch is in our own hands, after all.

This does not mean that I advocate bland reporting or entertainment without excitement. On the contrary, so far as investigative journalism is concerned, I respect and appreciate the media's interference. Not all public servants are honest in discharging their duties. It is appropriate, therefore, to have journalists, their noses as long as an elephant's trunk, snooping around and exposing wrong-doing where they find it. We need to know when this or that renowned individual hides a very different aspect behind a pleasant exterior. There should be no discrepancy between external appearances and the individual's inner life. It is the same person, after all. Such discrepancies suggest them to be untrustworthy. At the same time, it is vital that the investigator does not act out of improper motives. Without impartiality and due respect for the other's rights, the investigation itself becomes tainted.

With regard to the question of the media's emphasis on sex and violence, there are many factors to consider. In the first instance, it is clear that much of the viewing public enjoys the sensations provoked by this sort of material. Secondly, I very much doubt that those producing material containing a lot of explicit sex and violence intend harm by it. Their motives are surely just commercial. As to whether this is positive or negative in itself is to my mind less important than the question of whether it can have an ethically wholesome effect. If the result of seeing a film in which there is a lot of violence is that the viewer's compassion is aroused, then perhaps that depiction of violence would be justified. But if the accumulation of violent images leads to indifference, then I think it is not. Indeed, such a hardening of heart is potentially dangerous. It leads all too easily to lack of empathy.

When the media focuses too closely on the negative aspects of human nature, there is a danger that we become persuaded that violence and aggression are its principal characteristics. This is a mistake, I believe. The fact that violence is newsworthy suggests the very opposite. Good news is not remarked on precisely because there is so much of it. Consider that at any given moment there must be hundreds of millions of acts of kindness taking place around the world. Although there will undoubtedly be many acts of violence in progress at the same time, their number is surely very much less. If, therefore, the media is to be ethically responsible, it needs to reflect this simple fact.

Clearly it is necessary to regulate the media. The fact that we prevent our children from watching certain things indicates that we already discriminate between what is and is not appropriate according to different circumstances. But whether legislation is the right way to go about this is hard to judge. As in all matters of ethics, discipline is only really effective when it comes from within. Perhaps the best way to ensure that the output the various media provides is healthy lies in the way we educate our children. If we bring them up to be aware of their responsibilities, they will be more disciplined when they become involved in the media.

Although it is perhaps too much to hope that the media will actually promote the ideals and principles of compassion, at least we should be able to expect that those involved will take care when there is the potential for negative impact. At least there should be no room for incitement of negative acts such as racist violence. But beyond this, I don't know. Perhaps we might be able to find a way to connect more directly those who create stories for news and entertainment, with the viewer, the reader and the listener?

THE NATURAL WORLD

If there is one area in which both education and the media have a special responsibility, it is, I believe, our natural environment. This responsibility has less to do with questions of right or wrong than with the question of survival. The natural world is our home. It is not necessarily sacred or holy. It is simply where we live. It is therefore in our interest to look after it. This is common sense. But only recently have the size of our population and the power of science and technology grown to the point that they have a direct impact on nature. To put it another way, until now, Mother Earth has been able to tolerate our sloppy house habits. However, the stage has now been reached where she can no longer accept our behaviour in silence. The problems caused by environmental degradation can be seen as her response to our irresponsible behaviour. She is warning us that there are limits even to her tolerance.

Nowhere are the consequences of our failure to exercise discipline in the way we relate to our environment more apparent than in the case of present-day Tibet. It is no exaggeration to say that the Tibet I grew up in was a wildlife paradise. Every traveller who visited Tibet before the middle of the twentieth century remarked on this.

Animals were rarely hunted, except in the remotest areas where crops could not be grown. Indeed, it was customary for government officials annually to issue a proclamation protecting wildlife: 'Nobody', it read, 'however humble or noble, shall harm or do violence to the creatures of the waters or the wild.' The only exceptions to this were rats and wolves.

As a young man, I recall seeing great numbers of different species whenever I travelled outside Lhasa. My chief memory of the three-month journey across Tibet from my birthplace at Takster in the East to Lhasa, where I was formally proclaimed Dalai Lama as a four-year-old boy, is of the wildlife we encountered along the way. Immense herds of *kiang* (wild asses) and *drong* (wild yak) freely roamed the great plains. Occasionally we would catch sight of shimmering herds of *gowa*, the shy Tibetan gazelle, of *wa*, the white-lipped deer, or of *tso*, our majestic antelope. I remember, too, my fascination for the little *chibi*, or pika, which would congregate on grassy areas. They were so friendly. I loved to watch the birds, the dignified *gho* (the bearded eagle) soaring high above monasteries perched up in the mountains; the flocks of geese (*nangbar*); and occasionally, at night, to hear the call of the *wookpa* (the long-eared owl).

Even in Lhasa, one did not feel in any way cut off from the natural world. In my rooms at the top of the Potala, the winter palace of the Dalai Lamas, I spent countless hours as a child studying the behaviour of the red-beaked *khyungkar* which nested in the crevices of its walls. And behind the Norbulingka, the summer palace, I often saw pairs of *trung trung* (Japanese black-necked cranes), birds which for me are the epitome of elegance and grace, that lived in the marshlands there. And all this is not to mention the crowning glory of Tibetan fauna: the bears and mountain foxes, the *chanku* (wolves), and *sazik* (the beautiful snow leopard), and the *sik* (lynx) which struck terror into the hearts of the normal farmer – or the gentle-faced giant panda (*thom tra*), which is native to the border area between Tibet and China.

Sadly, this profusion of wildlife is no longer to be found. Partly due to hunting but primarily due to loss of habitat, what remains half a century after Tibet was occupied is only a fraction of what there was. Without exception, every Tibetan I have spoken with who has been back to visit Tibet after thirty to forty years has reported on a striking absence of wildlife. Whereas before wild animals would often come close to the house, today they are hardly anywhere to be seen.

Equally troubling is the devastation of Tibet's forests. In the past, the hills were all thickly wooded; today those who have been back report that they are clean-shaven like a monk's head. The government in Beijing has admitted that the tragic flooding of western China, and further afield, is in part due to this. And yet I hear continuous reports of round-the-clock convoys of trucks carrying logs east out of Tibet. This is especially tragic given the country's mountainous terrain and harsh climate. It means that replanting requires sustained care and attention. Unfortunately there is little evidence of this.

None of this is to say that, historically, we Tibetans were deliberately 'conservationist'. We were not. The idea of something called 'pollution' simply never occurred to us. There is no denying we were rather spoiled in this respect. A small population inhabited a very large area with clean, dry air and an abundance of pure mountain water. This innocent attitude toward cleanliness meant that when we Tibetans went into exile, we were astonished to discover, for example, the existence of streams whose water is not drinkable. Like an only child, no matter what we did, Mother Earth tolerated our behaviour. The result was that we had no proper understanding of cleanliness and hygiene. People would spit or blow their nose in the street without giving it a second thought. Indeed, saying this, I recall one elderly Khampa, a former bodyguard who used to come each day to circumambulate my residence in Dharamsala (a popular devotion). Unfortunately, he suffered greatly from bronchitis. This was exacerbated by the incense he carried. At each corner, therefore, he would pause to cough and expectorate so ferociously that I sometimes wondered whether he had come to pray or just to spit!

Over the years since our first arriving in exile, I have taken a close interest in environmental issues. The Tibetan government in exile has paid particular attention to introducing our children to their responsibilities as residents of this fragile planet. And I never hesitate to speak out on the subject whenever I am given the opportunity. In particular, I always stress the need to consider how our actions, in affecting the environment, are likely to affect others. I admit that this is very often difficult to judge. We cannot say for sure what the ultimate effects of, for example, deforestation might be on the soil and the local rainfall, let alone what the implications are for the planet's weather systems. The only clear thing is that we humans are the only species with the power to destroy the earth as we know it. The birds have no such power, nor do the insects, nor does any mammal. Yet if we have the capacity to destroy the earth, so, too, do we have the capacity to protect it.

What is essential is that we find methods of manufacture that do not destroy nature. We need to find ways of cutting down on our use of wood and other limited natural resources. I am no expert in this field, and I cannot suggest how this might be done. I know only that it is possible, given the necessary determination. For example, I recall hearing on a visit to Stockholm some years ago that for the first time in many years fish were returning to the river that runs through the city. Until recently, there were none due to industrial pollution. Yet this improvement was by no means the result of all the local factories closing down. Likewise, on a visit to Germany, I was shown an industrial development designed to produce no pollution. So, clearly, solutions do exist to limit damage to the natural world without bringing industry to a halt.

This does not mean that I believe we can rely on technology to overcome all our problems. Nor do I believe we can afford to continue destructive practices in anticipation of technical fixes being developed. Besides, the environment does not need fixing. It is our behaviour in relation to it that needs to change. I question whether, in the case of such a massive looming disaster as that caused by the greenhouse effect, a 'fix' could ever exist, even in theory. And supposing it could, we have to ask whether it would ever be feasible to apply it on the scale that would be required. What of the expense and what of the cost in terms of our natural resources? I suspect that these would be prohibitively high. There is also the fact that in many other fields – such as in the humanitarian relief of hunger – there are already insufficient funds to cover the work that could be undertaken. Therefore, even if one were to argue that the necessary funds could be raised, morally speaking this would be almost impossible to justify given such deficiencies. It would not be right to deploy huge sums simply in order to enable the industrialized nations to continue their harmful practices while people in other places cannot even feed themselves.

All this points to the need to recognize the universal dimension of our actions and, based on this, to exercise restraint. The necessity of this is forcefully demonstrated when we come to consider the propagation of our species. Although from the point of view of all the major religions, the more humans the better, and although it may be true that some of the latest studies suggest a population implosion a century from now, still I believe we cannot ignore this issue. As a monk, it is perhaps inappropriate for me to comment on these matters. I believe that family planning is important. Of course, I do not mean to suggest we should not have children. Human life is a precious resource and married couples should have children unless there are compelling reasons not to. The idea of not having children just because we want to enjoy a full life without responsibility is quite mistaken I think. At the same time, couples do have a duty to consider the impact our numbers have on the natural environment. This is especially true given the impact of modern technology.

Fortunately, more and more people are coming to recognize the importance of ethical discipline as a means to ensuring a healthy place to live. For this reason I am optimistic that disaster can be averted. Until comparatively recently, few people gave much thought to the effects of human activity on our planet. Yet today there are even political parties whose main concern it is. Moreover, the fact that the air we breathe, the water we drink, the forests and oceans which sustain millions of different life forms, and the climatic patterns which govern our weather systems all transcend national boundaries is a source of hope. It means that no country, no matter either how rich and powerful or how poor and weak it may be, can afford not to take action in respect of this issue.

So far as the individual is concerned, the problems resulting from our neglect of our natural environment are a powerful reminder that we all have a contribution to make. And while one person's actions may not have a significant impact, the combined effect of millions of individuals' actions certainly does. This means that it is time for all those living in the industrially developed nations to give serious thought to changing their lifestyle. Again this is not so much a question of ethics. The fact that the population of the rest of the world has an equal right to improve their standard of living is in some ways more important than the affluent being able to continue their lifestyle. If this is to be fulfilled without causing irredeemable violence to the natural world – with all the negative consequences for happiness that this would entail – the richer countries must set an example. The cost to the planet, and thus the cost to humanity of ever-increasing standards of living, is simply too great.

POLITICS AND ECONOMICS

During the last fifty years, we have witnessed an astounding increase in the financial wealth of the world. Yet although this has resulted in a standard of living higher than could ever have been imagined, it has been confined to a minority. There remains severe privation among perhaps half the world's population. Food, shelter and medicine are in short supply among too many of our brothers and sisters. Our basic sense of justice and fairness alone suggests that we should not be content with the way things are progressing. If it seemed likely that, carrying on as we are, we could eradicate poverty after, say, another fifty, or even after another hundred years, perhaps we would be justified in doing so. But this seems highly unlikely.

Of course I don't know much about economics. But I find it hard to avoid the conclusion that the wealth of the rich is maintained through neglect of the poor, especially by means of international debt. Saying this, I do not mean to suggest that the undeveloped countries have no share of responsibility for their problems. Nor can we put all social and economic ills down to politicians and public officials, I do not deny that even in the world's most established democracies it is quite usual to hear politicians making

~ 203

unrealistic promises and boasting about what they are going to do when elected. But these people do not drop out of the sky. So if it is true that a given country's politicians are corrupt, we tend to find that the society is itself lacking in morality and that the individuals who make up the population do not lead ethical lives. In such cases, it is not entirely fair for the electorate to criticize its politicians. On the other hand, when people possess healthy values, and where they practise ethical discipline in their own lives out of concern for others, the public officials produced by that society will quite naturally respect those same values. Each of us, therefore, has a role to play in creating a society in which respect and care for others, based on empathy, are given top priority.

So far as the application of economic policy is concerned, the same considerations apply here as to every human activity. A sense of universal reponsibility is crucial. I must admit, however, that I find it a bit difficult to make practical suggestions about the application of spiritual values in the field of commerce. This is because competition has such as important role to play. For this reason, the relationship between empathy and profit is necessarily a fragile one. Still, I do not see why it should not be possible to have constructive competition. The key factor is the motivation (*kun long*) of those engaged in it. When the intention is to exploit or destroy others, then clearly the outcome will not be positive. But when competition is conducted with a spirit of generosity and good intention, the outcome, although it must entail a degree of suffering for those who lose, will at least not be too harmful.

Again it may be objected that the reality of commerce is such that we cannot realistically expect businesses to put people before profits. But here we must remember that those who run the world's industries and businesses are human beings too. Even the most hardened would surely admit that it is not right to seek profits regardless of consequences. If it were, dealing in drugs would not be wrong. So again, what is required is that each of us develops our compassionate nature. The more we do so, the more commercial enterprise will come to reflect basic human values.

Conversely, if we ourselves neglect those values, it is inevitable that commerce will neglect them too. This is not just idealism. History shows that many of the positive developments in human society have occurred as the result of compassion. If we look at the evolution of human society, we see the necessity of having vision in order to bring about positive change. Ideals are the engine of progress. To ignore this and say merely that we need to be 'realistic' in politics and economics is severely mistaken. Consider, for example, the abolition of the slave trade.

Our problems of economic disparity pose a very serious challenge to the whole human family. Nevertheless, as we enter the new millennium, I believe there are a good number of reasons for optimism. During the early and middle years of the twentieth century, there was a general perception that political and economic power were of more consequence than truth. But I believe that this is changing. Even the wealthiest and most powerful nations understand that there is no point in neglecting basic human values. The notion that there is room for ethics in international relations is also gaining ground. Irrespective of whether it is translated into meaningful action, at least words like 'reconciliation', 'non-violence' and 'compassion' are becoming stock phrases amongst politicians. This is a useful development. Then, according to my own experience, I note that when I travel abroad I am quite often asked to speak about peace and compassion to quite large audiences – often in excess of a thousand. I doubt very much whether these topics would have attracted such numbers forty or fifty years ago. Developments such as these indicate that collectively we humans are giving more weight to fundamental values such as justice and truth.

I also take comfort from the fact that the more the world economy evolves, the more explicitly interdependent it becomes. As a result, every nation is to a greater or lesser extent dependent on every other nation. The modern economy, like the environment, knows no boundaries. Even those countries openly hostile to one another must cooperate in their use of the world's resources. Often, for example, they will be dependent on the same rivers.

And the more interdependent our economic relationships, the more interdependent must our political relationships become. Thus we have witnessed, for example, the growth of the European Union from a small caucus of trading partners into something approaching a confederation of states with a membership now well into the double figures. We see similar, though presently less well-developed, groupings throughout the world: the Association of South East Asian Nations, the Organization for African Unity, the Organization of Petroleum Exporting Countries, to name but three. Each of these testifies to the human impulse to join together for the common good and reflects the continuing evolution of human society. What began with relatively small tribal units has progressed through the foundation of city-states to nationhood and now to alliances comprising hundreds of millions of people which increasingly transcend geographical, cultural and ethnic divisions. This is a trend which I believe will and must continue.

We cannot deny, however, that parallel to the proliferation of these political and economic alliances there is also a clear urge toward greater consolidation along the lines of ethnicity, language, religion and culture – often in the context of violence following loosening of the bonds of nation statehood. What are we to make of this seeming paradox – the trend toward transnational cooperative groupings, on the one hand, and the impulse towards localization on the other? In fact, there need not necessarily a contradiction between the two. We can still imagine regional communities united in trade, social policy and security arrangements yet consisting of a multiplicity of autonomous ethnic, cultural, religious and other groupings. There could be a legal system protecting basic human rights common to the larger community which left the constituent communities free to pursue their desired way of life. At the same time, it is important that the establishment of unions comes about voluntarily and on the basis of recognition that the interests of those concerned are better served through collaboration. They must not be imposed. Indeed, the challenge of the new millennium is surely to find ways to achieve international – or better, *intercommunity* – cooperation wherein human diversity is acknowledged and the rights of all are respected.

CHAPTER FOURTEEN

PEACE AND DISARMAMENT

Chairman Mao once said that political power comes from the barrel of a gun. Of course it is true that violence can achieve certain short-term objectives. But it cannot obtain long-lasting ends. If we look at history, we find that in time, humanity's love of peace, justice and freedom always triumphs over cruelty and oppression. This is why I am such a fervent believer in non-violence. Violence begets violence. And violence means only one thing: suffering. Theoretically, it is possible to conceive of a situation where the only way to prevent large-scale conflict is through armed intervention at an early stage.

But the problem with this line of argument is that it is very difficult, if not impossible, to predict the outcome of violence. Nor can we be sure of its justness at the outset. This only becomes clear when we have the benefit of hindsight. The only certainty is that where there is violence, there is always and inevitably suffering.

Some people will say that while the Dalai Lama's devotion to non-violence is praiseworthy, it is not really practical. Actually, it is far more naïve to suppose that the human-created problems which lead to violence can ever be solved through conflict.

I am convinced that the main reason so many people say the path of non-violence is impractical is because the task seems so daunting: we become discouraged. Nevertheless, whereas formerly it was enough to wish for peace in one's own land, or even just in one's neighbourhood, today we speak of world peace. This is only appropriate. The fact of human interdependence is so explicit now: the only peace it is meaningful to speak of is world peace. Here observe that non-violence was the principal characteristic of the political revolutions which swept across so much of the world during the 1980s.

One of the most hopeful aspects of the modern age is the emergence of an international peace movement. If we hear less about it today than we did at the end of the Cold War, this is perhaps because its ideals have been absorbed into mainstream consciousness. But what do I mean when I speak of peace? Are there not grounds for supposing that war is a natural, if regrettable, human activity? Here we need to make a distinction between peace as a mere absence of war and peace as a state of tranquillity founded on the deep sense of security that arises from mutual understanding, tolerance of others' point of view, and respect for their rights. Peace in this sense is not what we saw in Europe during the four and a half decades of Cold War. The very premise on which it rested was fear and suspicion and the strange psychology of mutually assured destruction (aptly abbreviated to MAD). Indeed, the 'peace' which characterized the Cold War was so precarious, so fragile, that any serious misunderstanding on the part of either side could have had disastrous consequences. Looking back, especially with the knowledge we now have of the chaotic management of weapons systems in some quarters, I think it quite miraculous that we somehow escaped destruction!

Peace is not something which exists independently of us. But nor does war. It is true that certain individuals – political leaders, policymakers, army generals – do have particularly grave responsibilities in respect of peace. However, these people do not come from nowhere. They are not born and brought up in outer space. Like us, they were nourished by their mother's milk and affection. They are members of our own human family and have been nurtured within the society which we as individuals have helped create. Peace in the world thus depends on peace in the hearts of individuals. This in turn depends on all of us practising ethics by disciplining our response to negative thoughts and emotions, and developing basic spiritual qualities.

If real peace is something more profound than a fragile equilibrium based on mutual hostility, if ultimately it depends on the resolution of internal conflict, what are we to say about war? Although paradoxically the aim of most military campaigns is peace, in reality, war is like fire in the human community, one whose fuel is living people. It also strongly resembles fire in the way it spreads. If, for example, we look at the course of the recent conflict in the former Yugoslavia, we see that what began as a relatively confined dispute grew quickly to engulf the whole region. Similarly, if we look at individual battles, we see that if commanders perceive areas of weakness, they respond by sending in reinforcements – which is exactly like throwing live people onto a bonfire. But because of habituation, we ignore this. We fail to acknowledge that the very nature of war is cold cruelty and suffering.

The unfortunate truth is that we are conditioned to regard warfare as something exciting and even glamorous: the soldiers in smart uniforms (so attractive to children), with their military bands playing alongside them. We see murder as dreadful, but there is no association of war with criminality. On the contrary, it is seen as an opportunity for people to prove their competence and courage. We speak of the heroes it produces, almost as if the greater the number killed, the more heroic the individual. And we talk about this or that weapon as a marvellous piece of technology, forgetting that when it is used it will actually maim and murder living people. Your friend, my friend, our mothers, our fathers, our sisters and brothers, you and me.

What is even worse is the fact that in modern warfare those who instigate it are often far removed from the conflict on the ground. At the same time, its impact on non-combatants grows ever greater. Those who suffer most in today's armed conflicts are the innocent – not only the families of those fighting, but, in far greater numbers civilians who often do not even play a direct role. Even after the war is over, there continues to be enormous suffering due to land mines and poisoning from the use of chemical weapons – not to mention the the economic hardship it brings. This means that, more and more, women, children and the elderly are among its prime victims.

The reality of modern warfare is that the whole enterprise has become almost like a computer game. The ever-increasing sophistication of weaponry has outrun the imaginative capacity of the average lay person. Their destructive capacity is so astonishing that whatever arguments there may be in favour of war, they must be vastly inferior to those against. We could almost be forgiven for feeling nostalgia for the way in which battles were fought in ancient times. At least then people fought one another face to face. There was no denying the suffering involved.

And in those days, it was usual for rulers to lead their troops in battle. If the ruler was killed, that was usually the end of the matter. But as technology improved, the generals began to stay farther behind. Today they can be thousands of miles away in their bunkers underground. In view of this, I could almost see developing a 'smart' bullet that could seek out those who decide on wars in the first place. That would seem to me more fair, and on these grounds I would welcome a weapon that eliminated the decision-makers while leaving the innocent unharmed.

Because of the reality of this destructive capacity, we need to admit that whether they are intended for offensive or for defensive purposes, weapons exist solely to destroy human beings. But lest we suppose that peace is purely dependent upon disarmament, we must also acknowledge that weapons cannot act by themselves. Although designed to kill, so long as they remain in storage, they can do no physical harm. Someone has to touch a button to launch a missile strike, or pull a trigger to fire a bullet. No 'evil' power can do this. Only humans can. Therefore, genuine world peace requires that we also begin to dismantle the military establishments that we have built. We cannot hope to enjoy peace in its fullest sense while it remains possible for a few individuals to exercise military power and impose their will on others. Nor, for that matter, can we hope to enjoy true peace as long as there are authoritarian regimes propped up by armed forces which do not hesitate to carry out injustice at their bidding. Injustice undermines truth, and without truth there can be no lasting peace. Why not? Because when we have truth on our side, there is a straightforwardness, a confidence that comes with it. Conversely, when truth is lacking, the only way we can achieve our narrow aims is through force. But when decisions come about this way, in defiance of truth, people do not feel right – either the victors or the vanquished. This negative feeling serves to undermine the peace which is imposed by force.

We each have a role to play in creating a climate for genuine peace. When, as individuals, we disarm ourselves internally – through countering our negative thoughts and emotions and cultivating positive qualities – we create the conditions for external disarmament. Indeed, genuine, lasting world peace will only be possible as a result of each of us making an effort internally. Afflictive emotion is the oxygen of conflict. It is thus essential that we remain sensitive to others and, recognizing their equal right to happiness, do nothing that could contribute to their suffering. To help us in this, it is useful to take time and reflect on how war is actually experienced by its victims. For my own part, I need only think of my visit to Hiroshima some years ago to bring to life its full horror. In the museum there, I saw a watch that had stopped at the exact moment the bomb exploded. I also saw a small packet of sewing needles, the contents of which had been fused together in the explosion's heat.

Clearly we cannot hope to achieve military disestab-lishment overnight. Desirable as it may be, unilateral disarmament would be exceedingly difficult to achieve. And although if we wish to see a society in which armed conflict becomes a thing of the past, our ultimate goal must be the abolition of all military apparatus. Clearly it is too much to hope for the elimination of all weapons. After all, even our fists can be used as weapons. And there will always be groups of troublemakers and fanatics who will cause disturbance for others. Therefore, we must allow that so long as there are human beings, there will have to be ways of dealing with miscreants.

What is required, therefore, is that we establish clear objectives by means of which we can disarm gradually. And we must develop the political will to do so. With respect to the practical measures required to bring about military disestablishment, we need to recognize that it can only occur within the context of a broad commitment to disarmament. It is not enough to think merely in terms of eliminating our weapons of mass destruction. We must create the conditions favourable to our objective. The most obvious way of doing this is through building on existing initiatives. Here I am thinking of the efforts over many years to exercise control over the proliferation of certain classes of weapon – and in some cases to eliminate them. During the 1970s and 1980s, we saw the SALT (Strategic Arms Limitation Treaties) talks between the Eastern and Western blocs. We have had in place for many years a nuclear non-proliferation treaty to which many countries are already commited. And despite the spread of nuclear weapons, the idea of a universal ban is still alive. Encouraging progress has also been made towards the banning of land mines. At the time of writing, a majority of the world's governments have signed protocols renouncing their use. So while it remains true that none of these initiatives has so far fully succeeded in their aims, their very existence indicates recognition of the undesirability of these methods of destruction. They testify to humans' basic wish to live in peace. And they provide a useful start which is capable of development.

Another way in which we can move further toward our objective of global military disestablishment is by gradually dismantling our arms industry. To many, this suggestion will seem a preposterous and unfeasible idea. They will object that unless everybody agrees to do so simultaneously, this would be madness. And that, they will say, can never happen. Besides, they will add, there is the economic argument to consider. Yet if we look at the matter from the point of view of those who suffer the consequences of armed violence, it becomes very hard to deny our responsibility to overcome these objections by some means or another. Indeed, whenever I think of the arms industry and the suffering it enables, I am again reminded of my visit to the Nazi death camp at Auschwitz. As I stood looking at the ovens in which thousands of human beings just like myself were burned

– many of them still alive, humans who cannot even bear the heat of a single match – what struck me hardest was the realization that these devices had been built with the care and attention of talented workmen. I could almost see the engineers (all intelligent people) at their drawing boards, carefully planning the shape of the combustion chambers and calculating the size of chimneys, their height and breadth. I thought of the craftsmen who brought the design to fruition. No doubt they took pride in their work, as good craftsmen do. Then it occurred to me that this is precisely what modern-day weapons designers and manufacturers are about. They, too, are devising the means to destroy thousands if not millions of their fellow human beings. Isn't this a disturbing thought?

With this in mind, all individuals who undertake such work would do well to consider whether they can really justify their involvement. No doubt they would suffer if they gave it up unilaterally. No doubt, too, the economies of the arms manufacturing nations would suffer if these facilities were closed down. But would this not be a price worth paying? Besides, it seems that there are many examples in the world of companies which have successfully converted from weapons to some other form of manufacture. Also, we have the example of the world's one demilitarized state which we can consider in relation to her neighbours. If that of Costa Rica, which disarmed as long ago as 1949, is anything to go by, the benefits in terms of standard of living, of health and education are tremendous.

As to the argument that it would perhaps be more realistic simply to restrict arms exports to those countries which are reliable and safe, I suggest that this reflects a very short-sighted outlook. It has been demonstrated time and time again that this does not work. We are all familiar with the recent history of the Persian Gulf. During the 1970s the Western allies armed the Shah of Iran as a counterforce to the perceived threat from Russia. When the political climate changed, Iran itself was considered a threat to Western interests. So the allies began to arm Iraq against Iran. But then, when times changed yet again, these weapons were used against the West's other allies in the Gulf (Kuwait). As a result, the manufacturing countries found themselves going to war with their own client. In other words, there is no such thing as a 'safe' client for arms.

I cannot deny that my aspiration toward global disarmament and military disestablishment is idealistic. At the same time, there are clear grounds for optimism. One of these is the ironic fact that so far as nuclear and other weapons of mass destruction are concerned, it is extremely hard to conceive of a situation where they could be useful. Nobody wants to risk all-out nuclear war. These weapons are also an obvious waste of money. They are expensive to produce, it is impossible to imagine using them, and there is nothing to do but stockpile them, which also costs a great deal of money. Viewed from this perspective, they are utterly useless and nothing but a drain on resources.

Another reason for optimism is again the steady inter-twining of national economies. This is creating a climate in which notions of purely national interest and advantage are becoming less and less meaningful. As a result, the idea of using war as a means to resolve conflict is starting to look decidedly old-fashioned. Where there are human beings, there will always be conflict, this is true. Disagree-ments are bound to surface from time to time. But given today's reality of increasingly sophisticated weaponry, we have to find some way other than violence to resolve them. This means dialogue in the spirit of reconciliation and compromise. This is not just wishful thinking on my part. The global trend toward international politi-cal groupings, of which the European Union is perhaps the most obvious example, means that it is possible to envisage a time when maintaining purely national standing armies could one day seem both uneconomic and unnecessary. Instead of thinking only in terms of protecting individual borders, it will become logical to think in terms of regional security. In fact, this is already beginning to happen. There are, albeit as yet tentative, plans to integrate European defences more closely; a Franco-German army brigade has been in existence for more than ten years now. It thus seems possible, at least so far as the European Community is concerned, that what began purely as a trading alliance could eventually assume responsibility for regional security. And if this is possible within Europe, there is reason to hope that other international trading groups – of which there are many – could evolve to do the same. Why not?

The emergence of such regional security groupings would, I feel, contribute enormously to the transition from our current preoccupation with nation states to the gradual acceptance of less narrowly defined communities. They could also pave the way for a world in which there would be no standing armies at all. Such a scenario would, of course, have to evolve in stages. National armed forces would give way to regional security groupings. These could then gradually be disbanded, leaving only a globally administered police force. The main purpose of this force would be to safeguard justice, communal security and human rights worldwide. Its specific duties would be various, however. Protecting against the appropriation of power by violent means would be one of them. As to its operation, granted there are legal issues to be tackled first. But I imagine that it could be called in either by communities which came under threat – from neighbours or from some of it's own members, such as a violently extreme political faction – or it could be deployed by the international community itself when violence seemed the likely outcome of conflict, for example, of religious or ideological disputes.

Even though it is true that we remain a long way from this ideal situation, again it is not as fanciful as it may at first seem. Maybe this generation will not live to see it. But we are already accustomed to seeing United Nations troops deployed as peacekeepers. We are also beginning to see the emergence of a consensus that under certain circumstances it may be justifiable to use them in a more interventionist way.

As a means for furthering these developments we might consider the establishment of what I call Zones of Peace. Here I imagine either a part or parts of one or more country being demilitarized to create oases of stability, preferably in areas of strategic significance. These would serve as beacons of hope for the rest of the world. Admittedly, this idea is quite ambitious, but it is not without precedent. We already have one such internationally recognized demilitarized zone in Antarctica. Nor am I the only individual ever to suggest there could be more. The former Russian President Mikhail Gorbachev proposed just such status for the Sino-Russian borderlands. I myself have advanced the idea for Tibet.

Of course, it is not hard to think of areas in the world other than Tibet where neighbouring communities would benefit enormously from the establishment of a demilitarized zone. Just as India and China – both of them still relatively poor countries – would save a considerable proportion of their respective annual income if Tibet were to become an internationally recognized Zone of Peace, so there are many others on each continent from which a tremendous, wasteful, burden would be lifted if there were no need to maintain large numbers of troops on their borders. I have often thought, for example, that Germany is a most appropriate location for a Zone of Peace, lying as it does in the heart of Europe and taking into account the experience of the twentieth century's two world wars.

In all of this, I believe the United Nations has a critical role to play. Not that it is the only body devoted to global issues. There is also much to admire about the ethic behind the International Court at the Hague, the International Monetary Fund, the World Bank and others such as those dedicated to upholding the Geneva conventions. But, at present, and for the conceivable future, the UN is the only global institution capable of influencing and formulating policy on behalf of the international community. Of course, many people criticize it on the grounds that it is ineffective, and it is true that time and again we have seen its resolutions ignored, abandoned and forgotten. Nevertheless, in spite of these shortcomings, I for one continue to have the highest regard not only for the principles on which it was founded but also for the great deal it has achieved since its inception in 1945. We need only ask ourselves whether or not it has helped save lives through defusing potentially disastrous situations to see that it is more than the toothless bureaucracy some people say it is. We should also consider the great work of its subsidiary organizations, such as UNICEF, United Nations High Commission for Refugees, UNESCO and the World Health Organization. This remains true even if some of their programmes and policies and those of other world organizations have been flawed and misguided.

I see the UN, developed to its full potential, as being the proper vehicle for carrying out the wishes of humanity as a whole. As yet it is not able to do this very effectively, but we are only just beginning to see the emergence of a global consciousness (which has been made possible by the communications revolution). And in spite of tremendous difficulties, we have seen it in action in numerous parts of the world, even though at the moment there may only be one or two nations spearheading these initiatives. The fact that they are seeking the legitimacy conferred by a United Nations mandate suggests a felt need for justification through collective approbation. This, in turn, I believe to be indicative of a growing sense of a single, mutually dependent, human community.

One of the particular weakness of the United Nations as it is presently constituted is that although it provides a forum for individual governments, individual citizens cannot be heard there. It has no mechanism whereby those wishing to speak out against their own governments can be heard. To make matters worse is the fact that the veto system currently in place opens its workings to manipulation by the more powerful nations. These are profound shortcomings.

As to the problem of individuals not having a voice, here we might have to consider something more radical. Just as democracy is ensured by the three pillars of independent judiciary, executive and legislature, so we need to have a genuinely independent body at the international level. But perhaps the United Nations is not entirely suited to this role. I have noticed at international gatherings, such as the Earth Summit in Brazil, that individuals representing their country inevitably put their nations' interests first, despite the fact that the question at issue transcends national boundaries. Conversely, when people come as individuals to international gatherings – here I am thinking of such groups as the International Physicians for the Prevention of Nuclear War group, or the initiative on the arms trade by a group of Nobel Peace Laureates, of which I am a member – there is much greater concern for humanity itself. Their spirit is much more genuinely international and open. This leads me to think that it could be worthwhile to establish a body whose principal task is to monitor human affairs from the perspective of ethics, an organization that might be called the World Council of the People (although no doubt a better name could be found). This would consist in a group of individuals drawn, as I imagine it, from a wide variety of backgrounds. There would be artists, bankers, environmentalists, lawyers, poets, academics, religious thinkers and writers as well as ordinary men and women with a common reputation for integrity and dedication to fundamental ethical and human values. Because this body would not actually be invested with political power, its pronouncements would not be legally binding. But by virtue of its independence – having no link with any one nation or group of nations, and no ideology – its deliberations would represent the conscience of the world. They would thus carry moral authority.

Of course, there will be many who criticize this proposal, along with what I have said about military disestablishment, disarmament and reform of the United Nations on the grounds that it is unrealistic, or perhaps just too simplistic. Or they will say that it is not workable in 'the real world'. But while people are often content to just criticize and blame others for what goes wrong, surely we should at least attempt to put forward constructive ideas. One thing is for certain. Given human beings' love of truth, justice, peace and freedom, creating a better, more compassionate world is a genuine possibility. The potential is there. If, with the help of education and the proper use of the media, we can combine some of the initiatives suggested here with the implementation of ethical principles, we will have within our reach a climate in which disarmament and military disestablishment becomes totally uncontroversial. On the basis of this we will have created the conditions for lasting world peace.

CHAPTER FIFTEEN

THE ROLE OF RELIGION IN MODERN SOCIETY

It is a sad fact of human history that religion has often been a major source of conflict. Even today, individuals are killed, their communities destroyed and societies destabilized as a result of religious bigotry and hatred. It is no wonder that many question the place of religion in human society. Yet when we think carefully, we find that conflict in the name of religion arises from two principal sources. There is that which arises simply as a result of religious diversity – the doctrinal, cultural and practical differences between one religion and another. Then there is the conflict that arises in the context of political, economic and other factors, mainly at the institutional level. Interreligious harmony is the key to overcoming conflict of the first sort. In the case of the second, some other solution must be found. Secularization and in particular the separation of the religious hierarchy from the institutions of the state may go some way to reducing such institutional problems. Our concern in this chapter is with interreligious harmony, however.

This is an important aspect of what I have called universal responsibility. But before examining the matter in detail, it is perhaps worth considering the question of whether religion is really relevant in the modern world. Many people argue that it is not. Now I have observed that religious belief is not a precondition either of ethical conduct or of happiness itself. I have also suggested that whether a person practises religion or not, the spiritual qualities of love and compassion, patience, tolerance, forgiveness, humility and so on are indispensable. At the same time, I should make it clear that I believe that these are most easily and effectively developed within the context of religious practice. I also believe that when an individual sincerely practises religion, that person will benefit enormously. People who have developed firm faith, grounded in understanding and rooted in daily practice, are in general much better at coping with adversity than those who have not. I am convinced, therefore, that religion has enormous potential to benefit humanity. Properly employed, it is an extremely effective instrument for establishing human happiness. In particular, it can play a leading role in encouraging people to develop a sense of responsibility towards others and of the need to be ethical disciplined.

On these grounds, therefore, I believe that religion is still relevant today. But consider this too: some years ago, the body of a Stone Age man was recovered from the ice of the European Alps. Despite being more than five thousand years old, it was perfectly preserved. Even its clothes were largely intact. I remember thinking at the time that were it possible to bring this individual back to life for a day, we would find that we have much in common with him. No doubt we would find that he too was concerned for his family and loved ones, for his health and so on. Differences of culture and expression notwithstanding, we would still be able to identify with one another on a basic human level. And there could be no reason to suppose any less concern with finding happiness and avoiding suffering on his part than on ours. If religion, with its emphasis on overcoming suffering through the practice of ethical discipline and cultivation of love and compassion, can be conceived of as relevant in his time, it is hard to see why it should not be equally so today. Granted that in the past the value of religion may have been more obvious in that human suffering was more explicit due to the lack of modern facilities. But because we humans still suffer, albeit that today this is experienced more internally as mental and emotional affliction, and because religion in addition to its salvific truth claims is concerned to help us overcome suffering, surely it must still be relevant.

How then might we bring about the harmony that is necessary to overcome interreligious conflict? As in the case of individuals engaged in the discipline of restraining their response to negative thoughts and emotions and cultivating spiritual qualities, the key lies in developing understanding. We must first identify the factors that obstruct it. Then we must find ways to overcome them.

Perhaps the most significant obstruction to interreligious harmony is lack of appreciation of the value of others' faith traditions. Until comparatively recently, communication between different cultures, even different communities, was slow or nonexistent. For this reason, sympathy for other faith traditions was not necessarily very important – except of course where members of different religions lived side by side. But this attitude is no longer viable. In today's increasingly complex and interdependent world, we are compelled to acknowledge the existence of other cultures, different ethnic groups and, of course, other religious faiths. Whether we like it or not, most of us now experience this diversity on a daily basis.

I believe that the best way to overcome ignorance and bring about understanding is through dialogue with members of other faith traditions. This I see occurring in a number of different ways. Discussions among scholars in which the convergence and, perhaps more importantly, the divergence between different faith traditions is explored and appreciated are very valuable. On another level, it is helpful when there are encounters between ordinary but practising followers of different religions in which each shares their experiences. This is perhaps the most effective way of appreciating others' teachings. In my own case, for example, my meetings with the late Thomas Merton, a Catholic monk of the Cistercian order, were deeply inspiring. They helped me develop a profound admiration for the teachings of Christianity. I also feel that occasional meetings between religious leaders joining together to pray for a common cause is extremely useful. The gathering at Assisi in Italy in 1986, when representatives of the world's major religions gathered to pray for peace, was, I believe, tremendously beneficial to many religious believers insofar as it symbolized the solidarity and commitment to peace of all those taking part.

Finally, I feel that the practice of members of different faith traditions going on joint pilgrimages together can be very helpful. It was in this spirit that in 1993 I went to Lourdes, and then to Jerusalem – a site holy to three of the world's great religions. I have also paid visits to various Hindu, Islamic, Jain and Sikh shrines both in India and abroad. More recently, following a seminar devoted to discussing and practising meditation in the Christian and Buddhist traditions, I joined an historic pilgrimage of practitioners of both traditions in a programme of prayers, meditation and dialogue under the Bodhi tree at Bodh Gaya in India. This is one of Buddhism's most important shrines.

When exchanges like these occur, followers of one tradition will find that, just as in the case of their own, the teachings of other faiths are a source both of spiritual inspiration and of ethical guidance to their followers. It will also become clear that irrespective of doctrinal and other differences, all the major world religions are concerned with helping individuals to become good human beings. All emphasize love and compassion, patience, tolerance, forgiveness, humility and so on, and all are capable of helping individuals to develop these. Moreover, the example given by the founders of each major religion clearly demonstrates a concern for helping others find happiness through developing these qualities. So far as their own lives were concerned, each conducted themselves with great simplicity. Ethical discipline and love for all others was the hallmark of their lives. They did not live luxuriously like emperors and kings. Instead, they voluntarily accepted suffering – without consideration of the hardships involved – in order to benefit humanity as a whole. In their teachings, all placed special emphasis on developing love and compassion and renouncing selfish desires. And each of them called on us to transform our hearts and minds. Indeed, whether we have faith or not, all are worthy of our profound admiration.

At the same time as engaging in dialogue with followers

of other religions, we must, of course, implement in our daily life the teachings of our own religion. Once we have experienced the benefit of love and compassion, and of ethical discipline, we will easily recognize the value of others' teachings. But for this, it is essential to realize that religious practice entails a lot more than merely saying, 'I believe' or, as in Buddhism, 'I take refuge'. There is also more to it than just visiting temples, or shrines or churches. And taking religious teachings is of little benefit if they do not enter the heart but remain at the level of intellect alone. Simply relying on faith without understanding and without implementation is of limited value. I often tell Tibetans that carrying a *mala* (something like a rosary) does not make a person a genuine religious practitioner. The efforts we make sincerely to transform ourselves spiritually are what make us a genuine religious practitioner.

We come to see the overriding importance of genuine practice when we recognize that, along with ignorance, individuals' unhealthy relationships with their beliefs is the other major factor in religious disharmony. Far from applying the teachings of our religion in our personal lives, we have a tendency to use them to reinforce our self-centred attitudes. We relate to our religion as to something we own or as a label that separates us from others. Surely this is misguided? Instead of using the nectar of religion to purify the poisonous elements of our hearts and minds, there is a danger when we think like this of using these negative elements to poison the nectar of religion.

Yet we must acknowledge that this reflects another problem, one which is implicit in all religions. I refer to the claims each has of being the one 'true' religion. How are we to resolve this difficulty? It is true that from the point of view of the individual practitioner, it is essential to have a single-pointed commitment to our own faith. It is also true that this depends on the deep conviction that one's own path is the sole mediator of truth. But at the same time, we have to find some means of reconciling this belief with the reality of a multiplicity of similar claims. In practical terms, this involves individual practitioners finding a way at least to accept the validity of the teachings of other religions while maintaining whole-hearted commitment to their own. As far as the validity of the metaphysical truth claims of a given religion is concerned, that is of course the internal business of that particular tradition.

In my own case, I am convinced that Buddhism provides me with the most effective framework within which to situate my efforts to develop spiritually through cultivating love and compassion. At the same time, I must acknowledge that while Buddhism represents the best path for me – that is, it suits my character, my temperament, my inclinations and my cultural background – the same will be true of, for example, Christianity for Christians. For them, Christianity is the best way. On the basis of my conviction, I cannot therefore say that Buddhism is best for everyone.

I often think of religion in terms of medicine for the human spirit. Independent of its usage and suitability to a particular individual in a particular condition, we cannot really judge a medicine's efficacy. We are not justified in saying this medicine is very good because of such and such ingredients. If you take the patient and its effect on that person out of the equation, it hardly makes sense. What is relevant is to say that in the case of this particular patient with his or her particular illness, this medicine is the most effective. Similarly with different religious traditions, we can say that this one is most effective for this particular individual. But it is unhelpful to try to argue on the basis of philosophy or metaphysics that one religion is better than another. The important thing is surely its effectiveness in individual cases.

My way to resolve the seeming contradiction between each religion's claim to 'one truth and one religion' and the reality of the multiplicity of faiths is thus to understand that in the case of a single individual, there can indeed be only one truth, one religion. However, from the perspective of human society at large, we must accept the concept of 'many truths, many religions'. To continue with our medical analogy, in the case of one particular patient, the suitable medicine is in fact the only medicine. But clearly that does not mean that there may not be other medicines suitable to other patients.

To my way of thinking, the diversity that exists amongst the various religious traditions is enormously enriching. There is thus no need to try to find ways of saying that ultimately all religions are the same. They are similar in that they all emphasize the indispensability of love and compassion in the context of ethical discipline. But to say this is not to say that they are all essentially one. The contradictory understanding of creation and beginninglessness articulated by Buddhism, Christianity and Hinduism, for example, means that in the end we have to part company when it comes to metaphysical claims, in spite of the many practical similarities that undoubtedly exist. These philosophical contradictions may not be very important in the beginning stages of religious practice. But as we advance along the path of one tradition or another, we are compelled at some point to acknowledge fundamental differences. For example, the concept of rebirth in Buddhism and various other ancient Indian traditions may turn out to be incompatible with the Christian idea of salvation. This need not be a cause for dismay, however. Even within Buddhism itself, in the realm of metaphysics there are diametrically opposing views. At the very least, such diversity means that we have different frameworks within which to locate ethical discipline and the development of spiritual values. That is why I do not advocate a 'super' or a new 'world' religion. It would mean that we would lose the unique characteristics of the different faith traditions.

Some people, it is true, hold that the Buddhist concept of *shunyata*, or emptiness, is ultimately the same as certain approaches to understanding the concept of God. Nevertheless, there remain difficulties with this. The first is that while of course we can interpret these concepts, to what extent can we be faithful to the original teachings? There are compelling similarities between the Mahayana Buddhist concept of *dharmakaya*, *sambogakaya* and *nirmanakaya* and the Christian trinity of God as Father, Son and Holy Spirit. But to say, on the basis of this, that Buddhism and Christianity are ultimately the same is to go a bit too far, I think! As an old Tibetan saying goes, we must beware of trying to put a yak's head on a sheep's body – or vice versa.

What is required instead is that we develop a genuine sense of religious pluralism, in spite of the different claims of different faith traditions. This is especially true if we are serious in our respect for human rights as a universal principle. In this regard, I find the concept of a world parliament of religions very appealing. To begin with, the word 'parliament' conveys a sense of democracy while the plural 'religions' underlines the importance of the principle of a multiplicity of faith traditions. The truly pluralist perspective on religion which the idea of such a parliament suggests could, I believe, be of great help. It could help avoid the extremes of religious bigotry on the one hand, and the urge toward unnecessary syncretism on the other.

Connected with this issue of interreligious harmony, I should perhaps say something about religious conversion. This is a question which must be taken extremely seriously. It is essential to realize that the mere fact of conversion alone will not make an individual a better person – that is to say, a more disciplined, a more compassionate, a more warm-hearted person. In general, it is better for the individual to concentrate on transforming themselves spiritually through the practice of restraint, virtue and compassion than through conversion to another faith. To the extent that the insights or practices of other religions are useful or relevant to our own faith, it is valuable to learn from others. In some cases, it may even be helpful to adopt certain of them. Yet when this is done wisely, we can remain firmly committed to our own faith. This way is best because it carries with it no danger of confusion, especially with respect to the different ways of life that tend to go with different faith traditions.

Given the diversity to be found among individual human beings, it is of course bound to be the case that out of many millions of practitioners of a particular religion, a handful will find another religion's approach to ethics and spiritual development is more satisfactory. For some, the concept of rebirth and *karma* will seem highly effective in inspiring the aspiration to develop love and compassion within the context of responsibility. For others, the concept of a transcendent, loving creator will come to seem more so. In such circumstances, it is crucial for those individuals to question themselves again and again. They must ask, 'Am I attracted to this other religion for the right reasons? Is it merely the cultural and ritual aspects that are appealing? Or is it the essential teachings? Do I suppose that if I convert to this new religion it will be less demanding than my present one?' I say this because it has often struck me that when people do convert to a religion outside their own heritage, quite often they adopt certain superficial aspects of the culture to which their new faith belongs. But their practice may not go very much deeper than that.

In the case of a person who decides after a process of long and mature reflection to adopt a different religion, it is very important that they remember the positive contribution to humanity of each religious tradition. The danger is that the individual may, in seeking to justify their decision to others, criticize their previous faith. It is essential to avoid this. Just because that tradition is no longer effective in the case of one individual does not mean it is no longer of benefit to humanity. On the contrary, we can be certain that it has been an inspiration to millions of people in the past, that it inspires millions today, and that it will inspire millions in the path of love and compassion in the future.

The important point to keep in mind is that ultimately the whole purpose of religion is to facilitate love and compassion, patience, tolerance, humility, forgiveness and so on. If we neglect these, changing our religion will be of no help. In the same way, even if we are fervent believers in our own faith, it will avail us nothing if we neglect to implement these qualities in our daily lives. Such a believer is no better off than a patient with some fatal illness who merely reads a medical treatise but fails to undertake the treatment prescribed.

Moreover, if we who are practitioners of religion are not compassionate and disciplined, how can we expect it of others? If we can establish genuine harmony derived from mutual respect and understanding, religion has enormous potential to speak with authority on such vital moral questions as peace and disarmament, social and political justice, the natural environment and many other matters affecting all humanity. But until we put our own spiritual teachings into practice, we will never be taken seriously. And this means, among other things, setting a good example through developing good relations with other faith traditions.

AN APPEAL

That we have reached the last few pages of this book reminds us of the impermanence of our lives. How quickly they pass and how soon we will arrive at our final day. Within less than fifty years, I, Tenzin Gyatso, the Buddhist monk will be no more than a memory. Indeed, it is doubtful whether a single person reading these words will be alive a century from now. Time passes unhindered. When we make mistakes, we cannot turn the clock back and try again. All we can do is use the present well. Therefore, if when our final day comes we are able to look back and see that we have lived full, productive and meaningful lives, that will at least be of some comfort. If we cannot, we may be very sad. But which of these we experience is up to us.

The best way to ensure that when we approach death we do so without remorse is to ensure that in the present moment we conduct ourselves responsibly and with compassion for others. Actually, this is in our own interest, and not just because it will benefit us in the future. As we have seen, compassion is what makes our life meaningful. It is the source of all lasting happiness and joy. And it is the foundation of a good heart, the heart of one who acts out of a desire to help others. Through kindness, through affection, through honesty, through truth and justice towards all others we ensure our own benefit. This is not a matter for complicated theorizing. It is a matter of common sense. There is no denying that consideration of others is worthwhile. There is no denying that our happiness is inextricably bound up with the happiness of others. There is no denying that if society suffers, we ourselves suffer. Nor is there any denying that the more our hearts and minds are afflicted with ill-will, the more miserable we become. Thus we can reject everything else: religion, ideology, all received wisdom. But we cannot escape the necessity of love and compassion.

This, then, is my true religion, my simple faith. In this sense, there is no need for temple or church, for mosque or synagogue, no need for complicated philosophy, doctrine or dogma. Our own heart, our own mind is the temple. The doctrine is compassion. Love for others and respect for their rights and dignity, no matter who or what they are: ultimately these are all we need. So long as we practise these in our daily lives, then no matter if we are learned or unlearned, whether we believe in Buddha or God, or follow some other religion or none at all, as long as we have compassion for others and conduct ourselves with restraint out of a sense of responsibility, there is no doubt we will be happy.

Why, then, if it is so simple to be happy, do we find it so hard? Unfortunately, though most of us think of ourselves as compassionate, we tend to ignore these common-sense truths. We neglect to confront our negative thoughts and emotions. Unlike the farmer who follows the seasons and does not hesitate to cultivate the land when the moment comes, we waste so much of our time in meaningless activity. We feel deep regret over trivial matters like losing money while keeping from doing what is genuinely important without the slightest feeling of remorse. Instead of rejoicing in the opportunity we have to contribute to others' well-being, we merely take our pleasures where we can. We shrink from considering others on the grounds that we are too busy. We run right and left, making calculations and telephone calls and thinking that this would be better than that. We do one thing but worry that if something else comes along we had better do another. But in this, we engage only the coarsest and most elementary levels of the human spirit. Moreover, by being inattentive to the needs of others, inevitably we end up harming them. We think ourselves very clever, but how do we use our abilities? All too often we use them to deceive our neighbours, to take advantage of them and better ourselves at their expense. And when things do not work out, full of self-righteousness, we blame others for our difficulties.

Yet lasting satisfaction cannot be derived from the acquisition of objects. Similarly, no matter how many friends we acquire, they cannot make us happy. And indulgence in sensual pleasure is nothing but a gateway to suffering. It is like honey smeared along the cutting edge of a sword. Of course, that is not to say we should despise our bodies. On the contrary, we cannot be of help to others without a body. But we need to avoid the extremes which can lead to harm.

In focusing on the mundane, what is essential remains hidden from us. Of course, if we could be truly happy doing so, then it would be entirely reasonable to live like this. Yet we cannot. At best, we get through life without too much trouble. But then when problems assail us, as they must, we are unprepared. We find that we cannot cope. We are left despairing and unhappy.

With my two hands joined, I therefore appeal to you the reader to ensure that you make the rest of your life as meaningful as possible. Do this by engaging in spiritual practice if you can. As I hope I have made clear, there is nothing mysterious about this. It consists in nothing more than acting out of concern for others. And provided you undertake this practice sincerely and with persistence, little by little, step by step you will gradually be able to reorder your habits and attitudes so that you think less about your own narrow concerns and more of others'. In doing so, you will find that you enjoy peace and happiness yourself.

Relinquish your envy, let go of your desire to triumph over others. Instead, try to benefit them. With kindness, with courage, and confident that in doing so you are sure to meet with success, welcome others with a smile. Be straightforward. And try to be impartial. Treat everyone as if they were a close friend. I say this neither as Dalai Lama nor as someone who has special powers or ability. Of these I have none. I speak as a human being: one who, like yourself, wishes to be happy and not to suffer.

If you cannot, for whatever reason, be of help to others, at least don't harm them. Consider yourself a tourist. Think of the world as it is seen from space, so small and insignificant yet so beautiful. Could there really be anything to be gained from harming others during our stay here? Is it not preferable, and more reasonable, to relax and enjoy ourselves quietly, just as if we were visiting a different neighbourhood? Therefore, if in the midst of your enjoyment of the world you have a moment, try to help in however small a way those who are downtrodden and those who, for whatever reason, cannot or do not help themselves. Try not to turn away from those whose appearance is disturbing, from the ragged and unwell.

Try never to think of them as inferior to yourself. If you can, try not even to think of yourself as better than the humblest beggar. You will look the same in your grave.

To close with, I would like to share a short prayer which gives me great inspiration in my quest to benefit others:

> *May I become at all times, both now and forever*
> *A protector for those without protection*
> *A guide for those who have lost their way*
> *A ship for those with oceans to cross*
> *A bridge for those with rivers to cross*
> *A sanctuary for those in danger*
> *A lamp for those without light*
> *A place of refuge for those who lack shelter*
> *And a servant to all in need.*